Education and Dialogue in
Polarized Societies

Education and Dialogue in Polarized Societies

Dialogic Perspectives in Times of Change

Edited by
OLA ERSTAD, BENTE ERIKSEN HAGTVET, AND
JAMES V. WERTSCH

OXFORD
UNIVERSITY PRESS

Oxford University Press is a department of the University of Oxford. It furthers
the University's objective of excellence in research, scholarship, and education
by publishing worldwide. Oxford is a registered trade mark of Oxford University
Press in the UK and certain other countries.

Published in the United States of America by Oxford University Press
198 Madison Avenue, New York, NY 10016, United States of America.

© Oxford University Press 2024

All rights reserved. No part of this publication may be reproduced, stored in
a retrieval system, or transmitted, in any form or by any means, without the
prior permission in writing of Oxford University Press, or as expressly permitted
by law, by license, or under terms agreed with the appropriate reproduction
rights organization. Inquiries concerning reproduction outside the scope of the
above should be sent to the Rights Department, Oxford University Press, at the
address above.

You must not circulate this work in any other form
and you must impose this same condition on any acquirer.

CIP data is on file at the Library of Congress

ISBN 978-0-19-760542-4

DOI: 10.1093/oso/9780197605424.001.0001

Printed by Integrated Books International, United States of America

Contents

Contributors xi

1. The Importance of Dialogue 1
   Ola Erstad, Bente Eriksen Hagtvet, and James V. Wertsch
   1.1 Introduction 1
   1.2 The Importance of Dialogue 2
   1.3 The Current Dominance of Monologic Approaches 3
   1.4 The Dialogical Rationale of This Book: Key Theoretical Positions 6
   1.5 Dialogue and Learning 8
   1.6 The Structure of the Book 9

   ## SECTION 1: THE LEGACY OF ROMMETVEIT

2. The Role of Narratives in Dialogue and Intersubjectivity 15
   James V. Wertsch
   2.1 Introduction 15
   2.2 The Influence of Rommetveit 16
   2.3 Narrative as a Symbolic Tool 19
   2.4 American National Narratives as Coauthors 20
   2.5 Competing Narrative Templates 22
   2.6 Dialogism, Intersubjectivity, and Narratives 26

3. Ragnar Rommetveit on Contextures and Partially Shared Understandings 29
   Per Linell
   3.1 Introduction 29
   3.2 Ragnar Rommetveit 31
   3.3 On Rommetveit's Early Attempts to Describe Contexts of Languaging 32
   3.4 Authentic Situations I: Threatening Phone Calls 35
   3.5 Authentic Situations II: Situations Suggesting Sexual Abuse of Children 37
   3.6 Authentic Situations III: Hannah Arendt About Adolf Eichmann in Jerusalem 39
   3.7 Authentic Example IV: Putin's Speech on the War in Ukraine 40
   3.8 On Remote Contexts and Lost Opportunities 42

    3.9   Context Atrophy in Formal Linguistics and in Myopic Interaction Analysis   44
    3.10 Conclusion: A Note on Macro-Level Phenomena   45

4. Layered Attunement: Internal Dialogues of Intersubjectivity   50
Christian H. Bisgaard, Marc Antoine Campill, Enno von Fircks, and Jaan Valsiner
    4.1   Introduction   50
    4.2   Dialogical Negotiation Beyond Consciousness   60
    4.3   The Polysemic Multivoiced Self   61
    4.4   Relations Between Voices: Tensions and Their Negotiation   67
    4.5   General Discussion: Learning with Rommetveit   71

SECTION 2: SOCIETAL CONDITONS FOR DIALOGUE AND THE ROLE OF EDUCATION

5. The Limits and Potential of Dialogue to Counter Polarization in Educative Settings   77
Mariëtte de Haan
    5.1   Introduction: Is Dialogue Disabled in Polarized Settings?   77
    5.2   Dialogue as a Remedy for Polarization—The UNION Project   79
    5.3   What Can Dialogue Do in Situations of Polarization According to the Theory?   82
          5.3.1 Can We Design Inclusive Dialogical Spaces for Communities That Are Diverse?   82
          5.3.2 (How) Can Dialogue Function Between Parties with Rival or Incommensurable Worldviews?   85
          5.3.3 What Can We Learn from the Very Nature of Intersubjectivty and Its Ability to Bridge Opposing Worlds?   86
    5.4   Implications for Designing Dialogical Interventions   89
          5.4.1 Design Principles for Dialogical Interventions   90
    5.5   Conclusion: The Need to Go Back to the Rough Ground   92

6. Active Citizenship and Participation Through "Dialogues in the Square"   96
Maria Beatrice Ligorio, Giovanna Barzanò, Francesca Amenduni, Roberta Cauchi, Sergio Turrisi, Lorenzo Raffio, Claudia Ragazzini, and Ludovica Valentino
    6.1   Introduction   96
    6.2   Theoretical Framework   98
    6.3   "Dialogues in the Square": The Origins of the Project   102
    6.4   Participants and Partners   104
    6.5   The Development of Dialogues: Toward Action in a Public Space   106
    6.6   Experiencing Different Types of Dialogues   108

    6.7 A Snapshot from the Field: Triggering Cross-Generation
          Dialogue   110
    6.8 Constraints and Opportunities   113

7. A Dialogic Theory of Educational Technology   121
   Rupert Wegerif and Louis Major
   7.1 Introduction: Definitions and Scope   121
       7.1.1 What Is "Technology"?   123
       7.1.2 Theory and Practice as Dialogues in Different Timescales   124
       7.1.3 What Is "Education"?   125
   7.2 Dialogism   126
       7.2.1 The Dialogic Gap Is Constitutive for Meaning   126
       7.2.2 Dialogic Space   127
       7.2.3 The Inside:Outside and Outside:Inside Nature of Dialogic
              Relations   127
       7.2.4 We Learn as a Response to a Call   127
       7.2.5 Dialogic Double-Voicedness   128
       7.2.6 Learning as the Expansion of Dialogue   128
   7.3 The Theory of Educational Technology   129
   7.4 Conversation Theory   130
       7.4.1 Commentary on Conversation Theory   132
       7.4.2 Connectivism or Learning as Networking   132
       7.4.3 Commentary on Connectivism   133
   7.5 A Dialogic Theory of Educational Technology   134
       7.5.1 Education Technology for Connection   134
       7.5.2 Education Technology for Participation   135
       7.5.3 Education Technology for the Expansion of Time   136
   7.6 Discussion and Conclusion   137

SECTION 3: THE ROLE OF DIGITAL TECHNOLOGIES

8. Using Microblogging to Create a Space for Attending and
   Attuning to Others   145
   Ingvill Rasmussen and Paul Warwick
   8.1 Introduction   145
   8.2 Socioscientific Reasoning, Intersubjectivity, and
       Technology-Mediated Dialogue   147
   8.3 Microblogging in Classroom Interactions   149
   8.4 Vignettes of Classroom Attunement and Intersubjectivity   150
       8.4.1 Who Is to Blame If the Car Crashes?   151
       8.4.2 "The Computer Could Go Crazy"   154
       8.4.3 "I Think You Should Do That One"   157
   8.5 Attunement and Intersubjectivity in Technology-Mediated
       Learning   160

9. Engaging in Dialogic Activities in an Online Community: Expanding the Notion of Double Dialogicality — 167
Kenneth Silseth, Ola Erstad, and Hans Christian Arnseth
   9.1 Introduction — 167
   9.2 Dialogism and Coauthorship of Meaning — 168
   9.3 Digital Technology and the Expansion of Double Dialogicality — 169
   9.4 Engaging in Dialogic Activities in an Online Community—Space2cre8 as an Illustrative Case — 170
   9.5 Conclusion — 175

10. Intersubjectivity and Dialogue in Video Games — 178
Declan Saviano
    10.1 Introduction — 178
    10.2 Online Gaming and Notions of Intersubjectivity — 180
    10.3 Contextual Background — 181
    10.4 Elements of the Communicative Medium and Their Influence on Toxicity — 185
    10.5 Enculturation — 187
    10.6 Data and Analysis — 188
    10.7 Disagreement and Intersubjectivity—Online and Offline — 192
    10.8 Conclusion — 194

SECTION 4: LEARNING DIALOGUES AT HOME AND IN SCHOOL

11. Opportunities to Learn and Intersubjectivity — 199
Catherine Snow and Joshua Lawrence
    11.1 Introduction — 199
    11.2 Classroom/Supports for Active Learning — 202
       11.2.1 Engaging in Debate and Discussion — 202
       11.2.2 Using Worked Examples to Promote Reflection — 204
       11.2.3 Collaborative Learning with Authentic Tasks — 206
       11.2.4 Summary of Classroom Methods — 207
    11.3 Piercing the Autonomous Learner Shield in Professional Development — 208
       11.3.1 Engaging in Hybrid Debate and Discussion — 210
       11.3.2 Using Worked Examples to Promote Reflection — 211
       11.3.3 Collaborative Learning with Authentic Tasks — 213
       11.3.4 From Practices to Principles — 214

12. Code-Switching During Shared Reading in Bilingual Families — 219
Dilman Nomat, Vibeke Grøver, and Veslemøy Rydland
    12.1 Introduction — 219
    12.2 A Dialogic Perspective on Parent—Child Code-Switching in the Context of Shared Reading — 220

	12.3	The Present Study	222
	12.4	Methods	222
		12.4.1 Participants	222
		12.4.2 Procedure and Data Collection	223
		12.4.3 Coding and Analysis	224
	12.5	Results	224
		12.5.1 Code-Switching Patterns Over Time in the Seven Dyads	224
		12.5.2 Code-Switching as a Tool in Scaffolded Dialogues	227
		12.5.3 Child-Initiated Code-Switching and Parental Confirmation	227
		12.5.4 Child-Initiated Code-Switching and Parental Extension	229
		12.5.5 Parent-Initiated Code-Switching to Support the Child's Understanding	231
	12.6	Discussion	233
	12.7	Conclusion	235
13.	The Importance of Intersubjectivity in Teacher–Child Joint Story Construction		239
	Bente Eriksen Hagtvet, Silje Hølland, Ellen Brinchmann, Liv Inger Engevik, Jannicke Karlsen, and Jana Kruse		
	13.1	Introduction	239
	13.2	Teaching and Learning as Communicative Acts, Based on Intersubjectivity	240
	13.3	Intersubjectivity and Learning Dialogues	240
		13.6.1 Participants	240
	13.4	Intersubjectivity in a Developmental Perspective	243
	13.5	The Current Study	243
	13.6	Method	244
		13.6.1 Participants	244
	13.7	Results	248
		13.7.1 Teacher–Child Interactions at High-Level Intersubjectivity	248
		13.7.2 Teacher–Child Interactions with Wavering Intersubjectivity	256
	13.8	Summary and Discussion	262
		13.8.1. Co-construction of Stories and Levels of Intersubjectivity	262
		13.8.2. Mediating with Intersubjectivity	263
		13.8.3. Understanding Variations and Relations: Methodological Reflections	264
		13.8.4. Three Dimensions of High-I Teacher Mediation	266
	13.9	Implications	267

SECTION 5: COMMENTARIES

14.	Dialogue, Polarization, and Change: Reflections—A Commentary	273
	Jay Lemke	

15. Not Just Change: Dialogue in Times of Crisis—A Commentary 277
    Alfredo Jornet
    15.1 A Perennial Theme of Acute Contemporary Relevance 277
    15.2 Crisis, Not Just Change 278
    15.3 The Implications of Considering Crisis 280
    15.4 The Significance of Dialogical Perspectives in a Time of
         Planetary Crisis 283
    15.5 A Brief Illustration 284
16. Legacies and Prospects of Dialogue—Editor's Final Note 290
    Ola Erstad, Bente Eriksen Hagtvet, and James V. Wertsch
    16.1 A Final Note 290
    16.2 With Inspiration from Ragnar Rommetveit 291

Index 295

Contributors

1. The Importance of Dialogue

Ola Erstad, Professor, Department of Education, University of Oslo

Bente Eriksen Hagtvet, Professor Emerita, Department of Special Needs Education, University of Oslo

James V. Wertsch, David R. Francis Distinguished Professor and Director Emeritus of the McDonnell International Scholars Academy, Washington University, St. Louis

2. The Role of Narratives in Dialogue and Intersubjectivity

James V. Wertsch, David R. Francis Distinguished Professor and Director Emeritus of the McDonnell International Scholars Academy, Washington University, St. Louis

3. Ragnar Rommetveit on Contextures and Partially Shared Understandings

Per Linell, Professor Emeritus, the Department of Education, Communication and Learning, Gothenburg University

4. Layered Attunement: Internal Dialogues of Intersubjectivity

Christian H. Bisgaard, 'Bisgaard Performance' and Centre of Cultural Psychology Aalborg

Marc Antoine Campill, University of Salerno, Italy & IBEF-International Centre of Excellence on Innovative Learning, Teaching Environments and Practices Shanghai, RPC

Enno Freiherr von Fircks, Sigmund-Freud-University (Vienna, Austria) PhD Student, Master of Social and Political Psychology, Gestalt practitioner in Siegen (Germany)

Jaan Valsiner, Centre of Cultural Psychology, Aalborg University

5. The Limits and Potential of Dialogue to Counter Polarization in Educative Settings

Mariëtte de Haan, Professor, Faculty of Social Sciences, Utrecht University

6. Active Citizenship and Participation Through "Dialogues in the Square"

Maria Beatrice Ligorio, University of Bari

Giovanna Barzanò, Ministry of Education, Universities and Research

Francesca Amenduni, Sfuvet Swiss Federal University for Vocational and Training

Roberta Cauchi, I.C. Settembrini

Sergio Turrisi, Liceo Machiavelli

Lorenzo Raffio, Tony Blair Institute

Claudia Ragazzini, I.C. Settembrini

Ludovica Valentino, Liceo Machiavelli

7. A Dialogic Theory of Educational Technology

Rupert Wegerif, Professor, Faculty of Education, University of Cambridge

Louis Major, Senior Lecturer in Digital Education, Manchester Institute of Education, University of Manchester

8. Using Microblogging to Create a Space for Attending and Attuning to Others

Ingvill Rasmussen, Professor, Department of Education, University of Oslo

Paul Warwick, Emeritus Fellow, Homerton College, University of Cambridge

9. Engaging in Dialogic Activities in an Online Community: Expanding the Notion of Double Dialogicality

Kenneth Silseth, Professor, Department of Education, University of Oslo

Ola Erstad, Professor, Department of Education, University of Oslo

Hans Christian Arnseth, Professor, Department of Education, University of Oslo

10. Intersubjectivity and Dialogue in Video Games

Declan Saviano, Consultant, Premier Advisory Group & MSc in Digital Anthropology, University College London

11. Opportunities to Learn and Intersubjectivity

Catherine Snow, John H. and Elisabeth A. Hobbs Professor of Cognition and Education, Harvard Graduate School of Education

Joshua Lawrence, Professor, Department of Education, University of Oslo

12. Code-Switching During Shared Reading in Bilingual Families

Dilman Nomat, Doctoral Research Fellow, Department of Education, University of Oslo

Vibeke Grøver, Professor, Department of Education, University of Oslo

Veslemøy Rydland, Professor, Department of Education, University of Oslo

13. The Importance of Intersubjectivity in Teacher–Child Joint Story Construction

Bente Eriksen Hagtvet, Professor Emerita, Department of Special Needs Education, University of Oslo

Silje Hølland, Associate Professor, Oslo Metropolitan University

Ellen Brinchmann, Associate Professor, Department of Special Needs Education, University of Oslo

Liv Inger Engevik, Associate Professor, Western Norway University of Applied Sciences

Jannicke Karlsen, Advisor, The National Service for Special Needs Education, Oslo

Jana Kruse, Advisor and Teacher, The Waldorf School, Nesodden

14. Dialogue, Polarization, and Change: Reflections—A Commentary

Jay Lemke, Professor Emeritus, City University of New York

15. Not Just Change: Dialogue in Times of Crisis—A Commentary

Alfredo Jornet, Ramón y Cajal Research Fellow, University of Girona

16. Legacies and Prospects of Dialogue—Editor's Final Note

Ola Erstad, Professor, Department of Education, University of Oslo

Bente Eriksen Hagtvet, Professor Emerita, Department of Special Needs Education, University of Oslo

James V. Wertsch, David R. Francis Distinguished Professor and Director Emeritus of the McDonnell International Scholars Academy at Washington University in St. Louis

1
The Importance of Dialogue

Ola Erstad, Bente Eriksen Hagtvet, and James V. Wertsch

1.1. Introduction

Human beings have lived through major social transformations over the course of history. It is not uncommon for each generation to experience some sort of crisis and fundamental transition in ways of living. Although the pace and complexities of change may have increased steadily, developments during the last decade have created an awareness that something fundamental in the human condition is at stake, especially for young generations: a devastating environmental crisis, increasing globalization with large-scale migration, and mounting instability and polarizations among groups and nations. For better and for worse, we at the same time undergo great impacts of digitalization in our daily life and in ways of collaborating. Together these developmental trends constitute this book's point of departure and pivotal context.

A number of scholars in the social sciences and the humanities have addressed the cultural and psychological dimensions of living through social, economic, and political crises (Castells et al., 2012; Wertsch et al., 1995), and how "enduring struggles" (Holland & Lave, 2001) become manageable via social practices, typically in collaboration with more experienced adults or friends. These developments have challenged scholars to carry out research that contributes to increased understanding of complex sociocultural processes and how we as human beings can cope with them. A number of scholars have argued that dialogue is man's most promising tool when faced with apparently unsolvable situations. Some of their ideas are represented in this book.

With this volume we highlight a set of ideas, perspectives, and research findings which may elucidate the basis for the abovementioned changes. We also offer examples of initiatives and research results at macro and micro levels that may contribute to increased understanding of these ongoing challenges, and also of ways of coping with them. A specific focus is on how *education* may contribute constructively to the handling of these ongoing—and often destructive—challenges.

Our overarching objective is to elucidate how a dialogical perspective is reimagined today as a perspective that sheds light on hidden, but nonetheless important, aspects of contemporary challenges in political/cultural, digital, and educational areas. A dialogical perspective also invites reflections on fundamental values of communication and how these are taken care of by educational institutions and programs.

1.2. The Importance of Dialogue

The basic rationale underlying this book is built around three key issues as accentuated by Ragnar Rommetveit (1968, 1979, 1992): "perspectivity," "dialogicality," and "intersubjectivity." These ideas point to the way we position ourselves toward others by taking their perspectives in everyday conversations, online communities, and political discourse. In dialogues characterized by good will and mutuality the interlocutors typically achieve intersubjectivity (shared understanding) by speaking and listening from each other's perspectives. In dialogues intended to, for example, cheat, harm, lie, or ridicule, the speaker on the contrary most typically speaks on his/her own premises and intersubjectivity is often not obtained. With these interdisciplinary ideas as points of departure, we see education as a key social system where students learn skills and knowledge that are fundamental to social and cultural development, such as skills in taking the perspective of others, skills of communication, and skills of establishing intersubjectivity.

A fundamental question is then, to what extent, and how, education systems, curricula, and teachers' practices may develop a culture of mutual respect that may foster students' appropriation of attitudes and skills that enable them to cope with ongoing social and cultural transformations, such as for example the ongoing digitalization process. The ideas of perspectivity, dialogicality, and intersubjectivity, often jointly referred to as a "dialogical perspective" (Rommetveit, 1968, 1992) or "dialogism" (Bakthin, 1981), are the cornerstones of these ongoing transformations, and also of this book. These are ideas that will be discussed in many of the book chapters, in different ways and through a multitude of topics. We shall argue that, at all levels, the most basic and productive vehicle in these ongoing change-generating processes is dialogue. Dialogue may both be a response to an increasing focus on individualism in our culture and education systems, and a tool of guiding human beings through these times of increased individualism and polarization. On the positive side, dialogues may promote communication in multicultural contexts, facilitate political solutions, support technology-mediated skills and knowledge, and promote learning at schools, work, and elsewhere. New solutions and insights in complex societies are typically a result of collaboration and collective problem-solving; dialogue is also the tool of internal individual dialogues as reflection and thinking. The dialogue is, in short, a most sensitive and productive tool of progress, learning, and intimacy among human beings. However, it is also a powerful, potentially even destructive, vehicle for misunderstandings, poor learning, social distancing, and animosity — via lies, sarcasm, and threatening hate speech, as is today daily experienced in the media, most prominently in the forms of fake news and disinformation intended to create harm.

During these times of large macro- and micro-level changes, education plays a pivotal role in assisting individual and societal needs for change, whether in formal settings such as preschool, school, and universities or, more informally, during leisure time, in the workplace, or in adapted programs of continued education. Education for all is the tool by which progress, inclusion, and innovation is made possible, and this provides an underlying premise for this book. By this, our volume has the humanistic objective of studying interaction in different contexts for the purpose of showing the importance and powers of dialogue and how it may contribute to students' learning in school. This is in many respects contrastive to traditional aims and means of schooling, which not rarely holds a rather monological view on learning and teaching: from the teacher to the child.

1.3. The Current Dominance of Monologic Approaches

In the face of the supremacy of individualist and monological ways of thinking and behaving in modern western societies, a number of potentially threatening implications arise, among which we will highlight three ongoing trends: "polarization," "personalization," and "digitalization."

The term *"polarization"* in this context refers to a process of dividing groups into opposites, or of how social spaces become divided between people, both within and between groups and nations. By often involving divisions into two sharply contrasting groups, or sets of opinions or beliefs, processes of polarization tend to generate distrust in systems and disruption of what has been taken for given facts by tradition, news media and science. Today we see increased polarization between people, communities, and societies. Even global agencies like the UN are failing to create good conditions for polarization-reducing acts, with the result that conflicts often escalate.

Developments during the last decade have shown how complex processes of communication have infiltrated contemporary societies and how polarization has created communicative tensions between people, communities, and nations. One example is the era of the Trump presidency in the United States, which both created upheaval on a global scale, and increased polarization between people at the local level. Within the field of political science, the idea of polarization has emerged as a concept by which one may raise fundamental questions about "global threats to democracy," where "potential consequences for democracy include gridlock and paralysis, careening and instability, democratic erosion, and democratic collapse" (Somer & McCoy, 2019: 9). We can also see how increased polarization and lack of dialogue affect societies and make them unable to act on environmental threats and build new sustainable future models for societies and social living. This has given rise to new activism among young people against old models and institutions and also to civil disobedience. Embedded in this is always processes of power, as strongly highlighted by Manuel Castells (2009). A related term in this discussion is "friction" (Tsing, 2005), which has been used to challenge the widespread view that globalization invariably signifies a "clash" of cultures. Therefore, Tsing alternatively suggests using "friction" as a metaphor for the diverse and conflicting social interactions that make up our contemporary world. Frictions may come in many forms and indicate tensions in communication and dialogue as well as a split between diverse interests, also with the potential of creating new "energy" and solutions.

Of more immediate relevance for our purpose in this book are analyses of people's lives and how communities relate to processes of polarization. Intriguing examples can be found in the books *Our Kids: The American Dream in Crisis* by Robert Putnam (2015) and *Coming of Age in the Other America* (Deluca et al., 2016). Both books describe how communities in the United States that used to be oriented toward togetherness across social and economic boundaries, with schools and students reaching across diverse communities, have now become more divided and segregated. Today families and children from different backgrounds do not meet in any social spaces to build mutual understanding and dialogic interrelationship.

Similar processes can be seen in other countries, for example in Norway, in an ethnographic research project studying young people and families in the Grorud valley, a multicultural community in the Eastern part of Norway's capital, Oslo (Erstad et al., 2016). During the last two decades, this community experienced transitions of families and increased segregation, with families of ethnic Norwegian background moving out of the Grorud valley, and diverse immigrant groups moving in. It has become a target of political parties on the political right to portray this development as an example of increased polarization and difference and therefore a threat to what some consider "Norwegianness" as cultural identity.

A second quality of the times in which we are living is increased *personalization*, with an emphasis on individuals' achievements. In the field of education this is reflected in its focus on individual students' performances and test scores as reflected in grades and formal diplomas. As societies become increasingly polarized, we see an increased orientation toward person-centered and monologic perspectives in human communication, in societies at large and, more specifically, in educational systems. Other important competencies such as skills of communication and collaboration are less appreciated. This increasing focus on individual performances is presumably at least partly, due to the growth of "social" media, which are in fact more person-oriented than social in the sense that communication centers around the individual with "likes," "emojies," "personal timelines," and stories about the individual self.

In social theory, arguments are often forwarded about social development and transformation as being more focused on the person than the collective as entity (Biesta, 2006). In Biesta's critique of "learning" as linked to international tests, he argued in favor of a broader collective understanding of "education." This could well be an underlying argument for several of the chapters in this volume. During the last two decades we have seen a growth in application of assessment systems of students' individual performances. International tests have in many countries set the agenda for curriculum development, content orientation within subjects, and foci of teachers. The consequence is that the teachers' attention is geared more toward students' learning as individual achievements, than toward collective processes. Still there are developments that point to the efficacy of approaches that focus more on transversal topics—for example, civic education—and the complexities of social and environmental issues.

It follows from the above that increasing *digitalization* appears to be a crucial driver of monologic ways of thinking and behaving. Digitalization has had an unforeseen impact on the way we orient ourselves towards others and to the world around us. Even though the benefits and expectations of digital technologies have been acknowledged by many, developments during the last decade have made us more aware of the dangers and challenges also involved. One example is the growth of disinformation, conspiracy theories, and fake news pointing toward how distrust in social institutions create a sense of insecurity regarding how we can orient ourselves in an increasingly complex world of information. Another example is the way life online and the way we communicate digitally does not appear to create more openness towards other perspectives and opinions, but rather less, mainly due to the way algorithms are defined and coded within platforms like Facebook, Amazon, and Google—all global companies of immense power. This is often described as "filter bubbles" and "echo chambers," where the algorithms make us communicate with like-minded people building communities with people that think like we do. The implications include more online hate speech, sexual harassment, disrespect, marginalization and exclusion of people and groups, often perpetrated by anonymous users. These developments undermine coexistence across different communities and positions and challenge us as citizens in who we can trust and how we can orient ourselves in creating our own understanding of the world around us.

Digitalization has also had an impact on our education system and the ways we learn. Again, there are both benefits and risks associated with the digital tools we have available. As shown in this book there are examples of activities using digital tools where dialogic approaches are emphasized. However, the dominant force today has been towards machine learning, learning analytics of big data emphasizing what has become the prominent slogan of "personalized learning", and the growth of artificial intelligence (like ChatGPT). This means more adapted approaches on a personal level where learning is tuned to individual needs and abilities, and where the digital tools and system provide feedback on input by students. In its simplest forms these are simply technically more advanced tools than those used in the past, yet more developed tools may engage the learner in diverse activities of problem-solving.

We have above highlighted three ongoing trends, "polarization," "personalization" and "digitalization," which in different ways appear to enhance individualist approaches to development and learning. A striking trend characterizing the last decade regards how ways of communicating apparently become more polarized and filled with tensions, creating a sense of crisis. An implication of this state of affairs is that a deeper understanding of how these serious challenges of our societies may be approached more dialogically is needed. Much has been written about ongoing social processes and the challenges that humankind faces today, and from different perspectives. However, many of these perspectives suffer from a lack of studying the ecology of how social processes are intertwined with people and communities (Erstad et al., 2016). Also, they offer few ways of thinking about possible futures and ways to address these challenges. The basic argument for this book is that a dialogic approach as understood through communicative practices, language use, and diverse mediational means, as nurtured by the role of education in our societies, are fundamental ways to understand and create social futures.

1.4. The Dialogical Rationale of This Book: Key Theoretical Positions

We will now return to the key issues framing the orientation of this book: perspectivity, dialogicality and intersubjectivity, as presented in this chapter's introduction, highlighted by Ragnar Rommetveit (1968, 1992), and inspired by thinkers and philosophers, such as Mikhail Bakhtin (1984), Lev Vygotsky (1978), George Herbert Mead (1934), and Ludwig Wittgenstein (1968).

Throughout his life, Rommetveit argued that verbal meaning was determined by its context of use and that descriptions of reality depend on the perspectives and positions adopted by the dialogue partners when interacting. From this follows that word meanings as well as individuals' knowledge and language skills should be studied in the stream of life (Wittgenstein, 1968). As a social psychologist influenced by phenomenological philosophy, Rommetveit (1968, 1992, 1998) further argued that everyday spoken dialogue should be investigated from within, i.e. from the perspectives of the interlocutors and from the psychology of the second person.

By this, Rommetveit places the "dialogue in context" at the center of verbally transmitted meaning-making, be it verbal interactions among close friends, between interrogator and accused at police stations, between teacher and child in learning contexts, or between speaker and listeners at formal meetings. Rommetveit formulated a set of fundamental presuppositions of "the ideal dialogue," characterized by, among other qualities, authenticity: authentic communication aims at establishing intersubjectivity ("shared here and now") and is characterized by reciprocity, complementarity, and sincerity (Rommetveit, 1979). The speaker talks on the premises of the listener, and the listener complementarily interprets the message on the premises of the speaker. It is then that the ideal dialogue is, within the constraints of a culturally established "shared social reality," characterized by perspectival relativity (Hagtvet & Wold, 2009).

Rommetveit developed his ideas about language, thought, and communication largely as an alternative to mainstream linguistics, as advocated at the time by the Harvard MIT group, foremost by Noam Chomsky (1957), which promoted an individualist orientation and adherence to methodologies that did not encourage studies of interactively established meaning in everyday dialogue.

During the last two decades dialogism as a theoretical position (here, broadly defined as a "counter-theory" to monologism (Linell, 2009)), has gained recognition within the humanities and social sciences, both as an approach to increased understanding of sociocultural processes in general and to communicative practices in specific settings (Wegerif, 2013; Wertsch, 2002). It has been used in ways of studying how we interact with a multitude of texts and voices in everyday life and also how we communicate in the classroom, the court, the hospital, and other settings (Linell, 2009; Pianta, 1999).

Arguing that complex phenomena should be studied from multiple perspectives, it follows that Rommetveit's theoretical frame of reference is fundamentally interdisciplinary. The interdisciplinary quality of this book is in the spirit of Ragnar Rommetveit. It studies communication under different contextual constraints associated with the book's four sections (SECTION 1: The legacy of Rommetveit; SECTION 2: Societal conditions for dialogue and the role of education; SECTION 3: The role of digital technologies; and SECTION 4: Learning dialogues at home and in school). Thereby the chapters of this book are expected to shed light on dialogical challenges specifically associated with these four domains and, more generally, on prerequisites of successful communication within an overarching educational frame.

1.5. Dialogue and Learning

A main contribution of this book concerns its focus on dialogue and learning as a dual relationship. The dialogue is both a fundamental means and a vital aim of education, and the book covers both functions. As strongly underscored by sociocultural theory, the dialogue is an essential "tool" of teaching, learning, and processing of new knowledge—in the form of interactions between teacher and student, student and student, and learner and learner (the learner's "inner speech" (Vygotsky, 1978)). However, dialogue is also a crucial *aim* of learning—via the *role of education in providing for dialogic perspectives and skills*. This includes skills in taking the perspectives of dialogue partners, be they children, youngster or adults, in daycare, school, or families. Education is important not only in the sense that young people gain knowledge through interaction and are expected to learn the tools and skills of digital and analog communication, but also as a social mechanism for how they evolve as citizens and appropriate democratic ideals and thought patterns. Dialogues thereby provide a means for understanding how interaction and respect for other human beings are addressed and developed. This includes learning how to participate in and master democratic dialogues that are not characterized by hierarchical power structures but by egalitarian values and mutual intentions to achieve intersubjectivity (Habermas, 1984). As such we refer to, but also go beyond, Vygotskian studies of learning.

Something is at stake for public education systems in contemporary societies. This is reflected both in increased privatization of education in many countries and in the fundamental questions frequently raised by the media and researchers on the role of school and public education today and for the future. For example, in contrast to the last two decade-strong focus on testing and assessment of instrumental performance indicators of schools, teachers, and students at the national and international levels, recent curricula in countries like Norway and Finland indicate that broader aspects of education and Bildung are today being addressed, such as the cross-curricular topic of "life skills" (livsmestring) in the national curriculum of Norway (implemented in 2020). As a whole, the chapters in this volume underline the important discussion of how our public education system and quality education for all is of utmost importance for countering polarization in our societies. We hope this book will contribute to a broader public debate about these issues of utmost importance to civic dialogues and education.

1.6. The Structure of the Book

The contributors to this book have been influential in highlighting the potentialities of dialogic approaches within educational studies, in empirical research of teaching and learning practices (with and without digital technologies), in classroom settings as well as in dialogues between adult–child and child–child. At a concrete level, the objective has been to contextualize dialogism and education within present day challenges of how children and young adults live their lives with demanding life conditions and varied future options.

The chapters are grouped within four different sections implying different thematic orientations and levels of analysis. Section 1 provides theoretical perspectives of key importance in this field, referring to Ragnar Rommetveit and beyond. Section 2 is oriented broadly at societal, political, and community perspectives of importance for understanding communicative and dialogic practices. Section 3 mainly focuses on the importance of digital technologies in educational settings as resources for dialogic practices. Section 4 provides examples from classroom settings and learning dialogues between parent-and-child and teacher-and-child as micro-level analyses of dialogic practices. Finally, we have invited two scholars to provide personal reflections on the contributions of the volume and the topics presented, also with a short book-end Editors' Note, where we make concluding remarks framing this book.

The chapters offer a variety of interdisciplinary approaches to studies of learning across a range of domains: home, school, preschool, and local community. A common denominator is the role and meaning of immediate and distant social and cultural contexts in ongoing verbal communication and also on the impacts of different kinds of learning and of the development of digital technologies that play a role in the ways we communicate.

Each chapter in this book sheds light on essential communication challenges of our times. By revealing the circumstances by which dialogue contributes to increased intersubjectivity, as well as when it contributes to misunderstandings, ignorance, and frustrations, the authors point to some specific qualities of successful communication. Using this framework, we believe that this book will provide important insights into essential aspects of human living, learning, and growth in contemporary societies.

This edited collection brings together scholars from a number of European and North American countries to consider the potentials and pressing issues of dialogic perspectives on macro, meso, and micro levels. The contributors draw on various fields of scholarship including educational sciences, philosophy, linguistics, sociology, psychology, cultural studies, and literacy research. The book offers results from recent and ongoing research projects, and introductory and concluding essays frame the idea of the book and explore its implications for policy and educational practice.

References

Bakhtin, M. (1981). *The dialogic imagination: Four essays*. (C. Emerson and M. Holquist, Trans.; M. Holquist, Ed.). University of Texas Press.
Biesta, G. (2006). *Beyond learning: Democratic education for a human future*. Routledge.
Castells, M. (2009). *The rise of the network society*. Wiley-Blackwell.
Castells, M., Caraca, J., & Cardoso, G. (2012). *Aftermath: The cultures of the economic crisis*. Oxford University Press.
Chomsky, N. (1957). *Syntactic structures*. Mouton.
Deluca, S., Clampet-Lundquist, S., & Edin, K. (2016). *Coming of age in the other America*. Russell Sage Foundation.
Erstad, O., Gilje, Ø., Sefton-Green, J., & Arnseth, H. C. (2016). *Learning identities, education, and community. Young lives in the cosmopolitan city*. Cambridge: Cambridge University Press.
Habermas, J. (1984). *The theory of communicative action: Reason and the rationalization of society*. (Vol. 1). Beacon Press.
Hagtvet, B. E., & Wold, A. H. (2009). On the dialogical basis of meaning: Inquiries into Ragnar Rommetveit's writing on language, thought, and communication. *Mind, Culture, and Activity*, 10(3), 186–204. doi:10.1207/s15327884mca2003 2.
Holland, D., & Lave, J. (Eds.). (2001). *History in person*. School of American Research Press.
Linell, P. (2009). *Rethinking language, mind, and world dialogically: Interactional and contextual theories of human sense-making*. Information Age Publishing.
Mead, G. H. (1934). *Mind, self, and society*. Chicago University Press.
Pianta, R. C. (1999). *Enhancing relationships between children and teachers*. American Psychological Association.
Putnam, R. D. (2015). *Our kids: The American dream in crisis*. Simon & Schuster.
Rommetveit, R. (1968). *Words, meaning, and messages: Theory and experiments in psycholinguistics*. Academic Press.
Rommetveit, R. (1979). On the architecture of intersubjectivity. In R. Rommetveit & R. M. Blakar (Eds.), *Studies of language, thought and verbal communication* (pp. 93–107). Academic Press.
Rommetveit, R. (1992). Outlines of a dialogically based social-cognitive approach to human cognition and communication. In A. H. Wold (Ed.), *The dialogical alternative: Towards a theory of language and mind* (pp. 19–44). Scandinavian University Press.
Rommetveit, R. (1998). On human beings, computers and representational-computational vs hermeneutic-dialogical approaches to human cognition and communication. *Culture & Psychology*, 4(2), 213–233.
Somer, M., & McCoy, J. (2019). Transformations through Polarizations and Global Threats to Democracy. In *ANNALS, AAPSS, Special Issue 'Polarizing Polities: A Global Threat to Democracy*, 681, 8–22.
Tsing, A. (2005). *Friction: An ethnography of global connections*. Princeton University Press.
Vygotsky, L. S. (1978). *Mind in society: The development of higher psychological processes*. Harvard University Press.
Wegerif, R. (2013). *Dialogic education for the internet age*. Routledge.

Wertsch, J. (2002). *Voices of collective remembering: A narrative approach.* Cambridge University Press.
Wertsch, J. V., del Rio, P., & Alvarez, A. (1995). Sociocultural studies: History, action, and mediation. In J. V. Wertsch, P. del Rio, & A. Alvarez (Eds.), *Sociocultural studies of mind* (pp. 1–32). Cambridge University Press.
Wittgenstein, L. (1968). *Philosophical investigations.* Blackwell.

SECTION 1
THE LEGACY OF ROMMETVEIT

Drawing on ideas of Ragnar Rommetveit as a starting point, the three chapters in this section expand the notion of dialogue beyond the sort of face-to-face interaction at the heart of many of his analyses. These chapters make their contributions from different perspectives, in the process illustrating the power and generativity of Rommetveit's ideas about human dialogue and intersubjectivity.

In Chapter 3, Per Linell notes that many studies of dialogue focus on "'micro-social' phenomena in the daily lives of people's face-to-face interactions" and cites the school of discourse studies known as "conversation analysis" as a case in point. In contrast to this approach, he urges us to focus on "macro-social" relations, including global conversations about politics, trade, and the media. In pursuing this goal, he harnesses the notion of "communicative activity types." In this view, context is part of the starting point of studies of language and communication rather than something that can be added back in later. Linell illustrates these ideas with analyses of communicative activity types such as the "censured monological" language Vladimir Putin uses to justify Russia's invasion of Ukraine. The general point is that "sense-making practices must often invoke remote, or nonlocal, contexts of the participants' background knowledge, i.e. aspects that are not immediately present in the particular situation at hand."

In Chapter 4, Christian H. Bisgaard, Marc Antoine Campill, Enno von Fircks, and Jaan Valsiner take up a complementary set of issues by examining "layered attunement." They emphasize the hierarchical organization of human thought and communication and call for a new set of analytic tools to address it. Their goal is to understand the "negotiation of multiple simultaneously occurring inter- and intrapsychological dialogues" involved in navigating complex contexts in which individuals routinely operate.

Bisgaard et al. emphasize the complexity of communication contexts by examining the choices made during the COVID-19 pandemic. This involves conflicting voices from different perspectives and expanding the notion of dialogue in both time and space. In the cases they examine, individuals are, to be sure, influenced by the immediate physical context of the encountered situation, but this occurs with help of multiple dialogues with experiences in the past as well as with future imagined contexts.

James V. Wertsch, in Chapter 2, explores ways that narratives involve dialogue. Borrowing from L. S. Vygotsky, he argues that narratives are symbolic tools and that using them involves a kind of coauthorship. The symbolic tools we use have invariably been part of previous dialogues, which means they come with meaningful baggage already attached to them. For example, in using the expression "Make America great again!", this baggage is obvious in today's context, but the symbolic tools used to create any utterance come loaded with echoes of where they have been used. And another dimension of coauthorship shows up in how they are used (e.g. sincerely or mockingly).

Like other symbolic tools, Wertsch argues that narratives have these traits. This is true for "specific narratives" and for "narrative templates" as well as "aspirational narratives." Using any of these symbolic tools on a particular occasion involves dialogue in the form of coauthorship. But the power of narratives to grasp things together in particular ways gives them a coherent form that often goes on to allow for dialogic encounters between the narrative tools themselves. For instance, national narratives sometimes take on the form of counternarratives that seem to be more intent on refuting others, say, than on telling a national story on its own terms.

The common thread that runs throughout all three of the chapters in this section is that it is important to expand notions of dialogue and intersubjectivity into new territory. The dialogic stance that Rommetveit introduced remains intact, but it is now expanded well beyond what he discussed. The larger theme of this entire volume is that understanding dialogue in its various guises can be the key to dealing with some of today's societal problems, such as the polarization involved in populism and nationalism. The three chapters in this section seek to "get inside" dialogic encounters of various sorts to gain a better perspective on how dialogue can go so wrong and on what we might be able to do to address this pressing problem.

2
The Role of Narratives in Dialogue and Intersubjectivity

James V. Wertsch

2.1. Introduction

Ragnar Rommetveit's insightful reflections on dialogue and intersubjectivity have played an important role in theoretical and applied studies of human discourse and mind, and they continue to do so today. By injecting a phenomenological perspective into the debate, he expanded the field of inquiry into topics that transcend standard methods in psychology, linguistics, and discourse analysis. And during the last decades of his career, his impact grew even greater as he expanded his vision by drawing on ideas from Lev Vygotsky (1986) on sociocultural context and Mikhail Bakhtin (1981) on dialogism. The array of topics explored in this volume reflects the generative power that Rommetveit's ideas (1974) continue to have to this day.

In what follows, I build on his ideas as well as those of Bakhtin and Vygotsky about dialogism and intersubjectivity. These authors were interested in going beyond the isolated individual when answering the question, who is doing the speaking? Instead of being produced by atomistic, "unencumbered" individuals, utterance involves what Bakhtin scholar Michael Holquist (2002) called "coauthorship" by the words of others. My goal is to expand this vision by including narratives as powerful and pervasive forms of symbolic mediation in such coauthorship. They serve as what Kenneth Burke (1998) called "equipment for living" that makes it possible for us to size up social settings and actors quickly, unconsciously, and with great—but sometimes misplaced—confidence.

In addition to these figures, this chapter draws on ideas by several other contributors in this volume. For example, it resonates with Linell's notion of "double dialogicality," which emphasizes how dialogue between interlocutors also involves dialogue with the sociocultural conditions in which they are embedded. And it complements the claims of Silseth, Erstad, and Arnseth (Chapter 9, this volume) about how new media shape dialogue. The evidence I examine comes from spoken or written narratives that have a surface form in discourse; but in order to make sense of them, I also posit underlying codes in

James V. Wertsch, *The Role of Narratives in Dialogue and Intersubjectivity* In: *Education and Dialogue in Polarized Societies*. Edited by: Ola Erstad, Bente Eriksen Hagtvet, and James V. Wertsch, Oxford University Press.
© Oxford University Press 2024. DOI: 10.1093/oso/9780197605424.003.0002

the form of schematic "narrative templates" (Wertsch, 2021). The psychological counterpart of these underlying codes takes the form of habit as first outlined by William James (1890) over a century ago and on more recent ideas about "fast thinking" (Kahneman, 2011). My focus on narratives and narrative habits is designed to account for successful efforts in attaining intersubjectivity, but it also recognizes impediments to intersubjectivity that stem from how narrative tools can create powerful barriers to understanding.

This effort to expand the notion of symbolic mediation draws on discussions about narratives that have been part of Western scholarship since Aristotle. In recent decades these ideas have been elaborated by figures such as Peter Brooks (1984), Paul Ricoeur (1984), and Alasdair MacIntyre (1984). The resulting approach views human discourse and mind as mediated by narratives, and it involves both an effort to provide new insights into theoretical debates and an attempt to address practical challenges in a contemporary world filled with contention and conflict.

2.2. The Influence of Rommetveit

Rommetveit spent decades meditating on the nature of face-to-face interaction, or what Bakhtin called the "primordial dialogue of discourse" (1984). In Rommetveit's account, such interaction involves the negotiation of new meaning that cannot be reduced to the transmission of information from one individual to another. In contrast to views of intersubjectivity as some sort of easily attained state of agreement, he emphasized its partial and temporary nature, an observation that had implications for many disciplines and areas of practice. In doing so, he drew on constructs in semiotics, language philosophy, and discourse analysis and maintained a focus on interactive processes of communication as opposed to linguistic structure.

In the early years of his career, Rommetveit developed a strong reputation in Europe and North America for his research in social psychology, but his curiosity drove him to search for answers by drawing on other disciplines as well. The first time that I witnessed this curiosity in action was in the summer of 1976 when I visited Rommetveit and a group of colleagues at the University of Oslo. I was on my way back to the United States from a year as a postdoctoral scholar in Moscow and was anxious to learn more about his ideas, which I had studied in graduate school at the University of Chicago. But what I found was that he was interested in more than just revisiting the insights of his earlier writings. Instead, his spirit of inquiry drove him to delve into new issues, including those of concern to scholars such as Vygotsky (1986), Luria (1981), and A. N. Leont'ev (1981), and later to Bakhtin. In taking this approach, he was a model for his junior colleagues from all over the world to emulate—an internationally renowned senior scholar who was always open to further growth.

Along with many other students and colleagues, I profited immensely from these discussions in the decades after 1976. As I searched for ways to build on Vygotsky's ideas about the social origins of mental functioning, including in the "zone of proximal development" (Wertsch, 1985), for example, I came to appreciate how powerful Rommetveit's ideas could be exploring the forms of adult–child dialogue that underpinned mental development. When applied to adult–child interaction, his analysis of intersubjectivity as a temporary, partially shared understanding of the world suggested that child development can be understood from the perspective of drawing children into more adult-like levels of understanding. These ideas proved to be a natural extension of Vygotsky's ideas, and bringing Rommetveit's ideas about intersubjectivity into the discussion led to a budding industry of research in developmental psychology by Barbara Rogoff (1990), Rogoff and Wertsch (1984), and others.

I developed additional levels of appreciation for Rommetveit's ideas as we discussed the implications of Bakhtin's ideas about dialogism. For Bakhtin, dialogue is not just one form of discourse and thought but rather lies at the very core of what it means to be human. Instead of starting with a stand-alone, "unencumbered" individual (Sandel, 2009) as a unit of analysis and then building up to dialogue, Bakhtin emphasized that thought and discourse of individuals—and individuals themselves are inherently dialogic in origin and nature. This stands in opposition to assumptions of methodological individualism that underpin much of the research conducted in psychology, especially in the United States. Both Rommetveit and Bakhtin pushed the boundaries of dialogue and how to examine it. The former did this in his deep reflections on the limits and fleeting nature of intersubjectivity, which requires constant negotiation and construction; and Bakhtin made his contribution by expanding the notion of dialogue to deal with "multivoicedness," "hidden dialogicality," "speech genres," and other issues (Bakhtin, 1986a; Wertsch, 1991).

What follows is consistent with these ideas, but it seeks to expand on them by bringing narrative mediation into the picture. It is part of an effort to expand the answer we can provide to the Bakhtinian question for any utterance: "Who is doing the speaking?" The answer for Bakhtin was: at least two voices. First, there is an active speaker in a concrete context, producing a unique utterance, but the symbolic tools they employ introduce at least one other voice, making the utterance coauthored. And narratives are among the most powerful symbolic tools we have. In general, symbolic tools are not invented on the spot but come with a history of use attached to them. In Bakhtin's words, there is no "linguistic Adam" who produces entirely novel utterances from whole cloth. Instead, any utterance is part of a "chain of speech communication" in which words used in the present have a history and retain the "scent" of where they have been (Bakhtin, 1981). The resulting picture is one of dialogism, or multivoicedness in the form of coauthorship. Words don't speak themselves, they require a concrete speaker to make them into utterances; but at the same time symbolic tools introduce a history and structure of their own into what a speaker says.

This claim applies to all forms of symbolic mediation. For example, it means our utterances are shaped by a language's grammar with its own history and organizing principles. This is a point that cognitive anthropologist Lera Boroditsky[1] makes in describing how the use of verbs in an Australian Aborigine language requires the speaker to know where they are vis-à-vis points on a compass. In a humorous illustration Boroditsky uses in presentations to Western audiences, she asks people to close their eyes and point to the southeast. Not surprisingly, nearly all are clueless and point in all sorts of directions, but this is a task that small children who speak the (Aborigine) language do effortlessly. Such observations reflect how a grammar requires speakers of a language to develop the habits needed to make certain distinctions whenever they speak. Boroditsky traces this line of reasoning out in a way that reflects claims made by Benjamin Lee Whorf (1956) and others nearly a century ago about how different languages may encourage different world views.

Bakhtin (1986b) was fully aware of how grammar shapes discourse and thinking, but like Rommetveit, he took the unique, situated *utterance* rather than the abstract linguistic unit of a sentence as a prime unit of analysis. Instead of focusing on how the abstract structure of a language's grammar shapes thought, he was concerned with the impact of patterns of utterances found in "social languages" and "speech genres" (Bakhtin, 1986a) These give rise to the multivoicedness of any utterance that stems from the fact that the words we use bring along with them a rich history of social discourse. This is often an extended history, making it difficult to detect the extent to which utterances from the past, sometimes the distant past, influence what we say and think in the present.

In some instances, however, the use of a social language belonging to others can be quite obvious. If I were to drop the expression "make America great again" into the middle of a conversation with someone in the United States in 2021, the presence of a social language, namely that of Donald Trump and his followers, is so obvious that it is impossible to take this as an expression that emanates from nothing more than my own personal view. It is an expression that belongs to others, and using it allows others' voices to "infiltrate" my speech, regardless of whether I want this to happen or not. In such cases, the scent of where an expression has been is so strong that its meaning is populated with ideological

---

[1] https://www.youtube.com/watch?v=RKK7wGAYP6k

overtones that may lead people to refuse to use it or to use it only with mocking, ironic sense.

For Bakhtin, however, claims about the multivoiced nature of utterances extend far beyond instances where the voice of the other is so blatantly obvious. His claims apply to *any* utterance, a point he elaborated in a variety of ways. In the end we can no more speak without using a national language, such as English or Japanese, than we can without using "social languages" that belong to certain groups of speakers and "speech genres" that reflect speech contexts ranging from highly scripted ones in religious ceremonies to more flexible ones as in everyday discussions. When speaking in a highly scripted speech genre, such as that required in the military, for example, one can respond with "Yes sir!" or "Aye, aye, sir!", but not with "OK," "Yeah," or some other more informal speech style. In all cases of social languages and speech genres, Bakhtin's starting point was that we are using the words of generalized contexts of speech or generalized groups.

2.3. Narrative as a Symbolic Tool

In what follows, I expand on the ideas of Rommetveit and Bakhtin by bringing another form of symbolic mediation into the picture—narratives. These are often part of social languages and speech genres, but they introduce an additional form of symbolic organization. The study of narratives has long been part of scholarly inquiry in psychology, literary analysis, moral philosophy, and other disciplines. For my purposes, the ideas of the philosophers Paul Ricoeur (1913–2005) and Alasdair MacIntyre (b. 1929) are of particular importance. Both explored narratives as fundamental tools of human discourse and mental life. For them, as for many other analysts of narrative, such as the Russian semiotician Yuri Lotman (1976), narrative is a closed text organized around a plot that grasps together a set of events that occur across time into a coherent whole.

In examining the role of narratives in mediation and intersubjectivity, it is useful to return once more to the question: Who is doing the speaking? And to remember that the Bakhtinian answer is: At least two voices. One is the voice of a concrete individual speaking in a unique time, space, and social setting. The other is the voice, or voices, that have infiltrated the utterance the speaker is making, voices that reflect a history of past usage and bring the overtones of others into what the speaker says. Narratives play a crucial role in this regard, and if we see the world, especially the social world, through narrative lenses, it becomes important to understand the history and structure of these lenses.

It has long been recognized that plot is the crucial organizational feature of narrative structure. Plot is what gives narratives their status of "cognitive instruments" (Mink, 1978) and organizes discursive and mental processes in ways that differ from, say, the abstract logico-mathematical processes involved in syllogisms (Bruner, 1986; Luria, 1981). Part of what makes narrative mediation crucial for human discourse and thought is that narratives are such a ubiquitous part of everyday life, a fact that also allows them to operate in such unnoticed, unconscious ways that it easy to overlook their impact.

In an effort to unpack how this works, I introduce the distinction between "specific narratives," which include information about concrete individuals, times, places, and events, and "narrative templates" (Wertsch, 2002; 2021), which are largely devoid of such specific information. The latter rely on schemata of the sort discussed by Frederic Bartlett (1932) and Ulric Neisser (1967), and they reflect a sort of distilled remnant from countless experiences with specific narratives. In the case of national narratives, an illustration can be found in the "Expulsion-of-Alien-Enemies" narrative template that shapes discourse in the Russian national community. As I have outlined elsewhere (Wertsch, 2021), this is a general story line that begins with a setting in which Russia is peacefully existing and bothering no one, followed by a wanton and vicious attack by an alien enemy that turns into an existential threat to Russian civilization, which in turn, gives rise to a heroic effort by Russia, acting alone, to fight the enemy, followed by an ending about the expulsion of the invader. This narrative template organizes the understanding of multiple episodes of the past for this community, including the Great Patriotic War (1941–1945), the Napoleonic invasion of 1812, the Mongol invasions of the thirteenth century, and even communism (Wertsch, 2021). This Russian case illustrates a widespread pattern of using specific narratives and abstract narrative schemata in national memory.

2.4. American National Narratives as Coauthors

Like Russia and other nations, America has its own narrative tools that shape political discourse and national memory. As in other cases, these tools serve as more than neutral cognitive instruments. They are also a source of the emotional commitments and norms that come with the American collective identity project, and as such, they are a blueprint not only for what is, but for what *should* be.

In the American case, there are several candidates for a national narrative, but the one that is perhaps best known is the "City on a Hill" story. This can be traced to a sermon given by the Puritan John Winthrop in 1630 on a ship anchored off the New England coast. There, he preached to his congregants about their challenge and responsibility by drawing on Matthew 5:14: "Ye are the light of the world. A city that is set on a hill cannot be hid." In reality, as Abram Van Engen (2020) has noted, it was only in the nineteenth century that the use of this narrative began to appear in political discourse about how America can serve as a beacon of light for other nations as they move toward liberty, democracy, and prosperity. The City on a Hill reemerged as a theme during the Cold War and was invoked in the following decades by figures ranging from John Kennedy to Ronald Reagan and from Newt Gingrich to Barack Obama.

In this national narrative, America is presented as exceptional in its aspirations and accomplishments, including the claim that, in contrast to nations grounded in ethnicity or blood ties, America was based on Enlightenment principles and began with a covenant among free people. As such, it is viewed as an exceptional nation and as having a unique mission. These are claims that strike some in the United States, and especially people in other countries, as not only arrogant but hubristic and dangerous; and on more than one occasion, they have produced disastrous consequences. However, they continue to provide an underlying and seemingly unshakeable foundation for political discourse, as reflected in the fact that successful political leaders in the United States invoke them time and again to mobilize public opinion.

This is not to say this narrative is not contested, even in the United States. As Van Engen notes, the emergence of the City on a Hill narrative was part of a larger political struggle between one region and another in what would eventually come together to form the United States. Specifically, it reflected the perspective of New England citizens and elites that guided historical scholarship and public education in the eighteenth century. In many respects it was largely the *only* national narrative in public discourse at the time, reflecting the fact that the bulk of historians and textbook writers promulgating it were from this region.

Largely left out in this public discussion, however, was the perspective of slave-holding regions in the South. In the early years of America, racism and slavery could be found in all regions of the colonies, but the South witnessed the emergence of traditions that left room for slavery as a "peculiar institution" along with a commitment to the vision of the City on a Hill narrative. As in the case for many national narratives, this pattern of commitment to an exceptionalist view and grand mission somehow exists side by side with less savory episodes from that past, and the obvious contradictions are often handled by ignoring the latter or claiming they were aberrations in the overall story line.

In trying to sort this out, it is useful to consult some of the ideas of moral philosopher MacIntyre (1984). His focus is on identity and moral choices that individuals make for themselves, but they also apply to individuals as members of national communities. In a crucial passage he wrote, "I can only answer the question 'What am I to do?' if I can answer the prior question, 'Of what story or stories do I find myself a part?'" (1984, 216), meaning that narrative tools not only help us understand who we are, but have normative power in telling us what we should do. Furthermore, these tools are what might be called "off-the-shelf technology" (Wertsch, 1998) meaning narrative tools are not the creation or invention of individuals acting alone. Instead, MacIntyre noted, that "an understanding of any society, including our own, [begins with] . . . the stock of stories which constitute its initial dramatic resources (ibid., p. 216).

For MacIntyre, the City on a Hill story would count as an "aspirational narrative." Instead of an ending that takes the form of a known, concrete outcome that brings into focus everything that goes before, it takes the form of an imagined "telos" about where we are headed—and should be headed. In the case of national narratives, this means they are tools of a "national narrative project" (Wertsch, 2021) with an aspired-to, yet indefinite future outcome, or "telos" for the community. This contrasts with a closed text about historical events such as World War II, which has a concrete beginning and middle, and an ending that grasps together and gives meaning to the events and characters in the story and can give rise to narrative templates. To qualify as a narrative template means that multiple specific narratives are emplotted (Ricoeur, 1984) in accordance with the same general story line, where the sense of an ending is crucial.

A simple illustration of this latter type of narrative is a detective story with an ending that neatly wraps up preceding events, making it possible to understand the characters and their actions in the story and reveals "who done it." When Agatha Christie's hero detective Hercule Poirot convenes a group of potential suspects at the end of a murder case, we gain neat closure on who the perpetrator was and the meaning of the characters and events in the story. No such neat ending caps off aspirational narratives such as those of national narrative projects. The end point takes the form of an aspiration, a project being pursued rather than an actual event that has happened.

2.5. Competing Narrative Templates

Up to this point I have laid out some ideas of how narratives coauthor what we say and think, creating a dialogic encounter between the voice of a concrete speaking individual in a specific speaking context and the voices associated with narrative tools (cf. the "make America great again" story line noted earlier). But other forms of dialogism are often part of the picture when one community confronts another. This has parallels with the kind of face-to-face dialogic negotiation envisioned by Rommetveit, but in this case the negotiation is going on between communities, each equipped with its own narrative tools.

In the American case, for example, this plays out in how various accounts of the past challenge or coexist with the City on a Hill national narrative. This dialogic encounter often becomes complex and heated in discussions of slavery in America. For example, Van Engen writes about how slavery in the state of

Virginia gave rise to an alternative vision of the social order that challenges the City on a Hill story. Virginian Thomas Jefferson, author of the famous words that "All men are created equal" in the Declaration of Independence, owned slaves and treated them as such. While opposing slavery in many of his public pronouncements and labeling it a "moral depravity" and "hideous blot,"[2] Jefferson himself refused to free his slaves, including the mother of several of his children, even at his death.

Jefferson and other leaders from the South dealt with the obvious paradox and hypocrisy involved by acknowledging that slavery was a stain on America, but they did little to end it. Instead, they sidestepped it, passing it on to future generations, a failure that led up to the American Civil War of 1861–1865. Jumping ahead to today, figures as diverse as Barack Obama and Senator Mitch McConnell, a conservative Republican senator from Kentucky, continue to use "original sin" when speaking of slavery, suggesting that to this day slavery is viewed as an anomaly in America's national narrative. In this view, it exists alongside the City on a Hill story, which often ignores it or in other cases addresses it by taking credit for the fact that America had overcome its original sin.

Another possibility, however, is that the story of slavery is *not* some sort of paradoxical anomaly in America's narrative. Instead, it can be seen as reflecting a longstanding alternative narrative template that is part of a larger discussion that includes the City on a Hill narrative project. The roots of this alternative pattern can be traced to 1619, when the first African slaves were brought to what was to become Virginia. This was before the Puritans came to New England with their aspirational narrative of a City on a Hill, suggesting that the two narratives had different historical origins and trajectories.

In contrast to what transpired in New England, settlers in Virginia were pursuing a mercantilist vision of building profitable agricultural enterprises in the New World, a vision that did not focus on religious freedom or other teloi of a model society. In their story, African slaves were emplotted as means toward an end of creating wealth and as part of a society based on hierarchical order presided over by a landed gentry. The collective aspiration in this narrative was a stable and harmonious social order in the South based on a traditional agrarian economic system. Among other things, this presupposed the need to protect and defend against threats to this social order.

My goal here is not to add to the historical scholarship, something I am not equipped to do in any event. Instead, my focus is on the role of slavery in the formation of a national narrative and memory project during the four centuries since African slaves were first brought to the shores of what would become

---

[2] https://www.monticello.org/thomas-jefferson/jefferson-slavery/jefferson-s-attitudes-toward-slavery/

America. From the outset, slave revolts were of constant concern and showed up in a few landmark events in North America and the Caribbean. The successful slave revolt against French overlords in Haiti between 1791 and 1804 (Trouillot, 1995), for example, was part of the collective memory of white slaveholders in the South and elsewhere. A half-century later, John Brown, a radical White abolitionist sought to unleash slave revolts in the United States, the most famous episode being 1859 with his raid on Harper's Ferry. This attempted insurrection was put down by U.S. troops led by Robert E. Lee, who soon thereafter became a leading general for the Confederates in the Civil War. Brown was captured, tried, and hanged in 1859, but he was unrepentant to the end. What was heroic and inspiring for abolitionists and Black slaves, however, was threatening to slaveholders and the aristocratic society they hoped to preserve in the South, and as such, accounts of Brown's exploits were ignored or suppressed there.

Many hoped that the racism inherent in slavery would disappear after the Civil War and that Americans would rely on the City on a Hill narrative template to make sense of the reborn nation. But an undercurrent of racism remained in alternative candidates for a national narrative and retained its shadowy presence even during efforts to stamp it out. During the bitter Reconstruction after the Civil War, President Grant used military force in an effort to stamp out racism by disbanding groups such as the Ku Klux Klan, but the staying power of the alternative narrative template that guided some segments of Southern culture was displayed by the reappearance of the KKK in the following decades. This suggests the continued influence of a White supremacist narrative, often operating just below the surface of national political culture. It is sometimes depicted as something akin to a virus, something that can lie dormant in the soil for long periods but then reemerge as a destructive force.[3]

The alternative narrative in this case reflected a longstanding fear among many Whites in America of being overrun or replaced by "others." Initially, this applied largely to African slaves, but it also guided the understanding of non-Anglo-Saxon immigrants in the United States and was more widespread than just in the former Confederate states. A striking example of its pervasiveness can be found in the efforts of Madison Grant (1865–1937), a patrician from New York who was friends with Theodore Roosevelt, Andrew Carnegie, and other leading figures of his day. Grant's book *The Passing of the Great Race* (1916) was part of a budding eugenics movement of the time and ended up being a favorite of Adolf Hitler. During the same period, D. W. Griffith's blockbuster film "The Birth of a Nation" provided a racist retelling of the American Civil War.

Such developments suggest the continuing influence of an alternative narrative project focused on a general fear of "others" that continues to this day. *The*

---

[3] https://www.un.org/en/un-chronicle/virus-racism-enduring-dilemma-humanity

Passing of the Great Race, for example, has echoes in contemporary claims of "replacement theory" that explicitly sees threats coming from Black Americans, but also Jews, and just about everyone else in America who is not what Grant in 1916 would call "Nordic." Chants of "You will not replace us!" and "Jews will not replace us!" were front and center at the 2017 Unite the Right rally in Charlottesville, Virginia that shocked many in the United States but were supported by rightwing members of Congress and White supremacists. More recently, Fox News commentator Tucker Carlson has gone into detailed accounts of what replacement theory means for America and why he is so intent on showing the threat to Whites and why they must act against it by limiting immigration and imposing voter restrictions.

Again, my point is not to add to the historical scholarship on this issue but to point out an undercurrent of national memory that shapes American political culture. Namely, the developments I have recounted suggest the existence of a narrative project that provides an alternative to the City on a Hill story and is more coherent than is suggested by the dismissal of slavery and racism as "blots" or forms of "moral depravity."

So, how can we describe this narrative project and formulate its relationship with the City on a Hill story? The thread that connects slavery, replacement theory, and White supremacist thought in America is a schematic narrative project at a higher level of abstraction than what I have proposed so far. At this higher level of abstraction, a narrative about the fear of others in America, which also has parallels with the Russian Expulsion-of-Alien-Enemies story line, might be dubbed as a more general "Protect and Defend against the Other" storyline. This more abstract formulation does not include information about any particular national case and is concerned with the general need to protect one's group from all threats from outsiders. It is a sort of umbrella narrative with an abstract plot line that covers the Expulsion-of-Alien-Enemies narrative template for Russia as well as the fear of replacement in America. In both cases, it is a symbolic tool that helps a community imagine itself and others, and it often becomes more active and defined in times of confrontation. Thus, the recent reactivation of America's Protect and Defend against the Other narrative project came at a time of renewed disputes over racial injustice and the rise of the Black Lives Matter movement.

The Fear of Replacement by Others story line has taken on various guises over the history of America. As noted above, one of its earliest versions stemmed from fear of slave revolts, but in subsequent iterations, it has reemerged in connection with mass immigration, Communism, and racism against Black Americans. For nearly a century following the American Civil War, this took the form of "Jim Crow" laws and other efforts to maintain White supremacy.

In an ironic twist, those using the Fear of Replacement by Others narrative often defend themselves by saying *they* are the real patriots and wish to defend the City on a Hill story line by making sure that the population of "real Americans" remains intact to pursue the noble dream of the American founders. For them, the fear of being replaced by others is not a failing or blot on the national narrative of a quest for freedom. Rather, it is part of an effort to pursue another aspirational narrative and telos that in fact are consistent with the City on a Hill narrative. But the obvious, overriding goal for most adherents of the Fear of Replacement narrative project is to preserve self-serving forms of White supremacy.

2.6. Dialogism, Intersubjectivity, and Narratives

I have outlined a set of issues that seem so diverse as to defy efforts to find a common thread that relates them. These range from the early socialization of children through dialogic encounters with parents and teachers to the narrative templates and narrative projects that guide national communities. Some items on this list go beyond what Rommetveit explicitly said in any of his writings. However, based on decades of discussion with him and the spirit of his thinking, I think he might agree with the way I have expanded his ideas. The more general point is that much of what I have tried to discuss here rests on the basic insights Rommetveit provided about intersubjectivity and dialogism in human nature. For him, human communication invariably involves dynamic negotiation between two or more perspectives, a process of coming to understand what is meant by what is said. To the extent that we are successful in this, we arrive at a temporary, partially shared reality.

Rommetveit's claims also provide a foundation for investigating how human interaction can leave us with incomplete, conflicting, and otherwise unsatisfying outcomes. Instead of starting with assumptions about shared semantic codes and assuming that the end product is the transmission of messages from one speaker to another, he pioneered a perspective that focuses on the negotiation of meaning that is often good enough to get the job done. But his analysis also leaves open the possibility that our efforts to communicate have less than perfect outcomes.

When harnessed in studies of adult–child interaction and the zone of proximal development, the effort to achieve intersubjectivity can yield new, higher stages of mental functioning. In this view, growth in the cognitive functioning of a child is tied to higher levels of intersubjectivity in interaction. Rommetveit's ideas about dialogue and intersubjectivity also have useful applications when we focus on how narrative tools shape discourse and thought. By bringing narrative tools into our analyses, a host of additional applications of his ideas come into focus, including ways that the stock of stories from different communities can lead to impediments, frustration, and conflict in our efforts to communicate.

As I have argued elsewhere (Wertsch, 2021), this frustration can become so pronounced that the most realistic hope in some cases is to *manage* differences rather than believe we can transcend them. This may wade into more ominous territory than Rommetveit wished to take on, but if there is hope for dealing with issues such as dangerous standoffs between groups and nations, it will start by recognizing what we are up against and what we can imagine as a way of dealing with it—and the broad conceptual framework outlined by Rommetveit provides a perfect place to start. Indeed, this framework remains one of the best tools available for dealing with many of the issues that face us in today's world.

References

Bakhtin, M. M. (1981). *The dialogic imagination: Four essays* (M. Holquist, Ed.). University of Texas Press.
Bakhtin, M. M. (1984). *Problems of Dostoyevsky's poetics* (C. Emerson, Trans., Ed.). University of Minnesota Press.
Bakhtin, M. M. (1986a). The problem of speech genres. In V. W. McGee (Trans.), C. Emerson & M. Holquist (Eds.) *Speech genres & other late essays* (pp. 60–102). University of Texas Press.
Bakhtin, M. M. (1986b). The problem of the text in linguistics, philology, and the human sciences: An experiment in philosophical analysis. In V. W. McGee (Trans.), C. Emerson & M. Holquist (Eds.), *Speech genres & other late essays* (pp.103–131). University Texas Press.
Bartlett, F. C. (1932). *Remembering: A study in experimental and social psychology*. Cambridge University Press.
Brooks, P. (1984). *Reading for the plot: Design and intention in narrative*. Harvard University Press.
Bruner, J. S. (1986). *Actual minds, possible worlds*. Harvard University Press.
Burke, K. (1998). Literature as equipment for living. In D. H. Richter (Ed.), *The critical tradition: Classic texts and contemporary trends* (pp. 593–598). Bedford Books. (First published in 1938.)
Grant, M. (1916). *The passing of the great race; or, The racial basis of European history*. Scribner's Sons.
Holquist, M. (2002). *Dialogism*. Taylor & Francis, Ltd.
James, W. (1890). *The principles of psychology*. Dover Publications, Inc.
Kahneman, D. (2011). *Thinking, fast and slow*. Doubleday Canada.
Leont'ev, A. N. (1981). The problem of activity in psychology. In J. V. Wertsch (Ed.), *The concept of activity in Soviet psychology*. M. E. Sharpe.
Lotman, Y. M. (1976). *Analysis of the poetic text* (D. Barton Johnson, Trans.). Ardis.
Luria, A. R. (1981) *Language and cognition*. John Wiley & Sons.
MacIntyre, A. (1984). *After virtue: A study in moral philosophy* (2nd ed.). University of Notre Dame Press.
Mink, L. (1978). Narrative form as cognitive instrument. In R. H. Canary & H. Kozicki (Eds.), *The writing of history: Literary form and historical understanding* (pp. 182–203). University of Wisconsin Press.

Neisser, U. (1967). *Cognitive psychology*. Prentice-Hall.
Ricoeur, P. (1984). *Time and narrative*. University of Chicago Press.
Rogoff, B. (1990). *Apprenticeship in thinking*. Oxford University Press.
Rogoff, B., & Wertsch, J. V. (1984). *Children's learning in the "zone of proximal development."* Jossey Bass.
Rommetveit, R. (1974). *On message structure: A framework for the study of language and communication*. John Wiley & Sons.
Sandel, M. (2009). *Justice: What's the right thing to do?* Farrar, Straus and Giroux.
Trouillot, M. R. (1995). *Silencing the past: Power and the production of history*. Beacon.
Van Engen, A. C. (2020). *City on a hill: A history of American exceptionalism*. Yale University Press.
Vygotsky, L. S. (1986). *Thought and language* (A. Kozulin, Ed.). MIT Press.
Wertsch, J. V. (1985). *Vygotsky and the social formation of mind*. Harvard University Press.
Wertsch, J. V. (1991). *Voices of the mind: A sociocultural approach to mediated action*. Harvard University Press.
Wertsch, J. V. (1998). *Mind as action*. Oxford University Press.
Wertsch, J. V. (2002). *Voices of collective remembering*. Cambridge University Press.
Wertsch, J. V. (2021). *How nations remember: A narrative approach*. Oxford University Press.
Whorf, B. L. (1956). *Language, thought, and reality*. MIT Press.

3

Ragnar Rommetveit on Contextures and Partially Shared Understandings

Per Linell

3.1. Introduction

Dialogical theory, or dialogism, is a humanistic and social-scientific framework based on the thesis that human beings are interdependent with others, in particular, in making sense of utterances, actions, and environments. It is opposed to radical individualism[1], structuralism, and monologism, since it shuns monoperspectival positions that are lacking in pluralism and freedom of opinion.[2] Dialogism highlights perspectives like phenomenological description, ethics of solidarity, rational truths, and robust epistemologies (Rommetveit, 1992, 2008; Linell, 2009; Marková, 2016). This essay deals primarily with language, contexts, communication, and understanding.

In language sciences, the term "language" is used about both abstract language systems and situated[3] activities of languaging (*linguistic* practices; praxeology of language).

Two metatheories of language are formal linguistics and dialogism. The formal(ized), abstract objectivism would maintain that: 1. The language system is the first-order notion, and language use is merely secondary. 2. There are no essential theories of contexts or morality; language is simply neutral. 3. Minimal units of language are abstract objects (signs) like morphemes (lexical units) and grammatical constructions.

---

[1] "Individuals" here means that they are single organisms with free access to their own ideas, feelings, and volitions. Dialogism, by contrast, stresses that human beings are social persons with both personal identity and social relations (e.g. Nikulin, 2010: 72ff.).

[2] Yet, in contemporary Western societies we have recently been met with ideas such as fake news, "alternative truths," irrational arguments, beliefs in conspiracies—sometimes with and links to religiously founded, extreme positions of hate and intolerance of foreign groups that are typically non-dialogized (i.e. monoperspectival).

[3] Here, and below, I will use the term "situated" about single occasions at a particular place and time, with a specific physical environment and specific people with their concerns and various backgrounds.

Dialogism is action-based, assuming that: 1. Languaging is the first-order phenomenon, and language systems (experiences and knowledge of how to use language) are secondary (derived). 2. Contexts, actions, and morality are essential; commitments and position-takings are the substance for ethics of language and communication in context. 3. The minimal unit is something which can give rise to a response, such as agreement or disagreement in interaction or communication (Bakhtin, 1981).

Dialogism appears in two disguises. Scientific dialogism is descriptive and is supposed to provide truthful, empirically robust, and explanatorily adequate accounts of data, with a focus on self–other interactions, situations, and dialogues among culturally, cognitively, emotionally, and volitionally capable persons, rather than in individuals who are seen as contextless abstractions. Normative dialogism specifies ethical theories of how dialogue "ought to be," rather than "is" (good dialogue)—decent conduct, such as respect for self and others, etc.

More specifically, this article will deal with the work of Ragnar Rommetveit and his life-long struggle against exclusively formal theories of language and communication. I will select three (related) points of his. First, he would assume that linguistic practices (languaging, not his term) are primary (logically, socially, fylo- and ontologically); actions, interactions, and practices precede language systems, at least up to a point. In line with this, he would argue for a much wider range of relevant contexts and contextures.[4] Divergent cultures, concerns and interests often give rise to partially shared, or even opposite, understandings of subject matters by persons who get involved in communicative encounters. Participants are not simply individuals; they are social persons, usually with memberships in many cultures and subcultures. If we pay regard to these varied contextures, it will be natural to argue for "partially shared understandings," as a substitute for conventional ideas of "shared understandings" in communication. Monologists assume, often without much empirical validation, that people strive for and achieve symmetrical and complete common understandings. But most communication situations are in fact asymmetrical (parties contribute different

---

[4] The term "contexture" has been used by, among others, Aron Gurwitsch (1964) and Charles Goodwin (2011) and suggests that contextual configurations have a layered character and fuzzy "fringes" and they are temporally unfolding (cf. also Goodwin, 2018: 188); whereas contexts tend to be seen as rather stable and integrated systems. Alternatively, contexture suggests a field of contexts, rather than a single aspect of the environment of a message.

Linguistics, and perhaps psychology too, still supports simplistic assumptions about contexts, as if they were given environments linked to language. Gurwitsch too works with a partly structuralist and integrated, gestalt-psychological notion of the "field of consciousness." Zaner (1979), who was a student of Gurwitsch, emphasizes that consciousness is limited, has fuzzy boundaries, and is full of "incompletenesses." This comes closer to Rommetveitian ideas of understandings as being only "temporarily held and partially shared" (Rommetveit, 1974, p. 29).

actions); "complementarity" (Rommetveit, 1974, 1992) is therefore a more adequate principle.

3.2. Ragnar Rommetveit

Ragnar Rommetveit was born in 1924, and he became professor of psychology in Oslo in 1955. He passed away on June 11, 2017. Although a psychologist by training, his academic oeuvre was much broader, ranging from philosophy over social, cognitive, and developmental psychology to communication and language studies. In their obituary on Rommetveit, Hagtvet et al. (2020) divided his career into four phases. These phases could be seen as his successive scientific contextures. Here, I shall highlight a few of his main ideas and, in particular, his notions of contexts and contextures.

Ragnar Rommetveit's wondering about language and human existence went far beyond linguistics and social psychology. His relation to contemporary language sciences was largely one of skepticism and opposition. In his early work (1974), he was concerned with abstract linguistics—in particular, generative grammar and semantics or pragmatics based on ordinary logic ("premature formalizations,": 125). He was also convinced that the disciplinary divisions in academia led to "irrational compartmentalization of knowledge" (1974: 124). He promoted interdisciplinary studies influenced by both hermeneutic–dialogical and cognitive–computational approaches, and he spoke in favor of multi-method approaches (as demonstrated in Blakar & Rommetveit, 1979, and argued again in Rommetveit, 1998).

Having spent his early years in academia during an era still dominated by behaviorism in psychology and structuralism in linguistics, Rommetveit later turned to dialogism, claiming that it could bring meaning back into language studies and psychology. Sense, or meaning-making, i.e. events in perception, communication, and thinking always take place in a situation; we can never be "not in a situation." He stressed that the message potential of an utterance is strongly permeated by aspects of both semiotic actions (discourse) and contextures, and both prior actions and possible next actions ("what may be said next," 1974: 125) in the local context. Thus, it cannot be explicated only by recourse to truth-conditional and acontextual semantics applied only to context-less sentences.

Rommetveit made a clear distinction between the meaning of "abstract linguistic resources" (words and grammatical constructions) and meaning occasioned in particular situations. According to him, resources in the language system do not have fixated meanings, but rather potentials to give rise to partly different meanings *in situ*, always together with various contextual factors. These two are clearly different notions. In most of structural and generative linguistics, they had erroneously been regarded as roughly the same; they were seen as type vs token (occasioned copy). In addition, Rommetveit, already in *On Message Structure* (1974), made a distinction between meaning potentials (semantic potentialities) of the linguistic resources, on the one hand, and message potentials in situated utterances, on the other. Note that situated utterances and actions too—that is, the specific utterance tokens—interact with contexts and can be interpreted in divergent ways, as we will see in the examples given below.

In the last two decades of active work, Rommetveit came out as a leading dialogist (e.g. 1992, 1998, 2008). One of his points, arguably inspired by Mikhail Bakhtin's work, was that participants in communication must take on some responsibility for their utterances and other actions. If somebody asserts something publicly, he or she must remain epistemically responsible for the contents, unless there appear legitimate reasons to opt out. Similarly, if a promise is made, or a particular question asked, etc, the instigator must bear the moral consequences (Rommetveit, 1991, 1992, 1998).

In 2008 a substantial and partly popular summary of Rommetveit's thinking was published as *Språk, individuell psyke, og kulturelt kollektiv* (in New Norwegian), which provides a good picture of his later intellectual career. Social psychology is a moral science (Sarason, 1981; Bruner, 1990). Therefore, participants in cognitive and communicative activities entertain— along with intuitions, intentions, and thoughts—responsibilities and social commitments.[5]

Let me now bring up some examples illustrating Rommetveit's notion of "only partially" shared understandings in conversations between parties. I suppose that this is almost universally true of all constellations of participants, since participants are bound to belong to (widely or only slightly) different communities of context and culture.

3.3. On Rommetveit's Early Attempts to Describe Contexts of Languaging

Ragnar Rommetveit always insisted on the role of contexts and background knowledge in the explication of people's communication or lack of communication. However, instead of turning to empirical data, he first set about devising theoretically crucial examples which were made up, yet realistic, interactions.

---

[5] His scientific and scholarly work has been commented upon by several reviewers and commentators, e.g. Wold (1992), Wertsch (2003), Linell (2003), Kowal & O'Connell (2016), and Hagtvet el al. (2020) and in some interviews (e.g. Josephs, 1998).

Thus, he became an expert on inventing situations for which the standard semantic descriptions of literal meanings were not applicable. His favorite example concerned what Mr. Smith was doing as he, on an early Saturday morning, was mowing his lawn in his posh villa suburb. In this scenario, when he was toiling behind his manual lawnmower, his wife received two phone calls, and in both these conversations, Mr. Smith's current activity was topicalized but in quite different ways[6]:

(3.3a) First call: Mrs. Smith receives a phone call from her female friend (F), who is not a great fan of Mr. Smith. Well into the conversation, she (F) suddenly asks:
1. F: that lazy husband of yours, is he still in bed?
2. Mrs. S: no, he is already outside working, he is mowing
3.   the lawn.

(3.3b) Second call: Mrs. Smith receives a ring from her husband's colleague (C), his work-mate at the firefighters' station, who regularly calls when he wants to go for a fishing trip:
1. C: is your husband working today?
2. Mrs. S: no, he is not working, he is mowing the lawn.

Rommetveit returned to this imagined situation in several publications, often adding details of new interpretations. I will dwell only on a few of the remarkable features of the two calls. Mrs. Smith was able to issue two opposite, yet simultaneously true, accounts ("he is working" (3.3a: line 2); "he is not working" (3.3b: line 2)) about the very same physical situation. Rommetveit argued that this would be hard to reconcile with standard truth-conditional semantics. But without additional conversational data, an analyst would not be in a position to say much about the inferences that Mrs. Smith wanted to communicate (and presumably did communicate). In (3.3a), she seemed to say indirectly that Mr. Smith, who was after all toiling on his lawn, was not a complete lazy bone. In (3.3b), the relevant conclusion was that Mr. Smith, who was not on duty, i.e. he was "not working" (line 2), but free to go for a fishing expedition.

Mrs. Smith was arguably successful in both conversations, despite the contradictory information she seemed to provide. A possible conclusion might be that,

---

[6] Transcriptions are simplified. Note the following:
>> << enclose very rapid talk; > < enclose slow talk; note that numbers in (3.3a–c) refer to turns, not to lines as in conventional transcription.

I use *italics* for quotes from the texts of scholars and commentators. To avoid confusion, I will number examples using the same numerals as occur in the sections involved.

in the field of linguistic communication, we should deal with how sense-making is contextually accomplished; it is not something which can be calculated from details of language use per se. Words don't just have fixated (literal) meanings (Rommetveit, 1988).

But many people are not entirely convinced by the Smiths' example. Are Mrs. Smith's utterances *He is working.* (3.3a) and *He is not working.* (3.3b) really mutually opposite, with the same linguistic meaning "work" being not negated and negated, respectively? In (3.3a) Mrs. Smith meant to say "He is exercising his body," and in (3.3b) "He is not at work (so he can go fishing with you)." His whereabouts (his own garden) and what he is doing (mowing his own lawn) are references to the same physical situation. But what about the *social* situation? After all, Mrs. Smith's female friend and Mr. Smith's workmate have quite different relations to Smith, and these relations are presupposed in the callers' questions ("Is he still in bed?" vs "Is your husband working today?"). Are we not confronted with two words (*work$_1$* "exercising one's body" and *work$_2$* "being at one's workplace")? I think Rommetveit would have conceded this. But the point is that many theories of lexical meaning might be influenced by physical reference rather than social status (language as a means to represent the world of things rather than providing concepts for proper understandings). However, he would probably claim that we have one word "work" with a meaning potential to contribute meaning in at least two ways in different semantic or pragmatic situations.

Anyway, the Smiths' episode touches upon a central finding in interaction studies, namely the hybridity and multiplicity of contexts, situations, and activity types. Indeed, Rommetveit focuses on aspects of imagined situations in which participants—despite the potentially opposite conditions—did not arrive at shared understandings. This is an assumption that he seems to share with other pragmatic theorists.

Mrs. Smith and each of her callers would probably mutually understand their linguistic actions. But meanings of what people do or say are not necessarily shared in the same manner. Rommetveit enumerated several things that could potentially be associated with Mr. Smith's lawn mowing (cf. Rommetveit, 1991: 19) apart from "working" and "not working," activities such as beautifying his garden, keeping up property value in Scarsdale, getting a physical work-out, avoiding his wife, etc. But was "avoiding his wife" part of Mr. or Mrs. Smith's intended message, or was it a hostile interpretation made by some but not all bystanders? While some people may not come up with precisely this interpretation, it could be a controversial part of the "message potential" of Mr. Smith's activity. Coulter (1999: 167) notes: "What people may actually say is, of course, up to them. But what they then mean by whatever they say (if anything) is not solely up to them to say."

Anyway, Rommetveit was well-known for suggesting that participants often only "*partially* share" (italics added/PL) their understandings, which are—in addition—only temporarily shared and often changed over time as a result of participants' various utterances (e.g. Rommetveit, 1974: 29ff.). However, since most of his examples were made up, it would be important to demonstrate that his conclusions are even more evident in examples drawn from authentic languaging. The following sections (3.4–3.7) use data from such a set of mutually divergent situations, in which participants find it difficult to understand what the other is trying to say.

3.4. Authentic Situations I: Threatening Phone Calls

This example concerns telephone talks between a mafia blackmailer and a well-to-do banker. Viveka Adelswärd and myself (1994) analyzed a corpus of nine threatening phone calls that took place in the 1980s between a member of the American branch of the Italy-based mafia and Mr. Cuccia, an Italian banker. I shall here cite some fragments from one of these calls.[7]

(3.4a) M = a mafia member, V = the victim (Mr. Cuccia): turn numbers indicate how far into the call the turns occur:
M 70: now listen to me, Mr.Cuccia, listen to me. if you wanna act stupid like you don't know what I am talking about and you want me to say something I shouldn't say I will not *say* it. I am only telling you one thing, your time is getting short, my time is getting short, if I am destroyed I don't care whether it takes me a year me—it takes me two years, and the day you look when you feel that some tragedy, don't feel sorry just go to the mirror and look at the mirror and say that "well I was the cause of this tragedy."

Here we can see some characteristic features of threatening calls. The victim, Mr. Cuccia, who has evidently been instructed to carry out certain actions, is only vaguely told about what unfortunate consequences will be inflicted if he fails to do so. What should he do: against whom, when, where, and why? M will "not say something [he] shouldn't say" (line 3). In other episodes (not cited here), it transpires that the blackmailer would not describe his discourse as "threatening" Mr. Cuccia; he is just "giving [. . .] a fact of life" (Adelswärd & Linell,

---

[7] For a much more comprehensive analysis, I refer to Adelswärd & Linell (1994). All relevant details about the legal case, in which the calls were used as evidence, can be found in that article (p. 263 *et passim*). The original purpose of the paper was to explore the resource of vagueness in threatening phone calls. It should be pointed out that these exchanges took place long before electronic threats could be used as resources.

op.cit.: 275): M is just "informing" the victim of what may happen later. Any attempt on Mr. Cuccia's part to fish for more information will later be described as "playing games" (see (3.4c) below). But there is also, according to the blackmailer, very little time left (3.4a: lines 4–5). This is undoubtedly said to intimidate Mr. Cuccia even further. If M is "destroyed" (line 5), by the measures taken by Mr. Cuccia, or the absence of such measures, he vaguely predicts that a "tragedy" will happen; M's revenge will come within some quite indeterminate time period (lines 6–9). What the tragedy might involve is in fact specified by M later:

(3.4b)
M90: >>Cause if you don't, one of these days you go to work you get a phone-call you find out your wife was burned in the apartment or you may get a phone-call you find out your daughter's car blew up when she went into it or you get a phone-call and you find your son fell out the window in your chemistry company. And that's all I got to tell you. << Because right now I'm choked, I have no ways to go and my time is limit and if you make my time run out when my time runs out, your time=
V91: =look here look here eh eh now you listen to me=
M92: =no more, listen to me now=
V93: =no no you too you too you listen to me=
M94: =listen=
V95: =you listen to me=
M96: =((xx)) gotta do what I gotta to do, I am sorry I took you like a gentleman I feel=

This exchange is very asymmetrical. In the whole call the victim receives vague instructions about what he should do. (In addition, the requested actions would presumably be illegal.) The victim has no say; he—desperately and in vain—demands a chance to talk, but he doesn't get his voice heard (3.4b: turns 91–96). The threatener exemplifies his examples of upcoming attempted assassinations, with no information about when and where. When the victim tries to get more information, he is described as someone who "is playing games":

(3.4c)
V109: =why why don't you mention any *name* because you are talking to me=
M110: =let's not play games, let's not play games=
V111: =but I am not playing games eh eh (M: xx) I put you first one question (M: right) answer me one question, you are talking about Sindona or not?
M112: listen to me, I am not talking about anybody, you *know* what you're supposed to do=

At the theoretical level, practices like these don't fit formal linguistics and truth-conditional semantics. Yet, threatening phone calls might well be seen as a communicative activity type (Linell, 2010) or a communicative genre (Luckmann, 2002). They are totally dominated by the blackmailing party, who more or less constantly alludes to some dreadful events that will happen to the victim or his family. However, information about how, when, where, etc is not disclosed. Instead, the activity builds crucially on vagueness and uncertainty as interactional resources. The threatener makes no interpretations explicit; the victim is vaguely instructed to do something in a very intimidating situation but is not allowed to have his questions answered. Under these conditions, there can be no shared understanding. The only partially shared assumption is that there is a serious demand articulated by the dominant party. But the blackmailer cannot "say something he shouldn't say" (3.4a: lines 4–5). If he did, the threat would be seriously weakened, and we could even say that the exchange would no longer follow the conditions defining a "threatening phone call."

3.5. Authentic Situations II: Situations Suggesting Sexual Abuse of Children

The examples in Section 3.4 involve a case in which one participant, the mafia member, is clearly unwilling to make himself completely understood. In this section (3.5), the parties, i.e. children and parents, are unable to understand each other straightforwardly, despite the fact that both parties would surely want to.

Section 3.5 deals with cases of sexual abuse of children. I take the liberty of quoting a paper by Anna Margrete Flåm and Eli Haugstvedt (2013)[8] dealing with families in which young children had been exposed to sexual abuse, with little of shared understandings between victims, relatives, and perpetrators. In such cases, it is well-known that the victims are often quite reluctant to tell others, including family members, about their horrifying expectations and experiences. This may have to do with feelings of shared guilt and wishes to preserve trust in close relations.

Flåm & Haugstvedt point out that the children's brief utterances cited in the following excerpts could possibly be interpreted as implying a concealed reference to something dreadful and forbidden, but they remain quite indirect, vague, or ambiguous. In the first two examples (3.5a and b) the responses by the parents

---

[8] The investigation reported and discussed in Flåm & Haugstvedt (op.cit.) covered the cases of 20 children (17 girls, 3 boys), who were all acquainted with their abusers (Flåm, 2018: 46).

Flåm's (2018) dissertation, in which the paper cited is included, is built largely on Rommetveit's dialogism. The example has also been used by Marková (2016: 197).

do not include any reference to imminent risks of abuse to be inflicted on the girls at all.

(3.5a) *The time has come for the primary schoolgirl to do the dishes, as she has promised, at the family's neighbour's house. Before leaving home, she asks her father, who is standing close by: "Do I HAVE to wash the dishes even though I get paid?" The father thinks her question is a sign of laziness, which requires a reminder of her responsibility. He says: "You have to keep your promises. If [you] make a promise, you keep it." The girl leaves without pursuing the topic further.*

(3.5b) *The father, mother, and preschool daughter are visiting their [extended] family. The parents are going out and tell the daughter that her uncle is going to look after her along with her cousins, as he usually does. As they are about to leave, the girl calls out: "Do I HAVE to go to uncle?" The adults interpret this reaction as being a temporary reluctance for them to leave, which requires a comfort: "Yes, your uncle is looking after you. He is so kind." They leave.*

In retrospect, the girls' communicative contributions in examples (3.5a and b) are calls for help; compare the emphasis on the obligation in the key phrase "do I HAVE to . . . " Yet, the somber anticipation in the victims' questions can hardly be said to be outspoken *in situ*. In neither of these cases did the children disclose anything direct about sexual abuse. Their utterances or actions did not contain any allusions to anything evil for the parents, who didn't think along those lines at all beforehand. Only after a long delay did new information come forth by the children telling outsiders about sexual abuse. These outsiders then informed the parents. The police and childcare authority were contacted, and comprehensive sexual abuse was disclosed (Flåm & Haugstvedt, 637).

In some cases included in Flåm & Haugstvedt's data, adults had indeed developed apprehensions that opened up for more direct sense-making about abuse—and for later actions or questions and answers:

(3.5c) *The mother is about to leave for her night job. She goes to her teenage daughter's room to say good night, and opens the door silently. The daughter jumps up from the bed into a sitting position, and asks in a terrified voice: "Is it YOU, mommy? Do you HAVE to leave for work?" The mother thinks: "Such a strange voice. How scared she sounded! She was not like that before." Several nights later the mother wakes up to find her husband's side of the bed empty. She knows, without knowing how to explain it afterwards, that she has to go directly into her daughter's room. She finds her husband in her daughter's bed. Without the husband*

> *noticing, the mother calls the police at once. They arrive immediately. Comprehensive sexual abuse was disclosed.* (Flåm & Haugstvedt, 637)

All the data in Flåm & Haugstvedt's article deal with serious events in real life, and yet parents in Examples (3.5a and b) did not show any understandings of what the girls were worried about. Example (3.5c) could be said to include a sequence of relevant sense-making responses (the mother's silent thoughts). Yet, all the later disclosures of the truths, only made in retrospect, hinge upon the utterances documented; each extract contains the utterance "do I/you HAVE TO . . . ." These utterances are said "in a different voice" (intensified physical voice, exaggerated bodily stance, embodied signs of being stressed), a notion which can be dialogically understood (Flåm, 2018: 68). At a longer timescale, the early signs eventually led to crucial communicative and practical actions.

In these cases of sexual assault and abuse, some of the interlocutors were quite close, for example, the girls in (3.5a and b) and their relatives (father and uncle). But the young girls felt very uneasy about the impending situations (being alone with adult men). Their worries were not discussed beforehand with adult family members. Instead, the children were supposed to live up to accepted social norms, such as obeying their parents and sticking to promises once given. The girls had to contain within themselves internal dialogues and different expectations (nice and horrifying events), with some exceptions in (3.5c); but even there, the serious conflicts were mainly handled by the young person alone.

Sex and sexual transgressions are strongly morally loaded topics, and they belong to games of social sense-making that often contain relatively little verbal discourse. These exchanges of enticements and threats, attractions and repulsions are demonstrated in inner dialogue.

3.6. Authentic Situations III: Hannah Arendt About Adolf Eichmann in Jerusalem

What seems evident in examples (3.5a–c) is that the girls' parents in their immediate reactions only actualize local contexts. At the outset, they don't attend to other possible contextual environments, which may have been important for the girls—in particular, the *cultural*, global, and more general context, in this case the risk that adult men can have a sexual interest in children and adolescents, especially girls.

Let us consider a quite different case of a possible neglect of cultural contexts. The eminent phenomenologist philosopher Hannah Arendt reported in Arendt (1961) from the trial in Jerusalem of the Nazi concentration-camp boss Adolf

Eichmann. Arendt claimed that Eichmann was not a particularly evil person; rather, he was a relatively ordinary and banal person, who simply obeyed orders, even regarding the practical implementation of the Holocaust, and he did not hate Jews and other categories of victims. At least, these features in Arendt's rather journalistic book have been highlighted in its reception. Several critics have pointed out that Eichmann, and presumably many other Germans from the 1930s onwards, were perhaps "ordinary Germans" but not people who could have appeared in just *any* historical–cultural situation. There had been a long period of indoctrination and propaganda against Jews, a very long history of antisemitism in many European cultures, and large numbers of nationalists had been accustomed to looking at Jews as less-valuable people. It was normal to accept dreadful treatments of them. That attitude was largely a cultural–historical specificity, a global context, which peaked in the beginning of the 1940s (and a new surge might be building up at this moment).

On the face of it, this example concerns one intellectual (Arendt) encountering an obvious opposition from a large majority culture. The diverse moral positions were held by partly different groups of officials, intellectuals, and citizens, but partly the moral clash must have affected Arendt herself, in her silent mind and her internal dialogue (as well as in external confrontations with other individuals). Again, this is a conflict between communities, cultures, and contexts which generates only partly shared understandings.

3.7. Authentic Example IV: Putin's Speech on the War in Ukraine

I will end up with an even more provocative case, one which is a sign of changing times in the world (to hint at the title of this anthology). On February 24, 2022, Vladimir Putin announced in a televised speech that Russia was going to launch a military campaign in Ukraine. Putin said several things about this plan, but I will focus on only three highly controversial statements (here in rough translation): (3.7a) *"we will initiate a special military operation in Ukraine,"* which will involve (3.7b) *"denazifying Ukraine"* and (3.7c) *"demilitarizing this country."* First, the formulation "special military operation" (3.7a) sounds like referring to relatively small infringements by military means. Indeed, representatives of the official Russian regime have consistently refused to use the words "war" and "attack," just as the mafia member in (3.4) denies that he is threatening Mr. Cussia! However, the first two years of warfare were followed by a brutal total war involving heavy bombing and use of missiles, killing thousands of civilians, destroying lots of infrastructure (hospitals, schools, roads, bridges, military installations, railway stations, civil residence houses, etc).

The second goal, that of "denazifying" (3.7b) Ukraine, presupposes that nazists are frequent and still influential in the country, particularly in the government and other authorities. This is not true, even if the history of the country[9] (in pre-WW2, during WW2, and in the post-WW2 era) was strongly influenced by many nationalists, some of whom might be characterized as right-wing extremists or fascists. Russian politicians (and members of the Russian public) have begun to use the term "nazist" as generally applicable to all kinds of enemies. It is also ironic to hear this statement by Putin, who is himself a tyrannical leader and dictator acting in a fascist manner in this situation, when Ukraine has been a relatively free country with some democratic practices.

Finally, the goal of "demilitarizing" (7c) Ukraine flies in the face of both those attacked and a lot of observers in other European countries. In fact, Russia under Putin is now silencing, enslaving, and killing many of the grandchildren of the "brother people" who sacrificed their lives fighting for the Red Army in the Great Patriotic War (WW2).

In addition to a generally impoverished language variety, Newspeak, George Orwell's dystopian novel *1984* formulates some slogans that are very similar to Putin's statements (or, rather, the other way around). Orwell (1949, pp. 6, 18, 29) satirically tells us about a totalitarian system claiming that "War is Peace," "Freedom is Slavery," and "Ignorance is Strength." We can then add "Fake claims are valuable news" (Putin, Trump, and others).[10]

The contrast between Putin's statements and actions, and the views of so many "Westerners", is stark. In fact, there is also a deep rift between Putin's propagandistic language, as exemplified above and presumably supported by many indoctrinated Russian citizens, and the real actions exercised by this soldiers and military officers. Putin's actions are in themselves communicative actions, signs with the message potential of power and warning, addressed to his own co-patriots, the suffering Ukrainians, and many Western nations. There seems to be an internal lack of consistency (only partially shared coherence) between Putin's verbal claims and his actions. There seem to be many contradictions in Putin's logic and his "inner dialogue."

Putin addresses several audiences (contexts) with conflicting interests: his victims, his military, his supporting majority (?) at home, his enemies (and supporters) in the Western world. The last-mentioned opponents have been threatened, warned, and accused of making war with actions like economic sanctions.

---

[9] Primarily in eastern Ukraine (Donbass) (Walker, 2018).
[10] Another case of similarity with Orwell, this time with Doublespeak, is given in Pomerantsev's (2014) book on Putin's and post-Soviet history, which is called *Nothing is true, and everything is possible*. This fits Trump's slogans based on "alternative truths."

Yet, Putin's mind can be dialogically theorized as hounded by internal and external dialogues, and he will therefore end up in many situations of only partially shared understandings. There is a fundamental difference in the international debate of present-day Russia. In the West, the ideal discourse is influenced by skepticism and doubt. Russia, by contrast, prefers a censured monological narrative about the glorious past and present of the nation. If, however, we turn to normative dialogism (the ideas of "good dialogue"), Putin must be seen as one of the most demonizing, non-dialogizing, and dreadful despots in world history.[11]

3.8. On Remote Contexts and Lost Opportunities

With these examples in mind, let's now turn to some of Rommetveit's points in Sections 3.8 and 3.9 below.

One of Rommetveit's cherished ideas was the refusal to acknowledge "literal meanings" in normal words.[12] This was salient in the Smiths' example (Section 3.3), but it could be reinforced in the analysis of authentic linguistic practices; if we go back to Sections 3.4–3.7, it is clear that participants could not share fixated meanings of, say, "listen" (Section 3.4), "have to" (3.5), "evil" (3.6), and "nazi, fascist" (3.7), among others. In the rich dynamics of contextures, we trade on "partially shared," rather than "fully shared" understandings.

Rommetveit wished to analyze the nature of contexts and contextures (Section 3.4). Some of the contexts are backward-pointing, others are forward-pointing relations between actions. He was also concerned not only with local relations, but also with remote contexts that must be activated as motivations in the present situation: "(back)grounds," "surroundings," "connections," "circumstances," or "enabling conditions." These are participants' past experiences, including earlier conversations, communicative biographies, and cultural knowledge (including the language system). We recall events from memory, and we have dreams about the future.

Conversation analysis (CA) (Schegloff, 2007; Sidnell, 2009), by contrast, is basically a powerful and very strict and cogent method for the analysis of manifest verbal interaction in the situations at hand. CA's focus on only manifest actions is sometimes reminiscent of looking for the lost key only where the light is. Not all meaning in local relations is generated by immediately adjacent utterances, e.g. between question and answer. The overall conclusion is that CA is less successful when it comes to accounting for sense-making and communication.

---

[11] The factual historical background for some of Putin's rhetoric (Walker, 2018) cannot be used in defense of his outrageous decisions and conduct since February 24, 2022.
[12] *Terms* (in science, law, administration, etc.), by contrast, are *made* to be semantically stable.

Local (situated) sense-making practices must often invoke remote, or nonlocal, contexts of the participants' background knowledge, i.e. aspects that are not immediately present in the particular situation at hand. The situated sense-maker might retrieve knowledge of activity types and discursive genres (which are always wider than single occasions), or from their own biographical knowledge. These nonlocal circumstances may become operative in the present situation, if participants *make them locally relevant*. Prior contexts are by definition nonlocal, and we can discern at least three kinds:

(a) More or less remote communicative experiences, e.g. those having occurred in earlier conversations than the current one.
(b) These earlier events shade into larger biographical experiences, e.g. the parties' knowledge or assumptions about significant people.
(c) Cultural assumptions, such as knowledge about situation (or activity) types and about language, i.e. meaning potentials of words and constructions and varieties of language use.

Naturally, these more remote contexts are often only imagined and not engaged with full awareness by participants, but they must still be made relevant, i.e. brought into the discourse (silent or loud) in the situation.

Participants in a situated exchange may also anticipate possibly upcoming conditions; these are "possible next" contexts. However, prior contexts are richer and more numerous than future ones. The future becomes part of the present through projections, anticipations, inhibitions, speculations, hopes, and fears. When we shape our utterances in the immediate situation, we may have to consider their impact on possible future interactions with the other or third parties.

Remote meanings and contexts are clearly part of everyday sense-makings in communication, i.e. they belong to what Rommetveit (1974) called "message potentials." In positing such message potentials, or "message structures" (the term he used for his 1974 book), he pointed to the fact that the one and the same situated utterance will allow for several interpretations (3.3a and b).

As argued, remote contexts can function as parts of everyday sense-makings in situated communication, as nonlocal conditions made locally relevant by participants. Respondents to situated utterances can home in on different pragma-semantic potentials in terms of allusions (Schegloff, 1996), possible continuations, anticipations, and interpretations that previous utterances can give rise to. When we are confronted with data such as those in Sections 3.3–3.7, we may proceed to deep hidden meanings and psychological overtones.

Rommetveit (1987, 2008, and elsewhere) suggests that potential continuations and implications may appear as near at hand in the minds of participants.

Utterances are sometimes "pregnant" with possibilities for the future, to use the expression of Cassirer (1956: 8).[13] However, many of these "opportunities" are never disclosed on the spur of the moment, and they often remain "lost possibilities" (Rommetveit, 2008: 114). At other times, however, after some time lapse, participants can bring such (perhaps half forgotten or vague) thoughts into serious thinking and explicit language or, in other words, into their internal (and then perhaps externalized) dialogue. The mother in example (3.5c) finally did not let the opportunity slip out of her mind. Surely, this was also the case for the participants in both most of the threatening phone calls and the other events of the sexual abuse and their aftermath (Section 3.5).

Rommetveit claimed that possible continuations and vague anticipations of further dialogue may be part of real people's communication, even if they are not disclosed publicly, at least not for the time being. When we participate in communicative events, we may entertain embryonic versions of interpretations, associations, and ideas that are never properly developed, due to lack of access to the conversational floor, discretion, ignorance, shyness, imagined guilt, or whatever. Often, however, they remain silent, and then eventually evaporate.[14]

3.9. Context Atrophy in Formal Linguistics and in Myopic Interaction Analysis

As mentioned, Ragnar Rommetveit's publications in the 1970s were highly critical of formal grammar and pragmatics in linguistics. He criticised them for having an absurdly arid view of context. When he had moved into dialogism, he argued that Conversation Analysis too tended to be prone to "myopia" (Rommetveit, personal communication). CA focused exclusively on quite local contexts, that is, short verbal sequences in documented and audio- or video-recorded conversational data (or "talk-in-interaction"). On this point, CA maintains a behaviorist inclination with its third-person perspective. Their method is based on an admirable methodological rigor, but it reminds of searching for the lost key only where the streetlight is. It is myopic also in more general respects. It focuses too much on method at the expense of theory. From their point of view, the problem with lost opportunities (Section 3.8) is that they raise quite a few methodological

---

[13] Another concept is that of "avantgarde messenger" utterances (Jacobs, 1986), by which therapists sometimes anticipate future (but so far only implicit) developments in the exchange (Flåm, op.cit.: 75).
[14] The idea of "lost opportunities" was discussed by Rommetveit (1987, 2008: 114), referring to methods of the German philosopher Oevermann et al. (1979) and his "objective hermeneutics."

problems. Analyses of communication (and we could add, sense-makings in general) necessitate a much broader array of methods.[15]

Like virtually all dialogists, Rommetveit assumed that language, meaning and sense-making are rooted deep-down in socially shared knowledge rather than in individuals (although the latter are "shareholders" in language and culture; Josephs, 1998: 193). If you believe in the social nature of the mind (Valsiner & van der Veer, 2000), you can be either more of a constructionist or more of an interactionist. As Nystrand (1992) argues, Rommetveit was definitely the latter. This is in line with his insistence on the importance of contexts. It also concurred with his tendency to avoid terms like "structures" and "stocks of knowledge."[16]

The lack of sufficient common contextual anchorage oftentimes results in only partially shared understandings by participants in dialogue. But above all, contexts wither away in the accounts of many analysts. It is "context atrophy," which takes slightly different forms in formal linguistics and CA. In struggling with monologist sciences, e.g. formal linguistics and asocial (mainly individually oriented) psychology, one might say that he put Anglo-Saxon individualism into question.

3.10. Conclusion: A Note on Macro-Level Phenomena

As Wertsch (2003) points out, despite the point that we must look upon minds as "social" in nature, Rommetveit hardly applied dialogical notions to the collectivities of large groups, whole communities, nations, and global organizations. Why?

This issue makes me turn to the overall theme of this book, that of the large-scale structures and changes in the human cultural conditions of our time. Most dialogistic analyses of interaction and dialogue are concerned with "micro-social" phenomena in the daily lives of people's face-to-face interactions with one another in dyads or small groups. However, this book might require a focus on "macro-social" relations, perhaps at the level of worldwide politics, trade, media, etc. It seems to me that there are two main responses to this from dialogism. On the one hand, it could be suggested that worldwide policies are ultimately formulated and negotiated between real people, e.g. in governments and

---

[15] For sure, there were similarities between Rommetveit's dialogism and CA. In particular, CA works consistently with backward-pointing and forward-pointing relations of the utterance which systematically influence the local understanding of this same utterance. But the problem is that CA's analysis is *too local*.

[16] Rommetveit was skeptical about both "social representations" (Moscovici, 1984) and "social stocks of knowledge" (Berger & Luckmann, 1967), presumably because he found these notions too static.

parliaments, negotiations between representatives of states, in companies and industrial concerns, high-tech organizations, and so on. For example, Gillespie (2012) analyzed the sequenced moves made by Washington and Moscow in the Cuban crisis in 1962. Rommetveit (personal communication) regarded high-level diplomacy as a special communicative activity type in which parties very thoroughly calculate hierarchies of (sometimes hidden) intentions of the other. My example about Putin's assertions belongs here.

The other approach to large-scale events would be the metaphorical one. Dialogical theories are designed to work with the analyses of the interactional moves taken by participants who are mutually present in real encounters of daily life. Participants are real persons trying to trade positions. A metaphorical dimension might then lie in the transpositions from persons to whole nations, states, or companies portraying these as the participants in interactions, in "international relations." In some applications of Dialogical Self Theory (Hermans & Hermans-Konopka, 2010), such "units" may be treated as agents who exchange messages based on ideas and positions entertained by them. Some dialogists, e.g. G. H. Mead, argue that the consciousness of a nation "as a nation" presupposes interaction on an international plane. Dialogical notions such as trust, responsibility, and contexts, to mention just three, can clearly be applied at this level (Marková, 2016).

In other words, dialogism has a contribution to make at this grand level too. That macro-social entities in interaction are metaphorical interpretations is not to say that they are unimportant or nonexistent. Quite the contrary!

Acknowledgments

An earlier version of this paper was read at a conference to commemorate the work and life of Ragnar Rommetveit in Oslo on October 18, 2018. I wish to thank the organisers Ola Erstad and Bente Hagtvet. Work on this text was supported by a grant from the Swedish Research Council to LinCS, University of Göteborg (no. 349-2006-146). I thank Kerstin Norén for pertinent comments on an earlier version of this essay. Naturally I am personally responsible for all remaining mistakes.

References

Adelswärd, Viveka & Linell, Per. (1994). Vagueness as an interactional resource: The genre of threatening phone-calls. In W. Sprondel (Ed.), *Die Objektivität der Ordnungen und ihre kommunikative Konstruktion* (pp. 261–288). Suhrkamp.

Arendt, Hannah. (1961). *Eichmann in Jerusalem: A report on the banality of evil*. Penguin Classics.

Bakhtin, M. M. (1981). *The dialogical imagination: Four essays* (C. Emerson and M. Holquist, Trans.; M. Holquist, Ed.). University of Texas Press.

Berger, Peter, & Luckmann, Thomas. (1967 [1966]). *The social construction of reality*. Penguin Books.

Blakar, Rolv, & Rommetveit, Ragnar (Eds.). (1979). *Studies of language, thought and verbal communication*. Academic Press.

Bruner, Jerome. (1990). *Acts of meaning*. Harvard University Press.

Cassirer, Ernst. (1955-1957 [1923-1929]). *Philosophy of symbolic forms*, 3 vols. [Translation of German original *Philosophie der symbolischen Formen* (1923-1929)]. Yale University Press.

Coulter, Jef. (1999). Discourse and mind. *Human Studies, 22*, 163-181.

Flåm, Anna Margrete. (2018). "I need your eyes to see myself." On the inclusion of dialogues and an otherness of the other into psychology and clinical work. Explored through studies of contexts where children live with violence in close relationships. (JYU Dissertations 7). University of Jyväskylä, Faculty of Education and Psychology.

Flåm, Anna Margrete, & Haugstvedt, Eli. (2013). Test balloons? Small signs of big events: A qualitative study on circumstances facilitating adults' awareness of children's first signs of sexual signs. *Child Abuse & Neglect, 37*, 633-642.

Gillespie, Alex. (2012). Dialogical dynamics of trust and distrust in the Cuban Missile Crisis. In Ivana Marková & Alex Gillespie (Eds.), *Trust and conflict, representation, culture and dialogue* (pp. 139-155). London: Routledge.

Goodwin, Charles. (2011). Contextures of action. In J. Streeck, C. Goodwin, & C. LeBaron (Eds.), *Embodied interaction: Language and body in the material world* (pp. 182-193). Cambridge University Press.

Goodwin, Charles. (2018). *Co-operative action*. Cambridge University Press.

Gurwitsch, Aron. (1964) [2010]. *The field of consciousness* (R. Zaner, Ed.). Springer/Duquesne University Press.

Hagtvet, Bente, Linell, Per, Wertsch, James & Wold, Astri H. (2020). Ragnar Rommetveit: A full life. *Culture & Psychology, 26*, 1-12.

Hermans, Hubert, & Hermans-Konopka, Agnieszka. (2010). *Dialogical self theory: Positioning and counter-positioning in a globalizing society*. Cambridge University Press.

Jacobs, Theodore. (1986). On counter-transference enactments. *Journal of the American Psychoanalytic Association, 34*, 289-307.

Josephs, Ingrid. (1998). Do you know Ragnar Rommetveit? On dialogue and silence, poetry and pedantry, and cleverness and wisdom in psychology (An interview with Ragnar Rommetveit). *Culture & Psychology, 4*, 189-212.

Kowal, Sabine, & O'Connell, Daniel C. (2016). Ragnar Rommetveit's approach to everyday spoken dialogue from within. *Journal of Psycholinguistic Research, 45*, 423-446.

Linell, Per. (2003). Dialogical tensions: On Rommetveitian themes of minds, meanings, monologue, and languages. *Mind, Culture and Activity, 10*, 219-229.

Linell, Per. (2009). *Rethinking language, mind and world dialogically: Interactional and contextual theories of human sense-making*. Information Age Publishing.

Linell, Per. (2010). Communicative activity types as organisations in discourses and discourses in organisations. In S.-K. Tanskanen, M.-L. Helasvuo, M. Johansson, J. Karhukorpi, & M. Raitaniemi (Eds.), *Discourses in interaction* (pp. 33-59). John Benjamins.

Linell, Per. (2022). Languaging in real life: On contexts and communication beyond formal linguistics and conversation analysis. In N. Muller Mirza & M. Dos Santos

(Eds.), *Dialogical approaches and tensions in learning and development: At the frontiers of the mind* (pp. 49–65). Springer.

Luckmann, Thomas. (2002). On the methodology of (oral) genres. In: P. Linell & K. Aronsson (Eds.), *Jagen och rösterna: Goffman, Viveka och samtalet* (pp. 319–337). [Selves and voices: Goffman, Viveka and conversation]. (SIC, 42). Linköping, SE. Tema Kommunikation.

Marková, Ivana. (2016). *The dialogical mind: Common sense and ethics*. Cambridge University Press.

Moscovici, Serge. (1984). The phenomenon of social representations, In: R. M. Farr & S. Moscovici (Eds.), *Social representations* (pp. 3–69). Cambridge University Press.

Nikulin, Dimitri. (2010). *Dialectic and dialogue*. Stanford University Press.

Nystrand, Martin. (1992). Social interactionism versus social constructionism: Bakhtin, Rommetveit, and the semiotics of written text. In: Astri H. Wold (Ed.), *The dialogical alternative: Towards a theory of language and mind* (pp. 157–173). Scandinavian University Press.

Oevermann, Ulrich, Tilman, Allert, Konau, Elisabeth, Rambeck, Jürgen. (1979). Die Methodologie einer "objektiven Hermeneutik" und ihre allgemeine Forschungslogische Bedeutung in den Sozialwissenschaften. In H. G. Soeffner (Ed.), *Interpretative Verfahren in den Sozial- und Textwissenschaften* (pp. 352–433). J. B. Metzlersche Verlagsbuchhandlung.

Orwell, George. (1949). *Nineteen eighty-four*. Penguin Books.

Pomerantsev, Peter. (2014). *Nothing is true and everything is possible*. Public Affairs.

Rommetveit, Ragnar. (1972). *Språk, tanke og kommunikasjon*. Akademisk Forlag.

Rommetveit, Ragnar. (1974). *On message structure*. Wiley.

Rommetveit, Ragnar. (1980). On "meaning" of acts and what is meant and made known by what is said in a pluralistic social world. In M. Brenner (Ed.), *The structure of action* (108–149). Blackwell and Mott.

Rommetveit, Ragnar. (1987). Meaning, context, and control: Convergent trends and controversial issues in current social-scientific research on human cognition and communication. *Inquiry, 30,* 77–99.

Rommetveit, Ragnar. (1988). On literacy and the myth of literal meaning. In R. Säljö (Ed.), *The written world* (pp. 13–40). Springer-Verlag.

Rommetveit, Ragnar. (1990). On axiomatic features of a dialogical approach to language and mind. In I. Marková & K. Foppa (Eds.), *The dynamics of dialogue* (pp. 83–104). Harvester Wheatsheaf.

Rommetveit, Ragnar. (1991). On epistemic responsibility in human communication. In H. Rönning & K. Lundby (Eds.), *Communication. Readings in methodology, history and culture* (pp. 13–27). Norwegian University Press.

Rommetveit, R. (1992). Outlines of a dialogically based social-cognitive approach to human cognition and communication. In Astri Heen Wold (Ed.), *The dialogical alternative: Towards a theory of language and mind* (pp. 19–44). Scandinavian University Press.

Rommetveit, Ragnar. (1998). On human beings, computers and representational–computational vs hermeneutic–dialogical approaches to human cognition and communication. *Culture & Psychology, 4,* 213–233.

Rommetveit, Ragnar. (2008). *Språk, individuell psyke, og kulturelt kollektiv* [Language, individual psyche and cultural collective]. Gyldendal Akademisk.

Sarason, Seymour. (1981). An asocial psychology and a misdirected clinical psychology. *American Psychologist, 36*, 827–836.
Schegloff, Emanuel A. (1996). Confirming allusions: Toward an empirical account of action. *American Journal of Sociology, 102*, 161–216.
Schegloff, Emanuel A. (2007). *Sequence organization in interaction.* Cambridge University Press.
Sidnell, Jack. (2009). *Conversation analysis. An introduction.* Blackwell.
Valsiner, Jaan, & van der Veer, René. (2000). *The social mind: Construction of the idea.* Cambridge University Press.
Walker, Shaun. (2018). *The long hangover – Putin's new Russia and the ghosts of the past.* Oxford University Press.
Wertsch, James. (2024). The role of narratives in dialogue and intersubjectivity. In O. Erstad, B. Hagtvet, & J. Wertsch (Eds.), *Education and dialogue in polarized societies: Dialogic perspectives in times of change.* Oxford University Press.
Wertsch, James. (2003). Ragnar Rommetveit: His work and influence. Introduction to a special issue. *Mind, Culture, and Activity, 10*, 183–185.
Wold, Astri Heen. (1992). Introduction. In A. H. Wold (Ed.), *The dialogical alternative: Towards a theory of language and mind* (pp. 1–18). Scandinavian University Press.
Zaner, Richard. (1979). The field-theory of experiential organisation: A critical appreciation of Aron Gurwitsch. *Journal of the British Society for Phenomenology, 10*, 141–152.

4
Layered Attunement
Internal Dialogues of Intersubjectivity

Christian H. Bisgaard, Marc Antoine Campill, Enno von Fircks, and Jaan Valsiner

4.1. Introduction

In an ever-developing, globalizing society—globalizing in respect to both political and personal issues—we see an increasing diversification and intertwinement across cultural contexts in a digital age. Politics and culture are expanding across hitherto established boundaries due to the new digital learning context allowing for potentially increasing diversity in minimal communities as well as in individuals and societies. In this chapter, we will propose that the self is narratively structured through multiple dialogues stemming from multiple forces, and voices in a global field of opinions are affecting our meaning-making process. And with the increased access to information streams, news, opinion polls, subcultures, and social arenas globally through social media in a digital age, we will in this chapter investigate how we can grasp the complex arrangement of the self through dialogism. Therefore, to analyze contemporary social phenomena that is inherently based on human meaning-making, we propose in this chapter that it is crucial to understand and investigate dialogism. Further, we need to expand the notion of dialogicality that has hitherto been understood as closely linked with its etymological meaning.[1] In this chapter, we propose that we need to move beyond what has been proposed by the "dialogical self" theory (Hermans, 2002), by turning to Rommetveit's notions of intersubjectivity and attunement to the attunement of others and to semiotic mediation to understand dialogism in relation to the self, and aid the discussion of what could happen if there was no dialogue but only monologue.

---

[1] Dialogue stemming from dia = through and logue = words from point to point.

Christian H. Bisgaard, Marc Antoine Campill, Enno von Fircks, and Jaan Valsiner, *Layered Attunement*
In: *Education and Dialogue in Polarized Societies*. Edited by: Ola Erstad, Bente Eriksen Hagtvet, and James V. Wertsch, Oxford University Press. © Oxford University Press 2024. DOI: 10.1093/oso/9780197605424.003.0004

Ragnar Rommetveit left us with a legacy of unity of deep philosophy and human psychology that is fertile ground for further investigations into the depth of the socially subjective human mind. In this chapter, we elaborate on the general theme of intersubjective attunement through inserting the basic scheme of cultural psychology of semiotic mediation (Valsiner, 2007, 2014, 2020a) into the texture of Rommetveit's (1985, 1992) focus on human understanding that is context-specific yet universal in its organization. Due to the self being narratively structured, we will in this chapter emphasize the centrality of the dialogical meaning-making process of human beings. Further, we want to emphasize the necessity of moving beyond words in human meaning-making yet being established through words and the necessity of moving beyond dialogicality (understood as between two opposing voices) by applying a polysemic, multivoiced framework of the self that can be expanded to encapsulate the community self as well.

Inspired by the story of Mrs. Smith's accounts of the perspective reversal of her husband's use of the lawnmower in the garden on a Saturday morning (Rommetveit, 1992) we created our data in the fictional story of a young man, Max. Just like many young men, Max is deeply involved in playing football, loves his mother, and is not insensitive to the looks of young women. He is very much enmeshed in his network of intersubjective relationships and aware of the wider needs of societal survival under siege of a pandemic threat that reaches into his life through general subjective awareness of potential dangers. Such threats—epidemics, famines, wars, revolutions, earthquakes, and the like—have been with humankind over the millennia. It is through subjective pre-adjustment via semiotic mediation that human beings can both experience the miseries of these dangers and develop ways of psychologically buffering themselves against those—ending up with the survival and further proliferation of humanity through the active coping by our ever-inquisitive minds.

The story of Max unfolds in a series of encounters with his daily world, bringing to the readers the introspective narrative of his relations with the events he is experiencing. Introspection has been—and remains—the basic method in the psychological science (Valsiner, 2017), as it is the *via regia* to the depths of human subjectivity. Our contemporary derivate of that basic method—the developing use of autoethnographies—illustrates the recurrence of the basic principles of introspection in twenty-first century social science. Each of the italicized portions of Max's introspective moments is relevant for our further analysis of the processes of attunement, building further from Rommetveit's legacy.

Scene 1

It is morning, and Max has just opened his eyes ready for a new day. A very important day. Finally, the sport clubs have been allowed to reopen following the big virus lockdown.[2] Max jumps happily out of bed eager to get through the day so that he can once again be reunited with his friends and finally play football not just by himself in the garden but with his teammates. Running down the stairs, Max feels the excitement in his body, and he kisses his mom good morning—just like always. *Max knows that due to the big virus you should avoid close contact, yet in his family, they have been physically isolated with little risk of being contaminated for the last two months of lockdown.* Therefore, Max does not even consider if he should stop kissing his mother good morning. The school has reopened—yet online. And Max has slowly gotten used to this kind of schooling, even though it feels strange and distant to sit in your own living room and attend classes while at the same time not being able to see and talk to your classmates. *This strangeness of social distancing has decreased with the students having collaboratively created some new forms of "being together," without physically being together.* They talk together during breaks and recess over the online video platform provided by the school. And when school finishes, they interact online through various social media platforms. They watch movies together, take walks together, and even play games together—all online. Even though Max has accepted the situation and has started to get used to this social distancing, *it just does not feel the same today. Something is missing. Something is not as it used to be.* Max misses his friends and classmates, even though he is talking to them through his computer. Usually, Max is very active during classes, but today he is distant, disturbed, and silent, and the teacher and his classmates start wondering about his absence. They ask if something is wrong, *yet Max is not able to say what is wrong.* There is just something that feels different today, and he just looks forward to going to football this afternoon.

It is the feeling of estrangement, of missing something, of being disturbed and not being able to verbalize what is going on inside of Max that shows his struggle to make sense of the situation now when football is once again available, and the school is still attended online. This is exactly the effect of the pandemic, challenging our meaning-making of our world in its everyday occurrence. Here Max's struggle in making sense of the situation he encounters is a sign of the

---

[2] During the winter of 2019–2020, a deadly virus, COVID-19 spread throughout the world, forcing countries and communities to shut down to minimize social contact. Due to a lack of effective treatments, however, the virus still managed to spread.

usual/previous narrative (myth[3]) coming to an end: going to school together, gossiping about the teachers during the breaks, reading classics in language classes, forming an opinion and defending it with your whole body, approaching the girl or boy you really like during sports classes, is just not possible anymore, as it had been previously. The pandemic—which outside of the actual infections operates as another myth story—creates a rupture of the previous myth—structuring the flow of experience e.g. in the class. All these signs combined into a narrative or myth (Gupta & Valsiner, 2003) by Max are now differently available, and he has not yet made sense of the altered signs and symbols nor structured them into a new story allowing him flow in the new experience. This is exactly the function of myth: "Myths are a way of making sense in a senseless world. Myths are narrative patterns that give significance to our existence" (May 1991, p. 16). And just when Max was starting to get used to this online schooling (creating a new myth), and football has once again been made available, this disturbs the meaning-making process and hinders the creation of this new, socially distant schooling myth. Here, the estrangement and the negative emotions show that Max's world has become "mythless" or without narrative. The people living within a myth do answer the challenges of it in a goal-oriented manner. Going to school, as previously mentioned, is more than getting taught something passively, but as the Latin word "educo" suggests, it is to bring something to light, to make something grow where the social component (school as socialization) is inherently important.

In a general sense, Max is thrown into a liminal state by the new setting, between the old arrangement of signs having become obsolete in the pandemic and the challenge of making meaning of the signs in a new manner required by the conditions of the pandemic. It is exactly that "thrown-ness" of a human being into liminality that is a deeply existential issue (von Fircks, 2022) requiring handling of the consequences of that liminal state and the feelings of estrangement that come with it.[4] As we see later in the story of Max—but important to mention here—is that myth makes community possible (May, 1991) while the individuals within the community are also able to contribute to the myth by answering the deeply existential issue at stake.

How can the liminal state be described? The totality of our social field consists of forces that direct our meaning-making processes in our life space, according

---

[3] We, as authors of the present paper, are aware of the difficult stance with which myth is confronted in science and society. However, myth is more than a narrative, due to its function as the silent organizer of human life. In the end, it is just a purposeful arrangement of signs and sign complexes that is inherently important for the human being and his organization of life (Valsiner, 2014). As May (1991) explains it, it is the bridge between the conscious and the subconscious.

[4] Here, we can invent the term of the myth of liminality that goes back to the Eleusinian mysteries (Malvezzi, 2019) where boys in Greek antiquity were "left naked, without food and having only a knife" (ibid., p. 321), with the goal of finding one's consciousness or the conditio humana.

to Kurt Lewin (1951). Here, different forces, communities, and their myths are affecting how a person perceives his or her encountered situation and how he/she feels and tries to make sense of the encountered situations. At the same time, the person is affecting the forces in the field by his agentic affective relation to a desired future and further his generalizations from past experiences orienting his behavior and actions in the field, e.g. Max's absence, tense feelings, and the struggle to make sense of his feelings in scene 1. Consequently, Max's behavior is now affecting the other students, the teachers, and thus the forces in Max's life space (Lewin, 1936, 1942, 1951; Valsiner, 2006). This is exemplified in Figure 4.1.

In Figure 4.1, we see how the different forces through their myths are affecting Max's meaning-making of the encountered situation when Max is interacting with this external force on the boundary to the self between layers 2 and 3, and we see how this interaction is also affecting the forces which end up in a reciprocal effect of both the force and Max.

The effect on Max in the encountered situation results in the strongest forces making certain myths and signs more prevalent and available for Max in his meaning-making process. This morning, the strength of the forces; teammates and the coach have changed (see Figure 4.1). They now become more significant and the hitherto balance or hierarchy of strength between the forces in the life space is being affected. This leads to the tension in the meaning-making process and Max's feeling of strangeness in the situation. Yet at the same time, Max is affecting the forces in his life space, as we see with the wondering of his classmates and teachers asking him about his social and emotional absence. In Figure 4.1, this is illustrated by the force of the classmates and the teacher meeting Max's force in the interaction in the boundary between layers 2 and 3 and work back on each component. Thus, the interaction between forces results in a reciprocal effect of both Max in layers 1 and 2 and the external forces in layer 3.

In sum, this is what Rommetveit (1992) calls the "gradual reciprocal attunement" to the attunement of the others. However, the creation of intersubjectivity in scene 1, and thus the continuance of the myth has been hindered due to the significance of the interrupting forces in Max's life space following the reoccurrence of football. Modeling this liminal state of tension in Max's meaning-making of the situation and further the reciprocal attunement to the attunements of the others, we see in Figure 4.1 how the football club, the teammates, and the coach are external factors in level 3. Yet, these are not all present in scene 1 but a certain significance of these forces is perceived by Max due to the availability of the forces later this day.[5] Thus, it is mainly the internalized forces from the coach and the teammates, stemming from Max's personal past experiences, that have been made available and lead to Max's internal hierarchy of significant forces in level 1 being slightly altered due to the indirect presence of the forces from

---

[5] Some of Max's classmates are teammates as well.

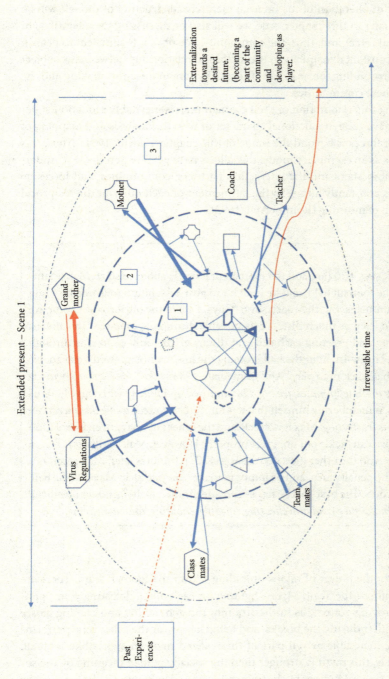

Figure 4.1. A model of Max's Polysemic Multivoiced self and the prevalent forces (voices) present in the encountered situation in scene 1. It is illustrated how the different layers in the PMS are affecting each other, leading to an individualized internalization of a PMS hierarchy in layer 1 and the following externalization. Further we see how forces in layer 3 affects each other. This affectation is possible in every layer between forces in the same layer as well as across layers.

football. This alteration of the internal hierarchical structure of the self will be discussed later in this chapter. And we will also be discussing the alterations in the external forces and, thus, the community. For now, it is sufficient to bear in mind the constant dynamicity in the reciprocal relationship between the subject and the surrounding forces in the life space in human meaning-making and the myths in these communities.

Applying this elaboration of the Lewinian Map is inevitably reductionist because we have created a fictional character of who the analysis and mapping of the field of forces is beyond the scope of this chapter (Lewin, 1951). Thus, this only serves as an exemplary model that allows us to get one step closer to understanding how Max's and the interaction partners, communities, and forces he encounters constantly attune to the attunement of each other in the reciprocal negotiation of meaning (Rommetveit, 1992).

Scene 2

The clock says 4:30 pm, and the football practice is about to start. Max is running to the football field, and he is about to give a fist bump followed by a hug to his teammates. But the coach says: "Guys! Due to the big virus situation, we will try to keep as much distance as possible during the practice. This means celebrating and greeting each other at distance. The only contact is through tackling. Throw-ins after the ball crossing the line are not allowed. Instead, we kick the ball back in to play." And immediately Max *takes one step back waving his hands to his teammates, feeling a bit annoyed and uneasy* with this big virus situation, remembering himself that it is for the *best to keep a safe distance, even though it is frustrating*. Max is not sick, and the other guys have been in isolation too, and we can tackle but not greet properly. However, Max thinks, *it is best to keep safe*. And the other guys do this as well. Ten minutes later, Max receives a cross in the penalty area, and he jumps to make a bicycle kick. Max hits the ball, and he scores. The best goal he has ever made. Immediately, *he jumps up and all his teammates surround him cheering, hugging, shouting, and high-fiving*.

Here we see the power of myths unfolding within the football team. There are two in conflict—the Team Myth—fighting for each other, defeating your opponent, improving your skills in the (training) match, taking and coming closer to one another during the breaks, and being happy for the other if he performs something incredible are all part of the realized myth in sports like football. Impressively, this myth is stronger than the socially guided meaning by the society (the Danger Myth) or by the trainer. Illustrated in Figure 4.1, we see how the virus regulations are present in the dialogical and reciprocal negotiation as well as the teammates and the coach, and this leads to the superiority of the Danger Myth over the Team Myth. In this situation, the players' internal dialogues are a result of the negotiation of forces in the PMS-model of the self, and thus layer 1 becomes dominated by I-positions as responsible teammate and responsible brother and son, while I-positions as engaged teammate is less dominant in the beginning of the scene.

We can see the dominance of the two myths changing places. The Danger Myth momentarily vanishes when the Team Myth jumps to dominance after the event (the outstanding goal). The event evokes a sudden overwhelming hyper-generalized[6] feeling that silences the Danger Myth, at least for a short moment. It is a field-like sign leading to cheering and joy. Team members' intersubjectivity—we can also say the mutual agreement upon the meaning-making of the signs, constantly negotiated and renegotiated—is the catalyst for the myth that is realized in rituals, such as cheering and celebrating the goal. Thus, the position I-as-engaged-teammate now momentarily dominates the I-positions in the situation both within the players' layers 1 and 2 and between the players in layer 3 in Figure 4.1.

The hegemony of the Team Myth is institutionally supported—the longer the feeling of celebration lasts, the better. It is not a coincidence that in sports clubs, especially in football clubs, there is often a clubhouse next to the pitch allowing the players to stay in their flow of experience and with their positive emotions even if the match is already over. Myth creates home wherein the community can live in. A counter-myth, such as the Danger Myth, might challenge it, but it is unlikely to be totally overcome.

Scene 3
However, after the celebration, a knot is felt in Max's stomach: "It was such a good goal, and I am happy for the goal *but what if one of us has the virus without knowing it?*" A *tension is felt throughout the group*, as it feels like the other players realize this rupture. The tense feeling within Max is especially severe due to his *felt responsibility for his vulnerable grandmother at home* who is particularly at risk to severe impact of the big virus; but at the same time, it is just so hard not to get carried away by the atmosphere at practice. Five

---

[6] Valsiner's (2007; 2014; 2020a; 2020b) theory of cultural psychology of semiotic dynamics emphasizes the abstractive generalization of signs that transcends to hyper-generalization of such signs. In the latter mode, the human psyche is overtaken by a complete field of meaningful feeling that cannot be described in fullness by words (only generalized labels—love, injustice, etc—are possible). It is implied in this theory that human beings function psychologically at that highest level of psychological use of signs, with episodic reduction from that level to the verbal communication (narrative) encounters.

> minutes later, Max scores another goal, and he is just about to give his teammate a high five, but just before the hands meet, both players stop, drop their hands, and just nod to each other.

What is crucial in Scene 3 is the interference of the worry from the there-and-then (grandmother at home) into the here-and-now (another good result on the field). Such interferences happen all the time as our minds wander beyond a particular setting—creating the perpetual dialogue between the AS-IS (here-and-now) and AS-IF (there-and then—Vaihinger, 1911) settings in the mind. Yet, the grandmother is not present in the situation—only in Max's internal dialogue, with the imagined dialogue of the mother and the grandmother in layer 2.

Most importantly, this internal dialogue with the imagined voices modulates the strength of the different forces in Max's life space and his Polysemic Multivoiced Self (PMS). We will return to this dynamic PMS later in the chapter. For now, it is important to note the effect of both external forces and imagined internal voices in the negotiation of meaning in the self and further how these external and imagined forces are also affected by the actions and meaning-making of the self (see this reciprocity in Figure 4.1).

Scene 4

At 6:30 pm, Max is riding his bike home from practice—*high from the feeling of finally seeing his friends*, playing, and having a great time during this big virus situation. He parks his bike in front of the house *and almost jumps to the door in excitement. When entering he cannot stop smiling and he is just about to hug his mother as she is to hug him too. Yet before touching, Max stops and steps back.* The mother seems confused. The co-created intersubjectivity of greeting with a hug was suddenly ruptured. The mother starts to wonder if she has done anything wrong, while Max at the same time is feeling guilty from hugging, cheering, and greeting at practice, thus potentially endangering his grandmother. Max thinks:

> "I want to hug her, but I might endanger grandma if I do 'cause mum is taking care of her all the time during this pandemic. I wish we would have never had that celebration huddle at practice, but I just could not help it. Everybody just did it."

This internal dialogue takes place at the junction where the Danger Myth again gains prominence over the Team Myth following the presence of the family myth. The latter's dominance in the field was affectively supported—even though the players came to an agreement during practice of not hugging and cheering in a huddle, the moment of elated success wiped out all the social contracts instigated by the Danger Myth. The relationships between different hyper-generalized sign fields are affectively—rather than cognitively—regulated. Such regulation involves both rapid changes in their dominance relations as well as the lingering ambivalence between the fields.

What happened in Scene 4? For Max, reflecting about what happened during practice, the cheering and hugging becomes a sign of violating the distancing rules, and he immediately thinks about the consequences (what could be) of it leading into the fear of life<>death for his beloved grandmother. The attunement toward the Other happens not only here-and-now—with real other people in contact—but also in the mind in relation to Others assumed to be somewhere else—real, or non-real (images of deities etc., e.g. indirect forces internalized in layer 2 and affecting the boundary negotiation between layers 2 and 3). Attunement to the Other is *subjectively layered*—different hyper-generalized affective fields/voices are situated in a hierarchy where their dominance relationship generates both the conduct and affective reflection upon it at the same time. The dominance hierarchy between forces/voices is dynamic and can be modulated by cognitive (circumvention strategies—Josephs & Valsiner, 1998) or affectively expanding conditions (e.g. where elation from success reverses the hierarchical order of the fields—see Scene 2).

The forces in the field of Max's life space become internalized as voices/hyper-generalized affective fields in Max's internal dialogue following Hermans (2001) Dialogical Self Theory. Hermans (2001), proposed the Dialogical Self Theory that focuses on the human self as consisting of a multitude of internalized (layer 1 in Figure 4.1) and imaginative positions (layer 2 in Figure 4.1) to make sense of the situations encountered. Due to the self being narratively structured, these positions are in the form of voices that are in dialogical negotiation. These voices both consist of the actual voices inter-psychologically (layer 3 in Figure 4.1) and the internalized and imaginative voices intra-psychologically (layers 1 and 2 in Figure 4.1).

Linking theoretical perspectives is productive. When talking about the voices as positions, we can start to align the Dialogical Self Theory (Hermans, 2001) with Lewin's Field Theory (Lewin, 1936, 1942, 1951) due to the spatial arrangement of the voices as positions in negotiation and across time and conditions. Different positions will be prominent and dominate the dialogue and thus the meaning-making process (Hermans, 2001).

As we saw in the elaboration of Figure 4.1, certain persons and objects external to the self are relevant and prominent; and these make certain internalized and imaginative voices prominent within the self that will be dominant in the dialogical meaning-making negotiation in that encountered situation due to the context conditioned (Valsiner & Capezza, 2002) strength of these forces (hence the width of the arrows in Figure 4.1). In another situation, different relevant forces will make different internalized voices dominant, and these will alter the dialogical negotiation of meaning. What is important to note is the continuance of the human being yet with different dominant voices in a *unitas multiplex*.[7] Thus, individuals are able to inhabit several I-positions which can create tension in the meaning-making process following contradictions and oppositions between the relevant voices. And as we see in the model (e.g. the strength of the forces and the perceived significance of these forces and internalized voices), some positions/voices are made available at relevant times and conditions, while others are out of consciousness and the subjective horizon at that point of time (Hermans, 2001). Further, these voices need not be actual other persons. Hermans (2001) also operates with collective voices that can be equal to the abovementioned myths in certain communities.

As previously elaborated, human meaning-making is not merely operating at a conscious level. We have seen the unconscious domains of the myths guiding our meaning-making processes in the situations we encounter. To further understand the parallel operating unconscious processes of human meaning-making and tacit knowledge construction, we will have to elaborate semiotic mediation that ranges far beyond the middle—narrative—domain of human communication processes.

4.2. Dialogical Negotiation Beyond Consciousness

Semiotic mediation entails that our meaning-making processes are sign creating, sign using, and sign leaving. Thereby, we understand and make sense of the situations we encounter by using signs, and the qualities of these signs allow us to pre-anticipate and adapt to the uncertainties of the future—in a way, trying to reach a desired future (Zittoun et al., 2013). In every situation, signs stand out and become available and interpreted by the individual in the contextual situation. The availability of these signs stems from our personal uniqueness as human beings following our unique personal pasts that have been reflected upon and made sense in, and thus the signs available for making sense in the future are flavored by our own unique personal pasts. Yet, as mentioned above, these past experiences are inherently social but differential since every person encounters

---

[7] Unitas multiplex means that our dialogical self is not an entity but a unity in multiplicity. The term was central for William Stern's personological theory of the self (1935; 1938).

these social situations differently and uniquely due to our individual differences in experiences as well (Branco & Valsiner, 2010; Valsiner, 2020a; 2020b). Put in another line according to the abovementioned myths, we are narratively understanding our lives. Thus we are not only internalizing external myths to our own narrative, but rather we are hierarchically ordering external myths in our personal narrative according to the significance of these myths/social experiences, and thus the social experiences will be socially differential. We can see this in Figure 4.1, where the internalized forces/myths are structured in a hierarchy of voices in layer 1 that strongly interacts with the imagined voices of non-present but still significant voices (there-and-then) in the here-and-now setting.

4.3. The Polysemic Multivoiced Self

The internalized hierarchical multivoiced self is called the polysemic multivoiced self (PMS), which is dynamic and potentially alternating according to the context conditions encountered (Valsiner & Capezza, 2002), the strength of the myths and forces in these contexts (Lewin, 1951), and thus the availability of certain signs (Valsiner, 2020a, 2020b).

In both the creation of the voice hierarchy in layer 1 of PMS and in the creation and usage of signs in the perception of the encountered situation, we are not just determined and constrained by past experiences through accumulative and deductive generalization. Further, every situation is not seen as a new unique situation that induces an inductive generalization of new meaning. *Instead, we are as human beings abductively generalizing past experiences into generalized signs and hyper-generalized sign fields* that flavor our future perception of situations without determining them (Salvatore & Valsiner, 2010; Valsiner, 2014, 2020a, 2020b). *In terms of the PMS this is seen as a tendency to a certain hierarchical order of the relevant voices due to their perceived significance in our abductively generalized past experiences.* Throughout our lives, we generalize our experiences and feelings into categories and point-like signs. Following PMS, this is seen as the dialogical negotiation of certain relevant forces and voices in the boundary between layers 2 and 3 and between layers 1 and 2, which might lead to a certain voice hierarchy in layer 1 being externalized in a certain behavior and meaning in the encountered situation (Valsiner, 2006). Further, these negotiations of hierarchies, and thus generalized feelings and categories, may be hyper-generalized into a nonverbal sign field hyper-generalized tendency to structure the voices in the PMS in a certain hierarchy, that is, guiding our future perception of the encountered situations just like an intuitive way of understanding the encountered situations (Valsiner, 2014). Thus, the signs having been generalized and hyper-generalized serve as representations of experienced situations and

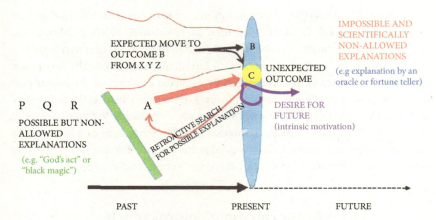

Figure 4.2. Abductive generalization in irreversible time illustrated by Valsiner (2020).

meanings, and these now guide our understanding of future situations entailing similar, or the same, signs. Thus, signs trigger and make available a certain hyper-generalized hierarchy in PMS, which allow us to pre-anticipate and pre-adapt to the uncertainties of the future. It follows that a semiotically mediated approach becomes an approach of internalizing, constructing, and reconstructing signs and experiences and thus our hyper-generalized voice hierarchy in PMS, in order to make sense of the future (Valsiner, 2006, 2014). And this future relatedness is linked with our goal-oriented nature as human beings (Branco & Valsiner, 2010; Valsiner, 2020a).

To go one level deeper in understanding abductive generalization and thus the creation of the hyper-generalized PMS, we will now outline abductive generalization following Figure 4.2. In our everyday lives, we are encountering new situations all the time due to the irreversibility of time, which means that every present has just become the past, and a new situation is emerging (Salvatore & Valsiner, 2010). If we are to consciously and verbally generalize and make sense of every situation schematically and categorically, we will not be able to live in the complexity of living a human life with all the new situations and signs encountered. Thus, we are not perceiving the encountered situations following only the usual schematization perceptive pathway. In parallel, a pleromatization perceptive pathway[8] is also operating (Branco & Valsiner,

---

[8] Pleromatization refers to an extension of the emerging sign forms in the situation allowing the individual to perceive the encountered situation affectively holistically, as when perceiving the atmosphere of a painting nonverbally but affectively and holistically felt (Valsiner, 2020a; 2020b).

2010; Valsiner, 2020a). This entails a holistic perception of the richness of the situation encountered in line with the gestalt psychological tradition. This pleromatic perception is guided by the before-mentioned hyper-generalized sign fields that are made available in the encountered situation and are operating as our "intuition" on behalf of our significant past experiences, that have been hyper-generalized into our intuitive hyper-generalized sign field flavoring our meaning-making in new situations (e.g. the hyper-generalized PMS). However, this meaning-making does not necessarily run smoothly, and tensions might be felt in our meaning-making processes (Valsiner, 2014). This is when situations offer signs and meanings of the signs, that are in opposition to or in conflict with our hyper-generalized sign fields of past significant experiences (e.g. when the forces in the life space and the dialogues in layers 1 and 2 are not equivalent with the hyper-generalized voice hierarchy available and guiding our meaning-making in the situation). Thus, we feel wonderment and surprise, and an abductive generalization has been initiated, wherein we revise and alter our generalized and hyper-generalized sign fields due to our new experiences (Salvatore and Valsiner, 2010). However, this revision or alteration might create tension, due to our hitherto understanding and feeling of the world now being questioned. This process of semiotic mediation is illustrated in Figure 4.2.

In Figure 4.2, we see how we are encountering a new situation in the present, and our past experiences have been generalized and hyper-generalized for us to pre-anticipate and expect a move XYZ to reach a desired outcome B in the situation. Yet, we experience outcome C in the situation (e.g. the wonderous or surprising situation mentioned above), and we feel a tension in our meaning-making process. A retroactive search in past experiences and a schematization of the signs encountered in the situation are initiated, and a new generalized sign of explanation A is created. And this might be hyper-generalized, which will then guide future pleromatic and schematic perceptions of future situations through both entailing explanations, XYZ and PQR.

Returning to Max, we see that he is experiencing a form of tension and wondering while feeling a knot in his stomach after practice thinking about his grandmother. He feels unease when attending online school waiting for football, and he feels a tension when greeting his mother after practice. These tensions might initiate a dialogical negotiation of meaning in layers 1 and 2 in the PMS model (see Figure 4.1), while simultaneously interacting with external forces in layer 3 being internalized through negotiation in the boundary between layers 2 and 3. Throughout everyday life, every situation encountered need not initiate this dialogical negotiation—hence the pleromatization perceptive pathway and further, due to the possibility of some voices in the voice hierarchy being so strong and influential in the hyper-generalized PMS that our the presently encountered situation does not introduce strong enough voices in layers 2 or 3. *Thus, our PMS is up-consciously enforcing a certain hierarchy leading to a certain meaning.* Yet, if enough tension is felt in the meaning-making process in the situation, Max will perform a dialogical reciprocal negotiation with the external forces at the boundary of layers 2 and 3. According to the strength of these forces, this reciprocal negotiation might result in affecting both the expression and strength of the internalized imaginative voice in level 2. Further, this tension felt in the meaning-making process and the altered strength of the forces might result in a new hierarchy in the PMS following the alteration of the forces in multi-logical negotiation of meaning. This multi-logical[9] order in the voice hierarchy is inevitable, due to the presence of several voices simultaneously. This new hierarchical order of voices following the tension will now guide Max's meaning-making and pre-anticipation in these situations (the externalization in Figure 4.1). Here, we draw parallels from the schematization process in semiotic mediation to the dialogical negotiation in dialogical self-theory (DST) (Hermans, 2001). Further, we want to propose the hierarchical ordering of the multi-logical self as a hyper-generalization process. Certain hierarchies of voices are hyper-generalized and will be up-consciously guiding voice hierarchies made available by the available signs and thus leading to certain pre-anticipations, meaning-making, and actions.

Going one step beyond conscious negotiation, we are proposing a model of the PMS that is a result of a multi-logical reciprocal negotiation of meaning between the internalized voices and the external voices in the boundary between layers 2 and 3 that leads to a certain hierarchical order of the PMS in layer 1 according to the perceived strength of the voices. This PMS might hyper-generalize into a hyper-generalized sense of self and thus a hyper-generalized PMS with a voice hierarchy guiding human meaning-making and conduct in the encountered situations. Thus, this step beyond conscious negotiation allows us to go two steps beyond Hermans' (2001) DST through our emphasis of the up-conscious dialogue, following the hyper-generalization principle in semiotic mediation that will inevitably lead to a hierarchically ordered multi-logue that will eventually externalize in a certain meaning-making and conduct in the situation either following the existing myth/intersubjectivity inherent in the minimal community or creating tension and thus inducing change in the minimal community myth.

---

[9] Multi-logue is an extension of dialogue, where we emphasize the presence of multiple voices and not only two at a time.

> ### Scene 5
>
> A year later, Max is about to attend a new football practice. Today is an exciting day. Max is joining a new football club. He felt he needed new challenges than those available in the old club and wanted to try something new and develop as a player. When arriving in the changing room Max shouts "Hi!" but no one is responding. All the players are silently listening to music not registering each other. A few moments later the coach arrives and starts speaking to two of the players on the team. Briefly after, these two players pick up a ghetto blaster, they put on a hip hop song and start dancing. The rest of the players join in a well-coordinated dance routine. Max gets *confused not knowing what to do, where to go, and how to act.* Still, no one is talking and suddenly two players start shouting, yet no words, just what seems like arbitrary sounds. The other guys jump two times on the spot and two new shouts follow. The rest jumps two more times and all the players start running out of the dressing room to the football field. Max is still standing without his football boots and feeling paralyzed. Quickly he changes and starts running to the field as well. Arriving on the field, he runs to the nearest player asking what just happened in the dressing room. The player (N) looks confused saying: "That in there? That is our mental prep to get in the zone for practice. Every team does that. That is a part of the game." Max thinks to himself that he has never seen anything like that before.

Here we see how the hyper-generalized PMS, and thus the tacit knowledge of a person, is countering the tacit knowledge of a new group (Polanyi, 1962) and how this leads to certain tensions in the meaning-making process. When joining the new football club, he has a goal of developing and being further challenged as a football player, and we see him feeling frustrated and being confused when the expected move from XYZ (his past experiences) to outcome B of saying "hi," greeting each other, and talking together is not met. Instead, outcome C of silence, dancing, jumping, and shouting is experienced, and we see the tension of Max being paralyzed. The surprise is especially severe in this situation, it almost seems as an explosion for Max as he has severe difficulty in making sense of the ongoing situation and further see how he could and should behave in the situation. In this chapter, we conceptualize this as a *gestalt explosion* when a situation is so new and different that it creates severe tension in the holistic and pleromatic perception of the situation. Further, he alone is not able to create signs that enable him to reach his desired future of improving as a football player. However, Max does create a new generalized sign that allows him to make sense of the situation—but not alone. Here Rommetveit's contribution of reciprocity in the inherently social nature of human being toward creating intersubjectivity linked with the extension of Herman's dialogical self to the polysemic multivoiced self becomes apparent in understanding Max's meaning-making process.

A crucial condition for the attunement toward the attunement of the other if we speak in Rommetveitian terms (Rommetveit, 1992) is the availability of a social guidance toward the meaning-making of a certain situation (the reciprocal negotiation in layer 3 and between layers 2 and 3). This is of great importance for creating intersubjectivity. Max does not know the meaning of the mental preparation, and he cannot grasp it because he simply does not know about it. There is a difficulty in arranging the signs of dancing among the other rituals into a theme or story which lead to feelings of confusion and insecurity. May (2007) elaborates on that when he explains that "I cannot perceive something until I can conceive it" (p. 236). This makes social guidance indispensable for the perception of the mental preparation as it happens and then in a second step the participation in it. Only when (N) suggests a potential meaning-making (mental preparation) of the event, can Max perceive it (e.g. N makes PQR available in Figure 4.2). It is hard to grasp a situation, to be attuned toward your team—as in the example of Max—when there is no such guidance within the feelings of uncertainty and ambiguity. The example shows that the significant other is necessary to overcome the tension of ambiguity and uncertainty or to enter into a meaning-making negotiation with the exact same purpose. By entering into dialogue with the significant other, we expand our meaning-making of the current situation trying jointly—in the example of Max and N—to stumble toward an interpretation of the situation, which is soon to be established when Max participates within the mental preparation. He then embodies the new, intersubjectively shared meaning.

In other words, following the model of the PMS, Max is not just internally having a dialogue in layer 1 trying to make sense of the encountered situation. Instead, he is being affected by the forces in layer 3 (the person N and the new teammates) and these forces are internalized—yet in a reciprocal negotiation and represented in the internalized imaginative voices in layer 2. These negotiations lead to the internalized voices of the forces having different strengths where the strongest internalized voices in the situation encountered drops toward the bottom of the PMS in layer 1 being the heaviest and most influential voices in the hierarchy (this is seen through both the number of connections with other voices and the subjectively perceived strength of the voice). Simultaneously the weakest voices float to the top of the self in layer 1 and have the fewest connections and the least perceived strength. Encountering the new teammates and their new routines initiated a new negotiation of the voice hierarchy in PMS further strengthened by the conversation with N. Yet, the creation of a new hierarchy might involve tension and take time. This will be further investigated with the implementation of our concepts of gestalt explosion and extinction.

> **Scene 6**
> Several days later, Max is attending another football practice, and the coach walks in, talks to two players, and they start dancing to the music. Earlier, Max told N that he has a hard time doing the dance and feeling ready for practicing. He feels a little left outside the community. Today N walks to Max and starts guiding Max through the dancing routine. Further, he gives cues to Max about when to shout, and just before running to the field, Max and N fist bump. It just felt right. Max was used to doing fist bumps in the old club, and N just went along naturally. However, when wanting to hug N as Max also did in the previous club, N said: "We should not do that. Even though COVID-19 is over, we could infect each other with diseases, so we should keep some distance at practice."

4.4. Relations Between Voices: Tensions and Their Negotiation

Tension and negotiation of different voices arise if the myths of multiple communities are contradictory and deny a simple coexistence of the voice's externalized conduct (rituals). *I cannot live in multiple communities if their myths and rituals harm each other continuously.* This makes the hierarchical ordering of different voices within the self indispensable. Thrown into that tension, the "I" can only make sense of the situation if the person circumvents it. Circumvention here means that the individual prioritizes one voice over another. Thus, a voice oriented toward a community may gain a dominant status over a personally important one, or vice versa. This is done practically by hierarchization of the multiple voices being in negotiation. This is a willful decision, a willful bias toward a community trajectory elicited by the semiotic marker and its (potential) consequences. It is noticeable at this point that releasing the tension that Max experiences in scene 5 in his meaning-making process can lead into the creation of a new voice as in the example of Max in his new football club in scene 6. The change in the multi-logical hierarchy of the self changes the perception of the ongoing flow of experience.

The difficulty of human interaction is characterized by individuals within one community having multiple different communities they feel attuned to. Person A and person B coming together in one community will eventually find they do not share all their other communities. And if they did, it is likely that these individuals might order all these tensive voices differently within their self, which marks the complexity of human interaction. This might explain the mutual disappointment of persons being temporarily in one community where one reveals beliefs that are distinct from the other about the centrality of the community and at a particular moment says something such as *"I thought you were more loyal toward our group."* Moving and living enables the active switching between attunement and non-attunement toward different communities. Signs and objects help the individual to push themselves toward the road of enabling or blocking that active switching.

Meaning-making explosion—the current sign-fields "breaking out" of their current borders—can be seen in meaning-making struggles following the tensions felt in the pleromatic perception of the encountered situations varying in strengths. New signs offering new meaning might not be easily created, as we see with Max being paralyzed in scene 5. Following an explosion, rearrangement of the hierarchical PMS needs to occur, and following the paralyzing explosion in scene 5 a fundamental rearrangement is needed. In other words, Max needs to abductively make PQR (in Figure 4.2) available. This is exemplified in Figure 4.3.

Following dialogue with N and reciprocal negotiation of meaning, Max internalizes voices from N and the myth of this new club, allowing him to once again create a hierarchically ordered PMS that enables him to create and interpret signs offered in this new community in an appropriate way, following the reciprocally negotiated intersubjectivity. This can be seen when N approaches Max and they end up fist bumping (e.g. the incorporation of a new voice). Max's newly created hierarchical PMS is seen in Figure 4.4.

In the process of semiotic mediation, human beings create hyper-generalized sign fields arranged in a myth-like story that intuitively guides our feeling in the world. Following the above model, we can conceptualize this hyper-generalized self as the PMS with some voices being more prevalent in most situations, while other voices are weaker and only present in few or limited situations. Thus, we propose a hyper-generalized self, constructed by the strong voices reconstructively internalized in our life space that guide our externalization of meaning in the encountered situations. Yet, the hyper-generalized PMS is not determining our externalizations. Our abductively generalizing nature as human beings allow us to create new signs and hierarchical orders in the hyper-generalized self that externalize slightly differently according to the situation encountered. Some voices might be stronger in some situations than others (teacher and classmates when Max is attending school), while some voices are present at all times (the grandmother due to Max's strong I-position, I-as-a-responsible-grandson). If enough tension is felt, a gestalt explosion calling for restructuring of the self might be induced. Here, we have taken one step beyond the DST by ordering the voices hierarchically.

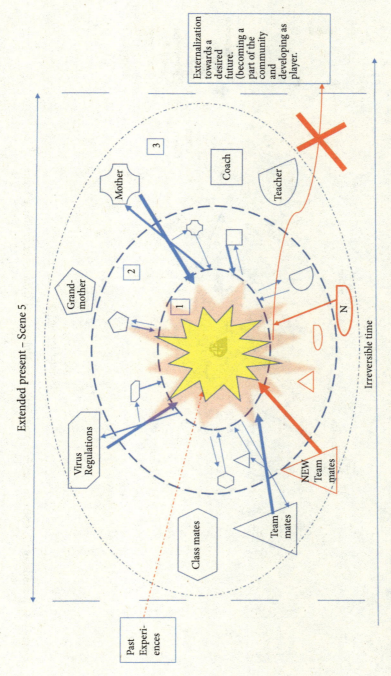

Figure 4.3. A model of the experienced explosion in scene 5 for Max, leading to the neccessity of restructuring his Polysemic Multivoiced Self.

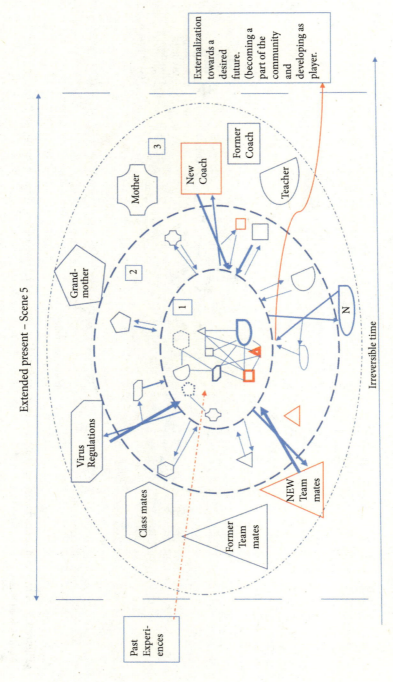

Figure 4.4. A model of the restructuration of Max' Polysemic Multivoiced Self after explosion in Scene 5.

4.5. General Discussion: Learning with Rommetveit

Rommetveit (1985, 1992) focused on a networking situation as a dialogue, as for example between Max and an individual N. This theoretical view would elaborate how two voices would negotiate their interpreted context-conditioned meaning of the situation, while attuning to the attunement of the other. In contrast to these beliefs, we have elaborated the conceptuality of PMS and meaning-making explosions and renegotiations based on a diverse understanding that not *a* dialogue but *multiple* dialogues are part of our everyday life.

Rommetveit's Mrs. Smith and our Max-the-Football-Player share much in common—rapid renegotiation of the metacommunicative frames in their action with others or within oneself. We are learning with Rommetveit not merely that context matters, but the ways in which it does and how to decompose the processes involved in it. The focus on it from the angle of the cultural psychology of semiotic dynamics—movement between experiencing and abstracting signs that become generalized and hyper-generalized—then returning to creating meaning in the particular here-and-now context altering it profoundly—opens the realm of possibilities for the polysemic multivoiced self to transform. It is not merely a shift of perspectives (as Mrs. Smith bluntly demonstrated) but the reorganization of the hierarchical self in layer 1. Therefore, we need to move beyond the original understanding of dialogicality of development through words from point to point.[10] We need to grasp the multiplicity of points that are inevitably present in the negotiation of the PMS that need not be a verbalizable process but can be a felt, pleromatic, and intuitive process available to us through conduct. A person of few voices in the hierarchical self has a monological perspective and thus a higher risk of losing oneself to fanatism[11]—be it determination to kill insects, minks, or enemies, or (on the positive side) spend all of one's resources in the cultivation of a monoculture (corn, potatoes, producing face masks or tanks, or giving birth to babies for them to become soldiers for "the fatherland"). While social institutions aim at turning society into a monocultural field, with Rommetveit we learn that this move toward homogenization can be socially toxic. Fortunately, it is also not achievable—as human beings abandon their temporarily fixed selves in their experiencing of their lives.

In this chapter, we have presented a new approach to dialogicality that allows us to expand the notion of dialogicality beyond time and space. With the PMS model of the self, we highlight the importance of looking at the individual in

---

[10] Multilogicality = dialogical meaning-making process in a polysemic multivoiced self, e.g. unitas multiplex.

[11] Few voices in the polysemic multivoiced self is not making us fanatics, but from the learnings in this article, fewer voices reduces our possibilities to escape fanatical thinking.

context: how this individual is interacting with the physical context in the encountered situation on the basis of his past experiences and, further, how the individual is interacting through multiple dialogues with other past-experienced context as well as future imaginary contexts. Thus, we pave the way for expanding the field of dialogicality beyond the individual—could we talk about a hyper-generalized polysemic multivoiced community self and thus community intuition? This is a field that needs to be investigated further. In the meantime, we have created a model that might aid the discussion and research of what happens when dialogue remains absent—both within the self and in the community.

References

Branco, A., & Valsiner, J. (2010). Toward cultural psychology of affective processes: Semiotic regulation of dynamic fields. *Estudios de Psicología*, *31*(3), 243–251.

Gupta, S., & Valsiner, J. (2003). Myths and minds: Implicit guidance for human conduct. In I. E. Josephs (Ed.), *Dialogicality in development* (pp. 179–195). Praeger.

Hermans, H. J. M. (2001). The dialogical self: Toward a theory of personal and cultural positioning. *Culture & Psychology*, *7*(3), 243–281. https://doi.org/10.1177/1354067X0173001

Josephs, I. E., & Valsiner, J. (1998). How does autodialogue work? Miracles of meaning maintenance and circumvention strategies. *Social Psychology Quarterly*, *61*(1), 68–83.

Lewin, K. (1936). *Principles of topological psychology*. McGraw-Hill Book Company, Inc.

Lewin, K. (1942). Field theory and learning. In H. B. Nelson (Ed.), *The forty-first yearbook of the national society of learning: Part 2, The psychology of learning* (pp. 215–242). Public School Publishing Company.

Lewin, K. (1951). Field theory in social science. In D. Cartwright (Ed.), *Selected theoretical papers* (pp. 238–303). Harper & Brothers Publishers.

Malvezzi, S. (2019). Self-fulfillment: The work of human existence. In P. F. Bendassolli (Ed.), *Culture, work, and psychology* (pp. 309–333). Information Age Publishing.

May, R. (1991). *The cry for myth* (1st ed.). Norton.

May, R. (2007). *Love and will*. W. W. Norton. (Original work published 1969.)

Polanyi, M. (1962). *Personal knowledge: Towards a post-critical philosophy*. Chicago, IL: University of Chicago.

Rommetveit, R. (1985). Language acquisition as increasing linguistic structuring of experience and symbolic behavior control. In J. V. Wertsch (Ed.), *Culture, communication, and cognition: Vygotskian perspectives* (pp. 183–204). Cambridge University Press.

Rommetveit, R. (1992). Outlines of a dialogically based social-cognitive approach to human cognition and communication. In A. H. Wold (Ed.), *The dialogical alternative. Toward a theory of language and mind* (pp. 19–44). Scandinavian University Press.

Salvatore, S., & Valsiner, J. (2010). Between the general and the unique. *Theory & Psychology*, *20*(6), 817–833. 10.1177/0959354310381156

Stern, W. (1935). *Allgemeine Psychologie auf personalistischer Grundlage*. Haag: Martinus Nijhoff.

Stern, W. (1938). *General Psychology From the Personalist Standpoint*. New York: Macmillan.

Vaihinger, H. (1911). *Die Philosophie des Als Ob: System der theoretischen, practischen und religiösen Fiktionen der Menscheit*. Renter und Reichard.
Valsiner, J. (2006). The semiotic construction of solitude: Process of internalization and externalization. *Sign Systems Studies, 34* (1), 9–34.
Valsiner, J. (2007). *Culture in minds and societies: Foundations of cultural psychology*. SAGE Publications India Pvt Ltd. https://dx.doi.org/10.4135/9788132108504
Valsiner, J. (2014). *An invitation to cultural psychology*. Sage.
Valsiner, J. (2017). *From methodology to methods in human psychology*. Springer.
Valsiner, J. (2020a). *Hyper-generalization by the human mind: The role of sign hierarchies in meaning-making processes*. Psychosozial Verlag.
Valsiner, J. (2020b). *Sensuality in human living: The cultural psychology of affect*. Springer.
Valsiner, J., & Capezza, N. (2002). Creating arenas for action: Videogames and violence. Keynote presentation at the Fifth International Baltic Psychology Conference. Psychology in the Baltics: at the crossroads August 23, 2002, Tartu, Estonia.
von Fircks, E. F. (2022). Daseinssemiosis: A new look at the phenomenology of Theodor Lipps. *Human Arenas, 5*(3), 592–608. https://doi.org/10.1007/s42087-020-00159-x
Zittoun, T., Valsiner, J., Vedeler, D., Salgado, J., Gonçalves, M., & Ferring, D. (2013). *Human development in the life course: Melodies of living*. Cambridge University Press.

SECTION 2
SOCIETAL CONDITONS FOR DIALOGUE AND THE ROLE OF EDUCATION

Section 2 consists of three chapters varied in thematic orientation and approach. The title of this section points toward some general issues in contemporary societies that have been a key concern of this book and which this section targets more specifically than the other sections. The societal conditions refer to human living and coexistence within societies and how this world is developing. As a section it refers to the former section, which is primarily theoretical in the issues raised, as well as the next two sections, which are more empirically based. As such, this section can be seen as a framing of issues brought up in other sections.

Across the chapters in this section there are two main issues raised. One crosscutting issue is the reflections on why and how dialogue is important, in contemporary societies, as an analytic lens on both possibilities and growing constraints for intersubjectivity and a common ground for mutual understanding and respect. As such, the three chapters all refer to Ragnar Rommetveit's ideas but apply these ideas in new ways to contemporary issues in our societies. However, the three chapters address this in very different ways. Still, together they point to important aspects of how to understand dialogue on different levels and as theoretical explorations and empirical foundation. The chapters refer to both possibilities and challenges within communities and societies, as well as different risks that dialogue always implies, especially in intercultural settings.

In Chapter 5, de Haan discusses the various theoretical viewpoints on the potential as well as the limitations of dialogue for reconciliation, creating mutual understanding, or defining common action in polarized settings. Ligorio and colleagues explore how active citizenship and social participation are developed through concrete actions concerning the improvement of public spaces in Chapter 6. And Wegerif and Major, in Chapter 7, draw attention to how cultural dialogues in contemporary societies are mediated by communications technology in various forms from words, through books, to the Internet.

The other cross-cutting issue raised in this section concerns the role of education. All three chapters ask fundamental questions about how we can understand the role of education in relation to dialogue and how through education we can promote dialogue on different levels and in different contexts. They all define education as an important societal mechanism to counteract the challenges of dialogue in our communities and societies. Education becomes a way to engage young people in interactions and participation to become citizens with an integral understanding of the importance of intersubjectivity and ways of expressing and listening to the other "I" dialogic acts.

de Haan investigates the potential of dialogical interaction in educational contexts that are characterized by opposition and conflict related to, for instance, social class, ethnicity, religion, or otherwise defined diversity. She emphasizes that dialogue is not an easy task that we can take for granted but something that must be pursued and struggled for among students within diverse communities. Ligorio and colleagues draw on a very interesting and important educational project called "Dialogues in the Square," involving two schools over several years in one community in Rome, Italy as a way to promote what they call "active citizenship." The project offers a rich array of opportunities for dialogue inside and outside the school as a broad landscape for dialogue between various human and nonhuman actors: students, teachers, classes, institutions, stakeholders, community, environment, and monuments. Wegerif and Major show how technology is now at the heart of education. They put forward a dialogic theory of educational technology intended to serve as a foundation for design to facilitate the dynamic interweaving of educational dialogues at different spatiotemporal scales, linking short-term face-to-face dialogues to long-term and more global dialogues. They argue that dialogic education with technology is an essential response to two of the biggest challenges of our time: the challenge of the Anthropocene and the challenge of the Internet Age. As such, this chapter also makes a bridge over to the next section in this book, focusing specifically on the role of digital technologies.

5
The Limits and Potential of Dialogue to Counter Polarization in Educative Settings

Mariëtte de Haan

We have got on the slippery ice where there is no friction and so in a certain sense the conditions are ideal, but also, just because of that, we are unable to walk: so we need friction. Back to the rough ground. (Wittgenstein, 1958: 146e)

5.1. Introduction: Is Dialogue Disabled in Polarized Settings?

In the past decade a new social urgency is felt to maintain and foster socially and culturally cohesive communities that allow the peaceful coexistence of groups of different (ethnic, religious, or socioeconomic) backgrounds. Citizens experience an increased "polarization," that is, an increasing sense of "us" versus "them," the lack of a shared worldview between social groups but also a lack of mutual acknowledgment and loyalty, articulated in increasing tensions and conflicts. For instance, Molina and Cadado (2014) report that in Europe a new sense of diversity is experienced, where diversity is seen increasingly as a problem, which even causes fear in large sectors of the population. Lianaki-Dedouli and Plouin (2017) argue that due to the forces of globalization, different cultures are imposed to a forced coexistence for which we haven't yet produced the collective capacity to imagine a common future.

Educative spaces, such as schools, are seen as sites where youth from different origins come together and learn to deal with "diverse others" and are prepared to become democratic citizens. However, presently these educative spaces *themselves* seem to experience this increasing tension. Schools experience a lack of social cohesion in their community, stronger outings of prejudice, and the inability to deal with "difference" (Gindi & Erlich, 2018). Marocco et al. (2019) report that there is increasing pressure on teachers to manage relational aspects of their educational duties related to handling diversity and promoting inclusion.

The chapter is inspired by my work with Utrecht city schools in the project UNION (de Haan, 2023) and the actual problems presented by teachers in a series of dialogues in roundtables in early 2018 on what is the matter with and could be done against polarization in schools, as well as the need to design new interventions that could tackle polarization. This project showed that dialogue as a method for reconciliation in situations of polarization, is as much promoted as it is criticized, rejected, or temporarily disregarded.

In this chapter I will examine theoretical approaches that in my view provide important insights into the role of dialogue between representatives of incommensurable life worlds. First, the chapter problematizes the social (meta) contract under which dialogue between different parties becomes possible. Second, it problematizes the (im)possibility for understanding between different parties, given that they belong to different sociocultural traditions. And third, it zooms in on the nature of intersubjectivity and how this translates to the role of dialogue in settings of conflict or disagreement.

Given the nature of the questions asked, I turn to a variety of disciplinary backgrounds. In answering the first question, I borrow mostly from political philosophy and the problem of representation in diverse societies. In answering the second question, I borrow from language philosophy and notions of the politics of difference, while in answering the third question, I draw upon dialogism and, in particular, Ragnar Rommetveit's theory of communication. All have in common that they problematize the issue of diversity and perspectivity and address the issue of how a priori-opposing and incommensurable perspectives can be bridged through dialogue.

I am using dialogue in this chapter as "authentic spoken interaction, i.e. on dyadic or polyadic dialogue in face-to face encounters" (Linnel, 1998: xi), which needs to be distinguished from "dialogism," which stands for conceptual and epistemological approaches that take dialogue as a starting point for understanding the social, text, etc. This is so, even though given the topic of the chapter, most of the approaches dealt with relate to some form of dialogism in this second sense. This implies that the chapter title "The Limits and Potential of Dialogue to Counter Polarization in Educative Settings," must be read first and foremost as a question about the possibility of dialogue as authentic spoken action in face-to-face encounters in situations of conflict and tension. As the chapter evolves, the meanings associated with "dialogue" will vary depending on the conceptual framing at hand. For instance, in some cases, dialogue refers to dialogue as an ideal, what dialogue should be, as is the case for Habermas' ideal speech situation. Polarization is understood here as a process marked by a perceived (increasing) sense of "us" versus "them" and is understood as a process by which already existing contradictions and agonies, which are in a sense a "normal" part of pluralistic societies, become more visible (see also de Haan, 2023).

Even though my focus in the chapter is on these conceptual models, my goal is to judge their relevance for practice. In my analyses I focus on the capacity these theories have to provide answers to practitioners and educational leaders that are dealing with concrete situations of polarization in education, making use of the three guiding questions mentioned above. The chapter's final ambition is to provide the conditions and conceptual underpinning to design dialogical models for interventions in educational settings that are characterized by polarized relationships.

The chapter is built up as follows. In section 5.2, I start with describing the context which was the direct cause to become interested in the question that guides this chapter: the project UNION. Section 5.3, which is the core of the chapter, deals with answering three key questions related to the role of dialogue in polarized settings, making use of a variety of different theoretical perspectives. Finally, in section 5.4, I will summarize what the implications of the findings in section 5.3 are for designing interventions that have as their aim to counter polarization and that see dialogue as the key to doing so.

5.2. Dialogue as a Remedy for Polarization—The UNION Project

In the UNION project, mentioned in the introduction, researchers worked together with the municipality and school boards to find solutions to prevent further polarization in the city schools. The participating schools ranged from the "white," "elite" "gymnasia" with almost only majority students, to schools with both a minority and majority student population, to schools with almost exclusively minority students. Although most of the teachers came from a majority background, teachers with a minority background were represented in all the roundtables. What was striking in these conversations was that teachers experienced a lack of dialogue, as well as a reluctancy to engage in it by both students and teachers. Rather than seeking out the others' perspective, it was the inability to do so that was often brought up in these conversations. The tensions that were mentioned most were between majority and minority students and teachers, while controversial issues would typically revolve around tensions between cultural-religious norms of Islam and "Western" secular norms, such as those related to the acceptance of sexual diversity. Engaging in a dialogue about such tensions was seen as extremely difficult, and, if accomplished, extremely hard work. Prejudices, lack of knowledge of the other were said to hinder mutual acknowledgment and listening to the other. Although this was a claim that involved all groups, representatives of the majority would blame minority students, in particular, for not listening and engaging in "decent and respectful" dialogue. The issue was, according to them, that minorities did not play the game by the rules. In contrast, for minorities, the issue was that they were excluded from "the game" in the first place.

The role dialogue can play in the prevention and solving of conflicts in educational settings is not a new topic, and much research has been devoted to documenting what methodologies and interventions are effective in this respect (see, for instance, the reviews by Paluck & Green (2009), Beelmann and Heinemann (2014) or Bettencourt et al. (2019)). Stimulating dialogue between groups that experience some form of distrust against each other is often one of the key elements in methodologies that aim to fight polarization. At the same time, dialogue seems to become harder as conflicts emerge (Sorensen et al., 2009), which is supported by the mentioned uneasiness of teachers to engage in dialogue in classrooms that are polarized. This paradox, that dialogue is both the preferred solution to solve a conflict and that which seems to be readily rejected, makes it necessary to ask some fundamental questions about the nature of dialogue and its capacity to mediate in polarized settings. The following three questions that underly our general question: "what can dialogue do in situations of polarization according to the theory?" form the leading questions for this chapter.

The first question that I would like to address is whether the spaces we have designed in our democratic societies to solve issues dialogically are designed properly so that diverse voices can be heard, dialogue is enabled in such a way that it allows and enables the participation of all, and difficult topics and controversy can be addressed rather than silenced.

For instance, research shows that established "ground rules for dialogue" or "meta contracts," that, for instance, define how to engage in dialogue, what to say or not say, and how to behave, etc, might not be inclusive. Even if such meta contracts appear neutral, they often tend to favor majority groups over minority groups, which makes it difficult to address controversies between these groups based on such meta contracts. Tammi and Rajala (2017) showed in an experimental study on deliberate communication in a multiethnic classroom how such meta rules of communication (in this case about how decision-making should take place, and who are the relevant stakeholders that should be involved in such decision-making) also reflect certain sociocultural norms, which can, unless thoroughly scrutinized and revised, lead to the exclusion of minorities. In a similar vein, Ponzoni et al. (2020) showed how, in the field of social work, newcomers are easily excluded from dialogue and that their contributions are effectively silenced by all kinds of procedures; they argue that new, experimental argumentative spaces are necessary if we want to ensure the voices of newcomers in democratic decision-making procedures. The question then becomes how or if we can make sure that argumentative spaces and their meta rules for communication are inclusive to the diversity of newcomers who come to claim their place in existing spaces for communication? How can we create just, inclusive, and welcoming dialogical spaces for all that appeal to and do justice to all groups to the same extent? Can such spaces for dialogue be neutral, and how do we make sure they are? And how can we design those spaces in a way that controversial topics are not avoided?

The second question I would like to address is whether dialogue will still work between parties that represent worldviews that are, or are considered to be, incompatible. Teachers dialogical conflict resolution skills seem to be challenged especially when they are confronted with conflicts and controversies resulting from incompatible worldviews (Marocco et al., 2019). Recent literature reviews show that professionals in education often find it extremely hard to address such controversies and have reported to ignore them (see for instance, Ho et al., 2017; Wansink et al., 2018). Dialogue then seems to be discarded as a means to bridging such seemingly incompatible positions. This raises questions about the ability of dialogue to mediate between positions that are seen as belonging to radically different ethnic, religious, and cultural life worlds.

Lastly, I would like to address a third, perhaps more fundamental question, which is how intersubjectivity (as the step by step process of creating understanding and bridging individual perspectives through interaction) functions in polarized settings. Research has shown that in situations of conflict, the participants in a dialogue seem less able to open up to the perspective of the other and have a tendency to defend their own position (de Hoog, 2013). Even though multi-perspectivity is considered a key literacy skill in our multicultural societies, many teachers struggle with mediating between multiple perspectives in their teaching, in particular when so-called controversial issues are addressed (Wansink, 2017). Given that perspective-taking seems to be much harder in polarized situations, and people have a tendency to act "defensively" and feel threatened (de Hoog, 2013), how can we understand this from our knowledge of how intersubjectivity happens in the first place? What can be learned from insights into the basic "grammar" of intersubjectivity to understand when dialogue is fundamentally threatened and potentially disabled? How can insights about the nature of intersubjectivity be helpful if full consensus is not within reach, but common action, or inhabiting the same space in a peaceful way, is necessary?

5.3. What Can Dialogue Do in Situations of Polarization According to the Theory?

5.3.1. Can We Design Inclusive Dialogical Spaces for Communities That Are Diverse?

According to Habermas's theory on communicative action (1998), the best possible way to address differences of opinion between diverse groups is to design public argumentative spaces that meet certain criteria. Fair procedures or meta rules must guarantee that the dialogues in such spaces are free and "uncoerced," fair, and inclusive. Examples of such meta rules are that no one is excluded on topics that are relevant for her/him, no information is withheld, the debate should be free of coercion, and should be open and symmetrical. All participants have the right and chance to initiate debates, question the agenda, and bring in arguments about the founding rules that apply to these argumentative spaces (Kapuur, 2002; see also Benhabib (1996) for a description of such conditions). These so-called ideal speech situations are not brought up by Habermas as descriptions or real situations but are rather meant as a normative model, to push and strengthen public participation in democracies. His theory on communicative action must be read against his aim to deliver what he calls a proceduralist view on democracy or "deliberative politics" (Habermas, 1998: 239) in which state power is legitimized by bringing about inclusive decision-making (Kapoor, 2002). This means that, according to Habermas, in modern democracies all norms, regulations, principles can only be valid once they follow from deliberation (and indirectly the reason and will) of those that fall under the regime of these rules, principles, norms, etc.

Habermas has explicitly addressed the issue of how his model of communication can be used given the diverse nature of modern democracies, and the potential conflict that can rise because of this diversity. Habermas is of the opinion that disagreement about values and notions of "what the good life is" is bound to be a fundamental characteristic of pluralistic societies. He does not assume that these different parties, with their fundamentally different worldviews, may just find consensus through leaning upon shared values (e.g. ideas of justice, humanity, and respect for others). In contrast, Habermas sees the potential for agreement in communicative action: "that form of social interaction in which the participants act on, or try to reach, a shared understanding of the situation—in regulating and reproducing forms of social life and the identities of social actors" (1998, editors introduction, n.p.). He claims that in these ideal, inclusive communicative practices, even participants who fundamentally differ in their vision on what the good life is, could "reach an uncoerced agreement on the validity of these kinds of norms on the basis of reasons that are acceptable to all" (n.p.). Habermas believes that fundamental differences between different subcultures do not have to impede dialogue in democratic societies, but on the contrary, dialogue is the main instrument for their political integration. This belief is founded on the distinction that he makes between concrete forms of life (ethnos)—which might fundamentally be opposed to each other in terms of values and norms—and a shared political culture (demos), based in rights of representation, constitutional principles, and procedures in the public sphere. According to Habermas, in this public sphere communities need to distance themselves from their beliefs and traditions to bring "universal principles of justice into the horizon of the specific form of life of [the] particular community" (Kapoor, 2002: 463).

This idea of an ideal speech situation, including the distinction between a shared, neutral dialogical space and concrete forms of life has been attacked by others, such as Mouffe (1999), who have argued that such a neutral coercion-free space to solve conflicts between different parties, is an illusion. She attacks Habermas' idea that rational debate should be seen as the primary form of political communication, that political questions can be decided upon rationally and dialogically, and that such rational exchange of arguments is the best way to—by a process of rational opinion and will formation—reach the ideal of the general interest.

Mouffe's model of "agonistic pluralism" (1999), based on her work with Laclau (Laclau and Mouffe, 1985) strongly opposes the idea that we are able to create neutral, public spaces in which a rational consensus can be reached based on dialogue, no matter how the regulations and conditions for this dialogue are set up. The reason for this is that she, unlike Habermas, postulates that power, conflict, and agonism can never be eliminated from such spaces.

Her objections are based on the idea that (1) the principles and procedures designed for such ideal speech situations always resonate these forms of life of a particular community and (2) thus can never be neutral or power-free.

Regarding the first point, she uses Wittgenstein's argument that there is no agreement apart from an agreement about the language that is used, which according to Wittgenstein can never be perceived apart from agreement on forms of life. This fundamentally opposes the idea that language (or a system of rules and principles that rises "above" these different forms of life) must be used to decide upon a debate between different forms of life. According to Wittgenstein there is no such general language that can be used to decide or debate upon which "form of life" should prevail. This is so because rules and procedures do not exist in isolation but must be seen as abbreviated/abstracted forms of life which are peculiar. Procedures always imply particular "ethics." By implication, finding "agreement" cannot happen at the level of the exchange of arguments/ "giving reasons" alone.

Her second fundamental objection to the idea that rational debate can be the primary form of arbitration between different groups is that we cannot strip dialogue of its inherent power relationships. Discourse is *in its very structure* authoritarian. Making use of Lacan's idea of the master signifier, she argues that power and authority are already given in discourse as discourses always have assumptions or meanings that are "beyond" or immune from argumentation. The same is true for how the regulations for dialogue are set up. Mouffe points out that certain procedures on how to dialogue might have already built-in injustices, to the extent that parties without already having a voice are not able to raise objections to the procedures.

The solution, according to Mouffe, is to address such relations of power directly. Her "agonistic pluralism" is based on the idea that in the very process of dialogue and interaction with the other, we need to deal with the agony it produces, just like in the famous quote from Wittgenstein in which he makes a plea to return to the rough ground (of agonism): "We have got on the slippery ice where there is no friction and so in a certain sense the conditions are ideal, but also, just because of that, we are unable to walk: so we need friction. Back to the rough ground" (1958: 146e).

While holding onto the idea that certain identities and differences are products of subordination and should constantly be challenged, Mouffe states that we need to start to see that such dialogical spaces can at best be seen as "domesticating hostility, only in trying to defuse the potential antagonism that exists in human relations" (1999: 754). The political is, according to Mouffe, already part of the dialogue, and we cannot but confront it within the dialogue. We must do this by accepting the other, not as an enemy, but as "adversary, somebody with whose ideas we are going to struggle, but whose right to defend those ideas we do not put into question" (755). In doing so, we should not strive for complete consensus, as this is a false ideal, but see the result of negotiations as the "result of a provisional hegemony, as a stabilization of power and that always entails some form of exclusion" (756).

Both these ideas from Habermas and from Mouffe hold important insights for designing spaces for argumentation in which diverse groups need to come to some form of (Habermasian) agreement or (Mouffian) provisional arrangement. Realizing with Mouffe that the design of these spaces never can be neutral, and that we must be aware of how power differences are played out within them, we might actually do so by taking up Habermas's challenge to constantly redesign the rules and procedures of such spaces to meet the needs of all.

5.3.2. (How) Can Dialogue Function Between Parties with Rival or Incommensurable Worldviews?

Although the issue of incompatible life worlds and the role of dialogue was briefly touched upon in the last section, here my focus is explicitly on the question of whether dialogue will still work between parties that have incompatible worldviews. I draw mostly upon Papastergiadis's work (2000) on the nexus between migration and modernity, the conflict of rival worldviews that it generates, and his notion of cultural translation. He addresses the problem of how one can think about the interaction between two meaning systems, cultures, languages, etc that are "different" or even might produce what Lyotard (1988) has called "a differend": "a case of conflict between (at least) two parties that cannot be equitably solved for a lack of rule of judgment applicable to both arguments" (132).

Papastergiadis gives the example of a mining company who lays a claim on an uninhabited piece of land in order to explore it. The mining company applies for the exploitation of it to a government agency. The claim on the land is rejected by an aboriginal community who argues that the land is inhabited by the spirits of their ancestors. Both claims make no sense in the life world of the other party, as the meaning of "inhabited," or the meaning of "owning land" depends on the life world it derives its meaning from. The spiritual language of the aboriginal community cannot be translated into the juridical and material language of the state system on which the mining company relies and vice versa. Now the question is whether a dialogue in such cases makes sense at all to move ahead. A solution would be to see this problem through the eyes of universalism, in which case one would need a superordinate system that provides a rule of judgment. Another solution would be to see it through the eyes of subjectivism, in which case both languages or systems are "locked up" in themselves and can, at best, coexist and truth would be a matter of perspective. However, Papastergiadis brings forward the idea of transculturation or cultural translation as a third, transformative concept. This concept departs from the position that dialogue between two or more conflicting life worlds with distinct meaning systems makes sense and requires a process of translation in which differences are acknowledged.

What is interesting in this account of transculturation is that it shows us that when two heterogenous genres meet through a dialogue, something different happens than just the "passing on" of meaning from one genre to the other. This can easily be understood when one realizes that expressions from one language cannot be fully translated into another language. However, something changes in the act of communication for both genres (or languages), while the act of translation is imperfect. It is imperfect in the sense that the meaning conveyed from one genre can only be picked up, in so far as the nature of the other genre has the means to interpret it. However, both genres change in the process of communication in order for communication to take place, the "original" meaning associated with one of the genres is "disrupted" or partly "broken" to incorporate it in the other genre and vice versa. As Papastergiadis states: "they no longer mean what they meant in *either* the source, or the target language [italics in the original]" (2000: 129).

These insights help us to understand that, in the act of communication, one party is inevitably doomed to be misrepresented in the language of the second, and vice versa; but that, at the same time, that transformation occurs through the very act of communication.

In theory, transculturation could also produce new meta-rules of judgment that could be formed based on the ongoing process of transculturation and transformed original genres. A slightly different position, which also rejects both universalism and complete relativism, is the idea by MacIntyre (1998) that a third position, language, or genre is needed to bring about dialogue between two incommensurable systems (as explained in Papastergiadis, 2000). This "third language," which should be equally distant from both systems, forms of life, belief system, etc, "possesses the conceptual range to comprehend accurately and represent the other two competing languages" (154). Such a third language should not make any claim to a universal truth or point of reference but should be multi-perspectival and, as such, recognize the specificity of several systems. Nevertheless, these third or meta-languages would still run the risk of being one-sided, possibly providing one party more power over this process than the others.

In sum, these notions provide important insights, particularly with respect to the possibility of overcoming fundamental differences through dialogue that is due to culturally incompatible systems. The notion of transculturation as well as the notion of a third language are conceptual tools for overcoming culturally informed incommensurability.

5.3.3. What Can We Learn from the Very Nature of Intersubjectivity and Its Ability to Bridge Opposing Worlds?

Having looked at the nature of argumentative spaces and their rules of judgment and the principle question of whether exchange is possible between two or more a priori-divergent life worlds, it makes sense to study the very process of intersubjectivity in such situations and how its nature might or might not be affected by the exchange of divergent positions. Given its premise that dialogue happens in socioculturally constructed settings and that it is inherently interwoven with these settings, Rommetveit's model of intersubjectivity (1979) is a good place to start to explore how communicative acts happen in opposing or conflicting life worlds. His ideas on the architecture of intersubjectivity or the grammar of communication could be seen as a magnifying glass to study communication between parties that are having trouble communicating. His ideas on how understanding through communication is, on the one hand, almost "automatically" anticipated and, on the other hand, can never be taken for granted provide an important lens to problematic communication.

Rommetveit's theory of communication can be seen as part of "dialogism" (Linell, 2003) being a strand of approaches often associated with the work of Bakhtin (1981), which builds on social constructivism and the notion that dialogue and the meanings it brings forward are contextual. Language is a thoroughly social phenomenon, and as Rommetveit states, "an utterance deprived of the context of human action is as absurd as the notion of a fall deprived of the gravitational field within which it takes place" (Rommetveit, 1979; 93). We must see dialogue and the meaning that is passed on within its "architecture of intersubjectivity." It is precisely these notions of the architecture of intersubjectivity in Rommetveit's theory that are a good place for further reflection in the context of this chapter. In particular I would like to highlight his insight that there is already a fundamental complementarity inherent in acts of communication of all kinds (Rommetveit, 1979). This implies that "taking the attitude of the other" is, according to his elaboration of intersubjectivity not a special skill that needs to be trained but "a basic and pervading feature of normal social interaction" (96). This skill is even so basic, according to Rommetveit, that it is almost inaccessible for conscious reflection of the speakers in such ordinary communicative acts.

What can be learned from this in the context of this chapter is the undeniable capacity of human communication for "other-orientedness" in communication, even if this does not mean that private worlds are transcended to the full. It points to the fact that communication is tuned toward transcending of private worlds, and therefore the tool "par excellence" for reaching out to the other. And it does such transcending work, even before we start to reflect on it, since a lot of what we do in our communicative acts happens as part of our communicative "grammar."

Communication aims to transcend the "private" and subjective worlds of its participants, and with this, it creates "states of intersubjectivity" (94). The intersubjectivity that is created depends on what is already known, assumed, and shared and the particulars of the here and now of the situation in which it is established. As participants in communication, we tend to anticipate what the other is meaning to say based on what we already know. So, intersubjectivity is also already anticipated and "in a sense taken for granted in order to be achieved." Communication typically is based "upon reciprocally endorsed and spontaneously fulfilled contract of complementarity" and on "mutual faith in a shared social world" (96) or a "pre-established shared *Lebenswelt* [italics in the original]"

(98). This means communication is also based on "decentration" of one's own subjectivity and, in the words of George Herbert Mead, on "taking the attitude of the other" (as cited in Rommetveit, 1979: 96).

Although Rommetveit did not explicitly address the role of dialogue as related to difference and pluralism in society (Wertsch, 2003; Linell, 2003), nor othering in the post-colonial sense, his work holds important elements to address these issues. To elaborate on this, I will address three different points that follow directly from his notion of intersubjectivity, as described above, but will also partly draw upon other writers who stand in the same tradition.

First, there is the notion of "decentration" which is a key concept in the establishment of intersubjectivity and allows us to see the perspective of the other. It relates to other concepts of other-orientedness, such as alterity in dialogism (Linell, 2003) and the notion of "estrangement" in Bakhtin, which have been used for the more explicit and conscious reconsidering of one's own position. Estrangement, for instance, has been associated with conscientization of the particularity or "strangeness" of one's own position, which then can lead to the reinterpretation of existing meanings or ideologies that were automatized in the discourse of the self (Tajima, 2017). It has been argued by Hermans & Dimaggio (2007), who also partly build upon Bakhtin that the notion of alterity, together with other qualities associated with a dialogue, can productively be marshaled in situations of uncertainty and ambiguity and creates openendedness in dialogue, which can challenge our potential for innovation and creativity. However, my first point is primarily, based on Rommetveit's notion of intersubjectivity, that decentration is already a natural part of human communication and secondly, as others such as Hermans & Dimaggio have shown, that this authentic capacity can be marshaled in situations in which other-orientedness needs to be pushed further without changing the basic "tenets" of communication.

Second, even if one could argue that such "decentration" is perhaps the easiest when we have mutual faith in a shared social world, and that in situations of polarization such shared worlds is the thing that is precisely lacking, the notion of partial shareholdership implies that such a lack of sharedness is only gradual. Rommetveit has shown that we can use terms and concepts and communicate successfully for "current, practical purposes" without sharing or having access to the full network of meanings these refer to, but that communication can also be "parasitic" to these networks. As Linell (2003) shows, Rommetveit also objects to the idea that in our communication we draw upon homogeneous collectivities that are fully shared: "We live in a "pluralistic social world," which is "only partially shared" and "only fragmentarily known" (e.g. Rommetveit, 1984). Understandings, our (partially) shared interpretations of utterances or situations, are temporarily established through dialogical interaction" (Linell,

2003: 221). Realizing that communication always happens or can successfully happen in partially shared access to discourse, language, and knowledge can help us to engage in communication with others with whom we assume to share less-common resources, while still expecting the communication to be successful. The fragmented nature of our access to and ownership of assumed collective heritages, language, and knowledge is a useful tool for thinking about assumed ethnic or otherwise fragmentations, divisions, or disunions, when we realize such fragmentations are already part of everyday communication anyway. Together with the notion that shareholdership can also be partly acquired through dialogue, these notions enable us to assume that dialogue is able to break through, add to, change, reinterpret, etc "old" meanings, including those associated with othering in a post-colonial sense.

Third, the so-called ethics of care that, according to Hagtvet & Wold (2003), are implicit in Rommetveit's notion of intersubjectivity, provides another interesting perspective in this respect. The idea that we depend on the other in dialogue to create self-understanding and identity is particularly important here. This implies that the other is granted "coauthorship" and epistemic responsibility and that the relationship is based on equality, trust, and respect (201).

In sum, despite the fact that Rommetveit's theory of intersubjectivity does not address the more political side of polarization, realizing that communication is an effortful attempt to overcome our private worlds more generally, that reaching common meaning is temporary, and that shared worlds are partial anyway, such insight might help us to build trust and common perspective with those for whom this might not be self-evident.

Building partial and temporarily shared worlds, while also realizing that through the principle of alterity this helps us to come to know who we are, might be the road that takes us out of a deep conflict or bridges incommensurable worldviews.

5.4. Implications for Designing Dialogical Interventions

(How) do the insights discussed above generate "useful," "relevant," or "practical" knowledge to understand the role of dialogue in a polarized situation, in the sense that it provides us with a model that goes beyond just describing what is going on to provide us with directions for action?

In my view, the answers to the questions posed at the beginning of this chapter can be foundations for an intervention on how to use dialogue in situations of polarization. First, they provide insight into how a common frame of reference can be built in situations where such frames do not exist a priori. Second, they provide the foundation for the translation between incompatible worldviews, and third, they provide guidelines for how to (re)design the spaces for dialogue, their ethics, and meta-rules for participation.

5.4.1. Design Principles for Dialogical Interventions

The insights of Rommetveit's theory of intersubjectivity as previously mentioned could be fruitfully applied in educational settings to foster dialogue between groups that experience polarization if focused on the following principles.

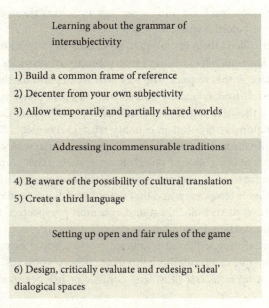

Figure 5.1. Design principles for dialogical interventions.

Learning about the grammar of intersubjectivity

1) *Build a common frame of reference.* First, interventions can focus on the very nature of communication, more generally, and teach students how it is actually a "normal" element of communication that you need to make an effort to bridge your—until then private—assumptions, ideas, norms by a series of communicative acts. The idea that you can stepwise build a common world, a common perspective by exchanging viewpoints is perhaps the most powerful and effective principle that should be highlighted in such interventions. In addition, the idea that certain assumptions are

not shared a priori and involve communicative effort should then be built into this first principle.
2) *Decenter from your own subjectivity.* Communication is all about decentration of one's own position all the time, and that this principle might sometimes be harder than other times, can be a second key principle that is helpful in dialogues in which conflicts or incommensurable points of view need to be bridged.
3) *Allow temporarily and partially shared worlds.* Taking partial and temporarily shared perspectives as an explicit goal, and a good enough goal, with the realization that this is how common meaning-making works overall anyway, is another important focus of such interventions.

These principles, which we can call "principles of the grammar of communication," can profit from the insights implied in the concept of cultural translation, particularly when specific culturally informed ideas, principles, and meanings hinder the communication and seem incommensurable.

Addressing incommensurable traditions

4) *Be aware of the possibility of cultural translation.* Making students aware that communication might be hindered by culturally informed principles, rules, ideas, etc that are perhaps not understood immediately by the other party is helpful. Moreover, making them aware that such impasses do not mean that translation and communication is senseless, but that dialogues have the capacity to at least partially disrupt earlier culturally informed opposing views in the act of translation is an important insight to work with. Inspiring students with the analyses of such translation processes and how these have changing capacity (exemplary or on-site dialogues) might be helpful and transformative.
5) *Create a third language.* Creating another genre, position, or vocabulary that is equally distant from what or who the parties represent in the dialogue, but is able to unite the opposing positions might be helpful. Such a third language can then bring multiple perspectives together and function as a common language of all parties.

Finally, the design of the argumentative space "itself," its meta rules, ground rules, or the principles of justice that define the fairness of the communication process, should be scrutinized. Habermas's ideal speech situation provides important principles to constantly redesign such spaces, while Mouffe's critique on them helps to keep an eye on the power struggles that are an inherent part of such spaces.

Setting up open and fair rules of the game

6) *Design, critically evaluate, and redesign "ideal" dialogical spaces.* Principles such as openness and symmetry, as well as the constant questioning of the agenda and issues of who participates in what debate, as documented by Habermas (1998) and Benhabib (1996), remain important. However, the key is to never take such dialogical spaces for granted and scrutinize them for equal opportunity, accessibility, and its inherent power dynamics about which Mouffe (1999) warns us.
7) *Confront the struggle of difference.* If acknowledging Mouffe's (1999) argument, we accept that the ideal speech situation does not exist and the political is always part of the dialogue, an important principle is to confront the political within and through dialogue. Such spaces should thus allow us to address opposing views and differences of interest in a respectful and peaceful manner.

If we look back to the context of polarization of the Utrecht city schools I started this chapter with, which probably is representative for many schools that experience a similar uneasiness with confronting the other, it seems that the schools lacked spaces for dialogue informed by the principles mentioned above. Rather the fear of incommensurable points of view, the lack of a critical evaluation of the fairness and inclusiveness of the dialogical spaces offered, and the reluctance to confront the struggle of difference was defining the situation that was expressed by these teachers. It is my hope that the design principles mentioned above can be helpful to these and similar schools to analyze their situation, inform their theories of change, and make corresponding decisions on what should be done.

5.5. Conclusion: The Need to Go Back to the Rough Ground

This chapter started with a plea to confront conflict rather than to avoid it. This means to accept a certain level of "messiness" and uncertainty. The idea of a "contact zone" by Mary Louis Pratt (2008) is a good metaphor that is able to bring together the design principles mentioned above, particularly in relation to the messiness or rough nature of dialogue between parties that suffer from conflict and have different access to power or represent incommensurable life worlds.

"Contact zones" are defined by Pratt (2008) as "social spaces where disparate cultures meet, clash, and grapple with each other, often in highly asymmetrical relations of domination and subordination—such as colonialism and slavery, or their aftermaths as they are lived out across the globe today" (7) and "establish ongoing relations, usually involving conditions of coercion, radical inequality, and intractable conflict" (8).

In these contact zones, new forced forms of copresence are created, in which the less powerful party struggles with the adoption of the cultural order of the dominant party, while finding ways to survive, sometimes adapting, sometimes resisting in the act of reproducing this cultural order (Pratt, 2008).

As Mouffe also states, these frictions somehow always need to be managed and dealt with. "Managed" here does not mean that these frictions are solved, or that there is inherent harmony, but that there is temporarily, relative steadiness and that the frictions are not acted upon momentarily.

In such zones, communication seems to happen on the "rough ground" shaped by the confrontation of difference. It is implied that full consensus is an illusion, while provisional cohesion, understanding, and power balances are the best one can hope for. However, as Wittgenstein argued, we need the rough ground with its friction to be able to walk. Without disregarding the fact that we need to address the "roughness" that the confrontation of diverse life views brings about, building upon a frame of reference that allows for multi-perspectivity, in the way MacIntyre proposes it (1998), is a necessary part of such an effort. The "ethics of care" implicit in Rommetveit's notion of intersubjectivity, according to Hagtvet & Wold (2003), provides a road to acknowledging the hard, or "rough" work of building on the architecture of understanding as an inherent part of building a code of "coauthorship" and "epistemic responsibility" (201) that implies, but at the same time also creates, trust and respect.

References

Bakhtin, M. (1981). *The dialogic imagination: Four essays* (C. Emerson & M. Holquist, Trans.; M. Holquist, Ed.). Austin: University of Texas.

Beelmann, A., & Heinemann, K. S. (2014). Preventing prejudice and improving intergroup attitudes: A meta-analysis of child and adolescent training programs. *Journal of Applied Developmental Psychology, 35*(1), 10–24. https://doi.org/10.1016/j.appdev.2013.11.002

Benhabib, S. (1996). Toward a deliberative model of democratic legitimacy. In S. Benhabib (Ed.), *Democracy and difference* (pp. 67–95). Princeton University Press.

Bettencourt, L., Dixon, J., & Castro, P. (2019). Understanding how and why spatial segregation endures: A systematic review of recent research on intergroup relations at a micro-ecological scale. *Social Psychological Bulletin, 2*(14), 1–24. https://doi-org.proxy.library.uu.nl/10.32872/spb.v14i2.33482

de Hoog, N. (2013). Processing of social identity threats: a defense motivation perspective. *Social Psychology, 44*(6), 361–372.

Gindi, S., & Erlich, R. R. (2018). High school teachers' attitudes and reported behaviors towards controversial issues. *Teaching and Teacher Education, 70*(4), 58–66. https://doi-org.proxy.library.uu.nl/10.1016/j.tate.2017.11.006

Haan, M. D. (2023). The "every day" of polarisation in schools; understanding polarisation as (not)dialogue. *Pedagogy, Culture & Society*. https://doi.org/https://www.tandfonl ine.com/doi/full/10.1080/14681366.2023.2237986

Habermas, J. (1998). In C. Cronin & P. de Greiff (Eds.), *The inclusion of the other. Studies in political theory*. Polity Press.

Hagtvet. B. E., & Wold, A. H. (2003). On the dialogical basis of meaning: Inquiries into Ragnar Rommetveit's writings on language, thought, and communication. *Mind, Culture, and Activity*, 10(3), 186–204. doi:10.1207/s15327884mca1003_2

Hermans, H. J., & Dimaggio, G. (2007). Self, identity, and globalization in times of uncertainty: A dialogical analysis. *Review of General Psychology*, 11, 31–61. https://journals.sagepub.com/doi/10.1037/1089-2680.11.1.31

Ho, L., McAvoy, P., Hess, D., & Gibbs, B. (2017). Teaching and learning about controversial issues and topics in the social studies: A review of the research. In M. M. Manfra & C. M. Bolick (Eds.), *The Wiley handbook of social studies research* (pp. 321–335). Wiley-Blackwell.

Kapoor, I. (2002). Deliberative democracy or agonisitic pluralism? The relevance of the Habermas–Mouffe debate for third world politics. *Alternatives: Global, Local, Political*, 4(27), 459–487.

Laclau, E., & Mouffe, C. (1985). *Hegemony towards a radical democratic politics*. Verso.

Lianaki-Dedouli, I., & Plouin, J. (2017). Bridging anticipation skills and intercultural competencies as a means to reinforce the capacity of global citizens for learning to learn together. *Futures*, 94, 45–58.

Linell, P. (1998). *Approaching dialogue: Talk, interaction and contexts in dialogical perspective*. Benjamins.

Linell, P. (2003). Dialogical tensions: On Rommetveitian themes of minds. *Meanings, Monologues, and Languages, Mind, Culture, and Activity*, 10(3), 219–229. doi:10.1207/s15327884mca1003_4

Lyotard, J. F. (1988). *The differend: Phrases in dispute* (G. G. Van Den Abbeele, Trans.). University of Minnesota Press.

MacIntyre, A. (1998). *Whose justice. Which rationality?* University of Notre Dame Press.

Marocco, D., Dell'Aquila, E., Zurlo, M. C., Vallone, F., Barajas, M., Frossard, F., Di Ferdinando, A., Di Fuccio, R., Lippens, M., Van Praag, L., Protopsaltis, A., Swertz, C., Arslan, P. Y., & Mazzucato, A. (2019). Attain cultural integration through teachers' conflict resolution skills development: The ACCORD project. *Qwerty—Open and Interdisciplinary Journal of Technology, Culture and Education*, 2(14), 11–30.

Molina, F., & Casado, N. (2014). Living together in European intercultural schools: The case of the Catalan school system (Spain). *European Journal of Education*, 49, 249–258. 10.1111/ejed.12044

Mouffe, C. (1999). Deliberative democracy or agonistic pluralism? *Social Research*, 3(66), 745–758.

Paluck, E. L., & Green, D. P. (2009). Prejudice reduction: What works? A review and assessment of research and practice. *Annual Review of Psychology*, 60, 339–367. 10.1146/annurev.psych.60.110707.163607

Papastergiadis, N. (2000). *The turbulence of migration: Globalization, de-territorialization and hybridity*. Cambridge: Polity Press.

Ponzoni, E., Ghorashi, H., & Badran, M. (2020). Naar een structurele plek voor het perspectief en de visie van vluchtelingen in beleidsvorming. (Towards a space for the *perspective and vision of refugees in policy making).* Institute of Societal Resilience, Vrije Universiteit.

Pratt, M. L. (2008). *Imperial eyes: Travel writing and transculturation.* Routledge.

Rommetveit, R. (1979). On the architecture of intersubjectivity. In R. Rommetveit & M. Blaker (Eds.), *Studies of language, thought and verbal communication* (pp. 93–107). Academic Press.

Sorensen, N., Nagda, B. R. A., Gurin, P., & Maxwell, K. E. (2009). Taking a "hands on" approach to diversity in higher education: A critical-dialogic model for effective intergroup interaction. *Analyses of Social Issues and Public Policy, 9,* 3–25. http://dx.doi.org/10.1111/j.1530-2415.2009.01193.x

Tajima, A. (2017). A dialogic vaccine to bridge opposing cultural viewpoints based on Bakhtin's views on dialogue and estrangement. *Integrative Psychological and Behavioral Science, 3*(51), 419–431. 10.1007/s12124-017-9394-6

Tammi, T., & Rajala, A. (2017). Deliberative communication in elementary classroom meetings: Ground rules, pupils' concerns, and democratic participation. *Scandinavian Journal of Educational Research, 62*(4), 617–630. 10.1080/00313831.2016.1261042

Wansink, B. G. J. (2017). *Between Fact and Interpretation. Teachers' Beliefs and Practices in Interpretational History Teaching.* Dissertation. Utrecht: Utrecht University.

Wansink, B., Akkerman, S. Zuiker, I., & Wubbels, T. (2018). Where does teaching multiperspectivity in history education begin and end? An analysis of the uses of temporality. *Theory & Research in Social Education, 46*(4), 495–527.

Wertsch, J. V. (2003). Introduction: Ragnar Rommetveit: His work and influence. *Mind, Culture, and Activity, 3*(10), 183–185. 10.1207/s15327884mca1003_1

Wittgenstein, L. (1958). *Philosophical investigations.* Blackwell.

6

Active Citizenship and Participation Through "Dialogues in the Square"

Maria Beatrice Ligorio, Giovanna Barzanò, Francesca Amenduni, Roberta Cauchi, Sergio Turrisi, Lorenzo Raffio, Claudia Ragazzini, and Ludovica Valentino

6.1. Introduction

Citizenship and participation are longstanding crucial issues in any education system. In the Italian curriculum, these two concepts have gained momentum in light of the United Nations (UN) 2030 Agenda[1] for Sustainable Development. The Agenda provides a comprehensive roadmap for an equitable, sustainable, and prosperous world, which includes 17 Sustainable Development Goals (SDGs) and 169 targets to be achieved by 2030. Italy is committed to implementing the SDGs by tackling the systemic obstacles which have so far prevented growth that is compatible with the sustainability of the planet, natural resources, and social equity. The issue of sustainability is also at the core of current education policies; a specific focus on active citizenship has been introduced in the curriculum. A recent law (92/2019) reframed "civic education" as a multifaceted discipline, concerning all subjects, across all school levels through a variety of methods (Surian, 2019). The new legal framework, followed by detailed guidelines, stresses the importance of the relationship between schools and their community and environment, and promotes initiatives that involve public and private institutions with the aim of engaging students in concrete ways. To this extent, the legislator intended to overcome the "marginalization" of citizenship education that had long characterized the Italian curriculum (Santerini, 2018). Citizenship education is expected to go far beyond the legal understanding of citizenship as a set of rights and duties. Its main aim is to empower learners of all ages to assume an active role in building more peaceful, tolerant, inclusive and secure societies as recommended in several official documents published by international organizations, such as the European Commission, UNESCO and Council of Europe (Barzanò & Zacchilli, 2018).

---

[1] https://www.un.org/sustainabledevelopment/development-agenda/

On the one hand, the new framework draws on the legacy of the many Italian schools that over the years have shown interest in the issues of citizenship education and have put in place innovative learning experiences (Pontecorvo, 2021). On the other hand, in Italy as in other countries, schools are aware of the difficulties in renewing their role and increasing their responsibilities in setting up a functional learning environment for citizenship education, ensuring the appropriate experiences of cognitive, intellectual and experiential learning required by every student (Cebrián, 2022; Mosa, 2021).

Citizenship education has been characterized by a series of theoretical and operational proposals connected to the concept of belonging to a community. These proposals have taken on various terms, from "civic education," to "civil coexistence," to "citizenship and the Constitution." In the Italian context, being an active citizen has for long meant primarily knowing and respecting the Constitution and being an active member of the community. Therefore, Italian schools—at all levels—highlighted the citizen-constitution-community triangulation as a means to exercise democracy. Recent changes in legislation are creating hopes for better spaces of action while, at the same time, causing concerns about the adequacy of schools to cope with the new requirements. This is particularly true in light of the UN 2030 Agenda. Many references to the SDGs are included in the text of the Law n. 92/2019. For example, the introduction of education on climate change and the need to safeguard the environment, human rights, education for health and wellbeing, and citizens' responsibility in actively participating in public life. Despite the ambitions of the new curriculum for citizenship education, many scholars are raising concerns about the preparedness of schools to effectively adopt it and move away from an education that is a mere transmission of knowledge, to one that is rich in opportunities for peer learning and learning throuh dialogue (Capobianco, 2021; Panizza, 2019; Tarozzi & Inguaggiato, 2018). As Palmerio et al. (2021) observe, Italian policy makers have never been really committed to developing the organizational conditions "that could actually make the declarations of principle feasible in practice" (p. 95).

Bombardelli and Codato (2017) offer a clear picture of the current status and role of civic and citizenship education in Italy based on: a) the analysis of official guidelines for schools produced by the Ministry of Education over a number of years, b) a brief review of academic research materials, and c) informal observations of teaching in schools. They conclude that, despite the evident interest in this topic from both teachers and students, significant changes in the approach to civic education in schools are necessary. Complaints about the limits of civic and citizenship education in the Italian school system are frequent. For instance, in a research conducted with a sample of 800 Italian students, 49.5% of them stated that they were not satisfied with the help they received at school for the development of their civic–political education, and only 20% stated that they sporadically participated in lessons of civic education throughout the school year (Rivelli, 2010).

Educational experiences capable of overcoming such criticisms are needed. In this chapter, we present one of these experiences, purposely designed to support active citizenship through participation in concrete activities tackling specific goals of the UN 2030 Agenda. The general idea is to involve students in redesigning an urban space—a square—near their school. In doing so, they explore and negotiate their sense of belonging to a larger community. The community involved includes not only classes that participate directly but also people living around the square: workers taking the underground, babysitters and parents with their kids, elders sitting on the benches, merchants whose shops overlook the square, runners passing by, religious people attending the nearby church, and even graffiti artists that decorated some of the square's walls. To engage in dialogue effectively with such a large community, it is essential to adopt an interdisciplinary approach involving all school subjects: history and philosophy, to explore the concept of the square, drawing parallels to the Greek *agora*; science, to acquire the right skills to observe the vegetation growing spontaneously in the square and deciding which plants would be best suitable for that environment; mathematics and geometry, to analyze the dimensions of the square and the relation between its different parts; art, to reflect on the role of the square to host and display art; literature, to develop interviews to be conducted with people associated to the square; visual arts to document the project through photos and videos.

In planning, executing, and analyzing this project, we used the dialogical approach as a theoretical framework. This approach helped us envision interconnections between all stakeholders involved and to connect various activities to the idea of a "dialogical citizenship." We propose this label as a way to make active citizenship more concrete and understandable.

The project has collected substantial documentation consisting of working documents, pictures, videos, texts, and field notes recorded by external observers or by teachers and students during the activities. We draw on this material to articulate the description of the experience and to extract its dialogic potentialities.

6.2. Theoretical Framework

Education for a culture of dialogue has long been an important mission of schools. The classroom is a place where students learn how to express themselves and how to listen to and learn from others. Nevertheless, the dialogical approach, recently introduced within the Italian context (Ligorio et al., 2018; Sansone et al., 2016), adds a new dimension: it is not enough being able to talk and listen to others, there is a need for genuinely considering other points of view to enrich one's perspective and acknowlede how others influence our own thinking. This avoids the risk of oversimplifying complex issues into a uniform vision of knowledge. Simultaneously, it fosters critical thinking as an integral part of the learning process. Simplification of reality is a rhetorical expedient often used in social discourses, particularly in some forms of public discourse, where ambiguous or misleading language can be used to deceive. For instance, argumentations based on the dichotomies "good" and "bad" or "us" and "them" are the bases of populist discourse all over the world. By reducing the discussion to a simple contraposition between, for instance, migrants and local people, populism argues that these two different categories of people have different rights and responsibilities, and consequently, a different social status (Mudde & Kaltwasser, 2017). The difference is so profound, according to populist assumptions, that a dialogue between these two parties is futile. There is nothing to be discussed: "them"—the migrants—are so different from "us" that values and norms that hold significance for 'us' are not equally applicable to 'them'. This is the case of, for instance, access to education, good jobs and salaries, and general respect in everyday life.

Critical thinking competencies are necessary to be able to identify deceptive language and logical fallacies in arguments. Critical thinking is the ability to evaluate, analyze, and interpret information about oneself, others, and the world (Ennis, 1993). Despite being traditionally defined as an individual ability, critical thinking is currently conceptualized as a dialogic practice (Kuhn, 2019) rooted in social interaction and information exchange (Mercier & Sperber, 2011). There is empirical evidence of the relation between dialogue and critical thinking. For instance, Kuhn and Crowell (2011) showed that students who were engaged in computerized dialogical activities produced better argumentation in individual essays on controversial issues compared to a control group who focused only on individual writing activities. Thus, dialogic education should address these issues. Education *through* dialogue is not enough: an additional step is required leading to education *in* dialogue. This implies bringing people together despite their differences and allowing a profound understanding of each other's point of view, rather than just acknowledging the differences (Barzanò et al., 2017; Wegerif, 2019).

The roots of dialogic education can be traced back to ancient philosophers like Socrates. More recently it includes thinkers as diverse as Freire (1996), who viewed dialogic education as a means of liberation from oppression, and Oakeshott (1991), for whom education is the process of engaging students in their cultural heritage, described as "the conversation of humanity." Bakhtin (1981), an influential source, as highlighted by Holquist (2003), for the recent theory of dialogic education, argues that to fully comprehend something it is imperative to engage in interactions involving multiple voices representing diverse viewpoints. In educational settings, dialogues can happen in many contexts between a variety of actors: teacher–pupil dialogue, small group dialogues, and dialogues between the whole class. Dialogues can also engage nonschool voices: experts, academics, artists, and societal institutions in a broader sense.

The relevance of dialogism can be understood considering also the connection that Rommetveit (2020)—building on authors such as Bakhtin (1981), Vološinov (1973), and Vygotsky (1979)—finds between the prevailing individualism in Western societies and a psychology not sufficiently attentive to the fundamentally social human nature. For these authors, at the basis of the development of our species lies the innate human need and capacity to understand each other, to guess and deliberately influence each other's intentions and, at the same time, to adapt oneself to feedback from others. Neglecting these dimensions to support individualism and classify people with predefined labels—as a great part of psychology does—would constitute a sort of demotion of the human capacity to develop and contribute to social progress. This complex vision of dialogicality should be taken into consideration when reflecting on the nature of contemporary society.

Specific attention should be paid to the role technology is playing in Western societies. Many authors (Kapitzke & Renshaw, 2004; Wegerif, 2007) contend that digital environments and tools play a crucial role in expanding and structuring the space for dialogues, enabling people to meet, discuss, and share information and ideas (see Chapter 7, by Wegerif and Major). Technology has the potential to facilitate communication between an unlimited number of voices (Trausan-Matu, 2019), reshape the concept of space and time for conversations (Ligorio & Ritella, 2010), and create a blended dimension where online and offline boundaries are blurred, fostering the development of intersubjective dialogue (Beraldo et al., 2021). Even the concept of community is reshaped by including contemporary contexts and concerns—economic, social, political, cultural, and ecological (Westoby & Dowling, 2013).

This complexity is not only welcomed in the dialogical perspective, but even necessary (Ligorio & César, 2013). Dialogism is a way to refuse oversimplifications and reductionist approaches when looking at human actions and thinking and to overcome social categories often used to stir up conflict. To unpack such complexity, a few criteria can be outlined:

(i) a dialogic orientation towards the other, a genuine interest in trying to understand the needs of others;
(ii) the recognition of social norms that support effective dialogue;
(iii) the need for the contribution of others in order to complete, refine and define one's own work/thought;
(iv) the co-construction of new meanings concerning not only concepts and knowledge but also the sense of identity (who I am, what I am capable of doing, who I want to be, etc.).

Altogether, these criteria can inform the way in which dialogism can be used to change class culture and support dynamics of integration, inclusion, and active citizenship.

Recently, the dialogical approach has been incorporated into the so-called Trialogical Learning Approach (TLA) (Hakkarainen & Paavola, 2009). The term "trialogical" refers to those processes where people are collaboratively and systematically developing shared and concrete "objects" together (Paavola & Hakkarainen, 2005). In trialogical learning settings, students collaboratively develop new objects of inquiry, such as knowledge artifacts, practices, ideas, models, and representations. These objects serve as catalysts for dialogical processes, where individuals not only engage with one another, but also channel their dialogues towards shared artifacts, actively contributing to their development. Dialogue is then shaped by the different phases of the object development, from the initial ideas to the realization of the final product, with participants adapting their behaviours in the dialogue to accommodate the object's changing nature. The border between dialogue and "trialogue" is not clearly marked, because both are based on dialogue and participation. The main difference between the two consists first in the focus of the dialogue, and second on the object development as a source for learning. Both trialogue and dialogue concur on the significance of social interaction, a concept originally formulated by Vygotsky (1978), as the primary catalyst for learning. Stetsenko (2005) suggested expanding the inter- and intra-psychological processes theorized by Vygotsky, emphasizing the importance of material social practices in object-oriented activities. She conceptualized learning as a transition among: a) material tool production; b) inter-psychological processes; c) intra-psychological processes or human subjectivity. TLA builds on Stetsenko's suggestions and sees the objects as being built collaboratively in the foreground. These objects must be meaningful and conceived for an external audience. This approach forces those building the objects to step into the perspective of the intended users, enabling a deeper understanding of their points of view. This process implies acquiring new knowledge and fostering a mindset that takes into account the attitudes of others. By engaging in dialogue while collaboratively constructing a meaningful object, the participants are compelled to genuinely comprehend each other and navigate away from unproductive discussions and entrenched individual stances.

Similar to the dialogical approach, TLA is also profoundly connected to the emergence of technology, in particular to its capability to transform intangible ideas into shareable digital artifacts. For instance, cloud and open-source tools provide several opportunities for collaborative work around shared objects. However, the use of technology is not enough to guarantee a trialogical process. The project presented in this chapter builds upon this framework and aspires to be an example of how dialogism can benefit from TLA to put in practice, expand, and enrich dialogues and interactions among different actors in a school context.

Figure 6.1. An overview of Piazza Annibaliano in Rome.

6.3. "Dialogues in the Square": The Origins of the Project

"Dialogues in the Square" (DiS) started in 2017, and it has the ambitious and challenging aim to involve students in the efforts to improve a historic square in Rome, Piazza Annibaliano, situated near their school (Barzanò et al., 2020). Despite undergoing restoration efforts in 2014, this significant urban space had fallen into a state of neglect. A new underground station, situated beside significant ancient monuments, is surrounded by litter and uncultivated flower beds. Figure 6.1 offers an overview of the square where both the underground station and monuments are visible.

The project followed a snowball development, initiated by one of those seemingly insignificant events that good teachers are quick to grasp. In November 2017, in a lively grade 3° class (average age 8) of a primary school located near the square, a student complained about the litter and broken bottles spread around the square. Others shared that they had come close to getting injured while walking to school. The teacher let the conversation develop, and the focus soon shifted to the problem of urban degradation, with the students very committed to understanding how to tackle it. When the circumstance was reported in the following school meeting, interest began to spread among teachers, and the idea of the project started its journey. The name "Dialogues in the Square" was chosen to stress how the practice of dialogue should be at the core of any possible intervention in a public space.

The school where this event occurred is part of Rete Dialogues,[2] a national network established in 2012 and comprising approximately 30 schools, all dedicated

---

[2] *retedialogues.it*

to global citizenship education. As information of the newly established DiS project started spreading within the network, an upper secondary school, also close to Piazza Annibaliano, decided to join in as a major actor, while several other schools from Rete Dialogues expressed interest in observing the ongoing processes with the aim of implementing similar initiatives.

DiS soon appeared to be a treasure trove of ideas that could strengthen the connections between the school and the larger community, providing meaningful opportunities for dialogue and fostering students' experiences of active citizenship. Several activities started to take place. Students from the two schools were encouraged to observe the square and engage in planning its renovation. Their plans were conceived as trialogical objects intended for both internal discussions and dissemination to communities beyond the school. Meetings were organised involving students from diverse schools, classes, and age groups to exchange updates, discuss challenges, celebrate achievements, and gather additional perspectives. Meanwhile, negotiations started with the local municipality to gain their support for the final interventions. Artists and experts from various fields were also involved to help students figure out suitable actions to improve the state of the square, eliciting its potential as a social and artistic site. Soon it became clear that the project presented an excellent opportunity for action-research (Stringer, 2007). A team of professional researchers started to engage with students and support teachers in the collection of qualitative evidence through video recordings and field notes.

Four areas of intervention on the square were identified for in-depth study, analysis, and subsequent planning. These areas were then included in a Memorandum of Understanding (MoU), between Rete Dialogues, the schools, the Municipality II of Rome, and other local associations. The four areas were:

1) History and narratives of the monuments visible in the skyline of the square to be displayed on information panels;
2) Murals to creatively represent values and ideas;
3) Green areas to contribute to the currently neglected flora;
4) Events to promote cultural and artistic initiatives.

These areas provided a clear and easily understandable framework throughout the project's duration. They served as a straightforward way to communicate the project's objectives to new students, teachers, and external audiences. Participants from previous years actively guided newcomers by explaining the project's goals, detailing completed work, and outlining future plans. Passing the baton to newcomers involved sharing not only knowledge around a project, but also the transmission of cultural values and the strong commitment to its outcomes. This is an important aspect already exploited in projects such as Fifth

**The 2030 UN Sustainable Development Goals
in Piazza Annibaliano, following the students**

A more sustainable square is a small part of a more sustainable world (Goal 4.7).

In this project we understood how important it may be to equip a square
so that it can fit the needs of different people (Goal 11.7).

We have many ideas on how to make the square a place of sustainability
where consumption and waste are minimized and recycling is made visible (Goal 11.7).

What better place than the square can represent the idea of gathering?
Working to improve Piazza Annibaliano we also work to improve our society (Goal 16.7).

Figure 6.2. UN 2030 Goals and DiS (authored by students from three classes of the project).

Dimension (Cole & Distributive Literacy Consortium, 2006). Intergenerational interaction is considered crucial for many reasons. It fosters a sense of community as students can model themselves after older peers and observe the continuity of activities over time. At the same time, they have the opportunity to suggest new ideas, thus experiencing the privilege of innovating the practices. New zones of proximal development are supported because of the scaffolding offered also by older "agents"—students from previous years—perceived as closer to them compared to teachers or experts.

The actions planned were also clearly linked to some specific goals and targets of the UN 2030 Agenda, as shown in Figure 6.2.

In the first four years of the project, several activities were undertaken with students, including developing comprehensive assessments of the problems of the square and a rich set of creative "dreams" for improvements. Meanwhile, significant research data was collected, including "thick descriptions" (Denzin, 2001) of events and processes, and evidence from "critical incidents" (Tripp, 1993), highlighting several meaningful aspects and nuances of dialogical processes involving various actors. New sponsors and artists joined the project in 2021, leading to the development of a new workplan for the improvement of the square. The next paragraph will offer an overview of the participants and partners of the project.

6.4. Participants and Partners

Almost 450 students with their teachers have been involved in the project so far. Table 6.1 provides an overview of the participants, with the shaded background indicating the duration of participation for each class. Around half of the students were active in the project for three to four years before leaving for higher levels of education, while some classes withdrew their participation due

Table 6.1. Overview of participants in the DiS project

		2017/2018				2018/2019				2019/2020				2020/2021				2021/2022				Students		
	Class	F	M	Tot.	Class	F	M	Tot.	Class	F	M	Tot.	Class	F	M	Tot.	Class	F	M	Tot.	F	M	Tot
PRIMARY age 6–10 grade 1–5	3A	13	12	25	4A	15	12	27	5A	15	12	27					2A	9	8	17	9	8	17
	3B	11	8	19	4B	13	8	21	5B	13	8	21									15	12	27
	2A	10	12	22	3A	10	12	22	4A	11	12	23	5A	11	12	23					13	8	21
	4D	8	14	22																	11	12	23
									3A	11	15	26									8	14	22
LOWER SECONDARY age 11–13 grade 6–8	1I	12	13	25					1H	12	13	25	2H	12	13	25	3H	12	13	25	11	15	26
	2H	20	10	30																	12	13	25
					2H	15	12	27	3H	15	12	27									12	13	25
													1H	11	9	20	2M	13	7	20	20	10	30
																	2H	11	9	20	15	12	27
UPPER SECONDARY age 14–19 grade 9–13	2F	16	5	21	3F	15	5	20	4F	15	5	20	5F	15	5	20					13	7	20
	2A	14	5	19																	11	9	20
													4L	22	3	25	5L	22	3	25	15	5	20
	2H	15	4	19																	14	5	19
													3L	24	4	28	4L	24	4	28	22	3	25
																	2L	21	4	25	15	4	19
													2F	21	6	27	3F	21	4	25	24	4	28
																					21	4	25
																					21	4	25
Tot part per year	9 classes	119 F	83 M	202	5 classes	68 F	49 M	117	7 classes	92 F	77 M	169	7 classes	116 F	52 M	168	8 classes	133 F	52 M	185	282 F	162 M	444
Total unique classes																					19		

to teachers moving to different classes. Between 100 to 200 students participated each year. The majority of students were female, mirroring the actual composition of the upper secondary school involved. About 40 teachers were involved with different levels of teaching experience and from different subjects (Literature, Latin, History, Maths, Religious Education, Art, Science).

Meanwhile, the number of partners increased, ranging from important public bodies to academic research institutions and private companies. The Accademia delle Arti e Nuove Tecnologie (AANT), a specialized institution for tertiary education, provided significant inspiration and support through its faculty and facilities.

Collaborative partnerships were also formed with other prestigious organizations, including the Associazione Amici di Villa Leopardi in Rome, the Fondazione Querini Stampalia in Venice, the University of Bari, the Parrocchia di Sant'Agnese Fuori le Mura in Rome, the Macro Museum of Modern Art in Rome and the World Wildlife Fund (WWF). The Bank of Italy and Cittadellarte Fondazione Pistoletto provided a financial contribution.

6.5. The Development of Dialogues: Toward Action in a Public Space

To offer an insight into how the dialogical dimension evolved, we provide a quick overview of the project's different phases. This includes the progress made but also the way in which the dialogical potentialities were exploited and how new voices entered into the project.

While the primary 'trialogical object' is the renovation plan for Piazza Annibaliano, several intermediate objects emerge throughout the project's development, fostering ongoing opportunities for dialogue. These objects include videos, presentations, and renderings created by and for the students. In Table 6.2, we outline the key phases of DiS and offer examples of these intermediate "trialogical objects."

Of course, the pandemic affected the DiS project. Online activities were intensified and further opportunities for observation were developed to recognize the impact the lockdown produced on the general setting of the square.

Throughout the project, a significant volume of data was collected. For the purpose of this chapter, we focus on approximately 100 field notes generated by teachers and researchers. These notes were documented either in physical form using pencil and paper or digitally. Additionally, we consider numerous interviews and focus group discussions involving both teachers and students, conducted by the research group. As part of the action-research framework, teachers received brief training on the format and purpose of field observation before collaborating with professional researchers.

Table 6.2. Overview of the phases of the project

Phase	Intermediate trialogical object	Contexts of dialogues	Link to the material
Year 1 (2017/2018) *diagnostic phase*: Analyzing the problems of the square and identifying potential opportunities	Interviews of people attending the square. Multimedia narratives to present the results of visits to the square and of the interviews collected for external audiences (other classes, parents, community)	Students' dialogue to balance details and synthesis. Dialogical negotiation between students and between students and teachers. Trialogical intermediate objects are presented to a large audience and it was asked for feedback; this triggered a larger dialogue	Students' videos (in Italian): https://retedialogues.it/phase1
Year 2 (2018/2019) *creative phase*: Moving into a museum to benefit from the inspiration of a creative space and planning with artists and experts	A series of meetings held at the Macro Art Museum in Rome as a pilot project to engage citizens. The meetings were called "Macro Piazza"	Dialogues between students, experts, and artists helping in developing students' ideas	A session with a film director at Macro Museum: https://retedialogues.it/phase2
Year 3 (2019/2020), the *reflection phase*: Engaging in dialogue remotely during the pandemic	A video produced collaboratively to replace a virtual party planned in presence in the square but cancelled because of the Covid-19 lockdown.	Technology-mediated dialogues between students and teachers remotely that also involved families and a general audience	"Dialogues in the square" a collective video to replace an in-person meeting: https://retedialogues.it/phase3
Year 4 (2020/2021) *towards executive planning*: Reflecting on different hypotheses about what is really sustainable to be implemented	A PowerPoint presentation reporting the state of the art of the project prepared by "expert" students to welcome new students joining the project.	Dialogues between *old timer* students authoring the presentation and the newcomers as main audience	Students' presentation of DiS to their peers: https://retedialogues.it/phase4
Year 5 (2021/2022) *time to act in the square*: Meeting the artists and the experts that will support the executive phase	Reports from the meeting with the street artist who will paint the damaged walls in the square. Sketches prepared to inspire the artist	Dialogues between the students and the artist to negotiate how they will bring their preparatory work into his mural	Meeting the artist and preparing sketches to inspire them

The research team—consisting of three units—enriched the development of the DiS project with comments, ideas, and suggestions and maintained ongoing discussions with the teachers, following their progress. In a few cases, class discussions were organized to enable students to report their progress and proposals to different audiences (researchers, members of the community, experts, etc.). Such meetings were audio-recorded and transcribed.

6.6. Experiencing Different Types of Dialogues

The involvement of a large group of partners created opportunities for a wide range of dialogical settings, where different actors were involved. The intertwining of a variety of interlocutors created virtuous loops. A synthetic but systematic view of the voices involved throughout the project and the nature of the dialogues occurring is shown in Table 6.3.

Table 6.3 reflects the richness and variety of dialogues that unfolded during the project, illustrating the strong commitment of all participants toward the aim of the project: restoring the dignity of Piazza Annibaliano not only as an important square but as a space intended to be experienced by various people.

We would also like to underline that each "voice" does not just express its own opinion. Often teachers talk on behalf of their students, reconceptualizing and synthesizing their points of view to make them intelligible to a specific audience—for instance, institutions. Other times, students incorporate teachers', experts', or even artists' voices into their work. This is evident looking at their products. For example, during the first year the products were based strongly on brainstorming sessions conducted in the classes. Students expressed their "dream" square drawing from literature, their travels to other cities, history books, and their fantasies, without taking into consideration practical constraints. However, when the local municipality was consulted, it became evident that these "dream" proposals required significant revisions. It was hard to give up these dreams, so further sources of inspiration were sought, and experts and artists were consulted. At that point, the aim of actually seeing the square restored based on students' suggestions in a short time appeared unfeasible. Teachers and students agreed that being an active citizen does not necessarily entail an immediate ability to change the social or physical world. Rather, it means to be able to recognize all stakeholders involved and to engage in a productive dialogue with all of them; this is what we call "dialogic citizenship." In this sense, the community became aware that one's 'voice' gains more impact when shared and embraced by others. As each voice is representative of a specific point of view, the "polyphony"—in its bakhtinian sense (Bakhtin, 1981)—generated is representative of a collective identity and a sense of belonging to a large community not

Table 6.3. Overview of voices and dialogues within the DiS project

Voices in dialogue	Focus of the dialogues
Teachers within the school	Following a strategic and dynamic agenda, teachers of different subjects need to be in close contact with one another, to engage in planning, follow developments, and cope with unexpected events
Teachers across schools/school levels	Planning activities and monitoring achievements across different school levels is challenging in ordinary school life. A good understanding of why it is relevant to focus on the square makes it functional to combine different experiences and sensibilities of teachers from different contexts
Teachers and institutions	A square is a public space where any official intervention must follow legal processes and procedures. Formal and informal contacts with local authorities regarding plans are essential to getting recognition and support
Teachers, artists, and experts	Inspirations provided by artists and experts are at the core of the planning. Capturing their voices in the dialogical context of a project on public spaces needs dialogues and actions. The presence of an artist working with the students requires preliminary contacts, negotiations, and mediations.
Teachers and students	School life may change dramatically when students are working side by side in a project, and any opportunity to improve the object is a powerful context of dialogue
Students within the class	The aim of building a meaningful knowledge based on plans, ideas, and proposals through collaboration is clear to everybody and provides a strong background for deep listening
Students in small groups	Small groups are intimate spaces where dialogue can be deeper and faster. Often this is where new ideas are generated and old ideas are evaluated redefined
Students across classes and schools	Relationships between classes are a powerful engine to assess new ideas and review the impact of what has been produced. The age difference may play a crucial role in enhancing a constructive sense of diversity
Students and institutions	Studying the urban space and figuring out how to produce meaningful impact puts students in dialogue with institutions, their practices, and regulations
Students, artists, and experts	Dialogue with artists and experts is rich in hints for creativity and challenges, it feeds dreams and hazardous proposals, which then need to match up with the realm of possibilities

Figure 6.3. The walls where the murals will be located.

confined into the "here and now" but includes the past—the monuments facing the square and the function embodied by squares in society—and the future—whoever will pass by the square. This led the students to engage in understanding how to leave a substantial mark on the square. Hence, the idea of placing a mural on the most damaged walls of the square (see Figure 6.3).

The mural is seen by students as an embodiment of their agency as active citizens, with the possibility to have an impact on the surrounding environment. At the same time, it is seen by both students and teachers as the fulfillment of a social responsibility. A process that involved complex tasks, including content negotiation, obtaining approval from local authorities, engaging with community members, and receiving support from artists.

6.7. A Snapshot from the Field: Triggering Cross-Generation Dialogue

An episode documented in a field note serves as a poignant illustration of dialogical citizenship. This event vividly portrays the dialogical environment that greeted new students when their teacher introduced them to the DiS project, describing the various activities undertaken by older schoolmates who had recently graduated after four years of involvement in the project. During their last year of school, the former students had invested much energy in discussing the potential content of the mural. Several ideas were explored in a dialogical context and refined in meetings with artists at the museum (see Table 6.3), both in class and online. The teacher was acting as a bridge between school-leavers and newcomers. The teacher told newcomers that their predecessors had devoured internet pages in search of ideas of what could be painted on Piazza Annibaliano's walls. Initially, the plan was to select a set of ideas and hold a vote among students and citizens to choose the most suitable content for the painting. Soon it was clear that this was not an effective way to proceed, and students started to explore the idea of combining elements from different proposals, to reach a sort of synthesis. Because of the pandemic, discussions continued online. Two clusters of ideas emerged (see Figure 6.4). The first one included four topics: a) nature themes such as birds—with references to a popular Italian song[3]; b) preservation of biodiversity, umbrella species, and charismatic species; c) endangered species in the Africa reflecting the African-themed street names surrounding Piazza Annibaliano; and d) depictions of nature inspired by Dante's Divine Comedy. The second cluster was inspired by two historical themes: e) folklore images, including sketches from famous films shot in Rome; f) history of suffering and civil resistance concerning four women Roman partisans, active during the Second World War, who received medals for their bravery.

A pivotal moment occurred when a student made a very critical, almost inflammatory, comment. They claimed that none of the proposals had a clear connection with the history of the square. This sparked an intense and lively dialogue among the students, leading to the emergence of a new, more comprehensive proposal. The suggestion was to draw inspiration from the mosaics found inside the old monuments situated in one corner of the square. The proposal included the idea of painting bees and ladybugs on these murals, as they are beneficial insects, aligning with the concept of endangered animals central to the first cluster of proposals. It was immediately clear that this was the "winning" proposal. No single author emerged for this idea, but everybody spontaneously set to work to better define it. The objective was to provide greater visibility to the square's monuments through these murals, allowing visitors to discover the remarkable mosaic treasures preserved within the monumental complex.

The tale of this adventure became a means for teachers to encourage dialogue between two generations of students. It highlighted the dedication of the former students to the project and their four years of hard work, culminating in the selection of the winning proposal for the mural.

Through interviews with teachers, we discovered that their primary goal was, in fact, to facilitate a dialogue between two student generations. Their intention was to integrate new students into the project while maintaining continuity with the previous generation. This involved preserving the existing work and infusing

---

[3] "Uccelli" by Franco Battiato.

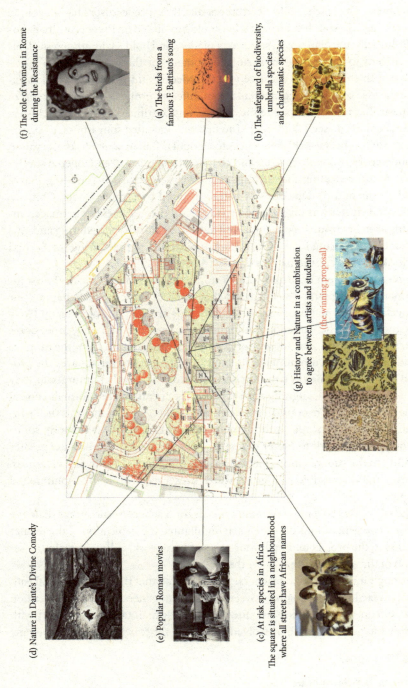

Figure 6.4. Students' proposals for themes to inspire the murals.

it with the fresh perspectives of the newcomers. In other words, a fertile cross-generational dialogue was initiated with the intention to further develop the ideas already emerged. Outgoing students see their work valued and appreciated, while new students had the opportunity to observe and reproduce mature social participation strategies. Participants fluidly transition between various roles, from the role of a teacher-like conductor, to observer, from media producer to mediator - all roles functional to the success of the project (Brown & Campione, 1994; Wenger, 1998). Participants learn through engagement in a common, meaningful project and by understanding someone else's perspective, striving to find commonalities and continuously attempting to evolve, and being open to new ideas and innovative solutions (Cole, 2009; Rogoff, 2008).

6.8. Constraints and Opportunities

The link between schools and the larger community is a crucial issue in the development of active and dialogical citizenship. To this extent, the opportunity to use the environment around the school has an enormous potential. The DiS project worked from this perspective, experiencing several limitations alongside many opportunities. The main constraints we found are outlined below.

- Enacting changes in urban spaces is extremely complex. What we have called the "diagnostic phase" in Table 6.2—in our case the identification of problems of the square (Piazza Annibaliano)—has been an exciting endeavor. Students engaged in deep observations, collecting and elaborating evidence, interviewing local residents, producing and sharing reportages, and receiving constructive feedback on their analyses. They invested all their fantasies and dreams ideating possible solutions, fostering a high degree of creativity and an intense dialogical atmosphere. However, when the time for planning concrete actions arrived, it soon became clear that any intervention to renovate the square would face many obstacles and require demanding negotiations with different stakeholders. Namely, challenges related to securing financial resources and obtaining official permits from various local authorities and art councils emerged. A delay in the students' schedule was unavoidable, which resulted in disappointment and a decrease in motivation for many students. The connection between quality of participation and quality of the urban space is a multifaceted and politically charged topic. Being aware of this connection and feeling empowered in contributing to this issue is a crucial aspect for dialogical citizenship.

- Planning was adventurous, in that the original timetable was continually disrupted and redrafted, due to unexpected events that risked spoiling the engagement and interest of both students and teachers. The Covid-19 pandemic created further difficulties. On numerous occasions, a sense of dispiritedness pervaded, as the obstacles were numerous, and students' self-efficacy (Bandura, 1992) was put to the test. Even minor alterations to a public space necessitate an abundance of documentation and permits. "*So many ideas and proposals .... and no way for us to have a real impact*" a student once commented with strong disappointment. During meetings, teachers questioned the extent to which this challenging project was beneficial, as they were concerned that it might unintentionally foster a sense of helplessness and disillusionment among the students, potentially contradicting the primary aim of educating for active citizenship. Besides the possibility to actually achieve all the objects that students and teachers may develop along the project, there is the positive side of learning to deal with real-life issues and contributing to the enhancement of the quality of urban spaces inhabited by their own community (Lukito, et al. 2021).
- The prolonged development of the project resulted in many students leaving school before they could see any tangible outcomes. Meanwhile, new groups of students joined the project without prior involvement, which meant they had to grapple with decisions made by their predecessors. This had a strong impact on teachers' planning, since it forced them to review and adapt processes and practices and caused a significant increase in their work. Some energy had to be diverted from curriculum content to the project design. This was also an opportunity for teachers to move away from frontal instruction and to recognize the potential of alternative teaching methods, such as dialogue between different generations of students and dialogue with entities outside the school.
- Working side by side with institutions outside the school—ranging from the exhausting bureaucracy of local authorities to the inspiring creativity of artists—is challenging. It means to be confronted with different agendas and schedules, different languages, mindsets, paces, and ways of working. This sometimes results in real difficulties in understanding one another. Institutions of various kinds (e.g. museums, cultural or scientific associations, etc.) commonly offer activities designed *for schools* such as guided tours, lectures, or workshops. However, these are usually top-down initiatives: even when carefully and cleverly conceived they often fail to leave space for a real dialogue. Involving institutions and experts in a project actually *with schools*, aiming at concrete goals, is demanding and sometimes exasperating. It implies finding a balance between different needs and worlds (e.g. the bureaucracy of permissions, the sponsors' needs for visibility, and

each artist's wish for freedom and independence). It is not enough to just interact with a counterpart. A real dialogue means attempting to understand other participants' perspectives and make your goals clear and convincing. The latter point implies an "inner" dialogue, which means reflecting on our own agenda, our own experience of dialogue, and the impact it has on our own development while avoiding implicit assumptions and suspending any judgement.

To some extent, several constraints encountered during the experience were eventually transformed into opportunities over time. In particular:

- The gap between the ambitious dreams students envisioned after their dialogues with artists and experts, and the real possibilities was significant and often disappointing. However, it became an opportunity to reinforce the dialogical atmosphere in the classes. According to a teacher of the team "*it resulted in a consolidated resilience: the students had many opportunities to comment, to share their concerns and hopes, they became familiar with this gap and saw it as a dynamic element which was even pushing their fantasy further.*"
- The broad engagement of partners with different characteristics and visions led the students to engage in a variety of languages and perspectives, allowing them to experience the complexity of the processes underpinning civic participation. Through this, students develop a deeper understanding of "otherness" (Bertau, et al., 2013). This offered an engaging scenario, rich in dialogical opportunities, where citizenship education can be explored in practice. Engaging in dialogical practices exposed students to critical reflections on controversial issues. For instance, they were engaged for a long time in a reflection concerning graffiti in the square. This reflection brought them to deal with different contradictions: what is the difference between an artistic expression and an illegal act of vandalism? Where is the fine line between the need to preserve the public decency of the square and censorship? These activities allowed students to shift from an absolutist stance to a perspective of multiplicity and epistemic assessment (Felton & Kuhn, 2007).
- Schools rarely offer students opportunities to provide a real contribution to their community with a clear impact. In the DiS project, Piazza Annibaliano is far more than just a learning object: teachers and students learn through actions that are expected to produce visible change and to have a real impact on the environment around their school. Besides building several artifacts, students also act as facilitators of processes and performances where there is a strong cooperation with and among adults, artists, experts, and professionals, as is the case for the artist involved in the murals.

- The main aims of DiS are clear and easy to understand from different complementary perspectives: improving the square by providing information about the history of its monuments, realizing murals on damaged walls, planting flowers and trees, and organizing participative events. These aims naturally drove any action to a transdisciplinary approach, creating a complex but suggestive operational context. Teachers of different subjects were involved, the actions required to proceed were compelling, and the pace was discontinuous. A strong need for flexibility and adaptation emerged, which led to a change in the traditional structure of teachers' planning and brought in new settings for dialogues and innovative practices. The project became an opportunity for professional development, where teachers could learn from each other and together with the students from an intergenerational perspective.
- Digital technologies played a pivotal role in several aspects of the project. They were essential for recording and documenting the initial inquiries that led to the identification of problems and potential solutions. They also facilitated research into the history of places and individuals, as well as communication among different classes and a broader audience for sharing artifacts and ideas. Additionally, when the pandemic lockdown disrupted original plans, technology allowed the project to adapt and continue online. During this period, an event that was expected to happen in the square was replaced by broadcasting a collective video produced by students online (see phase 3 in Table 6.2). The project became a test-bed for the use of technology in schools not just as a delivery tool but as a means to offer students and teachers several opportunities for improving their digital skills at the service of innovative approaches to the curriculum.

In conclusion, based on our experience, introducing effective educational practices designed to support active citizenship is complex—for at least two reasons. The first reason is methodological. To develop what we call "dialogical citizenship" required significant awareness of the importance of documenting all processes and activities. Initially, we observed that teachers only incidentally referenced critical moments, whereas researchers found these moments highly valuable. This stemmed from the fact that teachers were not accustomed to capturing and documenting such episodes. However, through project meetings and constructive dialogues, teachers came to recognize the necessity of systematic documentation for reflecting on the project's evolution. Simultaneously, researchers realized the importance of providing teachers with specific training in qualitative research methods.

A second reason concerns how schools are conceived and how they act within society. When targeting dialogic citizenship, schools cannot act as monads. They should establish interconnections with as many interlocutors as possible, especially if a dialogical approach is maintained. Encounters with partners of different nature, scope, and aims need to be well-orchestrated to avoid a cacophony where voices are not really interacting but simply expressing their positions. In this project, we noticed that many agencies were willing to perform activities *for* the schools. Yet conceiving schools as real stakeholders means to design and plan *with* them. Schools have significant potential to contribute to institutions, companies, and to the community in general. This perspective opens up a diverse range of collaborative opportunities for planning and executing concrete actions, initiatives, and "objects" that are actually useful to the broader community and effectively embodying the values of active and dialogical citizenship. How can we teach dialogical citizenship if we consider schools as simple repositories of knowledge and students only as receivers? It is crucial to recognize schools as significant stakeholders in broader cultural and social initiatives. Involving students in processes that have social and cultural impact—working on "trialogical" objects—means also to support a more effective learning. In the process of teaching dialogical citizenship, schools cannot just work around concepts and notions. The school community is part of the broader cultural dialogue, involving society at large. Preparing students capable of engaging in meaningful dialogue means forming citizens not only ready for the future but already active in the present. Schools should be conceived as parties entitled to contribute to social dialogue. They can contribute to overcoming the use of predefined and opposing categories, which lie behind monologues and often foment social conflicts. Our research highlights the significance of a dialogic perspective in society. It shows that the school community has a unique voice and can contribute to the broader cultural and social dialogue, orchestrating various voices when engaged in meaningful projects. Expanding this concept to a broader societal context, we could foster a more inclusive and dialogic society, where stakeholders view each other as genuine partners. In such a society, voices are not merely heard but also integrated and recognized as interdependent.

Acknowledgments

We would like to thank the students and the teachers taking part in the DiS activities with passion and commitment and Elena Zacchilli, head teacher of Liceo Machiavelli (Rome), who coordinated the project together with colleagues from Istituto Comprensivo Settembrini (Rome). Together with them, we thank the teachers of AANT, Accademia di Arti e Nuove Tecnologie (Rome) who offered their inspiration and technical support.

A special thanks goes to the artists and experts and to our partners for their precious cooperation in the field: Municipality II of Rome, Associazione Amici di Villa Leopardi, MACRO — Museum of Contemporary Art of Rome, AANT, Parrocchia di S. Agnese Fuori Le Mura Roma, Fondazione Querini Stampalia in Venice, the University of Bari, and WWF.

We would like to express our gratitude to the Bank of Italy that, together with Cittadellarte-Fondazione Pistoletto, granted a financial contribution to DiS within the framework of the project "Recreating a square or . . . an Urban Space."

References

Bakhtin, M. (1981). *The dialogic imagination: Four essays*. University of Texas Press.
Bandura, A. (1992). Exercise of personal agency through the self-efficacy mechanism. In R. Schwartzer (Ed.), *Self-efficacy: Thought control of action* (pp. 3–37). Hemisphere Publishing.
Barzanò, G., Amenduni, F., Cutello, G., Lissoni, M., Pecorelli, C., Quarta, R., Raffio, L., Regazzini, C., Zacchilli, E., & Ligorio, M. B. (2020). When the place matters: Moving the classroom into a museum to re-design a public space. *Frontiers in Psychology, 11*. https://www.frontiersin.org/articles/10.3389/fpsyg.2020.00943/full
Barzanò, G., Cortiana, P., Jamison, I., Lissoni, M., & Raffio, L. (2017). New means and new meanings for multicultural education in a global–Italian context. *Multicultural Education Review, 9*(3), 145–158.
Barzanò, G., & Zacchilli, E. (2018). Cittadinanza europea e cittadinanza globale: Tra appartenenze e valori [European citizenship and global citizenship: Between values and belongings] In P. Corbucci, & M. Freddano (Eds.), *I Quaderni della Ricerca* (Vol. 39, pp. 254–265). Loescher.
Beraldo, R., Annese, S., Schwartz, N., & Ligorio, M. B. (2021). Building intersubjectivity in blended problem-solving tasks. *Learning, Culture and Social Interaction, 31*, 100545.
Bertau, M., Gonçalves, M. M., & Raggatt, P. T. (Eds.). (2013). *Dialogic formations: Investigations into the origins and development of the dialogical self*. IAP.
Bombardelli, O., & Codato, M. (2017). Country report: Civic and citizenship education in Italy—Thousands of fragmented activities looking for a systematization. *Journal of Social Science Education, 16*(2), 73–85.
Brown, A. L., & Campione, J. C. (1994). *Guided discovery in a community of learners*. MIT Press.
Capobianco, R. (2021). For quality, equitable and inclusive education: Sustainability in the transversal teaching of civic education. *Formazione & Insegnamento, 19*(1), 252–265.
Cebrián, G., Mogas, J., Palau, R., & Fuentes, M. (2022). Sustainability and the 2030 Agenda within schools: A study of school principals' engagement and perceptions, *Environmental Education Research, 28*(6), 845–866.
Cole, M. (2009). Designing, implementing, sustaining, and evaluating idiocultures for learning and development: The case study of the Fifth Dimension. In S. Bekman & A. Aksu-Koç (Eds.), *Perspectives on Human Development, Family and Culture* (pp. 331–349). Cambridge University Press.
Cole, M., & Distributive Literacy Consortium (2006). *The fifth dimension: An after-school program built on diversity*. Russell Sage Foundation.
Denzin, N. K. (2001). *Interpretive interactionism*. Sage.
Ennis, R. H. (1993). Critical thinking assessment. *Theory Into Practice, 32*(3), 179–186.

Felton, M. K., & Kuhn, D. (2007). "How do I know?" The epistemological roots of critical thinking. *Journal of Museum Education*, 32(2), 101–110.

Freire, P. (1996). *Pedagogy of the oppressed*. Continuum.

Hakkarainen, K., & Paavola, S. (2009). Toward a trialogical approach to learning. In B. Schwarz, T. Dreyfus & R. Hershkowitz (Eds.), *Transformation of knowledge through classroom interaction* (pp. 73–88). Routledge.

Holquist, M. (2003). *Dialogism: Bakhtin and his world*. Routledge.

Kapitzke, C., & Renshaw, P. D. (2004). Third space in cyberspace. In *Dialogic Learning* (pp. 45–61). Springer.

Kuhn, D. (2019). Critical thinking as discourse. *Human Development*, 62(3), 146–164.

Kuhn, D., & Crowell, A. (2011). Dialogic argumentation as a vehicle for developing young adolescents' thinking. *Psychological Science*, 22(4), 545–552.Ligorio, M. B., & César, M. (Eds.). (2013). *Interplays between dialogical learning and dialogical self*. IAP.

Ligorio, M. B., & Ritella, G. (2010). The collaborative construction of chronotopes during computer-supported collaborative professional tasks. *International Journal of Computer-Supported Collaborative Learning*, 5(4), 433–452.

Ligorio, M. B., Sansone, N., & Cesareni, D. (2018). *Fare e collaborare: L'approccio trialogico nella didattica [Doing and collaborating: The trialogic approach in education]*. FrancoAngeli.

Lukito, Y. N., Kusuma, N. R., Arvanda, E., & Ummah, Z. R. (2021). Designing with users: A participatory design as a community engagement program in the city zoo. *ASEAN Journal of Community Engagement*, 5(1), 4.

Mercier, H., & Sperber, D. (2011). Why do humans reason? Arguments for an argumentative theory. *Behavioral and Brain Sciences*, 34(2), 57–74.

Mosa, E. (2021). La scuola come palestra di cittadinanza. Riflessioni e buone pratiche da Avanguardie educative [The school as a gym for citizenship. Reflections and good practices from educational avant-gardes]. *Scuola Democratica*, 12, 313–323.

Mudde, C., & Kaltwasser, C. R. (2017). *Populism: A very short introduction*. Oxford University Press.

Oakeshott, M. (1991). *On human conduct*. Oxford University Press.

Paavola, S., & Hakkarainen, K. (2005). The knowledge creation metaphor–An emergent epistemological approach to learning. *Science & Education*, 14(6), 535–557.

Paavola, S. & Hakkarainen, K. (2009). From meaning making to joint construction of knowledge practices and artefacts—A trialogical approach to CSCL. In *Proceedings of the 8th International Conference on Computer Supported Collaborative Learning, CSCL'09, Rhodes, Greece, June 8–13* (pp. 83–92). International Society of the Learning Sciences (ISLC).

Palmerio, L., Damiani,V., & Caponera, E. (2021). IEA's International Civic and Citizenship Education Study and the teaching of civic education in Italy. In B. Malak-Minkiewicz & J. Torney-Purta (Eds.), *Influences of the IEA Civic and Citizenship Education Studies* (pp. 91–102). IEA.

Panizza, S. (2019). La reintroduzione dell'insegnamento scolastico dell'educazione civica da parte d ella legge n. 92/2019, con a fondamento la conoscenza della Costituzione. Tra buone intenzioni e false partenze [The reintroduction of school education in civic education by law no. 92/2019, based on knowledge of the Constitution. Between good intentions and false starts]. *Diritti fondamentali.it Fasciolo*, 21–34.

Pontecorvo, C. (2021). La dimensione evolutiva nell'educazione civica e alla cittadinanza [The evolutionary dimension in civic and citizenship education]. *Scuola Democratica*, 12, 161–166.

Rivelli, S. (2010). Citizenship education at high school A comparative study between Bolzano and Padova (Italy). *Procedia-Social and Behavioral Sciences*, 2(2), 4200–4207.

Rogoff, B. (2008). Observing sociocultural activity on three planes: Participatory appropriation, guided participation, and apprenticeship. In K. Hall, P. Murphy & J. Soler (Eds.), *Pedagogy and Practice: Culture and Identities* (pp. 58–74). Sage.

Rommetveit, R. (2020). On dialogism and scientifically disciplined discourse-and conversation analysis. In R. Rommetveit (Ed.), *Theory and Methodology in International Comparative Classroom Studies* (pp. 38–60). Cappelen Damm Akademisk.

Sansone, N., Bortolotti, I., & Buglass, S. (2016). The trialogical learning approach in practices: Reflections from pedagogical cases. *Qwerty-Open and Interdisciplinary Journal of Technology, Culture and Education*, 11(2), 99–120.

Santerini, M. (2018). L'educazione alla cittadinanza nell'era della "post-verità." [Citizenship education in the era of "post-truth."] In S. Polenghi, M. Fiorucci, & L. Agostinetto (Eds.), *Diritti Cittadinanza Inclusione* [Rights citizenship inclusion] (pp. 35–46). Pensa Multimedia.

Stetsenko, A. (2005). Activity as object-related: Resolving the dichotomy of individual and collective planes of activity. *Mind, Culture, and Activity*, 12(1), 70–88.

Stringer, E. T. (2007). *Action research*. Los Angeles: Sage Publications.

Surian, A. (2019). I recenti orientamenti sull'Educazione alla Cittadinanza Globale: riflessioni e spunti per la rilettura dei piani di studio delle istituzioni scolastiche [Recent developments in Global Citizenship Education: reflections and suggestions on revising formal education curricula]. RicercAzione (IPRASE Trentino), Vol 11.

Tarozzi, M., & Inguaggiato, C. (2018). Implementing global citizenship education in EU primary schools: The role of government ministries. *International Journal of Development Education and Global Learning*, 10(1), 21–38.

Trausan-Matu, S. (2019). The polyphonic model of collaborative learning. In *The Routledge international handbook of research on dialogic education* (pp. 454–468). Routledge.

Tripp, D. (1993). *Critical incidents in teaching: Developing professional judgement*. Routledge.

Vološinov, V. N. (1973). *Marxism and the philosophy of language*. Seminar Press.

Vygotsky, L. S. (1978). *Mind in society*. Harvard University Press.

Vygotsky, L. S. (1979). Consciousness as a problem in the psychology of behavior. *Soviet Psychology*, 17, 3–25.

Wegerif, R. (2007). *Dialogic education and technology: Expanding the space of learning* (Vol. 7). Springer Science & Business Media.

Wegerif, R. (2019). Dialogic education. In *Oxford research encyclopedia of education*. Oxford University Press.

Wenger, E. (1998). Communities of practice: Learning as a social system. *Systems Thinker*, 9(5), 2–3.

Westoby, P., & Dowling, G. (2013). *Theory and practice of dialogical community development: International perspectives*. Routledge.

7
A Dialogic Theory of Educational Technology

Rupert Wegerif and Louis Major

7.1. Introduction: Definitions and Scope

Kurt Lewin famously said that there is nothing more practical than a good theory (Greenwood & Levin, 1998, p. 19). Following Diana Laurillard (2013), we understand education to be a design science like engineering or architecture. One core research method for education, as for any design science, is design-based research (DBR) in which different design principles are tried out and design frameworks are developed in a systematic and evidence-based way to be shared with the community. Design frameworks are often specific to projects. However, they are informed by more general theories or ways of seeing which, following Winograd et al. (1986), we refer to as foundations for design. In this chapter, we provide the provisional and tentative beginnings of a dialogic foundation for the design of education technology (Wegerif & Major, 2024).

Articles about education technology design often refer to theory when developing designs. However, these tend to be general theories of education such as the behaviorist theories behind much instructional design, or the constructivist and social constructivist theories behind the design of many learning environments. The problem is that theories of education alone do not always take the distinctive "voice" of technology into account. Technology, we claim, is inherently intertwined with education. As a result, we believe that the role of technology in shaping educational goals ought to be more explicitly acknowledged. Humans are now, and always have been, a combination of the biological and the technical. It follows from this that when technology changes, then what it means to be human changes—and thus, education also needs to change.

After explaining our understanding of theory and the importance of having a specific theory of education technology, the next question we want to address is why we need a distinctively dialogic theory of education technology. The advent of the Digital Age in a cultural historical timescale, and the advent of the Anthropocene in a geological timescale, both raise serious challenges for humanity—challenges to which technology-supported dialogic education offers, we argue, at least a partial response. The internet, which has emerged in recent decades as the new dominant mode of communication, has brought the majority of the human race together in what is essentially a single medium with the possibility of real-time, two-way dialogic interaction. While an extraordinary creation, this has presented many challenges. Initially seen as a potential support for democracy, the internet is now more commonly referred to as a threat to democracy with global social media platforms, such as Facebook, accused of encouraging extremism and the spread of "fake news." Part of the problem seems to be that the algorithms, designed to boost advertising revenue, reward extreme views, and messages expressing outrage get more visibility and "likes" than more moderate messages. In addition, social media often promotes "echo chambers," in which those with the same views are grouped together by a pattern of mutual liking that excludes diversity, challenge, and development (Geeng et al., 2020). In relation to education, the internet is accused of disrupting the cognitive development of children by encouraging distraction and leading to shorter attention spans (Carr, 2010; Greenfield, 2015). There is also a fear that the internet is leading to families who are "alone together," each on their mobile phones instead of talking together and so producing young people who are not able to connect to others except superficially (Turkle, 2011).

These concerns about democracy and childhood socialization are aspects of one big challenge of our time which is managing the transition from multiple, separate print-based cultures to a single, global internet-based culture. It is probably not coincidental that this transition to the Digital Age in what Vygotsky referred to as the cultural historical timescale, corresponds to an increasing awareness of the dawn of the Anthropocene in the much larger geological timescale. The Anthropocene is the idea that planet Earth has moved into a novel geological epoch characterized by human domination. Effects like global warming show that human actions are impacting on the quality of our environment such that collective self-regulation on a planetary scale has become essential if we are to continue not only to thrive but also, perhaps, simply to survive. The Anthropocene offers challenges that imply the need for us to collaborate across different countries in order to understand and to solve problems, such as global warming, which cannot be solved by any individual country acting alone. This suggests a need to design education to promote a possible global collective intelligence for the future. In this chapter and elsewhere (Wegerif & Major, 2024), we argue that a better theory of dialogic education with technology might help us address the challenges posed both by the Digital Age and the Anthropocene.

7.1.1. What is "Technology"?

Dialogic theory can be applied to understand the challenge of defining key concept words like "technology." The Greek word "dia" found in "dialogue" and "dialogic" can be translated as "across" and refers to an essential gap or difference defining "dialogic" in contrast to "logic." If "logic" refers to reason, then dialogic refers to "reason across difference." The essence of dialogic theory is that meaning occurs only when there is a difference between voices and perspectives. This dialogic theory tells us, for example, that the meaning of a key concept word in a dialogue is not given by its dictionary definition but by the difference that it makes in a context (Linell, 2009; Rommetveit, 1992). If we apply this dialogic insight to "education technology," often abbreviated in everyday contexts to "EdTech," we see that when educators use the term "EdTech" in schools and classrooms they are making a useful distinction between the main activities of education, teaching, and learning, and extra supplementary tools brought in to support those main activities. In an everyday sense, the term "educational technology" has a clear meaning. It does not refer to pens and paper or to blackboards and sticks of chalk; it does not refer to desks and chairs or to textbooks and the curriculum; rather, it refers to digital machines, their software, and their support systems.

However, stepping back from everyday classroom practice to take a more theoretical perspective on educational technology, we note that the close association of technology with physical machines, particularly digital machines, is quite recent. The Greek word "techné" that lies at the root of the modern word "technology" referred to techniques rather than to machines. Techné referred to pottery, weaving, and music making. On this model, pedagogy and the curriculum could also be included in the concept of educational technology. In fact, the first widespread use of the term "educational technology" in the 1950s and 1960s, returned to this Greek original meaning of techné by referring not so much to machines as to any systematic application of learning science in classrooms (Skinner, 1968).

It is interesting to note that in shifting our gaze from everyday current practice to theory we are not just going back in time, but more significantly, we are stepping back from the surface of time to take a larger temporal perspective. This stepping back to see from a larger perspective enables us to consider, for example, that the meaning or understanding of the term technology changes over time to refer to that which is experienced as new. This theoretical stance reveals that the apparently obvious everyday distinction of technology with non-technology, where technology means digital, is a local manifestation of a broader distinction between that which is new and requires thoughtful consideration in contrast to that which is already established and so can be taken for granted. Technology, it seems, is not so much a thing in the world as it is a way of looking at things in the world in terms of their function and their design.

Things that we take for granted as already established in education, such as the use of books and desks, are not always seen as a technology; they are part of the context within which and out of which we act. However, when something new comes along like, for example, wall chalk boards which arrived in classrooms in the early nineteenth century, then the question of function and design is raised for practitioners. Shifting from only having individual slates to also using a wall-mounted chalkboard was a challenge for practice: "When first introduced, the chalkboard went unused for many years until teachers realized that it could be used for whole group instruction. They had to change their thinking from individual slates to classroom slates" (Slade, 2001 quoted in Russell, 2006). New tools are technology not because they are digital but because decisions must be taken as to how to use them in ways that help to serve the perceived function of education.

7.1.2. Theory and Practice as Dialogues in Different Timescales

Plato and Aristotle understood theory to be contemplation of timeless truths as opposed to the more engaged stance of techné, which was about making things within time (or "poesis"). Epistemé (science) was said by Aristotle to refer to eternal knowledge, whereas techné, he claimed, referred only to things that changed in time (Aristotle, ca. 350 B.C.E/1925, ch. 3). This distinction between timeless truths and temporal practice has continued in the Western tradition of thought. This can still be seen today in the way in which fundamental science is sometimes contrasted to engineering and technology as if the one was finding timeless "laws of nature," and the other was about translating these into real-world contexts where they are applied to change things within time.

We agree with Aristotle that there is a useful distinction to be made between a theoretical perspective and a more practical perspective. Nonetheless, we disagree that they are fundamentally different in nature or that the theory perspective is outside of time: we claim that both are carried by dialogues within time but that they refer to dialogues operating at different scales of time. Conceptual understanding of the term technology from a more theoretical perspective still refers to the use of this term to signal a distinction within a dialogue. However, the dialogue of theory is longer-term and more global in its referencing than the dialogue of everyday practice.

The phrase "education technology" when used in everyday practical dialogues in classrooms refers to digital tools and so has a very different meaning from education technology as a concept in the longer-term dialogue of theory.

Conceptually, to think of something as technology is to think of it in terms of function and design. This is a contrast to the idea of pure or contemplative knowledge of the truth (epistemé) and also a contrast to unreflective practice. The key conceptual distinction here then is not about things in the world (laptops as technology and handwriting as not technology, for example) but about how we look at and think about what we do. Any aspect of education, if consciously approached as a question of the best design for a specific function, could be seen as technology and therefore as "education technology."

7.1.3. What Is "Education"?

If we look at how the term education is most commonly used in everyday language, we find that it refers to the education system of schools, colleges, and universities and is dominated by the closely linked ideas of literacy and numeracy. Despite the advent of the Digital Age, basic education still tends to be seen as reading, writing, and arithmetic, while more advanced education is still commonly associated with the mastery of knowledge contained in books (Pea & Cole, 2019).

To step back and take a more theoretical view of education, it helps to consider how education occurs in different cultures and at different times. Oral cultures, for example, understand education in a different way.

In oral societies, education tends not to involve schools, and nor does it involve the idea of knowledge in the form of representations that can be transmitted and stored in memory. As well as apprenticeship education through personal relationships (Rogoff, 2003), most oral societies have initiation ceremonies drawing young people into a living relationship with more generalized cultural voices sometimes referred to as "the ancestors" (Turner, 1987). There is usually overlap between what might now be classified as education for productivity and education for cultural identity. Ethnographic accounts suggest that in most truly oral cultures, many learning activities involve initiation into a living relationship with the appropriate ancestor. Malinowski brings out how the symbols of ancestors carved in the prow of fishing canoes in Melanesia were conceived as an essential part of productive technology (Malinowski, 2013, p. 116). In a similar way, the so-called "songlines" of Australian aborigines embed much useful productive knowledge in the form of a relationship with the land, animals, and plants and with the ancestors who first made the trails (referenced in the songs). Education into the songlines is not conceptualized as learning a store of useful representations, but rather as learning to hear the voices of the ancestors as they sing to the tribal member through features of the landscape (Watson & Chambers, 1989).

Stepping back to take a theoretical stance enables us to see the more general pattern that underlies both education in oral cultures and education in print literate cultures. Education can be characterized as guided induction into participation in the temporally long-term and spatially widespread dialogues of culture of which knowledge is an aspect. Knowledge cannot be separated from dialogues as it takes the form of answers to questions that are asked within dialogues, and answers change when the questions change as the dialogue develops. Education has two main interconnected functions: identity formation and the continuity of cultural practices. Guided induction into cultural long-term dialogues enables biological individuals and newcomers to the community to learn how to become "fully" human (i.e. culturally human as well as biologically human) by appropriating the culture which usually means learning how to talk with the ancestors and finding one's place among them. Guided induction into cultural practices is closely related to identity formation; it is about learning how to use the tools and techniques handed down by the ancestors and how to participate in dialogues about their use. In both strands, identity and practice, each generation explores and learns, both consciously and unconsciously, adding a little more to the stories and to the technologies of the culture and transmitting this additional information to succeeding generations.

7.2. Dialogism

We have already introduced the key idea of dialogic; that the meaning of a word in a dialogue is not fixed by its dictionary definition but depends upon its role within the dialogue. Significantly, the meaning of a word depends not only on what the speaker wants it to achieve but also on how it is actually taken up and used. This simple observation has profound consequences.

7.2.1. The Dialogic Gap Is Constitutive for Meaning

A difference between voices is essential for dialogue and for meaning. Dialogue occurs when two voices from different perspectives have to engage in a process of explaining things to each other. If two voices merge into complete unity then the dialogue between them ceases, and so the meaning ceases (Holquist, 2003). Voice is a term in dialogic theory for a unique perspective on the world that is the unit of analysis of a dialogue. Individual humans can speak with many voices. Things can also be given voice. Nations and abstract conceptual entities can similarly take on voice. Dialogism means that wherever there is meaning there is more than one voice in play.

7.2.2. Dialogic Space

Dialogic space is the space of possibilities that opens up when two or more incommensurate perspectives are held together in the creative tension of a dialogue (Wegerif et al., 2019). The use of the word incommensurate here is significant: it means that the different perspectives in the dialogue cannot be reduced to a single frame of reference or a single correct perspective. If that were to happen, the flow of meaning would cease. This dialogic space of multiple possible meanings is not reducible to any single "objective" external perspective. Externally a dialogue might be bounded within a classroom at a particular time taking place through audible words that can be recorded as sound waves and correlated with measurable neural changes, but internally it has a space of meaning that is unbounded and might range freely across many spaces and many times. This is not a simple ontological dualism; the inside and the outside of any given dialogue are inextricably bound up together as two aspects of the same unique dialogue.

7.2.3. The Inside:Outside and Outside:Inside Nature of Dialogic Relations

In any dialogue the person you are speaking to, the "addressee," is always already there at the beginning of the utterance just as you are there already on the inside when they frame their reply to you (Rommetveit, 1992). This can be understood if you think about where an utterance in a dialogue starts. If we respond to a question from a young girl playing with Legos, we use a different voice from when we respond to a line manager asking about productivity. In any dialogue we do not just address ourselves to the other as a physical object, a body, but we address them from within a relationship in which the words used are often as much theirs as ours.

This inside-out and outside-in nature of dialogues explains how education is possible at all. Education, as opposed to training, always requires what Bakhtin (2010) calls the persuasive voice that speaks to us as if from the inside.

7.2.4. We Learn as a Response to a Call

Learning occurs in education not only as constructivism suggests, as the active intention of learners trying to make sense of the world, but also as a response to being called out by the other, whether this other is conceptualized as a Specific Other, Generalized Other, or Infinite Other (Wegerif et al., 2019). Developmental studies suggest that the autonomous individual self, the self that decides what to learn, is not a starting point but a result of dialogic interaction in which the self of a new baby is called into being by their mother or other primary caregiver (Gallagher, 2020). In a similar way, each new "self position" (Hermans, 2018) is called into being within relationship with others. Sometimes these others are stand-ins for long-term dialogues and, following Mead, we call these "generalised others" (Mead, 1962). The mathematics teacher, for example, stands in for the long-term dialogue of mathematics. She does not only talk for herself but also for the whole living dialogue community of mathematics. Through the teacher mathematics calls to the students, and if they answer, then their voices are joined in that moment with the larger dialogue and they become, however peripherally, members of the dialogue community of mathematics; or, more simply, they become mathematicians.

7.2.5. Dialogic Double-Voicedness

Entering into dialogue implies a kind of double-identity or double-voicedness, which often looks like an oscillation between two identities over time. To simplify the experience for the sake of clarity: in the moment of speaking, we identify as one voice within the dialogue, and in the moment of listening we identify with the dialogue as a whole. This is not only true of face-to-face dialogues but of dialogues at every level including, for example, long-term cultural dialogues such as the dialogue of science. When we send a new article for review by a journal, we identify with that article and the specific contribution that it makes to the field; but when we review articles sent to us by a journal, we identify with the field of science that the journal represents and ask what contribution this article makes to the dialogue so far within that field. Being inducted into a dialogue is learning to be double in this way, both inside and outside at the same time.

7.2.6. Learning as the Expansion of Dialogue

Dialogic learning is not linear. Each new voice we acquire is a new perspective from which we can see the world. Acquiring a new voice does not necessarily mean that we must jettison our previous voices; more commonly we extend our repertoire of voices and expand our personal dialogic space, not so much progress from A to B as progress from A to A+B. Even when a new perspective is apparently much superior to an old one which it replaces (the way that Darwin's theory of evolution was superior to Lamarck's theory for example), the old voice does not completely disappear but hangs around in the dialogue as a site for alternative ideas to form. Recent discoveries about the inheritance of epigenetic traits have been described by some as a return to Lamarck; but if they are a return, this is only in relation to Darwin's perspective. The same is often true in individual moral development, sometimes voices we thought we had gone beyond, childish voices for example, have aspects such as innocence or playfulness that return revalued after a period of being rejected and marginalized.

Dialogic learning as the expansion of dialogue is both personal and collective. Each new discovery of science, for example, brings something into the dialogue that was previously outside of the dialogue. Every discovery, whether it is that slime mold can run mazes (Alexander et al., 2021) or that literacy changes the brain in a way that reduces holistic thinking (Dehaene, 2011), is not just a fact to add to a list of facts but is also a new way of seeing other things and so a new voice entering into the dialogue.

Dialogism does not imply that all voices should be equally valued. In the development of science and in the development of ethics, new voices often try to repress older voices and drive them to the margins for what appears to be good reasons at the time. However, it is seldom true that such repressed voices completely disappear from the dialogue. They remain as voices ready to return in new forms if new discoveries or changed circumstances call for them. The idea of learning as involving the expansion of dialogic space is perhaps a bit like the idea that ecological systems, such as the Amazon rainforest, evolve to support a diversity of organisms precisely because such biodiversity proves to be a good strategy for adapting to changing circumstances. In order even to understand why we should value some voices more than others, Darwin more than Lamarck for example, we need also to hear and to understand those other voices. Education needs to induct learners into a whole expanding dialogic space of culture if they are to understand judgments of true and false, right and wrong, as judgments always made in the context of a dialogue that is constantly evolving and the students themselves participating in and taking forward. Dialogic education is not so much about learning this or that, Darwin or Lamarck, but more about learning the whole dialogic space which gives significance to this or that.

7.3. The Theory of Educational Technology

When Gilbert Simondon (2017) argues that technology has its own drive to development, he does not mean that technology has agency on its own without humans being involved at all, but rather that biological organisms and technology form a couple, and it is this couple that has agency. The role of the engineer in a complex machine is not to impose their will on the machine from the outside, but to get to know the machine, to play with it and to understand it. By doing this, the engineer and the machine can generate a space of reflection and internal resonance. Simondon gives the specific example of the development of internal combustion engines with engineers anticipating how the machines can be better integrated internally and in relation to their environments. Similar arguments could be made about the role of educational theorists and designers in the development of education as a socio-technical system.

There is an understandable tendency to want to oppose human interests to technological interests and seek to return education to the needs of the authentic human. However, it is not possible to separate humans from technology. Homo sapiens emerged as a separate species of ape as part of the development of technologies of fire, flint tools, and language (Stiegler, 1998). Tensions occur because human technological evolution progresses at a different rhythm and timescale to human biological evolution. Some have argued that formal education was a response to the evolutionary challenge when technological systems developed too fast for biological systems to keep up (Geary, 2008). This view suggests that education augments biological humans with the technological skills that they need to support the larger socio-technical system that they are part of, such that this larger system can continue to reproduce and thrive.

The role of specific technologies, such as print literacy, in our thinking is perhaps becoming increasingly apparent because we are in a time of transition as significant as that which occurred when literacy replaced oracy as the dominant form of communication. In words written down by his student Plato, the oral thinker Socrates complained about the negative cognitive and moral consequences of writing that was, in his lifetime, sweeping through Greece (Plato, 2008). Ironically, we only know this because Plato wrote down Socrates' reflections on writing in the dialogue with Phaedrus, where he is reported as describing written words as like "orphans," "ghosts," and "dead seeds put out on flagstones in the heat of the sun" (Plato ca 400 B.C.E/2008). Today we hear very similar complaints from those concerned about the cognitive and moral dangers of the way young people are shifting away from print literacy to internet communication, which is more multimodal, more interactive, faster, and more fragmented (Poster, 2018; Pea and Cole, 2019).

7.4. Conversation Theory

If we accept the argument that what it means to be human is shaped by technology, especially the dominant mode of communication technology, then most theories of education that we use are now outdated because they uncritically assume the technology of print literacy. It follows that it might be useful to learn from more recent theories informed by advances in information and communications technology. One such theory is the "conversation theory" developed in the 1970s by cybernetician, Gordon Pask.

Conversation is understood by Pask as the most basic process of learning, the means by which voices (perspectives which could be human or machine) become informed about each other's "informings." Higher level coordinations take the form of "tokens" for lower-level coordinations (objects and events), which are themselves tokens for stabilities of sensorimotor activity and regular couplings with the environment. To form a "conversation," participants must formulate descriptions of themselves and their actions, explore and extend these descriptions, and carry forward the understanding that they generate together to a future activity. In order to learn, a person or system must be able to converse with itself and with others about what it knows (Pask, 1976: Sharples et al., 2010).

Pask influenced theories of education with technology put forward by later professors of Education Technology at the UK Open University, Diana Laurillard and Mike Sharples. Both Laurillard and Sharples, in their different theories of education with technology, claim to follow from Pask's conversational theory of learning that to be able to engage in productive conversation, all parties need access to a shared language and set of tools that enable the construction of shareable representations of whatever topics they are conversing about.

To elaborate, Pask's conversation theory has been applied by Sharples et al. (2010) and Laurillard (2002) to describe the processes involved in learning conversations supported by modern communications technologies. Sharples and colleagues develop and apply Pask in what they call "a mobile theory of learning" describing learning as a technology-mediated process of coming to know through conversations across contexts. Whereas learning was previously mostly described within institutional contexts, mobile technology it is claimed, allows for "seamless" learning between different contexts; but it does so through the conversational mechanism of feedback loops and resulting clarifications that Pask describes. Laurillard similarly develops and applies Pask in what she calls a "Conversational Learning Framework" (2002) which can be applied as a design framework for education in general (2011). Laurillard maintains that all complex learning involves "a continuing iterative dialogue between teacher and student, which reveals the participants' conceptions and the variations between them . . . . There is no escape from the need for dialogue, no room for mere telling, nor for practice without description, nor for experimentation without reflection, nor for student action without feedback" (Laurillard, 2002, p. 71). Laurillard's conversational framework is a theory of learning for the Digital Age, as the different aspects of dialogues and types of dialogue are matched to the affordances of different communications technology (e.g. attending to information through video then exploring through a web search, discussing in a webinar experimenting with a simulation, and finally expressing understanding using productive media which might be a word document or modeling software).

7.4.1. Commentary on Conversation Theory

Pask intended his theory of learning to work for machine learning as well as in hybrid human–machine contexts. Given that the technology he was working with, yes–no logic circuits, has no internality or awareness of how things feel, this implies the reduction of meaning to a single exterior surface. As system theorist Leydesdorff (2021) puts it, most technical theories, systems theory, and appeals to "big data" to understand learning assume an ontological monism that is incoherent. It is incoherent because there is no "view from nowhere" (Nagel, 1989). Biological systems begin at cell level precisely with a membrane distinguishing inside from outside. All that we know and can know must reach us filtered through—and generated by—such inside–outside membranes that separate systems.

Strangely, Pask's conversation theory is not dialogic. Dialogic meaning is not robotic interaction but an inter-illumination of different internalities that are external to each other. Dialogue works not by reducing differences to a single true external vision—a single text of explicit meanings expressed clearly in a shared language—but by expanding the shared space of reference and resonance (Bakhtin, 2010).

On the inside looking out, we are a perspective on the world or an opening on the world. Viewed by others on the outside, we are apparently located within one single objective or exterior world. In a dialogic ontology, the same duality is true of every figure since, as Bahktin said, "I hear voices in everything" (Bakhtin, 2010; Friedman, 2005). A figure, or concept term, or one of Pask's tokens, is only understandable in relation to its background or context. This relationship between figures and their grounds is not static but dialogic, giving rise to what Bakhtin called "an infinite potential for contextual meaning" (Bakhtin, 2010, p. 162). Dialogic learning, therefore, involves more than just making conceptual understanding explicit and external. It also encompasses the development of intuition and creativity by expanding empathy and understanding, even in situations where what has been learned cannot be verbally articulated. Whenever we teach a concept word, we also need to induct the student into the shared dialogic space within which the use of this word makes sense. Dialogic education is not therefore only about clarifying concepts and transferring explicit knowledge, but also about expanding the dialogic community or shared internality, such that those concepts have meaning.

7.4.2. Connectivism or Learning as Networking

"Connectivism" is claimed to be the first new theory of learning to emerge in the Digital Age. The theory came out of practice. Siemens and Downes taught a course called Connectivism and Connective Knowledge (CCK), at the University of Manitoba in 2008, with 25 registered fee-paying students but over 2,000 students online taking the course for free. The course used various technologies, including online broadcasting (RSS feeds), Second Life, blog posts in Moodle, and synchronous online meetings. These technologies supported processes that facilitate learning, selecting, and ordering resources—using tools like Flipboard—and creating, sharing, and accessing content using social media like YouTube and Flickr.

This 2008 course was described by Cormier and Siemens (2010) as a massive open online course (MOOC). Later, as MOOCs were developed using traditional transmission pedagogies, this first MOOC was retrospectively called a cMOOC (connectivist MOOC) in contrast to the sort of MOOCs run by EdX (created by MIT) and Coursera (originating out of Stanford) which were labeled as xMOOCs (eXtended MOOC, based on a traditional university course model). What makes cMOOCs different is the theory of connectivism created by Siemens and Downes (2005), which builds on the new affordances of the internet for education, viewing learning as networking and emphasizing the ability to traverse networks and integrate distributed knowledge.

Some critics have argued that this is not really a new theory but just a version of social constructivism. In response, Downes (2007) makes a clear distinction between constructivism and connectivism:

> In connectivism, a phrase like "constructing meaning" makes no sense. Connections form naturally, through a process of association, and are not "constructed" through some sort of intentional action. . . . Hence, in connectivism, there is no real concept of transferring knowledge, making knowledge, or building knowledge.

This is a very interesting claim. It challenges the cognitivist bias Downes claims lies behind all previous theories of learning, suggesting that learning is not just about memories in minds, but is also about real structures in the world. Non-human systems, machine learning programs or simple life-forms like slime mold, for example, can also learn to connect different sources of knowledge more efficiently in a way that helps them perform functions better (Alexander et al., 2021).

7.4.3. Commentary on Connectivism

As with conversation theory, the main theoretical problem with connectivism is the reduction of meaning to an exterior surface defined in terms of nodes and links. Linking nodes might explain how some computer programs learn, after all connectivism owes a debt to connectionism or building artificial neural networks that mimic some aspects of how the brain learns. It might also illuminate some kinds of cognition found in nature. But a dialogue between two people is not the same as a network linking two nodes because each partner in the dialogue has a kind of "internal" model of the other "external" person that they develop in the dialogue at the same time as reflecting on, and changing their own, thoughts and behavior as if from the perspective of a third party or witness position in the dialogue (Wegerif 2013). It is from this expansion of self-consciousness in dialogues that we learn to see from new perspectives and become "bigger" than we were.

7.5. A Dialogic Theory of Educational Technology

Combining a dialogic theory of education with the understanding of the central role of technology in education, and with what can be learned from the strengths and weaknesses of conversational learning theory and of connectivism, leads to the outline of a new dialogic theory of educational technology. This has three overlapping themes: connection, participation, and expansion.

7.5.1. Education Technology for Connection

Both the strength and weakness of connectivism as a theory of learning can be said to be the simplicity of its grammar: an ontology of nodes and links. However, education is not simply about forming networks; this might describe learning in some machines and some life-forms, like slime mold, but learning is only education when it impacts on identity and consciousness (Stojanov, 2017).

The idea of dialogic education has some overlap with the idea of education as networking, but it goes further by considering how learners expand their identity to include other voices. Essentially, dialogic education is about using the network to its full potential so that the network becomes a launching pad for new, more inclusive understanding, and a new dialogic community. The expansion of consciousness here is not based on a model of consciousness as tied to individual bodies, but of consciousness as an aspect of materially embodied dialogues. As Simondon explains, the "value of the dialogue of the individual with the technical object" is "to create a domain of the transindividual, which is different from the community" (2013, p. 343).

To give an example of how a dialogic theory of education technology builds on connectivism but goes further, let us consider how *Pol.is* works (https://pol.is/home). Pol.is, described as an AI-supported online debate and decision-making system, has been used in many contexts, perhaps most famously in Taiwan where it was introduced by digital minister Audrey Tang to improve democratic decision-making (Chang, 2021). Pol.is maps where people "are" in a dialogue, generating a kind of network with nodes being statements of opinion made by participants. Because of the map, participants can see where they share opinions or if they are at an extreme, and also exactly what they agree and disagree upon with others. In practice, the result of this software is to encourage people to converge on a shared solution through dialogue by deepening their understanding of divisive issues and valuing creative emergent solutions.

When an individual writes an opinion in a *Pol.is* debate, they naturally focus on their unique individual thoughts and experience. They locate themselves, through their "token," as a node in the network. However, stepping back and looking at the network they shift perspective to see themselves as if from the whole dialogue community. What develops from this is a more dialogic identity, both "my" voice on the inside talking outwards but also seeing or hearing the perspective of the dialogue, as if from the outside looking inwards to define and locate "my" voice as just one voice among others. In this process the individual does not lose their identity in the collective, but they expand their sense of identity to consider the point of view of the collective. They become more dialogic selves—double-voicedness as described previously—where "self" is not a static "thing" but a dynamic process, a continuous dialogue between inside and outside points of view. This approach to political decision-making was tried in Taiwan partly in response to the perception that traditional methods of democratic decision-making were no longer working well. While early days for this kind of experimentation, it is possible to hope that the combination of dialogic education and technologies such as Pol.is could enable people to reach out across ideological and community divides in the direction of the common good (Chang, 2021).

7.5.2. Education Technology for Participation

Pask's conversation theory claims that conceptual understanding emerges from dialogue and needs to be constantly refined and developed through a dialogue between many voices. We agree. However, this theory is limited in so far as it only seems to work for learning clear explicit concepts and does not aid in the understanding of dialogic space associated with those concepts. Its focus on the clarity of concepts fails to include the aspect of learning that is a shift in identity and an expansion of identity. As already outlined, the opening of dialogic space enables the expansion of identity as a double-voiced identity, taking on and becoming the dialogic community while remaining one voice within it. The dialogic space needed for education does not fall away once the key concept has been learned. That space remains essential to using and adapting the concept in new situations. It is a space of possibility needed for the emergence of innovation.

In educational design terms, this means that we need to open, widen, deepen, sustain, and focus dialogic spaces. Opening a dialogic space is often done by an educator who can point out an issue or a problem within a relationship with the student or students. Once a dialogic space has been opened, it is possible to widen it with a range of views which could be taken from voices on the internet, ranging from different interpretations of quantum theory or perhaps different ways to cook eggs. While this approach applies to every area of education, it is possibly most relevant to how we might be able to form a more collective and inclusive sense of global identity. Internet-mediated dialogues about identity issues between young people from different cultures have been shown to shift and expand identity in the direction of dialogic open-mindedness (Wegerif et al., 2019). Deepening is often a product of widening. The difference between views are sometimes such that conceptual frameworks which underpin them need to be examined and, in the process, deepened.

Technology can sustain these dialogues by giving them a physical form, perhaps a wiki, a web forum, or a website that is a focus for an online-mediated community of practice. Technology can also focus these learning dialogues by, for example, bringing together people with different views on the same concept so that they can teach each other (Abdu et al., 2022) or by potentially using a conversational agent to ask challenging questions, raising the key distinctions that the "human" interlocutors might not have raised (Tsivitanidou & Ioannou, 2021).

7.5.3. Education Technology for the Expansion of Time

Earlier in this chapter, discussing the concepts of technology and education, we highlighted the difference between local short-term practical dialogues and larger longer-term theoretical dialogues. Textbooks tend to represent the claims of the larger time context as if these were timeless truths. We suggest there are no truths outside of time but only cultural dialogues that education can help students participate in. Our dialogic theory of education technology is about how technology can be used to weave together small, local dialogues and long-term, more global dialogues of culture. This is a two-way movement, both a descent so that the insights carried by the larger dialogues can be brought to bear in interpreting immediate events, and an ascent, so that the larger longer-term level of dialogue can learn from each new experience and continue to develop. Successful education requires what Lemke called a "heterochrony" or bridge across timescales such that the timescale of local, face-to-face dialogues can be joined to the timescale of long-term, cultural dialogues (Lemke, 2000). Wertsch and Kazak (2011) suggested that concept words can be used in education as a kind of "ski lift" between levels of conceptual understanding from the more contextual to the more academic. We extend this metaphor to digital technology and replace the rather slow one-way ski lift metaphor with something more like a broad fiber-optic cable that can serve as a channel for electric sparks of dialogic inter-illumination.

The education technology literature offers many examples of how malleable artefacts can facilitate a dynamic dialogue between levels of time. One evocative example is the use of electronic whiteboards is reported by Sara Hennessy (2011), who describes how students could inscribe their own opinions about Elizabethan history on top of images of old works of art taken from that time. Learners then return to these, after further inputs and discoveries, to see how their views had changed over the scheme of work. Here, learners are not just learning about history, but actively participating in dialogues about how to interpret history. This sense of participation in the longer-term dialogue of history was then reinforced by the teacher guiding them to relate their views and points of disagreement to the debate continuing today among academic historians. The same shift from short-term dialogues, to long-term dialogues, applies in every area of the curriculum. For instance, we could move from everyday discussions of the meaning of "force" in the playground, to the concept of force that emerges from experiments like those conducted by Galileo, to listening in and vicariously participating in debates about conceptions of the meaning of force today in relation to gravity by research scientists.

The role of technology in the expansion of time is to link short-term dialogues to long-term dialogues, not only by providing a medium for the long-term dialogues but by providing dynamic links between the two timescales, connecting the experiment in the classroom, for example, to online video debates that carry forward the dialogue of science.

7.6. Discussion and Conclusion

In this chapter, we have put forward a dialogic theory of education technology intended to serve as a foundation for design. Our dialogic theory of education is that education is expanding dialogue, both by teaching students to be better at learning from dialogue with others and with otherness and through drawing them into participation in the long-term dialogues of culture. Communications technology has always played an essential role in mediating between different timescales, especially for educational purposes (i.e., the timescales of local, short-term dialogues and global, long-term dialogues). As mediating communications technology advances, so the form that education takes also has to change. Oral cultures facilitated an encounter with the living voices of tradition, the ancestors, using technologies such as masks, carvings, and cave paintings (Lewis-Williams, 2011). Inevitably each education system was limited to the members of the tribe, those who regularly spoke together face-to-face. Literate cultures have developed education systems for those who read the same print media, which understands itself as the transmission of objective knowledge, stored in the form of representations. The internet, with mobile and multimodal digital technologies, makes it possible to return to the dialogism of oral education. However, now, interconnected communications technology has the potential to support collective consciousness (Simondon's "transindividuality") at a global level. Dialogic pedagogy and technology design can first initiate students into dialogue as a means of learning, before then mediating between short-term local learning dialogues and longer-term global learning dialogues.

We began by outlining some of the challenges of the Digital Age and of the Anthropocene and claimed that a dialogic approach to the design of education and technology might help us to respond more effectively to these challenges. Having discussed how agency works in human–technology coupling, such that human engineers take on the function of anticipation in the larger machine of which they form a part, we are in a position to consider an alternative perspective. Indeed, it is possible to perceive our current state as the emergence of a global human–machine entity, shaped by the perspective of the future. Education technology is not just a way to reproduce our way of life, it is also a way to consciously design ourselves and to design our collective future. The reason we need a theory of education technology that goes beyond a simple theory of education is that the design process requires, as Simondon (2017) puts it, "a dialogue with technical objects." To design the future, we need to work constructively with the "voice" of technology as part of a broad synthetic vision of what flourishing means for the emerging global bio-socio-technical system of the future.

The theory of education technology that we propose as a foundation for design is taking dialogue seriously and designing for expanding dialogue. Provisionally and tentatively, we proposed a design framework for education technology consisting of a set of linked principles:

1. design for connection: drawing into networks through dialogic encounters with voices at different levels, the voices of individuals, and the cultural voices of generalized others;
2. design for participation: opening, widening, deepening, sustaining, and focusing dialogic spaces;
3. design for the expansion of time: building supports for a sustainable, two-way dialogic interaction between dialogues at different timescales from the short-term and local to the long-term and global.

Educational technology integrates the design of pedagogy and the design of technology. It is about the design of more dialogic selves as well as the design of technologically supported dialogic spaces. In a successful dialogue, a collective identity is formed without subordinating the individual voices involved. On the contrary, when dialogue works well, each participant feels expanded and enriched. One hope that we have for this dialogic theory of Educational technology is that it might help to facilitate a direction of overcoming not only the apparent alienation between humans and other humans, but also the apparent alienation between humans and technology. The vision motivating us is that an expanded dialogic collective consciousness might one day be able to appropriate the increasingly interconnected global network of technologies to promote a global flourishing that is more than simply human flourishing. It is as if we have been building a collective body together, a giant body with fiber-optic nerveways connecting a vast number of powerful and wonderfully intricate sensing devices and productive machines. But this new giant that we have built together lacks a soul. Dialogic education with technology is about how we can grow together to become the collective soul needed to inhabit our new collective body. We began this chapter with a rather negative story of how, if we want to continue to thrive and perhaps even to survive, we need to respond to the challenges presented to us by the Digital Age and by the Anthropocene. That is one way of looking at our situation—a reactive way. The proactive alternative version of this same story is that the convergence of the Digital Age and the Anthropocene offers an extraordinary opportunity, a chance to create something that has never been seen before in history: a planetary-wide, self-regulating organism. A dialogic theory of education technology is not going to achieve this epochal transformation all on its own (Wegerif & Major, 2024). However, we put this theory forward as one tool that might be useful: a foundation for the design of the kind of education needed if we are to flourish together in the future.

References

Abdu, R., Olsher, S., & Yerushalmy, M. (2022). Pedagogical considerations for designing automated grouping systems: The case of the parabola. *Digital Experiences in Mathematics Education, 8*, 99–124. https://doi.org/10.1007/s40751-021-00095-7

Alexander, V. N., Bacigalupi, J. A., & Garcia, Ò. C. (2021). Living systems are smarter bots: Slime mold semiosis versus AI symbol manipulation. *Biosystems, 206*, 104430.

Aristotle. (1925). *Nichomachean ethics: Book 6.* (W. D. Ross, Trans.). The Internet Classics Archive. http://classics.mit.edu/Aristotle/nicomachaen.6.vi.html (Original work published 350 B.C.E.)

Bakhtin, M. M. (2010). *Speech genres and other late essays.* University of Texas Press.

Carr, N. (2010). *The shallows: How the internet is changing the way we think, read and remember.* Atlantic Books.

Chang, A. W. S. (2021). Making our best move with Audrey Tang and Taiwan's digital democracy. *American Quarterly, 73*(2), 363–369.
Cormier, D., & Siemens, G. (2010). The open course: Through the open door—Open courses as research, learning, and engagement. *EDUCAUSE Review, 45*(4), 31–39.
Dehaene, S. (2011). The massive impact of literacy on the brain and its consequences for education. *Human Neuroplasticity Education, 117*, 19–32.
Downes, S. (2007). What connectivism is. https://halfanhour.blogspot.com/2007/02/what-connectivism-is.html
Downes, S. (2012*). Connectivism and connective knowledge: Essays on meaning and learning networks*. National Research Council Canada.
Friedman, M. (2005). Martin Buber and Mikhail Bakhtin. In Bela Banathy & Patrick M. Jenlink (Eds.), *Dialogue as a means of collective communication* (pp. 29–39). Springer.
Gallagher, S. (2020). *Action and interaction*. Oxford University Press.
Geary, D. C. (2008). An evolutionarily informed education science. *Educational Psychologist, 43*(4), 179–195.
Geeng, C., Yee, S., & Roesner, F. (2020, April). Fake news on Facebook and Twitter: Investigating how people (don't) investigate. In *Proceedings of the 2020 CHI conference on human factors in computing systems* (pp. 1–14). ACM. https://dl.acm.org/doi/10.1145/3313831.3376784
Greenfield, S. (2015). Mind change: How digital technologies are leaving their mark on our brains. Random House.
Greenwood, D. J., & Levin, M. (1998). *Introduction to action research: Social research for social change*. Sage.
Hennessy, S. (2011). The role of digital artefacts on the interactive whiteboard in mediating dialogic teaching and learning. *Journal of Computer Assisted Learning, 27*(6), 463–586. doi: 10.1111/j.1365-2729.2011.00416.x
Hermans, H. J. (2018). *Society in the self: A theory of identity in democracy*. Oxford University Press.
Holquist, M. (2003). *Dialogism: Bakhtin and his world*. Routledge.
Laurillard, D. (2002). *Rethinking university teaching: A conversational framework for the effective use of learning technologies*. Routledge.
Laurillard, D. (2013). *Teaching as a design science: Building pedagogical patterns for learning and technology*. Routledge.
Lemke, J. L. (2000). Across the scales of time: Artifacts, activities, and meanings in ecosocial systems. *Mind, culture, and activity, 7*(4), 273–290.
Lewis-Williams, D. (2011). *The mind in the cave: Consciousness and the origins of art*. Thames & Hudson.
Leydesdorff, L. (2021). Evolutionary and institutional triple helix models. In Loet Leydesdorff (Ed.), *The evolutionary dynamics of discursive knowledge* (pp. 89–113). Springer.
Linell, P. (2009). *Rethinking language, mind and world dialogically: Interactional and contextual theories of human sense-making*. Information Age Publishing.
Malinowski, B. (2013). *Argonauts of the western Pacific: An account of native enterprise and adventure in the archipelagoes of Melanesian New Guinea [1922/1994]*. Routledge.
Mead, G. H. (1962). *Mind, self, and society from the standpoint of a social behaviorist* (reprint). Chicago University Press.
Nagel, T. (1989). *The view from nowhere*. Oxford University Press.
Pask, G. (1976). *Conversation theory*. Applications *in education and epistemology*. Elsevier.

Pea, R., & Cole, M. (2019). The living hand of the past: The role of technology in development. *Human development*, 62(1-2), 14–39.
Plato. (2008). Phaedrus. (B. Jowett, Trans.). Forgotten Books.
Poster, M. (2018). *The second media age*. John Wiley & Sons.
Rogoff, B. (2003). *The cultural nature of human development*. Oxford University Press.
Rommetveit, R. (1992). Outlines of a dialogically based social-cognitive approach to human cognition and communication. In A. Wold (Ed.), *The dialogical alternative: Towards a theory of language and mind* (pp. 19–45). Scandanavian Press.
Russell, M. (2006). Technology and assessment: The tale of two interpretations (pp. 137–152). Information Age Publishing.
Sharples, M., Taylor, J., & Vavoula, G. (2010). A theory of learning for the mobile age. In *Medienbildung in neuen Kulturräumen* (pp. 87–99). VS Verlag für Sozialwissenschaften.
Siemens, G. (2005). Connectivism: A learning theory for a digital age. *International Journal of Instructional Technology and Distance Learning*, 2(1), 3–10.
Simondon, G. (2013). *L'individuation à la lumière des notions de forme et d'information*. Éditions Jérôme Millon.
Simondon, G. (2017). *On the mode of existence of technical objects*. Univocal Publishing.
Skinner, B. F. (1968). *The technology of teaching*. Appleton-Century-Crofts.
Stiegler, B. (1998). *Technics and time: The fault of Epimetheus* (Vol. 1). Stanford University Press.
Stojanov, K. (2017). *Education, self-consciousness and social action: Bildung as a neo-Hegelian concept*. Routledge.
Tsivitanidou, O., & Ioannou, A. (2021). Envisioned pedagogical uses of chatbots in higher education and perceived benefits and challenges. In *International Conference on Human-Computer Interaction* (pp. 230–250). Springer.
Turkle, S. (2011) *Alone together: Why we expect more from technology and less from each other*. Basic Books.
Turner, V. (1987). Betwixt and between: The liminal period in rites of passage. In Mahdi L, Foster S, Little M (Eds.), *Betwixt and between: Patterns of masculine and feminine initiation*. La Salle, Illinois: Open Court Publishing Company.
Watson, H., & Chambers, D. W. (1989). *Singing the land. Signing the land*. http://singing.indigenousknowledge.org/
Wegerif, R. (2013). Dialogic Education for the Internet Age. Routledge.
Wegerif, R., Doney, J., Richards, A., Mansour, N., Larkin, S., & Jamison, I. (2019). Exploring the ontological dimension of dialogic education through an evaluation of the impact of Internet mediated dialogue across cultural difference. *Learning, Culture and Social Interaction*, 20, 80–89.
Wegerif, R., & Major, L. (2024). *The Theory of Education Technology: a dialogic foundation for design*. Taylor & Francis/Routledge.
Wertsch, J. V., & Kazak, S. (2011). Saying more than you know in instructional settings. In Timothy Koschmann (Ed.), *Theories of learning and studies of instructional practice* (pp. 153–166). Springer.
Winograd, T., Flores, F., & Flores, F. F. (1986). *Understanding computers and cognition: A new foundation for design*. Intellect Books.

SECTION 3
THE ROLE OF DIGITAL TECHNOLOGIES

The most influential impact in contemporary societies during the last two decades, and of utmost importance in relation to conceptions of dialogues, is the growth of digital technologies. The process of digitalization is leading to fundamental social change affecting all spheres of social life. Digital technologies in all their diversity have moved from being mainly about information handling toward a dominance of communication and a flow of text production especially with the growth of social media. As such, these technologies have become the main means of human interaction in our societies. With the impact of social media we have moved from a positive attitude toward the possibilities represented by such technologies for global communication, to a much more dystopian and negative prospect by the implications these technologies now have on disinformation, hateful comments, lack of privacy, and limitations for genuine dialogues. Especially the last point has become a key concern during the last couple of years, as the algorithms of these technologies influence our daily life in different ways and structure the flow of communication and dialogue in certain ways, leading to more individualization and challenges to democratic processes in our societies—what is often referred to as "the filter bubble," "echo chambers," "trolling," and similar terms.

There is a growing understanding that provision of education becomes very important in highly digitalized societies, in ways to develop competencies and understandings, as well as core values that both take advantage of the communicative possibilities provided by digital technologies and how we deal with the challenges of technological developments mentioned above. Dialogic perspectives are at the center of these perspectives, as shown by the chapters in this section. Even though a common feature across the three chapters is about how digital communication technologies provide possibilities and challenges for developing dialogic approaches with young people, each chapter has its own distinct context based on diverse empirical approaches and different aspects of dialogic theory as linked to Rommetveit.

Rasmussen and Warwick, in Chapter 8, examine the potential for co-constructing knowledge in the context of classroom-based interactions, employing a microblogging tool based on data from an international research project in Norway and England. Their aim is to view technology-mediated classroom dialogue through the lens of the idea of attuning to the attunement of the other to achieve intersubjectivity in collaborative activities.

In Chapter 9, Silseth, Erstad, and Arnseth also draw on data from an international project. They discuss how digital technologies offer opportunities for dialogues across time and space between young people in different countries across the world. The chapter illustrates how many of the ideas about meaning-making and interaction put forward in this field by Rommetveit and others are still relevant and important for exploring the dialogues that emerges in online communities.

Saviano (Chapter 10) explores how dialogue in a particular digital setting can transform into something toxic. He uses participant observation data of the online computer game *League of Legends*, focusing on blame for negative in-game events as a central motivator. This form of online dialogue is discussed in relation to theorization of intersubjectivity.

The three chapters represent new contexts and approaches to familiar ideas and concepts from Rommetveit, especially on conceptions of intersubjectivity. And as Saviano asks in his introduction: "is dialogue within this new domain similar to offline dialogue, or is it something fundamentally different?" All three chapters present new and important understandings of this question.

8
Using Microblogging to Create a Space for Attending and Attuning to Others

Ingvill Rasmussen and Paul Warwick

8.1. Introduction

[I]n the most fruitful dialogues ideas emerge as a result of fruitful mis-understanding. What I mean by that is the following: A person says something, and I read something into it *beyond what he or she meant*. The meaning of one's own words may under optimal dialogical conditions be expanded and deepened by one's conversation partner's interpretation of them.

Ragnar Rommetveit, in conversation with
Ingrid Josephs (1998a, p. 200)

In this chapter, we examine the potential for co-constructing knowledge in the context of classroom-based interactions employing a microblogging tool (similar to X - formerly Twitter - and other social media platforms but designed for use in co-located interactions in the classroom). The aim here is to view technology-mediated classroom dialogue through the lens of specific ideas evident in the thinking of Ragnar Rommetveit—specifically, the idea of attuning to the attunement of the other (Rommetveit, 1998a) to achieve intersubjectivity in collaborative activities. In doing so, we draw on work from an international research project that examined the use of a microblogging tools in classrooms in Norway and England.

The purpose of this chapter is therefore to present a theoretical reflection on Rommetveit's ideas of attunement and intersubjectivity, informed by broad research findings related to the fields of classroom dialogue and technology mediated learning. In order to "breathe life" into, and provide context for, some of the arguments engaged in below, we draw on an example from our data to illustrate, emphasize and strengthen points made in the text. We present three vignettes of classroom practice from of our research to illustrate ideas about "the dialogic classroom" and technology-mediated learning; and, centrally, to revitalize ideas about intersubjectivity and attunement in light of contemporary classroom experiences.

Classroom dialogues that mix microblogging and face-to-face interactions have become a legitimate focus of investigation since young people today communicate extensively via this short multimedia text format on various social media platforms. Communication via multimedia posts have been seen as vulnerable to what might be termed "unfruitful mis-understanding"—to the projection and replication of biases—rather than as a space for open, reasoned dialogue and debate. This is particularly the case in areas where information paints a complex picture and where there is no simple solution to a problem. While discussions on X and other social media are vulnerable to the projection of bias, studies show that, when combined with "conventional" dialogue, co-located microblogs can provide students with numerous ways to share and explore their viewpoints and their developing ideas in a more fruitful manner, both within a group and more widely (Frøytlog & Rasmussen, 2020; Omland, 2021). Such a hybrid format for interaction, where messages have the permanence of writing (Ong, 1982; Dysthe, 1996) and can be manipulated for varying purposes in relation to the spoken dialogue, presents interesting opportunities for the examination of how students collaborate, make sense, and co-construct knowledge. Following this interest, we focus here on students working in a peer group and present an analysis of how a combination of spoken dialogue and microblogging might promote students' attention and attunement to the ideas of others and promote intersubjectivity across a classroom community.

As we have indicated, we exemplify our thinking with an analysis of a single lesson, in this case focusing on socioscientific issues (SSI). This choice is purposeful; in science education, the study of SSI encompasses "social dilemmas" that have no simple solution (Sadler, 2004, p. 513). We see engagement with SSI in the classroom as particularly well-suited to a dialogic pedagogy (Mercer, 2000; Michaels et al., 2008), which we discuss further below. At this point, however, we raise the idea that in circumstances where complex issues lack clear solutions, it is important to attend to different ideas and not arrive at a conclusion prematurely. In such cases, one key aspect of such collective knowledge-building practices concerns the collaborative and interactional work needed to achieve shared meanings or intersubjectivity, while maintaining an openness to exploration.

Classroom dialogues that mix microblogging and face-to-face interactions present changes—in comparison to "conventional" classroom dialogues—to the ways that others might influence us. In other words, when students take part in technology-mediated classroom dialogue, this changes the premise. Student groups are not constrained to the consideration of their own ideas or that of a single peer group; and the role of the teacher seems crucial in determining which ideas will be brought into play within the classroom community. Analyzing students' interactions in a lesson that focuses on SSI provides therefore an appropriate context in which to examine the idea of "attuning to the attunement of others" to achieve intersubjectivity through a combination of speech and the "voice" of technology.

8.2. Socioscientific Reasoning, Intersubjectivity, and Technology-Mediated Dialogue

Engagement with SSI is not constrained by a purely scientific frame of reference; moral, ethical, economic, religious, and societal considerations are also involved. Such work requires the consideration of a range of alternative or complementary perspectives and, usually, agreement within a group or community on a shared position to be taken forward. But intersubjective reciprocal processes are complex, especially when several modalities mediate interactions; a combination of oral, written, and spatial modalities—with digital objects of attention being manipulated in different ways—therefore makes analysis complex and interesting.

Rommetveit offered a theoretical framework that focused on dialogue as a bridge between the individual level and the societal level. He argued that we are "shareholders" rather than "owners of our language" and that we "co-author" meanings rather than "transmit" information from speaker to listener (cited in Heen Wold, 1992). Utterances are potentials to be realized, and this realization only happens if the listener attunes to the speaker and accept the speakers' premises. The fact that utterances are only potential messages raises the challenge of how we interpret utterances, given their vagueness and incompleteness. Such incompleteness or vagueness of language can act as a prompt to attend, and to create a relational or "dialogical space" that I and You need to step into to achieve intersubjectivity. We interpret this process as also an opening for creative and improvised language use, including fruitful as well as unfruitful understandings and misunderstanding.

The problem of making sense of the message potential in utterances, as described by Rommetveit, seems to be accentuated in technology mediated dialogues, and perhaps in particular when using platforms such as X that include short and often incomplete microblogs. It is worth noting, in this context, that microblogs in such social media platforms do not stand in the same sequential time-space order as the flow of face-to-face dialogues. The order of technology mediated communication is a result of the specific design of the platform and the temporal interaction of participants with it, bringing a potential additional layer of complexity to the idea of intersubjectivity in classroom interactions.

To add to the complexity, our view is that the teacher has a vital role in facilitating expectations and responsibilities with regards to classroom dialogue. Before we consider this role, however, our use of the terms dialogue and dialogic pedagogy requires clarification. A "dialogic pedagogy," while acknowledging the need for different modes of classroom talk (Mortimer & Scott, 2003), encourages specific forms of dialogue known to be productive for students' learning (Littleton & Mercer, 2013); in particular, it places an emphasis on the importance of reasoning, rational argument, building on the ideas of others, querying, explaining, and justification in co-constructing knowledge (Howe & Abedin, 2013; Mercer et al., 1999; Mercer et al., 2004). This talk has been termed "accountable talk" (Michaels et al., 2008), "academically productive talk" (Michaels & O'Connor, 2015) or "exploratory talk" (Mercer, 2000) and can be thought of as a social mode of reasoning in which people engage constructively with each other's ideas (Mercer et al., 1999, p. 97). Such dialogic features of talk seems instrumental in creating a "dialogic space" (Wegerif, 2006) for both attunement to the ideas of others and intersubjective engagement with the ideas being expressed by members of a classroom community.

In a "dialogic classroom," where attunement and intersubjectivity are intentionally considered, the teacher is key in framing the importance and nature of dialogic engagement between members of the classroom community. They can determine whether or not dialogic learning intentions are incorporated into lesson planning (Warwick et al., 2020); they can model and encourage dialogic interactions in whole class settings; they can help students to develop and use ground rules for talk in their group interactions (Mercer et al., 2004); they can focus group and class attunement on specific ideas and guide the intersubjectivity of participants in class dialogues; and they can determine the extent to which students reflect on their metacognitive understanding of talk as a learning tool. For these reasons, the teacher is a central element in our illustration of intersubjective engagement with SSI in the vignettes presented below.

More broadly perhaps, classrooms in which there is an intentional focus on dialogue are ones in which there is a focus on both the "message potential of utterances" and the ways in which words and phrases form the foundations of "fruitful mis-understanding." In considering "genuinely social-interactional and collective features of language" (Rommetveit, 1998b, p. 218) and the nature of dialogue across our data set (and our own teaching), we have noted that dialogue can be extended with words like "might be," "maybe," "I wonder if," "probably," "perhaps," and "possibly." Maine (2015) noted that such terms and phrases represent a "language of possibility," with such "potentiating" language creating a "space for the exploration of ideas" (p. 60). Here, Maine was drawing on Boyd et al. (2017, 2019, p. 2), who highlighted the use of specific words and phrases associated with speculation and reasoning in creating a "language of possibility space" for the open exploration of ideas.

We focus on the performative nature of this kind of talk, which views language as both shaped by and exerting effects on the social world (Enqvist-Jensen et al., 2017). The use of such words will of course be only a part of wider dialogic exchanges. But Boyd and Kong (2017) made it clear that, depending on context, they can act to: i) introduce reasoning, linking some markers to speculating and proposing; ii) indicate the hypothetical nature of claims or indicate the seeking of agreement through questioning, linking some markers to positioning or making claims; or iii) connect a reason to an assertion, either to deny such a link or to pose a question as a challenge, linking some markers to analyzing and generalizing. The use of such markers can perhaps be seen as similar to "hedging" in scientific writing, where language is used as a means of expressing "possibility rather than certainty and collegiality rather than presumption" (Hyland, 1998, p. viii). To us, the spoken language of possibility seems particularly suited to joint explorations between students about complex issues of SSI, to which there might not be a clear resolution; and our examination of the science lessons from this project, featured below, seems to add weight to this assertion. In such cases, attunement to the attunement of others, and the intersubjectivity that drives collective and individual knowledge construction, seem central.

8.3. Microblogging in Classroom Interactions

In the lesson that we present to support and illustrate arguments made here, the teacher uses the microblogging tool Talkwall to facilitate direct, real-time engagement with the wider ideas of the class. Talkwall is a microblogging tool designed to support the practices central to a dialogic pedagogy (Rasmussen & Hagen, 2015; Smørdal, et al., 2021). In the following, and in Figure 8.1, we briefly describe some of the functionality and affordances for attunement and intersubjectivity that our research has evidenced in Talkwall.

Talkwall is designed to facilitate students' collaborative discussions about a question or challenge, usually posed by the teacher. Students post short textual contributions to a shared "feed" with secure access through a generated PIN available to the students. These short contributions are therefore visible only to the class and can be interactively arranged on "walls" to promote further discussion—in effect, the posts become dialogic objects of attention. Talkwall seems, therefore, well-suited to a more open exploration of student ideas.

In terms of collaborative processes, microblogging technology such as Talkwall can facilitate direct, real-time engagement with the utterances, or message potentials, of the immediate community—in this case, the class. The

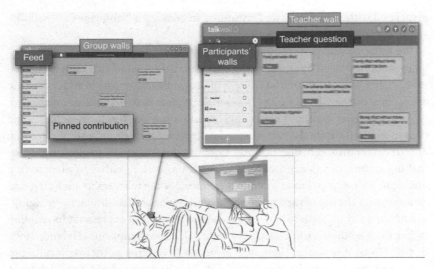

Figure 8.1. Talkwall.
Contributions are visible in the feed and can be pinned on group walls, edited. or built on. Students can organize ideas on their wall. Teachers control the teacher wall, which is displayed for participants. The teacher can also display the participants' walls.

ways in which other groups or individuals are attuning to the demands of a task are immediately evident, enabling intersubjective engagement with a range of ideas and perspectives. Thus, student groups are not constrained to the consideration of their own ideas; and the teacher can orchestrate the ways in which the ideas of others are directly employed by groups, influencing their views and perspectives (Chin & Osborne, 2010). However, the fact that such opportunities are present does not mean that they are redeemed in practice; whether the "action possibilities" of a combined oral dialogue and microblogging environment become "enacted affordances", thereby promoting and sustaining intersubjectivity, seems to depend very largely on the idea that that technology must be used in a way that is consistent with an appropriate pedagogy, to support students' collaborative sense-making processes in practice (Major et al., 2018; Warwick et al., 2020).

8.4. Vignettes of Classroom Attunement and Intersubjectivity

To illustrate how a combination of spoken dialogue and microblogging might promote students' attention and attunement to the ideas of others, we present episodes from a single lesson focusing on the pros and cons of autonomous vehicles. The lesson was designed and structured by the teacher to reflect many of the dialogic practices of science communities engaged in the study of SSI (Sadler et al., 2007). The lesson was divided into distinct phases to ensure an increasingly dialogically complex set of tasks, starting with a microblog activity in which the teacher elicited students' knowledge and what they wanted to learn. The "guide question" posed for the initial phase was "What do we know or want to know about autonomous vehicles?" with Talkwall employed as the medium for group responses. The class watched a video together on autonomous vehicles, gathering evidence of the advantages and disadvantages of autonomous vehicles from it; and with this information as a starting point, they discussed their own and other people's ideas about the question "What are the advantages and disadvantages of driverless cars?" Their conclusions were placed on the contribution feed of Talkwall, as individual groups came to agreement about which of their ideas they wished to present to the class.

The students were aged 11–12 years, which is the age of first-year secondary school students in England. The class of 23 boys and girls was divided into groups of three, with one iPad per group. The focus group for this lesson consisted of a triad of boys.

Our analysis, presented below, follows how the group of three boys makes sense of, attends and attunes to ideas, first in their group discussions and then to ideas from the wider classroom community presented digitally in microblogs. In Excerpt 1, we follow the peer group and their interactional work as they attempt to make sense of each other's ideas. In Excerpt 2, we see how the technology is integrated into the group dialogue. Lastly, in Excerpt 3, we follow how the students attend to ideas from the wider classroom community.

8.4.1. Who Is to Blame If the Car Crashes?

We enter the peer group dialogue in a part of the lesson in which the teacher asks his students to consider the question "What are the advantages and disadvantages of driverless cars?" The students are seated in groups, side-by-side, with Felix[1] in the middle, using one iPad for their own "group wall" (see Figure 8.2). Having watched the video together, the purpose of the interaction was to attune to and query, where appropriate, each other's ideas about the question posed by the teacher. In the analysis we will focus in on how the students use language to keep the dialogue open for exploration.

---

[1] All names are anonymized.

Figure 8.2. Attending to others' ideas via the feed.

> **Excerpt 1**
>
> 1. Zach: The disadvantages: Who is to blame if the car crashes? The manufacturer or the owner?
> 2. Felix: Not the owner, because the owner was just sitting in the car, basically.
> 3. Zach: Exactly! So was it their fault, or was it the manufacturer's?
> 4. Felix: No!
> 5. Zach: That is the question [speaks with staccato intonation while hammering hand on desk in a humorous way], and is it the manufacturer's fault if the car hits someone, or is it the owner of the car's fault?
> 6. Felix: If the owner has done nothing but sit in the car, then it's not their fault.
> 7. Zach: They could have raised the alarm, couldn't they?
> 8. Felix: Zach, what you're trying to say doesn't make much sense because Zach, it's like saying that if I'm sitting in a bus and someone else is driving it, if someone crashes the bus, and you're saying you can blame it on me.
> 9. Zach: No, because you don't own the bus.
> 10. Felix: Yeah...
> 11. Zach: But when you own the car, it's different.
> 12. Felix: Yes, but if they were like—say I was sitting on a bus and I don't own that bus, but the bus is driving itself, and then the bus crashes...

13.	Zach:	No, because the man is driving [the bus].
14.	Felix:	Zach, I don't get your [point].
15.	Tony:	What if it's a driverless car, then the driver's done nothing to stop the [inaudible].
16.	Zach:	I know, but if a pedestrian walked past, and the car ran him over, is that the person's fault for not looking out, or the car's?
17.	Tony:	Well, if the person can't do anything about it then it's only...
18.	Zach:	Well, they can raise the alarm. They could have pressed the brake, because I presume these cars have brakes.
19.	Tony:	Well yeah, but if that happens, it's only if the driverless car could actually press the brakes.
20.	Zach:	No, their operating [system] allow—[inaudible] steering [pointing to projector].
21.	Tony:	Yeah, so you could take control of the car, and if they had taken control of it, then they'd be held responsible. If they hadn't taken control of it, then maybe they wouldn't.

The excerpt commences with Zach suggesting that they start with the disadvantages of autonomous vehicles. Zach moves to develop the group's thinking by asking whether the manufacturer or the owner of the vehicle would be to blame if a crash occurs. In the turn that follows, Felix says that the owner would not be to blame because they have "done nothing but sit in the car." Zach agrees and builds on this point by again posing the question "Was it their fault or was it the manufacturer's?" His uptake indicates that he agrees with Felix's description that they have "done nothing but sit in the car" but that this does not resolve the ethical dilemma of blame. Zach pursues this in a humorous way when he speaks with a staccato intonation, saying that "That is the question"—(i.e. who is to blame when such a car crashes). Felix, on the other hand, stays with his argument that one cannot be blamed when one has done nothing, at which point Zach uses the language of possibility to explore what the owner could have done (raised the alarm).

In the exchanges that follow between Zach and Felix (turns 8–14), the distinction between occupant and owner is problematized, and they seem to misunderstand each other. The struggle to understand is clearly stated in line 14: "Zach, I don't get your point." At this juncture, Tony interjects, using the language of possibility to continue the exploration of the ethical dilemma of blame and autonomous vehicles; he poses a "what if" question (line 15). Here, we see that Zach says, "I know," which one might take as an attunement to Felix's utterance and the ethical dilemma of "blame." Zach then continues shifting the focus of the discussion from the driver and owner to an imagined person who is run over by an autonomous car. Zach asks if the person who is run over can be to blame (for not looking out). By so doing, he brings the idea of responsibility more to the fore. In line 17, we see how Tony attunes to this shift and that Tony follows up with a suggestion about what a driver "can" and "could" do (line 18). Zach and Tony continue to explore what "could" happen if the driver was able to take control of the car, referring to the film the class watched together, and the moral issue of responsibility is addressed (lines 20 and 21).

Moral issues and questions related to responsibility, agency, and control over technology are identified and put forward in the dialogue among the three boys. Here we see how, by using the language of possibility to explore the complexity of their original idea, the group engages with the range of possible outcomes to a scenario (Sadler et al., 2007). This exploration emerges despite their struggle to understand each other. The "what if" turn does not reject the previous turn but opens a dialogic space for further elaboration and expansion of complex moral questions. It is interesting to note that the group does not arrive at a conclusion but posts the moral question identified in their discussion on the group wall: "Who is to blame if the car crashes?"

The microblog post can be seen as a temporarily stabilizing of the flux of oral dialogue. In their dialogue, the students have taken the statement of another and attempted to move *"beyond what he or she meant"* (Rommetveit, 1998a, p. 200) and come to provisional collective agreement about the first thing they wish to know, based on the task of considering the advantages and disadvantages of autonomous vehicles. The three boys agree to form a moral question in relation to autonomous vehicles. Their question concerning such striving toward intersubjectivity and agreement is seen as central to engaging in productive dialogue in groups (Rommetveit, 1998). Clearly, agreement will not always be reached in group discussions, and provisional, tentative ideas are often the outcomes of such interactions. That said, here we see language providing "message potentials," relating what is said to the shared frame of reference for the task (Rommetveit, 1992). As the group moves to explore their shared or assumed knowledge and to express a relevant idea that might be posted, "what is made known draws both on what is said and what is taken for granted" (Edwards, 2020, p. 4).

8.4.2. "The Computer Could Go Crazy"

We will now follow the group as they continue to discuss the advantages and disadvantages of driverless cars. In Excerpt 1, they explore ideas from within the group about disadvantages. In Excerpt 2, they turn to the possible advantages—but after making some suggestions, they seem to run out of ideas. The purpose of the analysis is to show how the technology is integrated in the group dialogue as they attend to the blog contributions in the feed. It is important to return briefly and specifically to the role of the teacher here, as they mediate the interactions and learning through the ways in which they have set up tasks to be addressed through the technology, an idea that has been termed "vicarious scaffolding" (Warwick et al., 2010). But as we suggested above, the anticipated attunement to, and intersubjective engagement with, ideas within a group or wider classroom community are enabled through the active promotion of a dialogic classroom pedagogy; this too is the overarching responsibility of the teacher.

Excerpt 2

22. Felix: What are other advantages of [autonomous vehicles]? That was one disadvantage. An advantage could be, um . . .
23. Tony: . . . shorter travel times—
24. Felix: and pollution. [Typing] Travel times . . . [Typing[— ehmmm . . .
25. Zach: [points to the feed to a post from another group] Yeah, but the thing is, the computer could go crazy or run out of battery—cars have batteries already.
26. Felix: Yeah, yeah
27. Tony: —Yeah
28. Tony: Yeah [includes the post on their group wall] . . . . But, what else? What else do you think, Felix?
29. Felix: What happens if, like, an unsafe car goes out and begins driving? What if a car sends out, like, a wrong signal to the rest of the cars?

The excerpt starts with Felix inviting the others to pursue the task. He recollects that they have already identified one disadvantage. The pace of the dialogue is slow. Tony suggests shorter travel times as an advantage, to which Felix adds "and pollution." He himself seems to dismiss this addition, as instead he types Tony's suggestion "shorter travel times" in the blog. Again, the dialogue comes to a short stop. In line 25, Zach points to the feed and reads a post from another group: "the computer could go crazy or run out of battery." Note that he starts by adding an agreement—"Yeah"—and closes with the addition that "cars have batteries already." Felix and Tony (lines 26–28) acknowledge this suggested

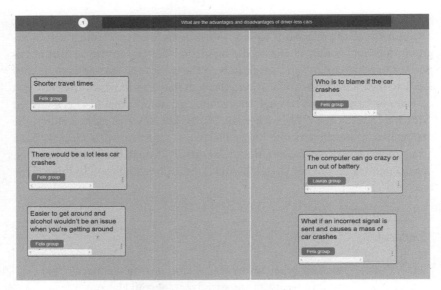

Figure 8.3. A recreation of the focus group's wall. *Their response to the teacher's first task: three advantages on the left and three disadvantages on the right.*

idea, introduced via the feed from the wider classroom community, and while Tony includes the blog on their "group wall," he invites Felix to add what else he might think (line 28). Felix elaborates on the topic of control over technology, as introduced in the blog from the feed, using the language of possibility. By so doing, he invites the others to explore further what might happen if an unsafe car begins to drive, and adds, "What if a car sends out, like, a wrong signal to the rest of the cars?" This initiation sparks an eager exploration in the group about the damages that this might cause.

As mentioned, in line 25, Zach comments on the blog that he points to in the feed (see also Figure 8.3). As such, Zach's utterance includes ideas produced by another group, his acknowledgment of that group's idea ("yeah"), and a correction or adjustment ("cars have batteries already"). This interaction with prior actions, the blog produced by another group, possible next actions, and the process of responding to the teacher's task reflect what Linell (2009) referred to as situation-transcending and double dialogicality (see also Silseth, Erstad, and Arnseth). The group's dialogue is taking place here and now, but in interaction with ideas produced by another group beforehand. This widens the *potential* frames of reference, in terms of the number of expressed ideas, with the students needing to grapple with multiple subjectivities. Here, the attempt to understand relies both on a shared understanding of the task and on the central role of language in creating and clarifying relational positions. It also relies, as we will see below, on groups giving appropriate levels of attention to ideas from outside their group.

Figure 8.3 displays the group's answer to the teacher's question posted on their "group wall" with three advantages and three disadvantages. Note that even though the students attend to an idea from another group introduced via the feed, the group mainly stays with their own ideas. All the blogs posted result from dialogues in the peer group, except for the blog attended to by Zack.

Observe also how the students use language. First, in line 28 and 29, the invitation from Tony to his peers "what else?" and the response "what if" from Felix. Both in this except and in Except 1, it seems that the group attunes to each other's inviting approach and that this helps them explore further ideas. The use of such invitations and the use of reasoning words is central to dialogic pedagogy, where the intention is to facilitate collaborative learning and exploration (Boyd & Kong, 2017; Mercer et al., 2004). Secondly, the boys frequently confirm each other's viewpoints (lines 25, 26, and 27). Such confirmations can be important to signal that we attend and attune to each other and/or signal intersubjective engagement. In technology-mediated settings, such signaling seems of particular importance as we give attention both to spoken utterances and to textual "utterances" on the screen.

One notable affordance of Talkwall is the "traveling" of knowledge and ideas from the classroom community. However, the presence of an opportunity, as we have made clear above, does not mean that it is redeemed in practice; what we observe here seems to be in line with that observation. The affordance of technology needs to be actualized by the task at hand. In the above excerpt, the students do attend to the feed but consider mainly their own ideas. It is thus interesting to observe in the next excerpt what happens when the teacher adds an additional task.

8.4.3. "I Think You Should Do That One"

In the last excerpt that we present, the teacher has just introduced an additional short task. After considering all the groups in his class and their blogposts in the whole class dialogue, he specifically asks the students to take a closer look at ideas from the wider classroom community. The students are given three minutes to discuss and select "three advantages on the left and three disadvantages on the right. Choosing others' "contributions—but not your own." In so doing, he draws the students' attention to the feed where more ideas are available for consideration. By selecting this excerpt, we draw attention to the importance of the teacher's task design and the relationship of the design to the students' uptake. We see that this task leads the students to consider the availability of knowledge and ideas from the wider classroom community made available in Talkwall. As such, the teacher's task design adds an additional layer and makes relevant affordances of the technology for widening the community of practice within the classroom. This illustrates the teacher's responsibility in designing and directing tasks that *require* attunement and engagement, within a shared task understanding, of the subjectivities of others.

In the following, we see the three boys' uptake of the teacher's task instruction.

Excerpt 3

1. Zach: I think you should do that one [pointing].
2. Tony: Yeah.
3. Felix: [reads out loud very quickly] Increasing the amount of homeless people because it can force driving inspectors, bus drivers, taxi drivers . . .
4. Zach: —'cause of loss of jobs—
5. Felix: Yeah, yeah yea:::h, that's a good one!
6. Tony: Because a lot of people will lose their jobs, won't they?
7. Felix: Yeah!

Excerpt 3 shows Zach attending to a blog by pointing and saying, "I think you should do that one." Both Felix and Tony acknowledge the suggestion. In this dialogue, the pace is quick, as indicated in the way that Felix reads aloud the content in the blog (line 3). Overlapping the reading is Zach's emphasis that a loss of jobs will result in increased numbers of homeless people. The dialogue can be characterized as cumulative (Mercer, 2000): all three are united in agreement that this is an important disadvantage. They also seem to agree that there is a connection between the introduction of driverless cars, loss of jobs, and homelessness. Note that both the blogs and the talk is quite indeterminate and that the communication is connected to pointing, attending, and reading of blogs.

The three boys in our focus group do attend to other ideas in the feed and are prompted to consider these ideas further. Students are not commonly encouraged in the classroom to consider others' ideas and build on them, but this is a practice that is central in dialogic teaching and learning, where it is seen as essential to listen and build on what others say. In the above example, we observe how the teacher utilizes technology for this purpose (Warwick et al., 2020). By using the affordances of access to the wider community in the feed, the teacher encourages the students to consider and select some. When microblogs are agreed for incorporation onto a group wall, the assistive memory affordance

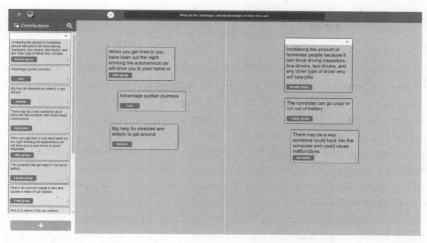

Figure 8.4. A recreation of the focus group's wall (with the feed included) and their response to the teacher's second task: "choosing others' contributions—but not your own."

of the technology means that they remain there. This contrasts with the volatility that characterize oral interactions. The blogs remain as placeholders of shared ideas—or objects of attention—and the ability to retain "markers" of intersubjective engagement. This implies that spoken dialogue can become more fragmented and is sometimes replaced by gestures, such as pointing to reinforce the derivation of utterances within the group, as seen in the except.

Thus far, we have been concerned with how microblogging tools might promote students' sustained explorations and support their co-construction of knowledge (Sadler, 2004; Tweney, 2012). We have aligned our thinking on this to specific ideas from the writings of Ragnar Rommetveit. We have considered specifically how a combination of spoken dialogue and microblogging might promote students' attention and attunement to the ideas of others and promote intersubjectivity across a classroom community. We identified three vignettes of classroom interaction that illustrate elements of our focus: i) students' active attention and attunement to the ideas of others to achieve intersubjectivity; ii) the use of language to keep the dialogue open for exploration and the potentially productive role of technology in this process; and iii) the teacher's task design and its uptake and interpretation by the students. Throughout, we have discussed the vital role of the teacher in creating a dialogic environment within the classroom, mediated by the affordances of technology. In the discussion that follows, we explore these ideas further, focusing specifically on the role of a language of possibility and the place of technology in attunement and intersubjectivity.

8.5. Attunement and Intersubjectivity in Technology-Mediated Learning

In this chapter we have shown that a teacher's dialogic pedagogy, and uptake of that pedagogy by students working in technology-mediated lessons, is an influence on both attunement to and intersubjective engagement with ideas in the classroom. In the context of lessons with an open, problem-solving agenda, it seems that the use of the "language of possibility" can facilitate exploratory dialogue, enabling the exploration of "fruitful misunderstandings" and the subjectivities of the classroom community; and, specifically, that "possibility markers" (Maine, 2015, p. 60) encourage students' active attention and attunement to the ideas of others. The students used such language to open dialogue for further exploration, with the language of possibility creating open prompts, allowing students to build on, justify, and challenge ideas. Encouraging such divergent thinking provided a nonthreatening way for students to consider the inherent complexity of SSI—a central component of socio-scientific reasoning (Sadler et al., 2007)—and to engage with the practice of idea improvement (Scardamalia & Bereiter, 2006). Such language can help students to experience and accept the provisional nature of ideas and the conditional nature of the relationship between them.

It has been argued that possibility thinking, characterized by a shift from what is to what might be (Jeffrey & Craft, 2004), drives creativity in the classroom (Craft et al., 2012). Building on Craft's (2002) work on "possibility thinking," Maine (2015) described a "dialogic space of possibility [that] includes and makes reference to the fluid and exploratory potential of the space between speakers" (p. 20). In these vignettes of classroom interaction, possibility markers have been used to create a space in which ideas may be explored, in the same way that Maine has described the use of phrases such as "maybe" and "I wonder if" (p. 60) in literacy lessons. She argued that other reasoning words, such as "because," "so," and "if" can be used to maintain the dialogic space of possibility and indicate a more exploratory form of co-construction; we see this point mirrored in the excerpts.

Boyd and Kong (2017) categorized reasoning words into three groupings: "language of possibility, reasoning links, and pressed for reasoning" (p. 78). They argued that the language of possibility "allows openness for diverse opinions and speculation" (p. 79). For example, "could" and "would" support elaboration by marking the hypothetical nature of a claim; "could" and "imagine" can be used to invite a specific form of elaboration that may be described as conjecture, suggesting that there is no definitive answer; and "might" and "believe" can be used to support reasoning. Advocates of dialogic approaches have frequently argued that utterances have dynamic meaning potentials, as opposed to static meanings (Norén & Linell, 2007; Rommetveit, 1992), and here we propose that such terms and phrases can be used to invite the articulation of interpretative meanings and to enable reasoning. In particular, Rommetveit (1992) points to the partial meanings that might be expressed by language, some of which have their meanings illuminated by the shared frame of reference or context, and some of which might only be illuminated through further probing in the dialogue. The language of possibility "allows" such probing, enabling individual or group subjectivities to become agreed, intersubjective perspectives.

Considering the potentially productive role of technology in this process of attunement and intersubjective engagement, the vignettes illustrate ways in which a particular microblogging technology can be integrated in the group dialogue as they attend to the blog contributions in the feed. The blogs are short, and the boys bring them into their communication by pointing, jointly attending to them, and jointly reading them. The short and often unfinished format seems to create room for further interpretation and negotiations of meaning, opening a space for attunement and possibility thinking. The analysis showed that exploration was a collective endeavor and that this process could be facilitated by ideas from the wider classroom community made accessible via the technology. We observed that the feed and the blogs became shared objects of attention, with the students attending and attuning to ideas of others. This created new meeting points in which different temporalities intersected (Linell, 2009; Ludvigsen et al., 2011); in line with others, we assert that the technology might here be seen as a "voice" and an "agent" in the interactions across the classroom (see also in this volume: Wegerif & Major, Chapter 7; Silseth et al., Chapter 9). Intersubjectivity is typically described as something that is shared between minds, and in this sense, technology might be seen as a facilitator of intersubjectivity. Matuk and Linn (2018), for example, argue that technology "can help to segment and scaffold the process by which students encounter and respond to ideas, allowing them time for greater reflection, and offering a finer-grained look at how they approach this task" (Matuk & Linn, 2018, p. 269). We observed this particularly when ideas created in another group were actualized through the Talkwall feed, commented on, and given provisional prominence on the group wall (Excerpt 2). Similarly, in this volume, Silseth et al. draw on Linell (2009) and his notion of "double dialogicality" to explore how digital technology mediate meaning-making between and across contexts. In our case, the layers may be seen as triple—we can talk about the oral dialogue within the peer group, the voice of the wider classroom community represented in microblogs on the feed, and the dialogue related to the blogs that are given specific attention by the group (exemplified in Excerpts 2 and 3).

The role of technology in enabling wider participation by the classroom learning community seems to be a particularly important context for exploratory work, in which the development of reasoning through dialogue is central. In using Talkwall or any similar tool to study SSI, it is important that the ideas of all students are not just referred to, but are actively explored, questioned, evaluated, and critiqued. Our analysis showed how engagement with microblogging contributions intellectually (through an embedded model of dialogue) and physically (through the affordances of the technology) enabled such explorations. Posting and manipulating contributions creates a contingent environment with the permanence and visibility of students' contributions. Particularly by browsing, selecting, and provisionally positioning objects of attention that they have created as microblogs, students can engage with a wide range of ideas and suggestions, using them to co-construct and make sense in relation to the task at hand.

This is all, of course, facilitated by the teacher's task design, that requires the students to work in groups and—in Excerpt 3—by an insistence on a focus on objects of attention that come from outside each group. But the role of the teacher, as we have indicated throughout, is much wider than this; technology is only potentially productive for learning, but in the classroom its use is always dependent on the culture and the pedagogy of the teacher (National Academies of Sciences, Engineering, and Medicine, 2018). As Matuk and Linn (2018) point out, the active engagement of the teacher is vital in developing classroom norms and practices whereby students feel comfortable with both contributing ideas and developing and critiquing the congruent and incongruent ideas of others. Considering this, meta-analyses show that the employment of exploratory talk in the class and in groups, and the use of the language of possibility, is not a "natural" or usual component of the design of learning experiences in classrooms (Howe & Abedin, 2013). The decision to implement an ethos and strategies that actively promote dialogic interaction, with a clear focus on attunement and intersubjectivity, was that of the teacher. As Stahl et al. (2014, p. 122) made clear, "No experienced educator assumes that just putting students into groups to talk with each other will result in rich dialog, effective knowledge building, or substantial learning. On the contrary, studies using diverse methods show that subtle guidance and the development of a classroom culture of certain social practices is necessary." Yet such a culture remains rare, and it is the teacher who decides, as our teacher decided, the extent to which such considerations are important for learning in their classroom.

Given a dialogic ethos, it is also the teacher who decides on how learning will be mediated, or scaffolded, through technology (Warwick et al., 2010), and here we have indicated the importance of task design and sequencing in this process (Amundrud et al., 2021). The design of tasks and activities is key in constructing opportunities to "learn to ask questions, obtain evidence, understand characteristics and limitations of scientific evidence, identify value positions or ideologies of both sides, and have access to appropriate social criteria for judging credibility of scientists" (Tal & Kedmi, 2006, p. 622). A recent synthesis of research by Darling-Hammond et al. (2020) adds weight to our assertion of the importance of the teacher in developing tasks and a supportive learning environment that fosters the epistemic engagement necessary to the study of SSI. This is, of course, challenging. There are numerous factors that might work against the wider classroom attunement and intersubjectivity that we believe is possible through co-located microblogging, and here we raise two. Firstly, the teacher requires some level of technical ability with the specific technology. However, we would suggest that it is much more important that the teacher has a clear idea of the cognitive and metacognitive learning that they wish to promote rather than high level technical competence. The intention must precede the means by which it might be achieved. The second issue that we would raise is that students—even those trained in dialogic interaction—tend to prioritize their own views, as it is cognitively challenging to even consider, let alone adopt, alternative viewpoints. Here, we found that the adoption of tasks where a number of responses may be equally valid, as in SSI, is a good "way in" to attunement and intersubjectivity; the importance of justification and reasoning can then come to the fore.

In this chapter, we have focused on peer group dialogue and the contribution that a specific technology might make to this already complex scenario of students working together on SSI. The group we observed attended and attuned to each other's ideas; they expanded on and deepened ideas put forward within the group and ideas made accessible via the technology. Furthermore, the "language of possibility" invited a specific form of elaboration that maintained openness to further explorations even when they misunderstood each other. If, as Rochelle and Teasley (1995, p. 70) stated in their seminal work, "collaboration is a coordinated, synchronous activity that is the result of a continued attempt to construct and maintain a shared conception of a problem," then microblogging technologies may assist the work of attunement and promote intersubjectivity and the co-construction of meanings through dialogue.

Acknowledgments

The DiDiAC research project is funded by the Research Council of Norway [FINNUT/Project No: 254761]. We particularly wish to thank the teachers and students who took part in the project. Student names are anonymized. The illustrations were made by Anja Amundrud.

We particularly thank Jan Dolonen and Victoria Cook for their thoughtful and detailed contributions to earlier versions of this chapter.

References

Amundrud, A., Smørdal, O., & Rasmussen, I. (2021). #Fact or #opinion: The educational design of a microblogging activity intended to engage students in productive interactions. *Technology, Pedagogy and Education*. https://doi.org/10.1080/1475939X.2021.1991997

Boyd, M., & Kong, Y. (2017). Reasoning words as linguistic features of exploratory talk: Classroom use and what it can tell us. *Discourse Processes*, 54(1), 62–81.

Boyd, M. P., Chiu, M. M., & Kong, Y. (2019). Signaling a language of possibility space: Management of a dialogic discourse modality through speculation and reasoning word usage. *Linguistics and Education*, 50, 25–35.

Chin, C., & Osborne, J. (2010). Students' questions and discursive interaction: Their impact on argumentation during collaborative group discussions in science. *Journal of Research in Science Teaching*, 47, 883–908. https://doi.org/10.1002/tea.20385.

Craft, A. (2002). *Creativity and early years education*. Continuum.

Craft, A, Cremin, T., Burnard, P., Dragovic, T., & Chappell, K. (2012). Possibility thinking: Culminative studies of an evidence-based concept driving creativity? *Education 3-13*, 41(5), 538–556.

Darling-Hammond, L., Flook, L., Cook-Harvey, C., Barron, B., & Osher, D. (2020). Implications for educational practice of the science of learning and development. *Applied Developmental Science*, 24(2), 97–140. https://doi.org/10.1080/10888691.2018.1537791

Dysthe, O. (1996). The multivoiced classroom: Interactions of writing and classroom discourse. *Written communication*, 13(3), 385–425. https://doi.org/10.1177/0741088396013003004

Edwards, T. (2022). Intersubjectivity. In J. Stanlaw (Ed.), *The international encyclopedia of linguistic anthropology*. https://doi.org/10.1002/9781118786093.iela0180

Enqvist-Jensen, C., Nerland, M., & Rasmussen, I. (2017). Maintaining doubt to keep problems open for exploration: An analysis of law students' collaborative work with case assignments. *Learning, Culture and Social Interaction*, 13, 38–49. ISSN 2210-6561. doi: 10.1016/j.lcsi.2017.02.001.

Frøytlog, J. I. J., & Rasmussen, I. (2020). The distribution and productivity of whole-class dialogues: Exploring the potential of microblogging. *International Journal of Educational Research*, 99, 101501. ISSN 0883-0355. 99. doi: 10.1016/j.ijer.2019.101501

Heen Wold, A. (1992). Introduction. In Astrid Heen Wold (Ed.), *The dialogical alternative. Towards a theory of language and mind*. Scandinavian University Press

Howe, C., & Abedin, M. (2013). Classroom dialogue: A systematic review across four decades of research. *Cambridge Journal of Education*, 43(3), 325–356.

Hyland, K. (1998). *Hedging in scientific research articles*. John Benjamins Publishing.

Jeffrey, B., & Craft, A. (2004). Teaching creatively and teaching for creativity: Distinctions and relationships. *Educational Studies*, 30(1), 77–87. https://doi.org/10.1080/0305569032000159750

Linell, P. (2009). *Rethinking language, mind, and world dialogically*. Information Age Publishing.

Littleton, K., & Mercer, N. (2013). *Interthinking: Putting talk to work*. Routledge.

Ludvigsen, S., Rasmussen, I., Krange, I., Moen, A., & Middleton, D. (2011). Intersecting trajectories of Participation: temporality and learning. In S. Ludvigsen, A. Lund, I. Rasmussen, & R. Säljö (Eds.), *Learning across sites: New tools, infrastructures and practices* (pp. 105–121). Cambridge University Press.

Maine, F. (2015). *Dialogic readers: Children talking and thinking together about visual texts*. Routledge.
Major, L., Warwick, P., Rasmussen, I., Ludvigsen, S., & Cook, V. (2018). Classroom dialogue and digital technologies: A scoping review. *Education and Information Technologies*, *23*(5), 1995–2028. https://doi.org/10.1007/s10639-018-9701-y
Matuk, C., & Linn, M. C. (2018). Why and how do middle school students exchange ideas during science inquiry? *International Journal of Computer-Supported Collaborative Learning*, *13*(3), 263–299. https://doi.org/10.1007/s11412-018-9282-1
Mercer, N. (2000). *Words and minds: How we use language to think together*. Routledge.
Mercer, N., Dawes, L., Wegerif, R., & Sams, C. (2004). Reasoning as a scientist: Ways of helping children to use language to learn science. *British Educational Research Journal*, *30*(3), 359.
Mercer, N., Wegerif, R., & Dawes, L. (1999). Children's talk and the development of reasoning in the classroom. *British Educational Research Journal*, *25*(1), 95–111.
Michaels, S., & O'Connor, C. (2015). Conceptualizing talk moves as tools: Professional development approaches for academically productive discussions. In L. B. Resnick, C. S. C. Asterhan, & S. N. Clarke (Eds.), *Socializing intelligence through academic talk and dialogue* (pp. 347–361). AERA.
Michaels, S., O'Connor, C., & Resnick, L. B. (2008). Deliberative discourse idealized and realized: Accountable talk in the classroom and civic life. *Studies in Philosophy and Education*, *27*(4), 283–297.
Mortimer, E., & Scott, P. (2003). *Meaning making in secondary science classrooms*. Open University Press.
National Academies of Sciences, Engineering, and Medicine. (2018). *How people learn II: Learners, contexts, and cultures*. The National Academies Press. https://doi.org/10.17226/24783
Norén, K., & Linell, P. (2007). Meaning potentials and the interaction between lexis and contexts: An empirical substantiation. *Pragmatics*, *17*(3), 387–416.
Omland, M. (2021). Technology-aided meaning-making across participation structures: Interruptions, interthinking and synthesising. *International Journal of Educational Research*, *109*, 101842. ISSN 0883-0355. doi: 10.1016/j.ijer.2021.101842
Ong W. J. (1982). *Orality and literacy. The technologizing of the word*. Methuen.
Osborne, J., Erduran, S., & Simon, S. (2004). Enhancing the quality of argumentation in school science. *Journal of Research in Science Teaching*, *41*(10), 994–1020.
Rasmussen, I., & Hagen, Å. (2015). Facilitating students' individual and collective knowledge construction through microblogs. *International Journal of Educational Research*, *72*, 149–161. https://doi.org/10.1016/j.ijer.2015.04.014
Rommetveit, R. (1992). Outlines of a dialogically based social-cognitive approach to human cognition and communication. In A. H. Wold (Ed.), *The dialogical alternative: Towards a theory of language and mind* (pp. 19–44). Scandinavian University Press.
Rommetveit, R. (1998a). Intersubjective attunement and linguistically mediated meaning in discourse. In S. Bråten (Ed.), *Studies in emotion and social interaction*, 2nd series. Intersubjective communication and emotion in early ontogeny (pp. 354–371). Cambridge University Press.
Rommetveit, R. (1998b). On human beings, computers and representational-computational vs hermeneutic-dialogical approaches to human cognition and communication. *Culture & Psychology*, *4*(2), 213–233.
Rommetveit, R. (2003). On the role of "a psychology of the second person" in studies of meaning, language, and mind. *Mind, Culture and Activity*, *10*, 205–218.

Sadler, T. D. (2004). Informal reasoning regarding socioscientific issues: A critical review of research. *Journal of Research in Science Teaching, 41*(5), 513–536.

Sadler, T. D., Barab, S., & Scott, B. (2007). What do students gain by engaging in socioscientific inquiry? *Research in Science Education, 37*(4), 371–391.

Scardamalia, M., & Bereiter, C. (2006). Knowledge building: Theory, pedagogy, and technology. In K. Sawyer (Ed.), *Cambridge handbook of the learning sciences* (pp. 97–118). Cambridge University Press.

Smørdal, O., Rasmussen, I., & Major, L. (2021). Supporting classroom dialogue through developing the Talkwall microblogging tool: Considering emerging concepts that bridge theory, practice, and design. *Nordic Journal of Digital Literacy, 2*, 50–64. ISSN 1891-943X.

Stahl, G., Cress, U., Ludvigsen, S., & Law, N. (2014). Dialogic foundations of CSCL. *International Journal of Computer-Supported Collaborative Learning, 9*(2), 117–125. https://doi.org/10.1007/s11412-014-9194-7

Tal, T., & Kedmi, Y. (2006). Teaching socioscientific issues: Classroom culture and students' performances. *Cultural Studies of Science Education, 1*(4), 615–644. https://doi.org/10.1007/s11422-006-9026-9

Warwick, P., Cook, V., Vrikki, M., Major, L., & Rasmussen, I. (2020). Realising "dialogic intentions" when working with a microblogging tool in secondary school classrooms. *Learning, Culture and Social Interaction, 24*, 100376. https://doi.org/10.1016/j.lcsi.2019.100376

Warwick, P., Mercer, N., Kershner, R., & Kleine Staarman, J. (2010). In the mind and in the technology: The vicarious presence of the teacher in pupil's learning of science in collaborative group activity at the interactive whiteboard. *Computers & Education, 55*(1), 350–362.

Wegerif, R. (2006). A dialogic understanding of the relationship between CSCL and teaching thinking skills. *International Journal of Computer-Supported Collaborative Learning, 1*, 143–157. https://doi.org/10.1007/s11412-006-6840-8

9
Engaging in Dialogic Activities in an Online Community
Expanding the Notion of Double Dialogicality

Kenneth Silseth, Ola Erstad, and Hans Christian Arnseth

9.1. Introduction

During the last few decades, digital technologies have radically transformed how we communicate and learn. Digitalization connects people from different parts of the world to form communities based on common interests and pursuits (Erstad & Silseth, 2023; Greenhow & Lewin, 2016; Ito et al., 2018). In these communities, people build meaning together and engage in dialogues about each other's social and cultural worlds. Even though the founding scholars of dialogism, such as Rommetveit (1974, 2003), were primarily interested in face-to-face dialogues, we believe that many of the ideas about meaning making and interaction put forward in this field are still relevant and important for exploring the dialogues that emerge in these online communities.

Drawing on a case study of intercultural education mediated through a designed social media platform called Space2Cre8 (S28), we discuss how digital technologies offer opportunities for dialogues across time and space. In S28, young people from different parts of the world came together to form a community and learn about each other's everyday lives. This provided us with a unique opportunity to explore and discuss dialogic activities within an online shared space. We are particularly interested in how these young people became acquainted, how they created profiles and presented themselves in this digital space, and what local and global cultural resources they drew on in their communication. The following research question guides the chapter: *What kind of dialogues emerge in the online community and what kind of resources are being activated?*

The structure of the chapter is as follows: Firstly, we will outline some assumptions about meaning making and dialogues found in dialogism.

Secondly, we will discuss dialogism as an approach to exploring relationships between practices that young people participate in. Finally, we provide illustrative data from the case study for discussing how we can understand the dialogues that emerge in this online community.

9.2. Dialogism and Coauthorship of Meaning

Dialogism is an epistemological approach to the study of language, cognition, and meaning making, as influenced by social, cultural, and historical factors (Holquist, 1990). It departs from a monologic stance, where language and meaning are viewed as static and predetermined, and language and meaning are considered as created and co-constructed in ongoing interactions between people and artefacts in activities situated in social practices (Valsiner & van der Veer, 2000; Wertsch, 1991). From this perspective, we are interested in studying how humans together engage in and with "an intersubjectively established, temporarily shared social world" (Rommetveit, 1974, p. 29), by means of digital technology.

According to Rommetveit (1974, 2003), the language we use when communicating with each other is never solely our own but rather something we are shareholders in. The meanings of words used in communicative activities are not ready-made but are remade in cooperation between people, in what Rommetveit (2003) called "coauthorship of meaning" (p. 216). This implies that people also co-construct knowledge and understanding of what is going on in encounters in and across settings and that we are taking part in a never finalized dialogue about multiple issues, topics, and orientations that we encounter throughout life.

We move through time and space and in and out of situations in which we as humans try to make meaning and temporarily construct a shared understanding of each other and what is going on (Lemke, 2000). When teachers and students talk about subject matter in classrooms, meanings about these issues are not ready-made but coauthored by the participants in the intersection between their preconceptions, understandings, and interests that together build a shared space for meaning, learning, and co-construction of knowledge and insights (Silseth & Arnseth, 2022; Williams & Ryan, 2020).

Thus, from a dialogic perspective, meaning is coauthored by interlocutors in specific practices that orient and attune to each other's contributions. However, the interlocutors also mobilize and orient to voices "belonging" to neighboring contexts and practices that might become relevant when engaging in activities—an issue we will address in the next section.

9.3. Digital Technology and the Expansion of Double Dialogicality

Digital technology has created new conditions for mediated interactions across time and space (Erstad & Sefton-Green, 2013). People situated in different places/spaces around the world can engage in synchronous and asynchronous communication. The internet provides students with social spaces for participation and offers multiple perspectives (Wegerif, 2013). Digital technologies can also facilitate dialogue in settings such as classrooms (Arnseth et al., 2018; Mercer et al., 2010; Rasmussen & Warwick, 2024). A teacher might use specific programs in her instructional work, which might prompt students to engage in dialogic activities. For instance, an interactive whiteboard can become a socially shared space where students and teachers can present ideas and perspectives on a curricular topic in a science education unit that can be used as resources in a whole-class dialogue.

However, we can also approach meaning making and learning with digital technology in a slightly different way; we can analyze meaning making activities with digital tools in one practice as standing in a dialogic relationship to other practices that students participate in. For example, between practices using digital technologies in classroom activities and how that connects, or not, to ways of using digital technologies at home, as part of gaming communities online, or when visiting a science museum. We can then study how people move between practices and contexts using digital technologies in different ways or study how elements from one context using technologies, for example at home, is brought up and used in another context, like in subject domains in the classroom.

To elaborate on this point, we will bring in Bakhtin's definition of "voice" and Linell's idea of "double dialogicality." First Bakhtin (1984) emphasized that when interacting, people bring in their attitudes, values, and interests that contribute to shaping the ongoing dialogue. In his definition of "voice," he emphasized that it ". . . also includes a person's worldview and fate. A person enters into dialogue as an integral voice. He participates in it not only with his thoughts, but with his fate and with his entire individuality" (p. 293). This implies that when people interact it is not only the object of talk he or she responds to but also the values, interests, positionings, and identities of self and others. Second, meaning making activities are also influenced by situational factors that frame the interactional work. From a dialogic standpoint, interactions (where meanings are made, and we become shareholders in meaning) are also considered to stand in a dialogic relationship to the context in which the interaction is situated. Linell (2009) defines the concept of double dialogicality in the following way: "In and through communicative and cognitive activities, there is dialogue within both situations and traditions; participants in the activities in question engage in both situated interaction and sociocultural praxis" (p. 52). This concept emphasizes that all dialogues between interlocutors are in dialogue with the sociocultural practice in which the interaction is embedded (see also Wertsch (2024) for a discussion of this concept).

Furthermore, as well as recognizing the dialogic relationship between interlocutors, and between the meaning making activity of interlocutors and the sociocultural practice in which the interaction takes place, we argue that we can add yet another level of dialogue. Resources that are used in communicative activities might also be mobilized and travel between sociocultural practices. One example is the mobile phone, which has become an advanced resource for a multitude of diverse communicative practices, that we carry with us all the time. If this is used by students when working on assignments in school, it is reasonable to assume that some of the literacy practices that students engage in outside school will be activated in the schoolwork, for better or worse. This further implies that experiences, interests, and identities developed from participation in many different practices that people have taken part in can potentially be mobilized in new situations and practices.

Thus, we can also speak of a dialogue between practices enacted through how interlocutors use resources to engage in specific activities over time. Developments of digital technologies have created new conditions for how different practices and contexts interconnect—both offline and online. When young people communicate through digital media, they bring with them their values, interests, and identities to their encounters, but they use other means to communicate than those used in face-to-face interactions. An interesting question is what happens when students are provided the opportunity to create a community, by means of digital technologies they are familiar with from outside school, in a school setting. In the following, we will present a case about social media use in an intercultural educational project and explore what types of dialogues emerge in this online community and what kinds of resources from practices, that are meaningful to the students, become activated in these dialogic activities.

9.4. Engaging in Dialogic Activities in an Online Community—Space2cre8 as an Illustrative Case

In the project Space2cre8 (S28), young people from the United States, India, Norway, South Africa, Australia, and the United Kingdom, connected through a social networking site with the same name. S28 was a closed social networking site, exclusively for youth in the participating schools and after-school programs, but had many of the same functions as more commercial sites such as Facebook. Each student created a personal profile, and they could also send messages, chat, write blogs, create discussion groups, add photos, music and/or videos to their own and each other's profiles.

In the local project in Norway, we followed a class of students at a lower secondary school during one academic year (data and findings from this project have also been reported in Erstad, 2014, 2016; Vasbø et al., 2014). The students' orientations and use of S28 represent different responses to this technology and the use of social media in a school context. For some of the students, the activities that were mediated by S28 became an extension of schooled activities and identities, while for other students it became a more interest- and friendship-driven activity and enabled students to mobilize multiple aspects of their selves. These ways of responding to the social media platform had an impact on the way students positioned themselves in interaction with others in the community.

Through the activities that were made possible by the S28 community and the social networking site, the students became part of dialogues on different levels of interaction. In the classroom, multiple dialogues about what S28 was all about, what kind of activities they could engage in, who the other members of the community were, and how they used social media outside school emerged during the project. During the academic year, several school projects were organized involving students in producing content for this shared space, which was further discussed within the community across participating countries. Examples were a video created by a group of Norwegian students as part of a project on "youth and alcohol use" and a presentation made by a boy in South Africa about hip-hop culture. Online, multiple dialogues emerged in interesting ways, and below we will describe and discuss some of these dialogues and what kinds of resources were being activated.

Creating profiles in S28. In their profiles, the students were supposed to present themselves to other participants in the S28 community. Below, we have listed some examples of how the students presented themselves in their profiles:

> Hi everybody, my name is Yasmin. I'm 13 years old and going on 8th grade at Greendale. My home country is Turkey. There I have a house and my aunts, uncles, grand-parents and my relatives lives there. My interest is to be with friends, shopping and much another fun things.
>
> My name is Kim. I am from Vietnam, but I live in Norway. I have 1 little sister and 1 big brother. I play the piano and I like it: D
>
> My name is Adil, I like football and my favorite team it's Manchester United FC. I play for Greendale IF. I'm born in Norway, but my parents are from

Macedonia and Kosovo. I speak Albanian with my family, but with my teachers and friends I speak Norwegian.

Even though this activity was not characterized as a dialogue in the ordinary sense of the word—as an interchange of verbal or written utterances—the profiles and how the members presented themselves can be viewed as a dialogic orientation to other members in the community, as an attunement to other students, possible connections, around the world. Interestingly, when presenting themselves in their profiles, most of the students chose to emphasize their ethnic origin more than their Norwegian belonging, even though most of the students were born and raised in Norway. This might be interpreted as a response to the fact that S28 was part of an intercultural education project, bringing together young people from different parts of the world and that the students saw this as important, but also relevant, information to the international audience. In addition to this aspect of their identities, many of the students also highlighted their interests and leisure activities. This might also be interpreted as a response to the fact that this project brought together youth from different countries and that, for instance, sports and shopping are considered part of global youth culture and might be a way of relating to other youth in the community.

According to Rommetveit, the meanings of words and sentences used in communicative activities are not ready-made but are remade in cooperation between people, meaning that a person who makes an utterance is never totally sure how others will interpret it. This is also the case when you try to communicate something about yourself through profiles on social media. You never know if people interpret who you present yourself to be in the way intended. Nevertheless, the profiles on S28 can be seen as part of an ongoing dialogue in the S28 community, where multiple and different experiences, interests, and identities from their everyday lives outside school, but also aspects of their more "schooled identities," are mobilized and activated. Thus, they are part of an ongoing dialogue in the community where students' voices reveal different aspects of themselves attuned to a possible audience and connections in the intercultural community.

Creating and maintaining online groups. What was especially interesting about these groups was they were created around aspects of their identities as attempts at creating dialogues on topics and issues that meant something special for the students. As with the profiles, the creators emphasized aspects of themselves as young people in an intercultural community, but these groups were designed as more direct invitations to interact through the social networking site. For example, one of the students started a group which he called "We who are from

Asia," which other students in the network joined. This student's parents were originally from Pakistan, and he saw the opportunity in the social networking site to play out this aspect of his identity and connect with other students across participating countries with the same cultural backgrounds. Other students started groups where pop-cultural interests became activated. One student created what she called the "Drew Bieber group," and introduced this group in the following way:

> Hi:D this group is about Justin Drew Bieber. Here you can learn about him, listen to his music, watch his videos and see some pictures of him. Go to my page to see his pictures and you can go to videos and watch his video (if you want) If you want to learn about him, just ask questions and I or someone who knows about him can answer.:D

For this student, S28 became a social space to position herself as someone who is deeply engaged in Justin Bieber and connect with other members around the world with similar interests. Thus, she used this network for pursuing interests that meant a lot to her in her everyday life; and through these types of activities, interesting relations between the activity in school and activities outside school emerged. Another student created a more general group about music and called it: "We like music" and introduced the group in the following way: "This group is for those who like music; it's just for fun. Join if you love music, all kinds of music." When making these groups, the students activate resources that connect to their cultural backgrounds as well as popular youth culture. Through this, different voices belonging to neighboring communities and practices that are important to the students become activated in the school through use of the social networking site.

Chatting activities in S28. Interestingly, students seem to respond to the chat function somewhat differently. Some of the students viewed it primarily as a schooled activity, where interactions were being framed around school topics, such as tests and grades. For others, the chat became a social space to engage in dialogues about everyday issues with members of the community from around the world and gain insights into each other's worlds. This shows how students' identities and interests influence the use of cultural tools. Below, we will zoom in on one of the students in the Norwegian class. Kuyna is originally from Kurdistan (Iraq). She attends Koran school in the afternoons and weekends and wears a hijab at school. She appears as a quiet student and to some extent withdrawn, but also values being with friends in and outside of her class. At home, she uses her computer for playing games, chatting via MSN, and doing homework. She does not use e-mail, nor does she have a Facebook profile but chats with friends and family that lives in Iraq. She views S28 as a safer space compared to other commercial sites. Below, we can see how Kuyna engages in a chatting sequence with another student in the intercultural community, here called Steve.

STEVE: Hi
STEVE: Hi
KUYNA: hi
KUYNA: what time is it there
KUYNA: ?
STEVE: hi
STEVE: its 9 in da mornin
KUYNA: :o
STEVE: wat time is it there?
KUYNA: its 18.20
KUYNA: 18.30
STEVE: o
STEVE: r u a boy or a girl
KUYNA: i am a girl
STEVE: o . . . nice
STEVE: how old r u?
KUYNA: 13 how old are you
KUYNA: ??
STEVE: 13, too
STEVE: where r u from?
KUYNA: ok
KUYNA: Iraq
STEVE: really
KUYNA: hehe yes
STEVE: is it like really hectic there?
STEVE: u kno, wit all da war and stuff
STEVE: wats it like there?
KUYNA: I'm not actually from iraq
STEVE: well . . . then where r u from?
KUYNA: I am from kurdistan but it is not a country but but Kurdistan is in Iraq
STEVE: o
KUYNA: yes
STEVE: so r u in kurdistan rite now?
KUYNA: now I am in Norway
KUYNA: I live in Norway

In the beginning of the dialogue, Kuyna and Steve are focusing on time differences regarding where in the world they are located and continue to address other aspects of their identities that they find interesting and relevant as young people taking part in an online community, such as age and gender. When they arrive to the issue of place and location, we can see an interesting turn in the dialogue, which also shows some of the complexity in these types of dialogues. It seems like Steve's question "where r u from?" leads Kuyna in the directions of thinking about her country of origin. Even though she is in Norway, she answers Iraq, which is still a very important part of her identity. In his response, it seems like Steve assumes that Kuyna is in Iraq. He follows up with questions about the challenging situation for people living in this part of the world, which is associated with war and conflicts. It seems like he really would like to know about her situation. However, instead of following up on his desire to know about the troublesome aspects of the everyday lives of people living in Iraq, Kuyna starts to adjust Steve's impression about her cultural background. In her response, Kuyna provides a brief account of the relationship between Kurdistan and Iraq, which to some extent is acknowledged by Steve, who responds by typing "o." By following up with the question "so r u in kurdistan rite now?" he once more makes visible that he assumed that Kuyna writes about where she is located, upon which Kuyna replies that she actually is in Norway.

This type of dialogue is clearly characterized as taking place across time and space. The students do not know anything about each other. The community of S28 brings Kuyna and Steve together, but they themselves need to carefully build intersubjectivity by attuning to each other through written communication for the dialogue to continue. There is a dialogue between these two young people, understood as an interchange of written utterances, but also a dialogue between their voices belonging to different cultural communities. However, we can also see the complexities and difficulties that emerge in these types of dialogues that are dependent on written communication across time and space.

9.5. Conclusion

In this chapter, we have argued that dialogism offers an interesting approach to address and discuss communicative activities in different practices in the context of digital technologies. By building on some of the ideas found in dialogism, we have explored how the use of digital technology in a school project, such as social media, is characterized by dialogic relations between persons, practices, and communities. It is our belief that developments of digital technologies fundamentally shift the communicative conditions that young people today are part of, creating both possibilities for relating to people in new ways but also dangers of polarization between groups of people as with so-called "echo chambers."

The expanding notion of double dialogicality refers to the new dimensions created by digital technologies by referring not only to people and situations when studying dialogues, but also to the extended relationship between different practices as connected by digital technologies across diverse time and space. As shown in our empirical case, we also believe that school and education have an important role to play in creating conditions and environments where children from different backgrounds can explore the dialogic potentials when participating in online communities. Our main points in summarizing ways that digital technologies can be used are:

First, digital technology enables people to communicate and engage in different types of dialogic encounters across time and space. In this chapter, this is seen in the profiles where students dialogically orient to other youth in an intercultural community, discussion groups about issues and topics they themselves found interesting and intriguing, and chat activities where students communicated about issues that matter to them across time and space, gaining insights into each other's everyday lives.

Second, dialogues through digital technology also seem to create dialogues between the practices that students traverse in their daily lives. Some of the youths used S28 as a resource for pursuing important part of their identities, enabling them to voice aspects of themselves to others in the community. S28 became a social space where experiences, interests, and ideas from neighboring practices became relevant resources for participating in the intercultural community.

In conclusion, digital technology makes new ways of interacting and being together possible. It enables dialogues between persons both in and across time and place and between practices and communities in which people and artefacts are situated. However, understanding how meaning making and learning are enacted and happen across social practices is complex. We argue that dialogism might be a promising way of approaching this complexity and a way forward for young people by elucidating the important role dialogic perspectives might have in our societies with extreme communication flows that young people must learn to navigate.

References

Arnseth, H. C., Hanghøj, T., & Silseth, K. (2018). Games as tools for dialogic teaching and learning. In H. C. Arnseth, T. Hanghøj, T. D. Henriksen, M. Misfeldt, R. Ramberg, & S. Selander (Eds.), *Games and education: Designs in and for learning* (pp. 123–139). Brill.

Bakhtin, M. (1984). *Problems of Dostoevsky's poetics*. University of Minnesota Press.

Erstad, O. (2014). The expanded classroom-spatial relations in classroom practices using ICT. *Nordic Journal of Digital Literacy, 1*(1), 8–22.

Erstad, O. (2016). Agentive students using social media: Spatial positionings and engagement in Space2cre8. In M. Walrave, K. Ponnet, E. H. Vanderhoven, J. Haers, & B. Segaert (Eds.), *Youth 2.0: Social media and adolescence* (pp. 79–99). Springer.

Erstad, O., & Sefton-Green, J. (2013). *Identity, community, and learning lives in the digital age*. Cambridge University Press.

Erstad, O., & Silseth, K. (2023). Rethinking the boundaries of learning in a digital age. *Learning, Media and Technology, 48*(4), 557–565.

Greenhow, C., & Lewin, C. (2016). Social media and education: Reconceptualizing the boundaries of formal and informal learning. *Learning, Media and Technology, 41*(1), 6–30.

Holquist, M. (1990). *Dialogism*. Routledge.

Ito, M., Martin, C., Pfister, R. C., Rafalow, M. H., Salen, K., & Wortman, A. (2018). *Affinity online: How connection and shared interest fuel learning*. New York University Press.

Lemke, J. (2000). Across the scales of time: Artifacts, activity, and meanings in ecosocial systems. *Mind, Culture, and Activity, 7*(4), 273–290.

Linell, P. (2009). *Rethinking language, mind, and world dialogically: Interactional and contextual theories of human sense-making*. Information Age Publishing.

Mercer, N., Hennessy, S., & Warwick, P. (2010). Using interactive whiteboards to orchestrate classroom dialogue. *Technology, Pedagogy and Education, 19*(2), 195–209.

Rasmussen, I., & Warwick, P. (2024). Using microblogging to create a space for attending and attuning to others. In O. Erstad, B. E. Hagtvet, & J. V. Wertsch (Eds.), *Education and dialogue in polarized societies: Dialogic perspectives in times of change*. Oxford University Press.

Rommetveit, R. (1974). *On message structure: A framework for the study of language and communication*. Wiley.

Rommetveit, R. (2003). On the role of "a psychology of the second person" in studies of meaning, language, and mind. *Mind, Culture, and Activity, 10*(3), 205–218.

Silseth, K., & Arnseth, H. C. (2022). Weaving together the past, present and future in whole class conversations: Analyzing the emergence of a hybrid educational chronotope connecting everyday experiences and school science. *Mind, Culture, and Activity, 29*(1), 60–74.

Valsiner, J., & van der Veer, R. (2000). *The social mind: Construction of the idea*. Cambridge University Press.

Vasbø, K. B., Silseth, K., & Erstad, O. (2014). Being a learner using social media in school: The case of Space2cre8. *Scandinavian Journal of Educational Research, 58*(1), 110–126.

Wegerif, R. (2013). *Dialogic: Education for the Internet age*. Routledge.

Wertsch, J. (1991). *Voices of the mind: A sociocultural approach to mediated action*. Harvard University Press.

Wertsch, J. V. (2024). The Role of Narratives in Dialogue and Intersubjectivity. In O. Erstad, B. E. Hagtvet, & J. V. Wertsch (Eds.), *Education and dialogue in polarized societies: Dialogic perspectives in times of change*. Oxford University Press.

Williams, J., & Ryan, J. (2020). On the compatibility of dialogism and dialectics: The case of mathematics education and professional development. *Mind, Culture, and Activity, 27*(1), 70–85.

10
Intersubjectivity and Dialogue in Video Games

Declan Saviano

10.1. Introduction

This chapter will explore how dialogue in a particular digital setting can transform into something toxic using participant observation data collected in 2019 from 309 games of the online computer game *League of Legends* on the North American server, focusing on blame for negative in-game events as a central motivator.[1] It will also consider the characteristics of this form of online dialogue in relation to psychologist and philosopher Ragnar Rommetveit's (1974) theorization of intersubjectivity (a social reality created and shared in dialogue), casting toxicity as an antagonistic reformation of intersubjectivity after the breakdown of an existing state of weak intersubjectivity. It will also show how the process by which intersubjectivity is achieved in online settings can be used to update Rommetveit's understanding of intersubjectivity to include cases of disagreement and antagonism offline, which Kowal and O'Connell (2015) note he rarely addressed. Finally, it will discuss how online dialogic spaces might facilitate states of intersubjectivity.

An immense amount of dialogue now takes place online. Thus, the question naturally arises: is dialogue within this new domain like offline dialogue, or is it something fundamentally different? And further, what is the relationship between online dialogue and intersubjectivity? Does online dialogue still create a shared social reality or, as Rommetveit (1974) suggested, is it a form of communication that reveals the difficulties of such a process more clearly than ever? The answer to these questions clearly depends on the site of investigation and the distinct insights offered by particular dimensions of the online experience, but Rommetveit's writings on intersubjectivity and dialogue can frame the discussion and speak to fallacies in popular discourse about online dialogue.

---

[1] Approval for anonymized data collection was granted by the Washington University in St. Louis Institutional Review Board on July 24, 2019.

Declan Saviano, *Intersubjectivity and Dialogue in Video Games* In: *Education and Dialogue in Polarized Societies*. Edited by: Ola Erstad, Bente Eriksen Hagtvet, and James V. Wertsch, Oxford University Press. © Oxford University Press 2024. DOI: 10.1093/oso/9780197605424.003.0010

Rommetveit's (1998) "hermeneutic–dialogical" perspective represents his view on dialogue. Here, dialogue is a means of achieving intersubjectivity—a social reality shared between interlocutors that exists in a constant state of co-creation, transformation, and recreation on the boundaries between the individual experiences of those taking part in it. However, he also noted that a perfectly shared social reality is extremely difficult to achieve because it is impossible for one person to ever fully know the experience of another. The construction of intersubjectivity through dialogue is therefore the process by which existing "conditions of uncertainty may . . . be transformed to conditions of social reality" (Rommetveit, 1974, p. 82). In addition, he emphasized that intersubjectivity "must be taken for granted in order to be achieved" (1974, p. 56) because it depends crucially upon shared presuppositions about linguistic factors, such as the meaning of deictic words, and cultural factors, such as the positionalities of the speaker and listener.

Through this perspective, online dialogue can be conceptualized as something that happens in a particular space with particular cultural templates for meaning and interaction, and which requires shared assumptions between interlocutors about their identities and reasons for communicating. To see online dialogue through the lens of intersubjectivity is to see it in an internal social context rather than, for example, to view it merely as externally determined communication as popular discourse often does. For example, one common colloquial perspective about digital dialogue is that it is the result of a system purpose-built for algorithmic behavioral manipulation. This view, which is prominent in both popular criticisms of social media, such as the documentary *The Social Dilemma*, and developer circles (cf. Seaver's 2019 ethnography of online recommendation algorithm developers), characterizes digital spaces as agents which create meaning and shape experience through manipulation rather than as spaces which take on meaning as a result of cultural use. Rommetveit's perspective offers a clear counterpoint to the context-free analysis of online dialogue exemplified by popular and developer discourse, centering the experience of the interlocutors and helping to set investigations of digitally mediated communication free of the analytically deterministic frameworks that so often characterize them. Because behavior-guiding principles are directly coded into the design of digital systems, it can be tempting to view the behavioral and cultural realities that develop in these systems solely as the result of such principles. While this perspective has valuable explanatory power to be explored later in this chapter, it also misses the ways in which interactions within digital systems can be dialogic. It also echoes earlier Chomskian attempts to describe language from a deterministic neurological perspective that Rommetveit positioned his initial theorization of intersubjectivity against (Rommetveit in Josephs, 1998). Seeing online dialogue through intersubjectivity thus conceptually unlocks the online world as a rich and diverse cultural space, brings attention to the ways in which disagreement and diverging contexts play a role in dialogue, and emphasizes the fluidity and generativity of new cultural practices across various online domains. Play is one such domain which, with the widespread popularity of online video games, has given rise to novel social settings and behaviors whose implications and effects have been the subjects of increasing attention in recent scholarship.

10.2. Online Gaming and Notions of Intersubjectivity

Online video gaming is one of the most popular pastimes in the world. According to the Entertainment Software Association (ESA), over 214 million people in the United States alone played video games per month in 2020 (51.1 million children, 163.3 million adults), with 63% of these players playing online and, therefore, in conjunction with other players in real-time as opposed to against a computer (ESA, 2020). The global total is even higher, with an estimated 2.7 billion people playing in 2020, or nearly 35% of the global population (ibid.). Only Facebook, with its gargantuan monthly user base of 2.9 billion, is a more popular form of digital media (Facebook, Inc., 2020). Indeed, video games have more global users than traditional cable TV and streaming services combined, which draw approximately 1.8 billion yearly global subscribers according to the Motion Picture Association of America.

These may be surprising figures. Put simply, video games are now an extremely popular form of digital entertainment. And while it is unknown what percentage of global gamers play offline and what percentage play online (and therefore engage in some form of social interaction during play), the 63% of US players who play online may be indicative of broader worldwide trends (ESA, 2020). A further distinction can be drawn between online players who communicate with others while playing and those who do not, but the specifics of this distinction are also unknown. Nevertheless, it is clear that people across the world spend significant amounts of time both playing and communicating with others in online video games. This is not a niche area of interaction.

What, then, is the nature of this constant communication? And what is intersubjectivity like in this context? Games with different communicative channels create different social worlds, but one particularly prevalent behavior that illuminates intersubjectivity in online gaming spaces is known as "toxicity." At its most basic, toxicity in the context of video game social interaction is colloquially understood as any in-game communicative behavior that is negative, mean-spirited, or hurtful to any person playing the game. It is a broad term which can refer to many specific types of behavior, including harassment, hate speech, bullying, "flaming" (directed insults), "raging" (generalized expression of anger at various sources), and "trolling" (deliberate tampering with another player's game experience)—the latter three of which are terms that have developed organically in the video game social environment to describe its unique forms of behavior. Like most behavioral phenomena, toxicity can take different forms in different contexts, but one of its defining aspects is its severity. Perhaps even more than toxicity in social media or other online discursive spaces, toxic interactions in video games are often startlingly vitriolic and involve utterances which would rarely be encountered in everyday offline interaction. Indeed, the phenomenon of road rage, in which drivers pull over after a driving conflict and begin to exchange insults or even blows, is perhaps the closest existing offline analogue to this form of toxicity, as it incorporates both the belligerents' anonymity to each other and the brevity and intensity of their exchange. But despite its offline rarity, toxicity has become an expected component of social interaction in many video games, unlike other less common online aggressive behaviors, such as cyberbullying. The uniqueness of its setting and characteristics make it a novel form of intersubjectivity consisting of extreme cases of antagonism and disagreement rarely encountered in other studies of social discourse. An approach to this phenomenon based on Rommetveit's writings about intersubjectivity thus seeks to understand dialogue from the perspective of the interlocutors rather than from an external perspective that sees it as a systematized behavioral reaction to specific events.

Toxicity is not exclusive to video games in new media. A cursory glance at Facebook or Twitter, especially in the dramatically polarized US media environment of the pandemic era, will show that antagonism abounds in other online settings. Detailed attention to the characteristics of digital dialogue in the video game setting is therefore important because it may reveal characteristics of online dialogue in other settings where, for example, critical political discussions are often held. Furthermore, using the concept of intersubjectivity to study dialogue provides a much-needed discursive counterpoint to the overly deterministic analyses of online dialogue described above.

10.3. Contextual Background

To reach an understanding of what dialogue looks like in this context, we must first examine the context itself—the game *League of Legends* (also known simply as League) is widely considered one of the most toxic online video game environments. Played on the PC platform, League is a Multiplayer Online Battle Arena (MOBA), a type of strategy game in which two teams, usually consisting of five players each, compete against each other to secure in-game objectives, with each player controlling one character in real-time. In League, each team tries to destroy the base of the opposing team while navigating the constantly changing game environment. Games generally last 20–40 minutes. All players begin the game with their characters, also known as "champions," at the same level of strength, and can increase this strength by gaining "gold" and "experience" by killing "minions" (weak, non-player characters which appear every 30 seconds), enemy "champions," or "monsters," such as dragons, which are always present. Players can use gold to buy items, which increase their strength, and experience, to increase the power of their character's unique abilities. In addition, all champions are restricted to the same bounded gameplay environment but cannot see all of it at once and must therefore compete with their opponents to gain vision of hidden areas. When "killed" by an opposing champion, a champion will return to the game after a set amount of time. There are currently 164 unique playable champions in League, each with five unique abilities, and over 100 unique items which all players can use in-game. With ten players in each game, a staggeringly high number of game states are possible. While even this description lacks a great deal of explanatory complexity, it should be enough to show that the game is quite complicated and requires players to focus a high degree of attention on team cooperation and communication in order to win.

Figure 10.1. A screenshot of a game of League, with players' usernames removed for privacy.

The nature of social interaction in League is fundamentally different from that of "ordinary" offline social interaction. Unless playing with friends, players are paired with four anonymous teammates against five anonymous opponents, with all players identifiable only by a username. During a match, communication is only possible via four avenues: in-game text chat visible to either one's whole team or to all players on both teams, pings (brief sound-icon pairings visible to one's own team that signify simple messages like "danger" or "on the way"), movement of champions on the screen (the most indirect form of communication but which nevertheless, like all actions, is a form of communication), and voice chat, which, at time of writing, was only available to players who are friends with each other in the game's rudimentary social networking system. The games considered in this research, which represent most League games, were fully anonymous and did not include voice communication. Textual communication is also possible before a match, when players enter a virtual pregame lobby with their team to select their champions and strategize, and after a match, where all players in a game enter the same postgame lobby to view match statistics. The game is fast-paced and demands attention and intense concentration, which makes longform communication either impossible or extremely inefficient within the constraints of a rapidly changing gameplay environment. This confluence of anonymity, limited communication channels, and fast-paced gameplay leads to a discursive environment full of brief, direct utterances which can be intense and affect-laden, and which are usually exclusively related to gameplay.

One might expect a game with such a high knowledge threshold and level of cooperation for success to produce a fairly benign social environment, but this is not the case. Although the game has an anti-toxicity system through which toxic players can be reported, reviewed, and potentially banned, toxicity is often quite prevalent in League (occurring at least once in 54% of observed games). Even the smallest mistake can sometimes elicit an extremely aggravated response, especially if harsh words have already been exchanged.

For example, consider the following brief interaction, which occurred over about 30 seconds in the postgame lobby between three players on the losing team. One of the players, [PLAYER 3], performed poorly and is being blamed by the others, but ultimately, they are all discussing what went wrong in their recently lost game. Ordinarily, a player's username would appear in-game in place of the "[PLAYER 3]" identifier, but all usernames in this and future examples have been removed for privacy. In addition, the name in parentheses after the redacted username refers to a player's champion. Players commonly refer to each other in-game by their champion's name rather than their username because it is easier to identify, being consistently paired with that champion's visual model across games.

> Example 1:
> [PLAYER 2] (Annie): xayah gets hooked[1]
> [PLAYER 1] (Leona): when you let him all in you?[2]
> [PLAYER 3] (Xayah): throughout the entire fu**in game
> [PLAYER 2] (Annie): and expects entire team to tp[3]
> [PLAYER 2] (Annie): on her
> [PLAYER 2] (Annie): imagine
> [PLAYER 3] (Xayah): BRUH
> [PLAYER 1] (Leona): you kept eating hooks
> [PLAYER 3] (Xayah): do you not realise leona
> [PLAYER 1] (Leona): all hook diet my dude
> [PLAYER 3] (Xayah): THE MOTHER FU**ER WAS GOOD AT HOOKS
> [PLAYER 1] (Leona): don't blame your sh*t on me
> [PLAYER 3] (Xayah): AND YOU COULDNT HIT AN FU**IN ULTI OR YOUR E[4]
> [PLAYER 1] (Leona): have fun losing more my dude
> [PLAYER 2] (Annie): hope you get perma'd[5]
> [PLAYER 3] (Xayah): you would literally watch me die
> [PLAYER 3] (Xayah): id fu**in kill yall ni***rs irl
>
> 1: In this example, "hooked" and "hooks" refer to the ability of a particular champion, a large hook that can pull enemy players towards him.
> 2: To "all in" is to commit fully to a fight such that one either wins or dies.
> 3: "tp" is an abbreviation for the teleport ability.
> 4: Each champion has four abilities, activated by pressing the Q, W, E, or R keys. "E" therefore refers to the ability activated by the E key, and "ULTI," which is short for ultimate ability, to the ability activated by the "R" key. To "hit" an ability is to activate it such that it achieves its intended effect.
> 5: "Perma'd" is an abbreviation of "permabanned," referring to a permanent ban from play usually enacted as punishment for egregious toxicity of the type displayed by Xayah at the end of this example.

It is evident from this example, which is not altogether uncommon, that dialogue in League is marked by an extensive and unique vocabulary system. The usage of such jargon reveals that an intersubjective state exists within the social world of the game that is accessible only to those who understand its terminology. Furthermore, many players often operate synchronously without ever needing to engage in dialogue. Just as basketball players take up positions around the court during a game and expect their teammates and opponents to do the same without ever needing to explicitly communicate about it, League players position their champions and use their abilities according to the state of the game largely without communication. Thus, players' nonverbal interactions are crucial to establishing the shared cultural and social templates upon which dialogic intersubjectivity is built. Indeed, players say a good deal more during toxic interactions than average interactions in a game of League. In contrast, a typical average interaction looks like this:

Example 2:
[PLAYER 1] (Thresh): bot no summs[1]
[PLAYER 1] (Thresh): drag now[2]
[PLAYER 2] (Master Yi) is on the way
[PLAYER 2] (Master Yi) is on the way
[PLAYER 2] (Master Yi): ok drag

1: "bot no summs" means the enemy players covering the bottom position of the map have no available summoner spells, powerful fighting tools.
2: "drag" refers to the dragon, a monster located in the bottom part of the map that gives bonuses to the team that kills it.

Communication in the above example is brief and meaning-laden. Players are talking exclusively about in-game events and objectives, and there is no conflict. Information about an enemy team's weakness and a potential way to capitalize on that weakness is communicated and confirmed by two teammates, and nothing beyond this needs to be said. It is again evident that intersubjectivity (albeit rather weak) exists between the players here, given that they can all clearly communicate critical information about a complex game state with very few words.

10.4. Elements of the Communicative Medium and Their Influence on Toxicity

Before discussing intersubjectivity further, it is helpful to consider the influence of League's communicative medium on toxicity from the external psychological perspective discussed in the introduction. In particular, two elements of League's design may indeed play a role in eliciting toxic behavior: anger and anonymity. Firstly, toxicity is characterized and may also be engendered by the anger that arises from the confluence of certain gameplay factors—high competitiveness, high engagement and attentional demand, and a negative in-game event. This can be understood through Berkowitz's frustration–aggression hypothesis, which suggests that the frustration of efforts to achieve a desired goal is a prerequisite for aggressive behavior, among other behavioral effects (Berkowitz, 1989). More specifically, frustration of a goal is understood to generate a sort of unspecified or formless negative affect within individuals, which can subsequently find expression as aggression or anger. This analysis has been shown to apply to the video game context (Breuer et al., 2015), revealing that toxicity in League may appear as a reaction to the frustration of certain in-game goals—a process that can be mapped onto the occurrence of negative in-game events, given that negative events ultimately frustrate the goal of winning the game. But regardless of whether toxicity in League is caused by anger that leads to a breakdown in intersubjectivity or vice versa, responding to negative events and blame with toxic behavior is a common and well-understood part of social life in League. Moreover, it represents a unique use of language generated by particular facets of the digital medium in which communication occurs.

Anonymity is another important component of toxic behavior that shapes the discursive environment of League and other digital spaces and can be conceptualized in this context through psychologist John Suler's theory of the online disinhibition effect. This is the phenomenon in which internet users often behave differently online than they would offline because, among other factors, behaviors which are normally prohibited offline due to social norms or the potential of negative repercussions are possible online when those social constraints are removed in an anonymous setting (Suler, 2004). League's environment certainly lacks strong social repercussions, as it is highly unlikely for players to encounter one another after a match is over. There are millions of players on the North American server alone, and the odds of seeing the same person twice are miniscule. As a result, players can freely be toxic to each other without fear that those to whom they are toxic will ever be positioned to retaliate against them in a way that affects their immediate gameplay experience. While some players do remember toxic encounters and sometimes talk about them, as in Example 3, they will rarely, if ever, be forced to confront those players again.

Various other factors certainly contribute to the development and prevalence of toxicity. League's high degree of competitiveness, its violent content, the largely young and male demographics of its player-base, and the offline circumstances or individual personalities of toxic players may all be significant contributors. But none of these factors alone explain why this type of behavior occurs so readily *here*, in this particular digital medium. Each can be briefly addressed. Firstly, competitiveness cannot explain toxicity alone because many physical games are competitive and yet develop a culture of tolerance and respect. Violent content cannot explain it alone either since violence has generally been supplanted by competitiveness as the driving factor behind video games' link to toxic behavior (Adachi & Willoughby, 2011). Furthermore, the toxicity of a young male demographic would have to manifest in offline situations as significantly different from the toxicity of, for example, young women, to be considered a relevant factor. Finally, the influence of circumstance and personality on toxic behavior in League is difficult to clarify given existing literature.

10.5. Enculturation

It is within this setting that players develop the ability to participate intersubjectively in League through a process of enculturation, just as intersubjectivity in daily life is built up through a process of socialization. Players are enculturated to the game's social norms as they move up from beginner status and learn both ordinary communication and toxic communication. This is evidenced by the differences in communication and behavior between beginner and veteran players. When they first join the game, players must complete several rounds of "bot" tutorials in which they play against AI enemies. In these games, allies are extremely helpful to each other. They type longer messages than veteran players and are often very supportive of each other as they learn—they ask questions, give answers, and share tips and skills that they are learning, often as they learn them. They express joy at successfully executing plays and laugh at their own and each other's mishaps rather than criticize them as veteran players are wont to do. Not all veteran players are critical, of course—some are highly positive—but on the whole, they are more toxic than beginner players.

However, as players graduate into games with human-controlled enemies and the occasional veteran player, the social landscape begins to change. Firstly, veteran players are a lot more skilled than novice players and have higher expectations for their teammates' performance, and games begin to demand more concentration as a result. This leads to changes in communicative style. Long messages are replaced with short, to-the-point utterances as novice players spend less time talking with each other and more time focused on gameplay. Furthermore, veteran players were observed engaging in toxic behavior toward new players as early as the sixth game played on a new account, and with regularity after the seventh game (players were identified as veteran by their extensive match histories, which can be publicly viewed). Toxicity thus emerges for the first time as a behavior early in the League experience and appears quite obviously as the single most interesting component of in-game social interaction. Players talk about it a lot—after all, they are first exposed here to a unique and as-yet-unknown behavior which shapes social interactions in the setting into which they have just entered and which they are trying to understand. They must learn to distinguish toxic behavior from non-toxic behavior to better communicate with veteran players who are already doing the same. Thus, toxicity appears as part of League's intersubjective environment.

Crucially, given the paucity of social norms within League, the concept of toxicity can actually serve to unite players and provide common ground upon which they can find shared experiences and become more involved with each other in the context-starved social world of the game. Importantly and perhaps surprisingly, this means that toxicity can facilitate intersubjectivity. For a brief illustration of this phenomenon (a more detailed example is included in the following section), consider the following example from a pregame lobby in which Player 1 begins describing their experience with a particularly toxic player, only for Player 3 to immediately respond antagonistically:

Example 3:
[PLAYER 1]: just played with the most toxic player ive seen in a while
[PLAYER 2]: how
[PLAYER 1]: legit ran it down my lane for reason and then started saying the hard r in chat[1]
[PLAYER 3]: don't dude
[PLAYER 3]: damn dude
[PLAYER 3]: I don't remember askin
[PLAYER 1]: k dont be toxic
[PLAYER 3]: no u

1: "ran it down my lane" refers to intentionally allowing one's champion to be killed by the enemy team, making them stronger and making the game harder for one's own team.

Note here how Player 3 understands what Player 1 has said but responds dismissively, showing that both players have a similar understanding of toxicity despite the fact that Player 3 has chosen to stifle the cordial dialogue that was developing between Player 1 and Player 2.

10.6. Data and Analysis

The process through which toxic interactions begin is crucial to understanding how toxicity has become a mainstay of League's social environment and to understanding the specific characteristics of this uncommon form of dialogue. Following an analysis of participant observation data consisting of 557 separate instances of toxicity, blame was revealed to be the centrally motivating factor behind toxic interaction between allied players.[2] These interactions develop according to the same relatively straightforward pattern: something goes wrong in-game; a player or players instigate communication about the event that is usually negative in character; blame is cast; the blame is contested; further

---

[2] Toxicity also occurs between players on opposing teams, but this is quite similar to trash talk and does not represent a sufficiently unique form of dialogue to warrant separate consideration.

communication devolves into toxicity. It is important to note that the specific direction of the blame and the players involved in both casting and receiving this blame are largely irrelevant to the emergence of toxicity. Indeed, the only commonality between the myriad situations in which blame is cast before toxicity erupts is that someone is blamed for the disadvantageous event—it does not matter who is blamed, who is blaming, or whether responsibility for the negative event is correctly attributed. Common negative events include a champion's death, a lost fight, the failure to secure a critical objective, or even other toxic behavior on the part of one or more players. The following example, which occurred over a period of less than a minute after a lost fight, when most of the involved players were dead and could freely type without controlling their champions, illustrates how blame serves as a catalyst for toxic behavior:

> Example 4:
> [PLAYER 1] (Samira): wait ur level 9
> [PLAYER 1] (Samira): what
> [PLAYER 2] (Shen): yah
> [PLAYER 2] (Shen): its almost
> [PLAYER 2] (Shen):;lie
> [PLAYER 2] (Shen): i have been camped[1]
> [PLAYER 2] (Shen): the entire game
> Enemy team has scored an ace![2]
> [PLAYER 2] (Shen): been dove[3]
> [PLAYER 2] (Shen): under my tower
> [PLAYER 3] (Nunu): nah shen
> [PLAYER 2] (Shen): 4 tiemws
> [PLAYER 2] (Shen): and you
> [PLAYER 2] (Shen): mother fu**rs
> [PLAYER 3] (Nunu): you would lose to any topp laner
> [PLAYER 2] (Shen): have done nothing
> [PLAYER 3] (Nunu): LMFAO
> [PLAYER 4] (Zyra): and we are getting drag?[4]
> [PLAYER 3] (Nunu): so bad
> [PLAYER 4] (Zyra): holy
> [PLAYER 3] (Nunu): just dodge next time[5]
> [PLAYER 1] (Samira): dude just sstop typing and play
> [PLAYER 2] (Shen): and?
> [PLAYER 4] (Zyra): just cry more
> [PLAYER 3] (Nunu): angry a**
> [PLAYER 3] (Nunu): pklayer

> 1: "camped" refers here to "camping," when an enemy player repeatedly assists a player's lane opponent.
> 2: This is an auto-generated message that occurs when all players on the allied team are dead at the same time.
> 3: "dove" refers to a "tower dive," when a player or players fight an enemy player under the safety of their own tower, a risky play which is difficult to correctly execute unless one team has a significant numbers advantage in the situation.
> 4: "drag" refers to the dragon, a monster which gives a significant bonus to the team which kills it.
> 5: "dodge" refers to quitting a game during the pregame lobby before it has begun, forcing the other players back into the matchmaking process.

Here, a seemingly innocuous question from Samira about Shen's level is all that is required to spark a toxic interaction because, at this point, the average level in the game was 12, making Shen severely under-leveled and therefore a liability for his team. Shen interprets this as blame, defending himself by blaming his team for not assisting him when the enemy was attacking him. Nunu responds to this accusation by further attacking Shen, and a toxic interaction develops. The players here are, in a roundabout way, talking about what went wrong in the fight they just lost, but this dialogue has morphed into something toxic.

Blame represents a rupture in the tenuous state of intersubjectivity that exists before a negative in-game event. As in Example 2, players generally share an understanding of the game prior to a negative event and can operate effectively with little to no dialogue. When players see each other performing the correct in-game actions without needing to communicate, they can safely assume that they are operating with some level of common familiarity. But it is often the case, as in Example 4, that a negative event creates differing perspectives on how to play the game going forward or reveals the existing differences between players' perceptions of the game state. The presuppositions players held about the shared social reality inhabited by their team are revealed to be illusions when, for example, a team is "aced." It is a wonder that such an intersubjective breakdown is not expressed more often since, from this perspective, it is clearly difficult, if not impossible, for players to come to the same set of presuppositions about in-game behavior and communication. How can players know what level of performance to expect from their teammates when they are all encountering each other for the first time? How can they establish any sort of common ground or trust with teammates with whom they will only communicate for 20–40 minutes, and even then only through hurried utterances? As discussed above, what little common ground exists is predicated on common terminology and on generalized or colloquial understandings of the social reality of gameplay learned through enculturation. Moreover, players clearly try to fix the problems that arise in-game so they can win, but the communicative medium effectively prohibits them from engaging in measured dialogue with each other and spurs them to communicate as forcefully as possible in as short a time as possible.

What, then, does toxic behavior between players reveal about intersubjectivity in League? Is it merely the end of whatever weak intersubjectivity existed previously, the final result of a total breakdown in dialogue? It is probably better understood as the opposite. Intersubjectivity relies on taking the perspectivity of the other by means of culturally produced templates of meaning that complement the shared social reality created by the direct focus of the language used, and these templates differ depending on the setting and content of dialogue (Rommetveit, 1974). Since toxicity is both a social norm in League, due to the enculturation process described in previous sections, and a behavior that players learn and understand together despite its antagonistic nature, it can therefore be understood as a reformation of the flimsy state of intersubjectivity that existed prior to a negative event. In other words, it may be considered a perverted continuation of intersubjectivity in the form of a hostile style of dialogue that serves as the only remaining commonality between players whose shared social reality has been revealed as illusory by negative events and blame. Rommetveit might describe it as a state of intersubjectivity that is "short of perfection, yet not so deficient that nothing can be made known" (Rommetveit, 1974, p. 38).

Rather than representing merely a deliberate termination of constructive dialogue, then, toxicity is paradoxically both a termination and continuation of existing dialogue. In a sense, it is the termination of one dialogue style and the genesis of another—a continuation of intersubjectivity with a different tone or characteristic, the substitution of an incongruous categorization strategy for in-game events with a shared categorization strategy for correcting poor behavior and expressing disappointment or discontent. As shown in Examples 1 and 4, toxic interactions can simultaneously be discussions about a negative event and expressions of antagonism guided by a common cultural reference frame. Thus, the vitriol exhibited by toxic players is not a complete breakdown in intersubjectivity (to the extent that intersubjectivity can be achieved through text-based communication in an anonymized online setting) as much as it is a strange and unique attempt to reestablish it through a language specific to a particular online social context. Players engaged in toxic dialogue with each other are, for better or worse, connected in a way that other players in the game are fundamentally not part of. Such a linkage could explain why toxic interactions extend for far longer than normal interactions, sometimes taking the place of gameplay itself as the primary activity in which players engage.

But what about cases of one-sided toxicity and Rommetveit's understanding of intersubjectivity as taking the attitude of the other? Previous examples have shown how toxicity often develops between two or more players, but it can also occur in the behavior of only one player, as in the following example which shows a toxic behavior known to the gaming community as "raging." Raging is closer to a rant or tirade than to directed insults, and in this example, Player 1 begins to lash out in the postgame lobby at everyone involved in the game out of frustration with his teammates' poor play.

> Example 5:
> [PLAYER 1] (Sylas): like HOW THE F*** DOES SOMEONE DO THAT AND STILL LOSE
> [PLAYER 1] (Sylas): cause this person is clearly trolling
> [PLAYER 1] (Sylas): i fu***ng hate this game man
> [PLAYER 1] (Sylas): "Hi my name is as***le, and I'd like to make you frustrated and waste your time to the tune of about 4 hours of games
> [PLAYER 1] (Sylas): cause I FEEL WORTHLESS INSIDE
> [PLAYER 1] (Sylas): AND ITS THE ONLY ENJOYMENT I FU***NG GET
> [PLAYER 1] (Sylas): IS MAKING REAL PEOPLE FRUSTRATED
> [PLAYER 2] (Veigar): ez bro
> [PLAYER 2] (Veigar): just a gme
> [PLAYER 2] (Veigar): game
> [PLAYER 1] (Sylas): i HOPE YOU ALL GET FU***NG CANCER AND YOUR MOM TOO

Surely players engaged in one-sided toxic behavior do not adopt each other's attitudes, as shown in this example, where Player 2 unsuccessfully attempts to calm Player 1 down. One-sidedly toxic players do not adopt the attitude of the players to whom they are toxic with respect to the attribution of responsibility and blame for gameplay failures. Instead, they adopt a general attitude toward gameplay failures that they have likely seen in the context of other matches, and, indeed, other games besides League. With whom are toxic players engaged in dialogue, then, if the attitude they take is unrelated to that of the players with whom they are communicating? It appears to be the attitude of the generalized cultural reference frame itself, the attitude of an imagined toxic player given form.

10.7. Disagreement and Intersubjectivity—Online and Offline

This analysis of online dialogue has revealed that intersubjectivity can exist even in cases of extreme disagreement through the mediating influence of shared cultural reference frames. But might this be the case for face-to-face intersubjectivity as well? While Rommetveit rarely explicitly addressed cases of disagreement like toxicity in his work, he did note that his formulation of intersubjectivity was not equated with or limited to situations of dialogic consensus (Josephs, 1998). For example, he describes how productive insights may be generated through incongruities of understanding such as when a teacher interprets a students' question through their own more knowledgeable background and thereby generates a new analysis of the topic of discussion. But dialogue in Rommetveit's example is undertaken in good faith, contrary to examples of toxicity where the interlocutors are not interested in reaching a shared conclusion. So how, then, can the persistence of intersubjectivity in bad-faith, face-to-face dialogue be understood?

Toxicity usually occurs as a result of the breakdown of more stable discussion—that is, it is a perversion of good-faith dialogue rather than an isolated or unprompted incident of bad-faith dialogue. This may characterize some face-to-face disagreements as well, since disagreements generally do not spring into being from nothing. Instead, they require an established frame of reference within which two interlocutors can hold opposing viewpoints, the establishment of which happens in good faith except in cases of manipulation and other situations in which one person is deliberately lying from the beginning. It is thus not difficult to imagine how even bad-faith, face-to-face disagreements can be considered forms of intersubjectivity—that is, dialogues where a shared social reality is constructed.

The architecture of toxic intersubjectivity can also help explain the nature of face-to-face intersubjectivity. As described in the previous section, cases of one-sided toxicity in League can be reinterpreted as dialogues with assumed cultural reference frames rather than with other players. This implies that a person's utterances and the cultural reference frames that each interlocutor uses to interpret the utterances of the other can be separate objects of dialogic engagement, as in Example 5. In online and offline bad-faith disagreement, then, we might find a dialogue that begins between two people but quickly transitions to a dialogue between one person and the reference frame of another and vice versa, with each person unable or unwilling to take the other's perspective and reach a more stable state of intersubjectivity. This is what happens in Example 5—Player 1, who is raging, refuses to acknowledge the helpfully motivated interjection of Player 2 as helpful, instead responding to it as if it were part of the toxic reference frame with which he (the gender of the champion) is already engaged. Both players are engaged in dialogue here, but they do not share the same cultural frame of reference. Instead, Player 1 assumes that the words of Player 2 represent the reference frame of a toxic player to which he himself is already committed.

Crucially, this incongruity in intersubjective dialogue is only possible because both players occupy the same social environment with a common set of communicative styles and reference frames that each can understand, and which can therefore overlap and be mistaken for each other—here, the frame of a toxic player and the frame of a helpful player. And while the absence of body language and tone of voice certainly plays a role in Example 5 and would perhaps resolve similar incongruities in face-to-face disagreements by more directly revealing the difference in reference frames, the general architecture of intersubjectivity in the disagreement remains the same online and offline. Rommetveit's formulation of intersubjectivity as including an "unequivocal direction of communication" between the speaker, "I," and the listener, "you," (1974, p. 37) might therefore be restructured in cases of disagreement to instead take place between the speaker "I" and the reference frame they reference, which could be called "it." Here, the speaker erroneously assumes that their interlocutor shares their reference frame, but the fact that they are communicating within a cultural environment that includes multiple speaking styles that both understand and access nevertheless allows intersubjectivity to persist in their dialogue. Each is, in effect, using the other as a vehicle to engage in dialogue with an assumed set of cultural ideas rather than directly with their interlocutor.

10.8. Conclusion

All this suggests the need to make Rommetveit's notion of intersubjectivity more expansive and flexible to incorporate the particularities of the novel spaces in which dialogue now frequently takes place. In doing so, however, it is important to remain focused on the central thrust of the theory—the imperfect but nevertheless attempted creation of a shared social reality—when considering digital communication because it can help orient discussion toward the ways in which experience is co-created in spaces lacking an easily identifiable material substrate. In understanding offline face-to-face communication, body language and subverbal cues undoubtedly play a critical role in forming and maintaining shared social worlds, but it is difficult to find analogues to these in online spaces. With its focus on language, which serves as the mediating influence on an incredibly large segment of digital communication, intersubjectivity can be a critical tool for understanding how communication works online. Furthermore, it can encourage a contextual attention to the specific qualities of the digital medium that shape the parameters of dialogue—that is, what can and cannot be said, how it can be said, and the cultures that develop around such ways of speaking that then influence further communication. Furthermore, insights from this discussion of online dialogue can shed light on the architecture of face-to-face disagreements, which include cues like body language but might nevertheless be structured similarly to online disagreements.

Despite the questions Rommetveit raises about intersubjectivity's true potential for accessing the inner mental life of our interlocutors, it remains a multifaceted experience that can take a variety of forms capable of creating a shared social reality in physical dialogue. Intersubjectivity in this particular online context, however, is considerably different. It is anemic by comparison, its fullness stunted by the constraints on language imposed by an anonymous medium that demands incredibly high levels of attention be directed at everything but linguistic interaction. But even here, communication thrives—even here, intersubjectivity is reestablished after breakdown from whatever fragments of commonly understood communication exist. Rommetveit's theory of intersubjectivity thus also reveals that digital communication may remain similar in its basic mechanisms to offline communication. The truly unique aspect of these examples of toxicity is not the fact that a space where such behavior can thrive has been created, but rather the adaptability of human communication to entirely novel spaces that differ drastically from the offline world and the ways in which this adaptation lays bare the structure of human communication.

Herein lies the central contribution of this research to understanding the importance of a dialogic perspective. Despite the novel setting and unlikely form of intersubjectivity that appears in few other areas of social discourse, the dialogic perspective provides a useful framework for interpretation and analysis of these interactions. Rather than turning to entirely new theoretical models to explain digital communication, we can recognize the crucial similarities between online and offline communication through the application of existing models, update those models, and thereby gain a foothold in discussions surrounding the distinction, or lack thereof, between online and offline life and culture. This perspective is also particularly important when considering phenomena such as online polarization and the rise of violent, exclusionary populist movements. Just as in cases of video game toxicity, the breakdown of dialogue and intersubjectivity necessary for cooperative functioning and discourse is also a central problem in online dialogic phenomena such as these, and the development of a theoretical account of the pattern of interaction of video game toxicity can begin a systematic inquiry into understanding and potentially solving these issues.

References

Adachi, P. J. C., & Willoughby, T. (2011). The effect of video game competition and violence on aggressive behavior: Which characteristic has the greatest influence? *Psychology of Violence*, 1(4), 259–274. https://doi.org/10.1037/a0024908

Berkowitz, L. (1989). Frustration–aggression hypothesis: Examination and reformulation. *Psychological Bulletin*, 106(1), 59–73. https://doi.org/10.1037/0033-2909.106.1.59

Breuer, J., Scharkow, M., & Quandt, T. (2015). Sore losers? A reexamination of the frustration–aggression hypothesis for colocated video game play. *Psychology of Popular Media Culture*, 4(2), 126–137. https://doi.org/10.1037/ppm0000020

Entertainment Software Association. (2020, July 15). 2020 Essential facts about the video game industry. https://www.theesa.com/resource/2020-essential-facts-about-the-video-game-industry/

Facebook, Inc. (2021). Review of "Facebook reports second quarter 2021 results." Facebook, Inc. https://investor.fb.com/investor-news/press-release-details/2021/Facebook-Reports-Second-Quarter-2021-Results/default.aspx

Josephs, I. E. (1998). Do you know Ragnar Rommetveit? On dialogue and silence, poetry and pedantry, and cleverness and wisdom in psychology (An interview with Ragnar Rommetveit). *Culture & Psychology*, 4(2), 189–212. https://doi.org/10.1177/1354067X9800400203

Kowal, S., & O'Connell, D. C. (2015). Ragnar Rommetveit's approach to everyday spoken dialogue from within. *Journal of Psycholinguistic Research*, 45(2), 423–446. https://doi.org/10.1007/s10936-015-9404-0

Motion Picture Association. (2019). 2019 THEME report. https://www.motionpictures.org/research-docs/2019-theme-report/

Orlowski, Jeff. (2020). "The Social Dilemma | Netflix." *Netflix*. https://www.youtube.com/watch?v=uaaC57tcci0

Rommetveit, Ragnar. (1974). *On message structure: A framework for the study of language and communication.* Wiley.

Rommetveit, Ragnar. (1998). On human beings, computers and representational-computational vs hermeneutic-dialogical approaches to human cognition and communication. *Culture & Psychology*, 4(2), 213–233. https://doi.org/10.1177/1354067x9800400204

Seaver, N. (2019). Captivating algorithms: Recommender systems as traps. *Journal of Material Culture*, 24(4), 421–436. https://doi.org/10.1177/1359183518820366

Suler, J. (2004). The online disinhibition effect. *Cyber Psychology & Behavior*, 7(3), 321–326.

The state of online gaming—2020. (n.d.). Organization: Edgio. https://www.techrepublic.com/resource-library/research/the-state-of-online-gaming-2020/

SECTION 4
LEARNING DIALOGUES AT HOME AND IN SCHOOL

A shared focus of the three chapters in this section is mediated learning in school and teacher training education (Chapter 11), in the home, in young dual language learners' (DDLs) acquisition of first and second language (Chapter 12), and in preschool and early schooling when children in typical and untypical language development learn how to construct stories (Chapter 13). Important background sources are Rommetveit's ideas of language and communication and other theorists, such as Vygotsky (1978) and Bruner (1985). Specifically, the authors have appropriated Rommetveit's assumption that the aim of authentic "I-You" communication is to establish intersubjectivity, that is shared meaning or shared understanding.

In Chapter 11 (Opportunities to Learn and Intersubjectivity), Catherine Snow and Joshua Lawrence argue that planned attention to intersubjectivity and to procedures that generate intersubjectivity is an essential—yet often ignored—component in effective learning, both in school and in teacher training education. A basic assumption is that learners who are actively engaged in constructing meaning in dialogical activities (such as discussion, reflection on others' thinking, and task collaboration) learn more efficiently and "retain their learning" more effectively than when learning individually. They also claim that learning is sharing rather than transmitting and collaboration rather than individual accomplishment (Kennedy, 2016), and discuss how intersubjectivity is central to these activities and to the participants' learning.

In Chapter 12 (Code-Switching During Shared Reading in Bilingual Families) D. Nomat, V. Grøver, and V. Rydland shed light on bilingual language learning via an empirical study of how young dual language learners (DDLs) living in multilingual contexts were exposed to, and learned to make use of, their two languages while sharing books. Specifically, they studied code-switching, that is the alternating use of more than one language in the same conversation (Myers-Scotton, 1993). Their foci of study were the characteristics of code switching, how it changed over time, and how parents used code-switching to scaffold their child's participation in the dialogues and in learning the two languages. Framed in a dialogical perspective which assumed that language learning originates in social interaction, the study shows *how* dialogical learning plays a crucial role in bilingual language development.

In Chapter 13 (Learning Dialogues When Interaction is Challenged: A Study of Teacher–Child Dialogues in Preschool and Early Schooling), B. E. Hagtvet, S. Hølland, E. Brinchmann, L. I. Engevik, J. Karlsen, and J. Kruse also investigated how young children shared books with adults. However, the adults were now the children's teachers, and the children were preschoolers and young school children in typical and delayed language development, in addition to children with Down Syndrome. The authors discussed how the teachers and children interacted during their co-construction of pictured stories; more specifically, they discuss how they negotiated and maintained intersubjectivity and how the teachers contributed to their joint story construction. The assumption is that intersubjectivity between teacher and child is a crucial mediator for the children's learning.

A unifying quality of the chapters is their focus on "learning dialogues," that is dialogues aiming at "passing on" knowledge or skills from a more experienced person (e.g. the teacher or parent) to a less experienced person (the learner). By this design, their role relationship was asymmetric: one individual (a teacher or parent) had a responsibility to support the child's/student's learning. At the same time, both "teachers" and "learners" varied in skills and experience. The uniting methodological quality of the three studies regards both their basis and their dialogical focus of study: with face-to-face dialogues as their point of departure, they see intersubjectivity between the more experienced and the learner as both a source and a mediating tool for learning.

11
Opportunities to Learn and Intersubjectivity

Catherine Snow and Joshua Lawrence

11.1. Introduction

One of Rommetveit's recurrent dilemmas was the distinction between the "I" and the "You," or the question of when human cognition remains within the skin/skull of an individual, and when it transcends the individual and incorporates others (Rommetveit, 1976. 1998, 2003). The challenge of figuring out the boundaries of individual cognition has been discussed as a theoretical issue by many (see Hagtvet et al., 2003; Linell, 2003; Wertsch, 2003). The issues Rommetveit raised have also been influential in how researchers with more applied interests think about the conditions for productive learning in schools. We believe that in this respect Rommetveit's concept of intersubjectivity is particularly productive. Intersubjectivity describes the dynamic psychological relationship between people engaged in productive shared dialogue or inquiry. Intersubjectivity arises during communicative acts; in other words, it is an inherently social phenomenon in Rommetveit's view. His work demonstrated how complex and dynamic conversations can be, and in doing so raised questions about how relationships that generate intersubjectivity are achieved and maintained and what the alternatives are. His inquiry surfaced questions about communication that are critical to education, which is ultimately the process of expanding students' understanding and knowledge. We argue that these outcomes are best achieved through dialogic processes that generate intersubjectivity. This conceptualization is not always given sufficient attention in analyzing classroom practice or in preparing and supporting teachers; instead, researchers too often isolate students by focusing on their learning or isolate educators by focusing on their teaching. We take from Rommetveit's conceptualization the lesson that both learners and educators, and the relationship between them, must be attended to in any analysis (1998). For instance, does communication in our schools acknowledge the social world in which teachers and students work and live? Who controls the topics of communication and how are social power dynamics, including the right to speak and the right to disagree, understood? In this chapter, we begin to address these questions by focusing on two specific contexts: the classroom and the preparation of teachers for the classroom.

The basic claim we will argue for in this chapter is simple: learners who are actively engaged in constructing meaning learn more efficiently and retain that learning more effectively (National Research Council (NRC), 2000; National Academies of Sciences, Engineering, and Medicine (NASEM), 2018). There is overwhelming evidence that active engagement in learning externally prescribed content requires opportunities for cognitive collaboration—working with well-designed learning tasks, with the guidance of experts, and with the collaboration of peers (NRC, 2000). In this chapter, we buttress the understanding of how to promote these features of active learning by relating them specifically to intersubjectivity—a conceptualization of learning as sharing rather than transmitting and as a collaboration rather than an individual accomplishment (Kennedy, 2016). We illustrate this perspective by documenting approaches to classroom teaching and to professional development that emphasize engaging in debate and discussion, authentic problem-solving, and collaborative learning, using worked examples to promote reflection, and collaborative learning with authentic tasks. We argue that these activities align with Rommetveit's conception of intersubjectivity and support student learning (NRC, 1999; NASEM, 2018).

Teachers face a recurrent dilemma in navigating the demands of nurturing students' minds while at the same time being responsive to the multiple institutional demands to cover a certain amount of content and to prepare students for consequential assessments (Hart et al., 2015). They may in response default to a transmission mode of teaching—in other words, a focus on the transfer via lectures or assigned readings of declarative knowledge from the teacher's mind to the students' minds. It is now widely accepted that the transmission model does not reflect the realities of learning (NRC, 2000). We will argue here that approaches to instruction that have been shown to be effective deviate from the transmission model and adopt instead methods that center intersubjectivity. Again, recognizing that the concept of *intersubjectivity* has multiple meanings that vary with context of use, we define it here as the sharing of understandings or knowledge across two minds, in other words, minds working together through communication and a common focus of reflective attention. The challenge for those interested in improving classroom practice is to support teachers in navigating the tensions between the need for true intersubjectivity in the classroom and the many achievement pressures teachers and students face.

We see precisely the same dilemma—how to give learners access to expertise in ways that exploit the potential of intersubjectivity but also satisfy external standards for content and efficiency—playing out in the design of preservice teacher education programs and professional development (PD).

Traditional approaches to PD involve offering multi-hour workshops that consist of lectures from speaker-experts—the so-called "Spray and Pray" approach. While these workshops are judged effective if the speaker is sufficiently entertaining, there is no evidence that they change teacher practice. Rather, at best they improve teachers' declarative knowledge but fail to support enacted knowledge (Snow et al., 2005) because they do not provide pillars of effective professional learning (opportunities to process the new information interactively, opportunities to consider how specific practices and materials would influence student learning, the intersubjectivity-supporting opportunities for instructional coaching) (Kennedy, 2016). We argue that this approach reflects precisely the same dilemma as choices about teaching practices in elementary and secondary classrooms: school administrators are responsible for providing a certain amount of PD covering certain mandated topics, and they default to the transmission model to meet those demands. Are there alternative approaches that would maximize teacher learning of the content by exploiting what we know about promoting active engagement with it rather than passive reception of it? We argue there are, and that those alternatives also exploit the potential of intersubjectivity.

What is wrong with the transmission model? It ignores, and thus undercuts, the active role of the learner in making sense of new learning—a role that, we argue, requires many adjustments in teaching practices: giving learners greater voice, distributing responsibility for tasks in novel ways, and attending to cognitive and affective engagement. If the transmission model default is indeed to be banished or diminished, though, then we are confronted with the need to consider the implications for how to change what goes on inside the classroom. The transmission model is represented in familiar and still common practices in the elementary and secondary classroom: teachers lecturing, assigning readings, assessing comprehension by focusing on recall of information in the texts, and examining students on the learning accrued. What practices should be implemented instead, to exploit the value added of shared cognition and active learning in pursuing deep understanding and enactable knowledge? And how do future and current teachers learn about those practices? How do they learn to implement classroom procedures which deviate so radically from the ones into which they themselves were inducted as students?

In this chapter, we will briefly review research on three teaching practices with the goal, first, of demonstrating their effectiveness, and second, of exploring what their effectiveness suggests about mechanisms of learning. In each case, we will explore how we see intersubjectivity as central to these activities and to their effectiveness in leading to learning. The three practices are: engaging in debate and discussion, using worked examples to promote reflection, and collaborative learning arrangements with authentic tasks. An overarching goal is to consider the potential and the limits of intersubjectivity in educational practice, and to explore how its features promote active learning by utilizing the affordances of shared cognition, not just in the elementary or secondary classroom but also for professional training and development.

11.2. Classroom/Supports for Active Learning

11.2.1. Engaging in Debate and Discussion

The three classroom practices we review here all violate the transmission model—the notion that teachers can simply transmit their own knowledge to their students. Of them all, topic-centered discussion is perhaps the most intriguing because it disrupts most powerfully the autonomous model of learning, and thus enables us to explore the power and the limits of intersubjectivity in educational practice. Classroom discussion disrupts a related feature of the typical classroom as well—the teacher-centered distribution of speaking privileges. Classroom discussion is of practical as well as theoretical interest precisely because it is widely recognized as academically productive and because claims about its relationship to outcomes we value, such as reading comprehension, writing, and critical thinking, have generated a widespread interest in promoting it.

The case of classroom discussion also crystallizes the practice dilemma because, despite the consensus about its value, it is in fact rather rarely implemented in classrooms. We argue that its rarity in elementary and secondary classrooms is not surprising when we consider a) that it is genuinely difficult to manage, b) that it can take more time than is scheduled for the topic in question, c) that many teachers are anxious about how to ensure well-managed, orderly classrooms during open discussions, and d) that very little preservice or in-service preparation focuses on discussion. As we will review in the second part of this chapter, teacher education and PD settings adopt transmission methods (lectures, assigned readings) as the default, offering models of topic-centered discussion as a skillfully deployed pedagogical practice only infrequently (Snow et al., 2005).

What is the evidence for the value of discussion in the classroom? Dozens of publications have described what good classroom discussion looks like (a small sample includes Aukerman, 2013; Hennessey et al., 2016; Howe et al., 2019; Mercer et al., 2009; Murphy & Firetto, 2017; Wilkinson et al., 2015; Wilkinson et al., 2017) and shown in some small-scale studies that students benefit (e.g. Reninger & Wilkinson, 2010), but large scale and rigorous demonstrations of positive effects are rarer. Murphy et al. (2009) conducted a meta-analysis that showed positive effects on reading comprehension and/or critical thinking for discussion-based pedagogical approaches like "collaborative reasoning," "instructional conversations," and "questioning the author," though surprisingly little empirical work had been carried out evaluating some of the more intensive approaches (Socratic dialogues, Paideia seminars), and results for some other approaches were absent or mixed. Nonetheless, there was robust support for the claim that discussion-based pedagogies support reading comprehension and even more robust support for positive effects on critical thinking.

One intensively studied and widely implemented approach to supporting critical thinking is collaborative reasoning, launched by Richard Anderson at the turn of the millennium. Collaborative reasoning (CR) produces strong effects on critical thinking and argumentation (Chinn & Anderson, 1998; Reznitskaya et al., 2001). The CR approach has been incorporated into various interventions developed and evaluated by scholars not directly related to the CR originators (e.g. Malloy et al., 2020; Silverman et al., 2021; Traga Philippakos & MacArthur, 2020), where positive effects have been found for students' argumentative writing quality. The practice has also been extended from its original design focused on student-managed discussions of ethical dilemmas arising from brief stories (Clark et al., 2003) to approaches more embedded in curricular content (Jadallah et al., 2010), with the advantage that then teachers are more willing to devote adequate classroom time to the activities.

Similarly, the Word Generation program launched by the Strategic Education Research Partnership (SERP) originally used relatively brief texts and activities to promote classroom debates about civic and moral dilemmas (e.g. Should physician-assisted suicide be legal? Should rap music be censored? Should grades be a basis for eligibility for membership on school sports teams?). Videos of these debates taken from public school classrooms can be viewed at https://www.serpinstitute.org/wordgen-weekly/discussion_and_debate. After Snow et al. (2009) showed positive but limited effects of the original Word Generation curriculum, SERP expanded the program to include science and social studies content aligned with state content standards but also incorporating both mini-discussions and full-scale debates into every unit (e.g. Were the Pharoahs wasteful spenders or wise investors? Was it better to live in Athens or in Sparta?). Word Generation shows positive effects on vocabulary even in its "light" version and, in the more intensive version, on reading comprehension and perspective-taking as well (Jones et al., 2019). Its positive effects on a measure of academic language skills are particularly strong for second-language speakers of English.

In short, discussion and debate have been shown to promote academic skills, such as critical thinking, reading comprehension, and writing that are only minimally responsive to transmission teaching. We argue that understanding how these positive effects emerge requires recognizing the role of intersubjectivity—the dynamic, relationship-based, communicative process in which individuals come to understand others' perspectives and incorporate others' information and points of view into their own thinking.

11.2.2. Using Worked Examples to Promote Reflection

Worked examples in math are exactly that: problems that have been worked out for the learner, sometimes correctly, sometimes incorrectly, sometimes in pairs that contrast in approach or correctness, often followed by one or two unworked examples to which students can apply the newly learned skill (see Sweller et al., 1998). Worked examples contrast with the standard practice in math class of giving students many similar unworked problems in the hope they will practice and master the algorithm leading to a solution. Evidence strongly suggests that responding to questions about just a few worked examples (see Figure 11.1) is more effective than solving multiple problems on one's own (Hoogerheide et al., 2014). The question is what mechanism explains this effect, and what does it have to do with intersubjectivity?

The examples in Figure 11.1 show the kinds of annotations students working on these problems are expected to make. The annotations reflect the students' efforts to figure out the cognitive processes of the (fictive) student who provided the original solution. Thus, though each student processes the worked examples individually and autonomously, the task requires identifying what someone else was thinking in order to explain that other person's successive steps to a solution. As a result, learners are forced to compare their own thinking processes to someone else's, just as they are when actually confronted with another student in a collaborative learning setting or in a classroom discussion. Worked problems thus require intersubjectivity despite the absence of face-to-face interaction and use the work of "the other" to provoke reflection and analysis.

Most typically (though not exclusively) implemented in math classes, worked examples are meant to replace the repetitive practice problems (often pages full of them) that have been shown to be ineffective in helping students master math principles (see Booth et al., 2015; Rittle-Johnson, 2006; Star & Rittle-Johnson, 2009). Many explanations have been offered for why lots of practice problems may not be effective in promoting learning in addition to their unparalleled capacity to decrease student interest. Students sometime focus so intently on the mechanical computational processes (adding or dividing correctly, keeping track of numbers when carrying) that the cognitive capacity needed to understand the similarities across problems is unavailable. Furthermore, students who are applying an algorithm incorrectly practice consolidating their errors, thus undermining or postponing correct performance. Alternately, pages full of problems may be completed correctly by students who are never challenged

OPPORTUNITIES TO LEARN AND INTERSUBJECTIVITY 205

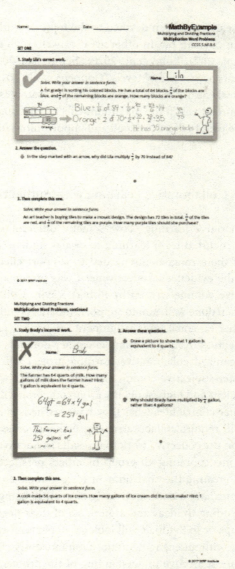

Figure 11.1. An example of one worksheet from Math by Example (https://www.serpinstitute.org/math-by-example).

to actually understand the deeper principles behind the solutions they are producing. Mechanical application of the algorithms is typically sufficient to complete traditional math assignments, and teachers may never realize that students are missing the big idea behind the application of the algorithm—the reason it works.

A wealth of research has been devoted to the topic of worked examples, not just in the domain of math but in other areas as well, such as medical education (Hartman et al., 2021; Kuhn et al., 2020; Shen & Tsai, 2009). The approach works with students across ability levels (Coppens et al., 2019) and across different content areas. Clearly, though, well-designed examples and sequences of examples are required to elicit the maximum effect (Atkinson et al., 2000), and attention has to be paid to cognitive load and opportunities for transfer (Paas & van Gog, 2006).

11.2.3. Collaborative Learning with Authentic Tasks

The term "collaborative learning" covers many different specific classroom practices, from structured team learning to casual student groupings. An extensive review of the arrangements needed to support effective collaborative learning, and of the evidence of effectiveness, was presented as early as 1995 in a comprehensive volume written by Robert Slavin. Collaborative learning arrangements, when done well, aim to support students of different ability levels in working together on some task, assignment, or project, learning from each other and all benefiting from their complementary domains of expertise or interest. A well-organized collaborative learning project will support students in engaging in inter-subjective communication. The tasks will be designed so that the most efficient and highest quality group outcome will only be achieved when each member contributes what they have learned. Furthermore, a well-organized task will require collaborative engagement across members in providing feedback on the collective work that results in iterative improvement on the final project incorporating all group members perspectives. Any teacher will confirm that creating the environment for productive collaborative work is not easy. Students have a hard time navigating challenging content while simultaneously attending to ideas and arguments of their peers (Kuhn & Udell, 2007). Some groups or individuals will look for opportunities to arrive at a solution or outcome without engaging in the simultaneously challenging work of establishing an intersubjective understanding of the problem space. We argue that for teachers to facilitate this kind of intersubjective learning they must encounter the value of such practices for themselves, in their own professional lives—a topic we turn to in the second part of this chapter.

Despite the challenges, the evidence is clear that collaborative learning is effective. For instance, the CORI science and literacy program (Guthrie, 2003), requires that a collaborative group of students draw information from a variety of textual, digital, and human sources, in order to satisfy the demands of a joint project. Each individual in the group has access to unique knowledge stores, so an optimal outcome requires reconciling and integrating those various resources into a shared understanding. CORI produced gains in reading comprehension as well as science knowledge.

There is evidence that collaborative learning arrangements promote engagement and critical thinking for university as well as elementary and secondary students (Gokhale, 1995; Laal & Ghodsi, 2012), and computer-supported collaborative learning is now widely implemented and has been extensively evaluated (Cress et al., 2021). As is the case for collaborative learning in face-to-face elementary and secondary classrooms, its effectiveness in university settings and in distanced, computer-mediated settings depends on the presence of an array of conditions, including norms for group member behavior, selection of tasks at the appropriate level of difficulty, and an appropriate mix of learners. When those conditions are in place, collaborative learning is both more effective and more motivating than individual learning (Krupat et al., 2016; Li et al., 2011; Slavin, 1995).

Collaborative learning arrangements are now widespread in various learning environments—much more so than either worked examples or topic-focused discussion. It has a longer history and its champion, Robert Slavin, developed an array of tools to support effective implementation of collaborative learning. It may be more familiar than worked problems, and easier to implement than whole-class discussion, which requires careful management of topic and process, leading to a lower threshold for adoption.

The question that requires more speculation is precisely what mechanism explains the effectiveness of collaborative learning. There is evidence of greater positive affect among students in collaborative than individual learning settings. We can only assume that translates into higher motivation and perhaps more time on task. But is there strong evidence that intersubjectivity—the exchange of information, the interdependence of the learners in formulating a final product—explains its influence on outcomes? Future researchers could devise ways of asking this question more directly.

11.2.4. Summary of Classroom Methods

Of course discussion supports, such as collaborative reasoning and word generation, as well as approaches like worked problems and collaborative learning, show variable effectiveness. However well designed a program is to support teachers and promote implementation, many competing pressures (such as the need to cover a certain amount of content, worries about "losing control" in the classroom, and the unaligned expectations of administrators) inevitably arise. It thus seems to us to be crucial to identify the key active ingredient of these successful intersubjectivity-boosting approaches to classroom activity, recognizing that those key active ingredients could perhaps be added to a wide variety of teaching approaches and curricular contents. What is common to collaborative learning, worked examples, and discussion-based pedagogy? We hypothesize that the common ingredient here is the piercing of the autonomous learner shield, the recognition of the value a) of making students' thought and analysis permeable to others' perspectives and b) of creating conditions under which students are expected to apprehend the thoughts and perspectives of others. If that is indeed the right analysis, if intersubjectivity is the key active ingredient, then we can start to seek out ways to introduce intersubjective activities more planfully and more widely, perhaps relying on mechanisms like collaborative reasoning or word generation, worked examples, or collaborative learning to introduce these practices but at the same time nurturing opportunities for intersubjectivity wherever they arise, for example, soliciting students' views with open-ended questions, systematically exposing students to multiple perspectives on a single issue, and exploiting unexpected responses to questions or solutions to problems as opportunities to probe each other's thinking.

11.3. Piercing the Autonomous Learner Shield in Professional Development

We hope we have demonstrated how engaging in debate and discussion, using worked examples to promote reflection, and collaborative learning with authentic tasks offer opportunities for intersubjective communication between students and that these practices improve student learning. The work of Rommetveit on intersubjectivity has also significantly influenced research into teacher PD by emphasizing professional learning as a collective endeavor. The idea of intersubjectivity highlights the need for teachers to have a shared understanding of the importance of their work together (Rismark & Sølvberg, 2011). Discussion might be the paradigmatic format for establishing an intersubjective relationship, and Rommetveit's work has influenced how researchers understand both online and face-to-face discussion in professional learning initiatives. Like real-life gatherings, networked learning communities offer participants the opportunity to obtain and create common knowledge by entering a socially shared world of understanding (Helleve, 2007). Online communities allow for joint interpretation and discussion of ideas, shared practices, and pedagogical strategies. When combined with face-to-face discussions, which build and reinforce the sense of collective action and shared understanding, learning communities may provide a way to support intersubjective learning communities and sustained professional learning.

The Sustainable Coaching and Adaptive Learning for Education (SCALE) model is an approach to professional learning designed to scale research-based practices through a hybrid coaching model. Teachers engaged in SCALE use an online platform to access research-based learning and classroom resources and evaluate their use collectively. In contrast to PD models that emphasize an external expert, the SCALE model supports the local coach's instructional leadership capacity and the teachers' collective knowledge. When professional learning initiatives are led by members of a school community, they can scaffold a local shared understanding of a new practice so that it can be adapted and adopted by a community. When skillfully implemented, local coaching results in practices being adopted naturally: they become part of the way "things get done" by that group of teachers rather than "just another thing" they are required to do.

We draw on data from one school implementing the SCALE model. The Rapids High School is a small school in rural Ohio. All 15 academic teachers participate in the SCALE project there. The work described here was led by a site leader supported by a state grant to become a literacy coach. The coach launched the work with teachers in February 2021 by leading an investigation into what makes literacy challenging across different content area classrooms. All teachers became familiarized with the online learning platform and the cadence of online and in-person meetings. Next, we describe work done there in the fall of 2021 to help unpack the potential of this model to support collaborative professional growth through discussion, examining strategies as worked examples, and how authentic collaboration tasks support reflection at Rapids High School.

The coach and school leadership, with input from faculty, decided to focus on supporting student classroom discussion and debate through the SCALE model during the fall of 2021. The coach and a consultant developed a 6-part cycle of inquiry and action related to research on the importance of discussion and a set of research-based instructional strategies to foster classroom discussion and debate. Each week, teachers in the cycle watched a webinar or read a research review selected and posted by the site leader. Teachers responded to structured questions in the online cohort learning area and to each other with comments. The site leader reviewed these responses during weekly meetings with an external consultant, and together the coach and consultant determined how best to meet the needs and challenges of each teacher. The site leader and consultant co-planned local meetings with teachers. They developed agendas that leveraged online responses during in-person meetings of the site leader and teachers. During the in-person meetings, the use of discussion protocols was the norm. The face-to-face interactions used structures that supported active listening and engaging topics and were similar to the structures teachers were being asked to implement in their classrooms. The SCALE model was developed to provide teachers with extended discussions of sophisticated content and sufficient opportunities to build an understanding of each other's perspectives and establish an intersubjective understanding of how new practices should be implemented schoolwide. The format also provided opportunities for the teacher group to examine research-based strategies.

11.3.1. Engaging in Hybrid Debate and Discussion

We report on the teacher's online and offline discussions in response to the first thread. The second author interviewed the coach, examined notes taken from the coach's meetings with the teachers, and examined summary data on program participation and online engagement data. There was variability in how much individual teachers responded online. The responses to the first post were the longest on average (M characters = 1,316, SD = 470). The most extended response to the first post (2,313 characters) was four times longer than the shortest response (477 characters). Participation rates were relatively high, with 100 percent of teachers responding to the first three posts. Across 6 posts, there were 72 responses (80% of the 90 response opportunities) though most of the non-completion was to one post.

We now look in more detail at the content of the teacher's work. The goal of the first post was to give a vehicle for teachers to reflect on and discuss the quality of discussion in their classrooms. The coach shared a link to a rubric developed to help teachers evaluate discussion in their classrooms (https://www.serpinstitute.org/wordgen-weekly/discussion_and_debate) and asked teachers to respond to the following prompts:

> Review the attached Word Generations discussion rubric. During class, use this rubric to evaluate students and answer the reflection questions below:
> 1.) For context, please describe the class discussion topic.
> 2.) What scaffolding did you provide before or during the discussion?
> 3.) Where do you feel like most of your students lie on this rubric when given chances to talk in your class? Are there any areas that you feel students struggle with the most?

Teachers' online responses to questions 1 and 2 were single sentences, but responses to question 3 were more detailed, informative, and thoughtful. One math teacher wrote, "Students could support/explain why they chose their answer, but they needed teacher prompting. They did use more than one sentence to explain their viewpoint, used a sprinkling of vocabulary words, and a few students questioned others' ideas." Another teacher wrote, "From what I have seen many of our students are too afraid to have a view that is different from their peers. When we get opposing views, the discussion will turn into raised voices and repetition of the same 'points' over and over." Teachers responded to each other with the "like button." The coach and one other teacher also replied publicly to two other teachers, so while there was evidence of peer-to-peer communication, it was limited. Rather, the responses demonstrated that teachers understood and reflected on the materials and were, for the most part, engaged. There is no evidence that this online learning itself created opportunities for intersubjective learning between participants. There was no opportunity to build a shared understanding because of the unbalance in the responses and timing of replies. The coach reported that she did not believe the online work would have resulted in the kinds of collaboration and teacher ownership that was eventually developed.

Instead, the coach believed that the online responses supported high-quality, face-to-face meetings allowing teachers to build on one another's ideas and establish a collective understanding of their work together. She identified two mechanisms by which the online work supported the face-to-face meetings. The first mechanism was logistical. She found that since participants in the face-to-face meeting came prepared, and she could use the limited amount of PD time she had with the teaching teams effectively. Meeting time was spent in deep conversations and reflection since all teachers came prepared and with something to contribute. The second mechanism relates to the development of intersubjectivity in face-to-face meetings. She noted that not every teacher read other teachers' responses, but a subset of teachers clearly did and brought other participants' ideas forward to the team meetings. She reported that in doing so, these participants became very influential in highlighting the responses from among the group that were most likely to resonate with everyone. By bringing forward ideas that had been shared online in the face-to-face meetings, these teachers ensured that even members who did not read each other's work online could benefit from the collective reflection conducted in the online space.

The coach's reflections and notes suggest that a consensus about the quality of discussion in the school had been established through the first hybrid discussion sequence. This consensus helped the teachers in the next steps of the inquiry process.

11.3.2. Using Worked Examples to Promote Reflection

There is fundamental conflict between the methods used to develop research-based education practices and scaling their implementation. On the one hand, research helps us understand approaches that have been effective on average across many contexts, and therefore are not based on any particular school.

On the other hand, each school community is unique, has its local history and commitments, and has its own approaches to teaching and working together. If we want to bring a new idea or approach to a school, we should contextualize the innovation for local commitments. When research-based practices are brought to schools, the mechanism used to share the findings does not always appropriately emphasize the importance of adaptation in implementing new instructional approaches or interventions (Kim et al., 2017). In some cases, research-based practices are presented as instructional "recipes" that do not need to be adapted but only implemented with fidelity. This approach to scaling promising practices provides limited scope for teachers to create a shared understanding of the practices and how they can be of maximal value for their local context. For research to scale effectively, we need an approach that leverages world-class research and innovative ideas but brings them to each school community in a way that allows the school community to build its unique, shared, collective understanding of what these practices mean to them and how they should be adapted and adopted.

In the SCALE model, teachers examine, test, and share instructional strategies and discussion protocols as examples rather than recipes. Rather than presenting a particular strategy as something which needs to be implemented formulaically, SCALE schools explore particular strategies as examples of a principle and work together to develop alternatives and reflect on the pros and cons of different approaches. In Rapids High School, the coach wrote to teachers on the online learning platform and asked teachers to "Think about a particular text, lesson, or class that you want to host a class discussion with in the next few weeks. We often want to try a new approach with the groups that are doing well already. However, what we really want to know is if new approaches are going to help us with our most reluctant groups or individuals, or with teaching material that has been challenging in the past." Even though the shared strategies had firm research bases, teachers were asked to test them for themselves and share their results with the group. Teachers responded to the online prompt with unique reasons for strategy selection. A government teacher selected the Rebuttal Battle (https://readingways.org/blog/argumentative-writing). She selected this strategy to test to see if it could help students to "anticipate how their opponent might respond: interpret claims differently; point to drawbacks" and "be ready with a comeback and refute the counter argument by showing how/why it is invalid." Another teacher wanted to test a structured discussion protocol to see if the use of the protocol would result in more balanced conversation. In particular, she wanted to curb some dominant participants so that all students had the opportunity to contribute. She noted that she changed the protocol that had been provided. "I added a section for students to make notes . . . while other students were speaking. We also discussed which talk moves would be helpful to use while students were in the discussion—students picked out appropriate talk moves prior to the discussion beginning." In these cases, teachers treat research-based instructional strategies as targets of reflection, like the "worked examples" given to students; because they were examples rather than recipes, the teachers were free to collaborate on changing, adapting, and mixing with other resources to determine approaches that worked for their school. Examining specific strategies this way seems to have created space for the teachers to reflect more intentionally on the task and on their own instruction.

11.3.3. Collaborative Learning with Authentic Tasks

Collaborative learning has been identified as one of the essential components of research-based professional development (Garet et al., 2001). Specifying the dimensions of collaborative work and discerning the quality of that work in teacher professional development is not easy. In this section, we describe one collaborative learning exercise that the math team engaged in during the SCALE PD initiative. This work was, for these teachers, the culmination of the six-week learning cycle. It built explicitly upon the shared understanding established through the hybrid discussion and the shared understanding that discussion quality in math classrooms could be better. It was also the direct result of the shared inquiry into the exemplar-based instructional strategies. The math team determined that none of the strategies they examined met their needs or were likely to be widely adopted in the math classroom in Rapids High School. These foundational discussions were essential in that they provided a mutually shared understanding of the purposes and goals of the work and provided an obvious and actionable authentic task: create a new strategy for the math department that would support student discussion of math concepts.

The first mention of the department's Error Analysis Protocol was in response to the fourth post. Most of the teachers selected an existing strategy to try, but several of the math teachers responded online about a strategy that had not been mentioned before. For example, "I have been using the Math Department's Error Analysis Protocol. In my classes I have them work in partners instead of small groups. Each group needs to go through 5 guided questions, making sure they start on question 1 and work towards question 5. I allow them to use whiteboards to write their thoughts down while they are discussing with their partner, but nothing can be written on their Error Analysis Paper until they have spoken with either myself or [another teacher]." The coach reported that the team began strategizing the creation of their own strategy in weeks two or three of the initiative, so that by the time the teams were asked to test the strategy, they already had a pilot version. For several weeks, teachers implemented and innovated on their protocol. Students were presented with a math problem with an error. Working with a partner or in a small group, they were asked to identify the key elements of the problem, identify the error made by the student, indicate why they thought the error was made, identify some ways the student could have checked their answer, and solve the problem correctly. They were to do the work on the whiteboard and only complete the Error Analysis Protocol when one of the teachers had checked their work.

Teachers in this professional learning project created a unique approach to the solution that was felt by the team to address the specific needs of their student and content area. The resulting solution was widely implemented in math classrooms, and was even brought into other departments, as demonstrated by this post from a biology teacher: "My biology classes used the Error Analysis Protocol developed by the math team. Luckily we aren't doing math, but we are interpreting and creating DNA and mRNA strands to start our protein synthesis unit. I created DNA sequences and mRNA sequences that had errors in them. Each group needed to a) find the error, b) correct the error, and c) discuss why the error might have occurred." Results like these demonstrate why the concept of intersubjectivity has been, and is, influential in thinking about professional development research. Hybrid discussion seems to have played a central role in establishing a shared consensus about the goals of the work and the commitment to an authentic inquiry process. The examination of specific strategies as exemplars rather than recipes encouraged creative adaptation. The math department saw a need to create a novel approach that they tested and shared with other departments through a collaborative learning process.

11.3.4. From Practices to Principles

We have evidence that certain practices—topic-focused discussion, using specific cases or worked examples as targets of reflection, collaborative learning—can improve learning outcomes for students in classrooms and for teachers in PD settings. We argue that these practices all promote active learning by replacing transmission models with models that exploit intersubjectivity—providing insights into others' minds. They also promote reflectivity, by requiring learners to explain their own thinking to others or themselves. Learning situations in which these intersubjective and reflective practices are implemented also are likely to be characterized by higher learner engagement and motivation, greater learner autonomy, and a more equitable relationship between novice and expert.

The practices we suggest promote intersubjectivity and reflectiveness and create learning conditions with many positive features:

- Embedding the learning task in social contexts;
- Decentering the role of the expert;
- Requiring explanation of one's thinking rather than simply reporting an answer;
- Requiring the use of language to bring thinking into the public sphere where it can be examined;
- Converting traditionally passive learning activities into more active ones;
- Giving learners greater autonomy in how to achieve their goals.

These features are as relevant to professional learning settings, those designed to help teachers align their practices with one another and with research guidance, as they are to classroom instruction intended to promote literacy and math skills, critical thinking, and progress through a set curriculum. Yet they are precisely the features that can most easily be undermined by pressures from accountability assessments, content standards, pacing guides, and demands for fidelity to research-based instructional or intervention protocols. If we are indeed going to promote active learning of the kind made possible by classroom practices that promote intersubjectivity and reflectivity, then we need to align the institutional structures to that goal as a prerequisite to improving both professional learning and classroom teaching.

References

Atkinson, R. K., Derry, S. J., Renkl, A., & Wortham, D. (2000). Learning from examples: Instructional principles from the worked examples research. *Review of Educational Research*, 70, 181–214.

Aukerman, M. (2013). Rereading comprehension pedagogies: Toward a dialogic teaching ethic that honors student sensemaking. *Dialogic Pedagogy*, 1, 1–31.

Booth, J., Cooper, L., Donovan, S., Huyghe, A., Koedinger, K., & Paré-Blagoev, J. (2015). Design-based research within the constraints of practice: Algebra by example. *Journal of Education for Students Placed at Risk (JESPAR)*, 20, 79-100.

Chinn, C. A., & Anderson, R. C. (1998). The structure of discussions that promote reasoning. *Teachers College Record*, 100, 315–368.

Clark, A., Anderson, R. C., Kuo, L.-J., Kim, I., Archodidou, A., & Nguyen-Jahiel, K. (2003). Collaborative reasoning: Expanding ways for children to talk and think in school. *Educational Psychology Review*, 15, 181–198.

Coppens, L. C., Hoogerheide, V., Snippe, E. M., Flunger, B., Van Gog, T. (2019). Effects of examples and modeling examples on learning. *Computers in Human Behavior*, 41, 80–91.

Cress, U., Rosé, C., Wise, A.F., & Oshima, J. (Eds.). (2021). *International handbook of computer-supported collaborative learning*. Springer.

Garet, M. S., Porter, A. C., Desimone, L., Birman, B. F., & Yoon, K. S. (2001). What makes professional development effective? Results from a national sample of teachers.

American Educational Research Journal, 38, 915–945. https://doi.org/10.3102/000283 12038004915

Gokhale, A. (1995). Collaborative learning enhances critical thinking. *Journal of Technology Education (JTE), 7*(1), https://doi.org/10.21061/jte.v7i1.a.2

Guthrie, J. T. (2003). Concept-oriented reading instruction: Practices of teaching reading for understanding. In A. P. Sweet & C. E. Snow (Eds.), *Rethinking reading comprehension* (pp. 115–140). Guilford Press.

Hagtvet, B. E., & Wold, A. H. (2003). On the dialogical basis of meaning: Inquiries into Ragnar Rommetveit's writings on language, thought, and communication. *Mind, Culture, and Activity, 10*(3), 186–204. doi:10.1207/s15327884mca1003_2

Hart, R., Casserly, M., Uzzell, R., Palacios, M., Corcoran, A., & Spurgeon, L. (2015). Student testing in America's great city schools: An inventory and preliminary analysis. *Council of the Great City Schools.* October. 1–162.

Hartmann, C., Van Gog, T., & Rummel, N. (2021). Preparatory effects of problem solving versus studying examples prior to instruction. *Instructional Science, 49*, 1–21. https://doi.org/10.1007/s11251-020-09528-z

Helleve, I. (2007). In an ICT-based teacher-education context: Why was our group "the magic group"? *European Journal of Teacher Education, 30*, 267–284. https://doi.org/10.1080/02619760701486118

Hennessy, S., Rojas-Drummond, S., Higham, R., Márquez, A. M., & Maine, F., Ríos, R. M., García-Carrión, R., Torreblanca, O., & Barrera, M. J. (2016). Developing a coding scheme for analysing classroom dialogue across educational contexts. *Learning, Culture and Social Interaction, 9*, 16–44.

Hoogerheide, V., Loyens, S. M. M., & Van Gog, T. (2014). Comparing the effects of worked examples and modeled examples on learning. *Computers in Human Behavior, 41*, 80–91. https://doi.org/10.1016/j.chb.2014.09.013

Howe, C., Hennessy, S., Mercer, N., Vrikki, M. & Wheatley, L. (2019). Teacher–student dialogue during classroom teaching: Does it really impact on student outcomes? *Journal of the Learning Sciences, 28*, 462–512.

Jadallah, M., Miller, B., Anderson, R., Nguyen-Jahiel, K., Zhang, J., Archodidou, A. & Grabow, K. (2010). Collaborative reasoning about a science and public policy issue. In M. McKeown & L. Kucan (Eds.), *Bringing research to life* (pp. 170–193). Guilford Press.

Jones, S. M., LaRusso, M., Kim, J., Kim, H. Y, Selman, R., Uccelli, P., Barnes, S., Donovan, S., & Snow, C. (2019). Experimental effects of Word Generation on vocabulary, academic language, perspective taking, and reading comprehension in high poverty schools. *Journal of Research in Educational Effectiveness, 12*, 448–483. https://doi.org/10.1080/19345747.2019.1615155

Kennedy, M. M. (2016). How does professional development improve teaching? *Review of Educational Research, 86*, 945–980. https://doi.org/10.3102/0034654315626800 4

Kim, J. S., Burkhauser, M. B., Quinn, D. M., Guryan, J., Kingston, H. C., & Aleman, K. (2017). Effectiveness of structured teacher adaptations to an evidence-based summer literacy program. *Reading Research Quarterly, 52*(4), 443–468.

Krupat, Richards, J. B., Sullivan, A. M., Fleenor, T. J., & Schwartzstein, R. M. (2016). Assessing the effectiveness of case-based collaborative learning via randomized controlled trial. *Academic Medicine, 91*, 723–729. https://doi.org/10.1097/ACM.0000000000001004

Kuhn, D., & Udell, W. (2007). Coordinating own and other perspectives in argument. *Thinking and Reasoning, 13*, 90–104.

Kuhn, J., Van den Berg, P., Mamede, S., Zwaan, L., Diemers, A. D., Bindels, P., & Van Gog, T. (2020). Can we teach reflective reasoning in general practice training through example- based learning and learning by doing? *Health Professions Education, 6*, 506–515. https://doi.org/10.1016/j.hpe.2020.07.004

Laal, M., & Ghodsi, S. M. (2012). Benefits of collaborative learning. *Procedia - Social and Behavioral Sciences, 31*, 486-490.

Li, N., Chang, L., Yuan Xun Gu, & Duh, H. B.-L. (2011). Influences of AR-supported simulation on learning effectiveness in face-to-face collaborative learning for physics. *2011 IEEE 11th International Conference on Advanced Learning Technologies, 320*–322. https://doi.org/10.1109/ICALT.2011.100

Linell, P. (2003). Dialogical tensions: On Rommetveitian themes of minds, meanings, monologues, and languages. *Mind, Culture, and Activity, 10*(3), 219–229. doi:10.1207/s15327884mca1003_4

Malloy, J. A., Tracy, K. N., Scales, R. Q., Menickelli, K., & Scales, W. D. (2020). It's not about being right: Developing argument through debate. *Journal of Literacy Research, 52*, 79–100.

Mercer, N., Dawes, L., & Staarman, J. (2009). Dialogic teaching in the primary science classroom. *Language and Education, 7*, 353–369.

Murphy, P. K., & Firetto, C. M. (2017). Quality talk: A blueprint for productive talk. In P. K. Murphy (Ed.), *Classroom discussions in education* (pp. 101–134). Routledge.

Murphy, P. K., Wilkinson, I. A. G., Soter, A. O., Hennessey, M. N. & Alexander, J. F. (2009). Examining the effects of classroom discussion on students' high-level comprehension of text: A meta-analysis. *Journal of Educational Psychology, 101*, 740–764.

National Academies of Sciences, Engineering, and Medicine. (2018). *How people learn II: Learners, contexts, and cultures.* The National Academies Press. doi: https://doi.org/10.17226/24783

National Research Council. (2000). *How people learn: Brain, mind, experience, and school* (Expanded Edition). The National Academies Press. https://doi.org/10.17226/9853

Paas, F., & Van Gog, T. (Eds.). (2006). Recent worked examples research: Managing cognitive load problem-example and example-problem pairs on gifted and nongifted primary school students' learning. *Instructional Science, 47*, 279–297. https://doi.org/10.1007/s11251-

Reninger, K. B., & Wilkinson, I. A. G. (2010). Using discussion to promote striving readers' higher level comprehension of literary texts. In J. L. Collins & T. G. Gunning (Eds.), *Building struggling students' higher level literacy: Practical ideas, powerful solutions* (pp. 57–83). International Reading Association.

Reznitskaya, A., Anderson, R. C., McNurlen, B., Nguyen-Jahiel, K., Archodidou, A., & Kim, S. (2001). Influence of oral discussion on written argument. *Discourse Processes, 32*, 155–175.

Rismark, M., & Sølvberg, A. (2011). Knowledge sharing in schools: A key to developing professional learning communities. *World Journal of Education, 1*, 150–160.

Rittle-Johnson, Bethany. (2006). Promoting transfer: Effects of self-explanation and direct instruction. *Child Development, 77*, 1–15.

Rommetveit, R. (1976). On the architecture of intersubjectivity. In L. H. Strickland, F. E. Aboud, & K. J. Gergen (Eds.), *Social Psychology in Transition* (pp. 1–16). Springer, Boston. https://doi.org/10.1007/978-1-4615-8765-1_16

Rommetveit, R. (1998). On human beings, computers and representational-computational vs hermeneutic-dialogical approaches to human cognition and communication. *Culture & Psychology, 4*, 213–233.

Rommetveit, R. (2003). On the role of "a Psychology of the Second Person". *Studies of Meaning, Language, and Mind*, Mind, Culture, and Activity, 10(3), 205–218. doi:10.1207/s15327884mca1003_3

Shen, C.-Y., & Tsai, H.-C. (2009). Design principles of worked examples: A review of the empirical studies. *Journal of Instructional Psychology*, 36, 238–244.

Silverman, Proctor, C. P., Harring, J. R., Taylor, K. S., Johnson, E. M., Jones, R. L., & Lee, Y. (2021). The effect of a language and literacy intervention on upper elementary bilingual students' argument writing. *The Elementary School Journal*, 122(2), 208–232. https://doi.org/10.1086/716897

Slavin, R. (1994). *Cooperative learning: Theory, research and practice* (2nd Ed.). Pearson.

Snow, C. E., Griffin, P., Burns, M. S., & NAE Subcommittee on Teaching Reading. (2005) *Knowledge to support the teaching of reading: Preparing teachers for a changing world.* Jossey-Bass.

Snow, C. E., Lawrence, J. F., & White, C. (2009). Generating knowledge of academic language among urban middle school students. *Journal of Research on Educational Effectiveness*, 2, 325–344.

Star, J. R., and Rittle-Johnson, B. (2009). Making algebra work: Instructional strategies that deepen student understanding, within and between algebraic representations. *ERS Spectrum*, 27, 11–18.

Sweller, J., van Merrienboer, J., & Paas, F. (1998). Cognitive architecture and instructional design. *Educational Psychology Review*, 10, 251–296.

Traga Philippakos, Z. A., & MacArthur, C. A. (2020). Integrating collaborative reasoning and strategy instruction to improve second graders' opinion writing. *Reading and Writing Quarterly*, 36, 379–395. https://doi-org.ezp-prod1.hul.harvard.edu/10.1080/10573569.2019.1650315

Wertsch, J. V. (2003). Introduction: "Ragnar Rommetveit: His Work and Influence". *Mind, Culture, and Activity*, 10(3), 183–185. doi:10.1207/s15327884mca1003_1

Wilkinson, I. A. G., Murphy, P. K., & Binici, S. (2015). Dialogue-intensive pedagogies for promoting reading comprehension: What we know, what we need to know. In L. B. Resnick, C. S. C. Asterhan, & S. N. Clarke (Eds.), *Socializing intelligence through academic talk and dialogue* (pp. 37–50). American Educational Research Association.

Wilkinson, I. A. G., Reznitskaya, A., Bourdage, K., Oyler, J., Glina, M., Drewry, R., Kim, M.-Y., & Nelson, K. (2017). Toward a more dialogic pedagogy: Changing teachers' beliefs and practices through professional development in language arts classrooms. *Language and Education*, 31, 65–82. https://doi-org.ezp-prod1.hul.harvard.edu/10.1080/09500782.2016.1230129

12
Code-Switching During Shared Reading in Bilingual Families

Dilman Nomat, Vibeke Grøver, and Veslemøy Rydland

12.1. Introduction

As an essential strategy for supporting the language development of young dual language learners (hereinafter DLLs; Dowdall et al., 2020; Raikes et al., 2006), shared reading has been shown to promote both the first (Roberts, 2008) and second languages (Grøver et al., 2020) of DLLs. During parent–child shared reading, the parent and child engage with a children's picture book and develop a story together. For DLLs, shared reading offers an opportunity to communicate using both languages. However, little is known about the specific ways in which young DLLs and their parents use their first and second languages during shared reading. Our study therefore examines how parents and children in bilingual families use their two languages as resources when reading a picture book together.

We use the term code-switching to refer to the alternating use of more than one language in the same conversation (Myers-Scotton, 1993). Code-switching is a social phenomenon that serves various functions. For instance, it helps speakers express acknowledgement and acceptance of others' preferred language use (Gafaranga, 2010) and negotiate meaning (Yahiaoui et al., 2021). Code-switching may be more or less deliberately used by the communication partners. Nonetheless, the act of code-switching may have implications for the interaction (Kheirkhan & Cekaite, 2015) and in supporting the child's understanding (Kabuto, 2010; Kremin et al., 2022).

In this chapter, we use a dialogic approach to examine how parents and children use their two languages while reading shared books. The dialogic perspective approaches language learning as originating from social interaction. The dialogism we have in mind is grounded in the social interactionist ideas of seminal authors, such as Vygotsky (1978), Bruner (1985), and Rommetveit (1992), who emphasize the central role of dialogue and interaction in learning and development. Rommetveit (1992) wrote extensively about how language in everyday conversation allows participants to negotiate a situated meaning

Dilman Nomat, Vibeke Grøver, and Veslemøy Rydland, *Code-Switching During Shared Reading in Bilingual Families*
In: *Education and Dialogue in Polarized Societies*. Edited by: Ola Erstad, Bente Eriksen Hagtvet, and James V. Wertsch, Oxford University Press. © Oxford University Press 2024. DOI: 10.1093/oso/9780197605424.003.0012

in accordance with fluctuating human concerns. He also discussed how participants of interactions can make sense of each other and establish shared attention through "attunement to the attunement of the other" (p. 23). More specifically, two key constructs within dialogic theory are useful in shedding light on language learning within parent–child dialogues: the Vygotskian term "the zone of proximal development" (Vygotsky, 1978) and its extension, "scaffolded dialogue" were introduced by Bruner (1985) to describe a process by which parents tailor their interactional support to the children's needs and abilities. For instance, parents might engage with children to broaden and enrich their experiences by building on their existing knowledge. Importantly, in a scaffolded dialogue, the parent recognizes the child's intentions and responds to input and clues from the child (e.g. when a child labels an object in a picture book). Scaffolding also involves responding to the child's signals in a way that builds a "scaffold" around the child, thereby allowing them to participate in dialogues and express themselves in a way the child would not be able to do on their own. Recent developments in the Vygotskian position have further emphasized the role of social interaction in educationally informed approaches to language learning (Grøver et al., 2019). Following Snow (2019), we "conceptualise adult–child interaction as a Vygotskian envelope for learning, in which understanding the social mind, i.e., others" communicative intentions, becomes the source of knowledge about language (p. 260).

The present chapter sheds light on how young DLLs living in multilingual contexts are exposed to and learn to make use of their languages while sharing books with their parents. This study responds to recent calls to uncover in-depth insights into parent–child code-switching in the context of shared reading (e.g. Gonzalez-Barrero et al., 2021).

12.2. A Dialogic Perspective on Parent–Child Code-Switching in the Context of Shared Reading

Code-switching between parents and their children is a common practice in bilingual homes and in their shared reading activities (Gonzales-Barrero et al., 2021; Kabuto, 2010; Kremin et al., 2022; Muysken et al., 1996). From a dialogical perspective, by emphasizing the role of social interaction in learning, code-switching provides specific functions that help speakers communicate and express their intentions and emotions (Pavlenko, 2004). Code-switching may signal convergence toward other's language use and preferences. Previous studies have suggested that parents may have unique motivations to code-switch with their children (e.g. Byers-Heinlein, 2013; Gafaranga, 2010; Kremin et al., 2022; Muysken et al. 1996). Indeed, parents have been found to use code-switching strategically to facilitate their children's comprehension and learning. For instance, Byers-Heinlein (2013) found that parents' most commonly reported reason for code-switching in interactions with their children (one-and-a-half to two-year-olds) was to teach them new words. Relatedly, Kremin et al., (2022) found that the most apparent motivation for parents' code-switching was to facilitate their children's understanding and to teach them vocabulary words, noting that bilingual parents may use code-switching "to scaffold bilingual vocabulary acquisition" (p. 2). Muysken et al. (1996) examined the functions of code-switching during shared reading in a sample of 25 five-year-old DLLs and their mothers in the Netherlands who spoke Papiamento and Dutch. Code-switching was more frequent when the mothers referred to new concepts with which the children were unfamiliar and when they corrected statements. In other words, the mothers used code-switching to scaffold the child's understanding and learning. Kabuto (2010) conducted a longitudinal case study of her English–Japanese bilingual daughter (from when she was two to seven years old) to examine her code-switching during shared reading. During the reading interactions, the child's father was mostly focused on the reading objective itself, which mainly involved developing a story together from the pictures of the book and not on what language his daughter used. The acceptance of her code-switching therefore functioned as a tool to stimulate her language learning. Moreover, the parent's and child's code-switching practices changed over time, reflecting a complex process of negotiation. Similarly, Gafaranga (2010) found that bilingual parents code-switched from their first language (Kinyarwanda) to their second language (French) to acknowledge and accept the children's preferred use of the second language.

Studies also suggest that code-switching patterns in parent–child dyads during shared reading activities may change over time. For instance, Pan (1995) studied parent–child code-switching in the context of shared reading of a wordless picture book in Chinese–English families with a preschool child. She demonstrated that the children used the second language (English) more over time, which might reflect the children's increased integration into the larger society and increased exposure to the second language as they grew older. In a study of seven-to nine-year-old Spanish–English bilinguals, Sheng et al. (2013) found that older children code-switched more from their first language to their second language than the other way around.

These developments might reflect children's sensitivity to the context (Bail et al., 2015; Byers-Heinlein, 2013; Paradis & Nicoladis, 2007). For instance, a bilingual child from a language minority background is presumably less likely to use their first language at preschool, where most people would not understand their language. Children's language practices also differ depending on the family member with whom they are communicating, as discussed by Lanza (1997).

12.3. The Present Study

While shared reading is important for DLL's language learning, the specific ways in which parent–child dyads use code-switching during this activity remains poorly understood. Although previous studies have documented the various benefits of shared reading, little research has examined how DLLs alternate between their languages and whether such alternation serves any specific purposes during shared reading. By adopting a dialogical perspective, the present study examined the characteristics of code-switching in parent–child dyads during shared reading at home. We applied a qualitative approach using a three-wave longitudinal case study design, which allowed us to obtain in-depth insights into parents' and children's code-switching practices, while also allowing us to map changes in code-switching over time. The subsample used in this study included seven Kurdish-Norwegian immigrant families who agreed to audiotape three shared readings at home over a five-to-six-month period. The families used Kurdish as their first language and Norwegian as their second language.

The study aims to answer the following research questions:

RQ1: What characterized code-switching over time during parent–child shared reading?
RQ2: How did parents use code-switching to scaffold the child's participation in dialogues?

12.4. Methods

12.4.1. Participants

For the purpose of this study, we included parent–child dyads that, at the onset of the study, primarily used Kurdish during the reading session. The exclusion of three dyads—two because they used Norwegian only and one because the child was the only speaker in a monologue-like recording—resulted in using seven dyads in the analyses. The children (five boys and two girls) were all four or five years old. A bilingual research assistant conducted structured interviews with the parents to obtain information about their families' home language and literacy environment. All children were born in Norway and attended preschool full time. The age of preschool entrance ranged from 20 to 41 months ($M = 31.86$, $SD = 6.69$).

The participants were from Kurdish-Norwegian immigrant families. The parents in each family shared the same first language (Kurdish), which differed from their second language (Norwegian). The parents were born outside of

Norway and had lived in Norway for 5–17 years. The parents' education level varied from primary school to master's degree or higher. For most parents, the highest level of education was high school.

The Kurdish language includes several dialects. In the present study, six of the dyads spoke Sorani-Kurdish and one spoke Badini-Kurdish. All parents grew up speaking Kurdish during childhood. Most of them mainly used Kurdish in their everyday lives at home and with their children. However, according to the parents, the children varied in terms of the language they spoke with their parents. All parents reported in the interviews that the main language spoken at home at the onset of the study was Kurdish. Moreover, all children in the sample were firstborn, and only two children had grandparents and relatives residing in Norway, suggesting that the children were mostly exposed to Kurdish through their parents. Most parents reported reading to their children on a daily basis, and when doing so, they used a combination of Kurdish and Norwegian.

12.4.2. Procedure and Data Collection

All seven parent–child dyads were part of a larger language intervention study by Grøver et al. (2020) that primarily took place in preschool but that also included a book reading component at home. As part of the intervention, the parents received four books to share with their children during the preschool year. The first three books were wordless, while the fourth included text in both Kurdish and Norwegian.[1] To reduce text diversity, we built the analysis on three books that built a narrative through pictures only. Wordless books offer bilinguals unique opportunities to use either language or alternate between them without having to take into consideration the language choice offered by a text.

Parents shared the first book at the beginning of the preschool year and the second and third books at two-to-three-month intervals. The time between reading the first and third books was thus five to six months. Parents (either the mother or the father) were asked to share each book several times and to audio-record one reading of each book. The same parent read with the child over time. While five dyads returned all three recordings, Dyad 6 did not return the recording of the third book and Dyad 7 did not return the recording of the second book. All parents were asked to use their preferred language and to share the book as they typically would.

---

[1] The sample of books was not expected to be familiar to families living in Norway and included *Frog Where Are You?* (Mercer Mayer), *Pancakes for Breakfast* (Tomie DePaola) and *One Frog Too Many* (Mercer Mayer). The books were read by the families in that order.

12.4.3. Coding and Analysis

The audio recordings were transcribed using the CHAT transcription format (MacWhinney, 2000) by a native Kurdish-speaking research assistant. In addition, all audio recordings and transcriptions were verified by the first author (also a native Kurdish speaker). To answer research question one, we first operationalized *code-switching occurrence* as an utterance that involved a switch from Kurdish (the primary language) to Norwegian. This switch from Kurdish to Norwegian applied to anything from a single word to a full sentence. We obtained the proportion of code-switching utterances by dividing the number of utterances that included code-switching by the total number of all utterances multiplied by 100. Second, we operationalized *initiations* of code-switching as parents' or children's initiation of a switch from Kurdish to Norwegian. Finally, to examine who of the speakers initiated a turn to Norwegian and who subsequently initiated a return to the primary language, we operationalized *returns* as parents' or children's attempts to return to the primary language (Kurdish). The first author and a research assistant (both native Kurdish speakers) coded six recordings (20% of the transcripts) independently. Differences were discussed to reach agreement. We examined inter-rater reliability using Cohen's weighted kappa. Cohen's weighted kappa for code-switching occurrences, initiations, and returns, were .86, .91, and .96, respectively.

To answer research question two, we used an inductive approach to examine the interactional context of code-switching in the different dyads. We analyzed the reading sessions of all seven dyads across all three waves. For illustration, we draw examples from reading sessions involving dyads 1, 2, and 4 because they differed from each other in important ways. These three dyads differed in their patterns of code-switching both at the onset of the study and over time (see Figures 12.1 and 12.2), illustrating how code-switching can change in unique and complex ways.

12.5. Results

12.5.1. Code-Switching Patterns Over Time in the Seven Dyads

Of the total utterances (N = 2850) produced by the parents in all seven dyads during the three waves, 9.83% were instances of a combination of Kurdish and Norwegian (median 7.48%). However, we observed much variation, ranging from 2.55% to 39.33%, in the frequency of parents' code-switching utterances. Of the total number of utterances (N = 1146) produced by the children in all

CODE-SWITCHING... BILINGUAL FAMILIES 225

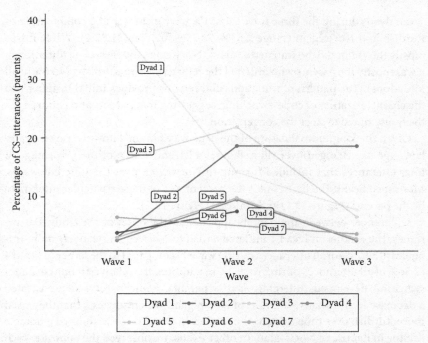

Figure 12.1. Percentage of parents' total utterances that included code-switching from Kurdish to Norwegian.

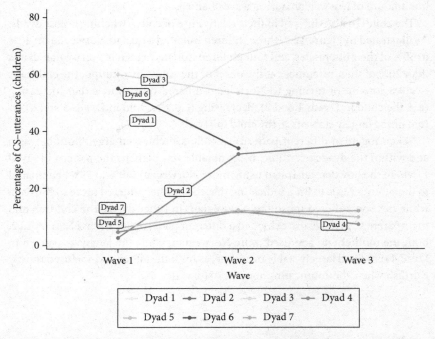

Figure 12.2. Percentage of children's total utterances that included code-switching from Kurdish to Norwegian.

seven dyads during the three waves, 22.51% were instances of a combination of Kurdish and Norwegian (range 2.53%–78.79%, median 31.82%). While it was mostly the children who initiated a turn to Norwegian (60.88% of all initiations), it was mostly the parents who initiated the returns back to Kurdish (84.76% of all initiations). The pattern of initiations and returns provides initial insights into the characterization of code-switching, suggesting that parents and children actively attempted to steer the conversation.

Given the longitudinal nature of the data, we examined how the seven dyads' language use changed over time. Figures 12.1 and 12.2 plot the percentage of total utterances that included turning to Norwegian over the different waves. More specifically, the figures plot the percentages of these particular utterances by the parents (Figure 12.1) and children (Figure 12.2).

Differences between the parents appeared at the onset of the study. For instance, the mother in Dyad 1 initiated a turn to Norwegian relatively more frequently (39.74% of all utterances during wave 1) compared to the father in Dyad 4 (2.56% of all utterances during wave 1). In addition, the relative amount of code-switching developed differently across parents. Some parents demonstrated a decrease in the relative amount of Norwegian, which suggests that they used more Kurdish over time, such as the mother in Dyad 1, who exhibited a notable decline in her use of Norwegian. In other dyads, we observed the opposite, such as the mother in Dyad 2, who increasingly used more Norwegian. Meanwhile, the father in Dyad 4 exhibited a more stable pattern over time, demonstrating a low amount of Norwegian during waves 1 and 3.

The children also differed in their relative use of code-switching across dyads. As illustrated in Figure 12.2, three children initiated a turn to Norwegian in 40% to 60% of their utterances, and four children initiated a turn to Norwegian in less than 20% of their utterances at the onset of the study. In addition, the children's relative amount of turning to Norwegian differed over time, either increasing (e.g. the child in Dyads 1 and 2), decreasing (e.g. the child in Dyads 3 and 6), or remaining largely stable (e.g. the child in Dyads 4, 5, and 7).

Taken together, different patterns of code-switching emerged both between and within the dyads over time. Most notable was perhaps the pattern in Dyad 1, where the boy demonstrated using more Norwegian (40% to 79%) compared to the mother (39% to 8%), indicating that the mother adhered more to Kurdish, while her son adhered mostly to Norwegian. In other dyads, the children and their parent's language use exhibited a different pattern. For instance, in Dyad 2, both the mother and son used more Norwegian, while the language pattern in Dyad 4 remained largely stable over time, as both the father and son used mostly Kurdish when communicating about the storyline.

We selected our sample based on these three dyads (Dyad 1, Dyad 2 and Dyad 4) to ensure variation when examining how parents used code-switching in scaffolded dialogues. These differences highlight the complex language profiles of the dyads.

In the next analysis, we examined how parents in these dyads engaged in code-switching when engaging in scaffolded dialogues.

12.5.2. Code-Switching as a Tool in Scaffolded Dialogues

Our analysis indicated that parents used Kurdish and Norwegian as a tool to scaffold their child's participation during shared reading. A combination of both languages was observed in instances where the parent attempted to guide and support the child's understanding. Overall, the parents supported the children in three different ways, as characterized in the following sections.

12.5.3. Child-Initiated Code-Switching and Parental Confirmation

The first category illustrates how the parents confirmed the child's contribution. In this category, parental confirmation refers to confirmation that the child is understood. Example 1 is drawn from Dyad 2 at the onset of the study. As demonstrated in Figures 12.1 and 12.2, both the mother and son used more Norwegian over time. In Example 1, the dyad spoke about the protagonist and his dog, who went to the forest. The example starts with a question from the mother in Kurdish (line 1).

Example 1.[2]
Dyad 2, (boy, 51.97 months).
1. MOT: Înca, biçokeke u segeke çon bû kuwê?
 Afterwards, where did the child and the dog go?
2. CHI: *Skogen.*
 The forest.

---

[2] We present the examples using multi-linear transcription since the dyads did not speak in English. In the examples, words spoken in Kurdish are written in roman script and words spoken in Norwegian are written in italics. The examples are translated directly to English and are therefore not always grammatically correct.

> 3. MOT: Ewan çon bo *skogen*.
>   They went to *the forest*.
> 4. MOT: *Skog* yanî daristan.
>   *Forest* means forest.
> 5. CHI: Daristan.
>   Forest.

The son answered the question in Norwegian (line 2). Next, the mother confirmed that she understood what the child was saying. She mainly used Kurdish but repeated the same word introduced by her son in Norwegian (line 3). The mother then told him what the Norwegian word was in Kurdish (line 4). The child repeated the Kurdish word (line 5) after the mother introduced it. The example illustrated that the mother attuned to her son's choice of words. She then built on her son's knowledge of the word in Norwegian by offering him the word in Kurdish. With guidance from the mother, the son was able to use the word in Kurdish (line 5).

As illustrated in Example 2 (drawn from the first book), the parents also confirmed their understanding without using Norwegian. The example involves a dyad (see Dyad 4) that mostly used Kurdish for all three book readings, as shown in Figures 12.1 and 12.2. In this example, the father and son speak about the protagonist, who was looking for a lost frog. In line 1, the father asks his son, in Kurdish, where the protagonist went.

> Example 2.
> Dyad 4 (boy, 61.09 months)
> 1. FAT: Kurik kîve çû?
>   Where did the boy go?
> 2. CHI: Kurik çû def (.) def *hullet* da.
>   The boy went to the (.) the *hole* inside.
> 3. FAT: Çû ser darê sehkete nav konêda, ew konêt nav darîda û sehketê +/.
>   Went up on the tree to look inside the hole, the holes inside the tree and looking +/.
> 4. CHI: Ê, konî.
>   Yes, hole.

The boy first attempted to answer in Kurdish, paused briefly—potentially signalling that he wanted to find the Kurdish word—and then continued by saying "hole" *(hullet)* in Norwegian (line 2). The father confirmed that he understood what the child was saying without providing a translation, unlike the mother in Example 1; rather, he explained what the protagonist was doing and emphasized the word "hole" by saying it twice in Kurdish (line 3). The son then successfully said the word in Kurdish (line 4). Thus, Example 2 illustrates a different method of parental confirmation compared to Example 1, though both ways led to the children learning words in Kurdish. The parent's confirmation seen in this example is also reflective of a type of extension, which we examine in more detail in the next section.

12.5.4. Child-Initiated Code-Switching and Parental Extension

The second category illustrates how the parents extended the topic, as briefly illustrated in Example 2. Example 3 is drawn from Dyad 2's reading of the third book. Mother and child spoke about the protagonist and his friends, who were happy and smiled as they were reunited with their little frog. The example starts with a question from the mother, who asks her son, in Kurdish, what the protagonist and his friends were doing.

> Example 3.
> Dyad 2 (boy, 51.97 months)
> 1. MOT: Wanîş çiyan kirdûwe?
>   What are they doing?
> 2. CHI: *Bli bû smil.*
>   Become a *smile*
> 3. MOT: Pêyan xoşe.
>   They are enjoying it.
> 4. MOT: *Smile* yan kirdûwe.
>   They are *smiling*.

The son answered using both Kurdish and Norwegian (line 2) to indicate that they are smiling. The mother extended her son's utterance by providing a short explanation, in Kurdish, for why they were smiling (line 3). She then repeated the Norwegian word that the child introduced (line 4). By building on her son's contribution to the dialogue, the mother emphasized and clarified his input while still using the Norwegian word that he had introduced. As demonstrated in Figures 12.1 and 12.2, Dyad 2 used more Norwegian when reading the third book. However, although the mother in Dyad 2 appeared to accept her son's use of Norwegian words, she occasionally negotiated what language to use. This negotiation is illustrated in Example 4, which is also drawn from the third book.

The mother points to a spider depicted in the book and asks her son what the word was in Kurdish (line 1).

Example 4.
Dyad 2 (boy, 51.97 months)
1. MOT: Ewe çîye, înca?
   Now, what is this?
2. CHI: *Edderkopp.*
   Spider.
3. MOT: Be Kurdî çi elên be *edderkopp*?
   What do they call *spider* in Kurdish?
4. CHI: *Edderkopp.*
   Spider.
5. MOT: Be Kurdî çi elên?
   What do they say in Kurdish?
6. CHI: *Edderkopp!*
   Spider!
7. MOT: Calcaloke +/.
   Spider + /.
8. CHI: *Edderkopp!*
   Spider!
9. MOT: Calcaloke.
   Spider.
10. CHI: *Edderkopp! +/.*
    Spider! + /.
11. MOT: Ewe çîye, înca?
    Now, what is this?
12. MOT: Ewe malî calcalokekanîye.
    This is the spider's house.
13. CHI: *Det er sånn edderkopp!*
    It is a spider!
14. MOT: Ê, de başe, *edderkopp*.
    Okay, fine then, *spider*.

As shown in line 2, the boy responded to the mother's invitation to name the spider depicted by saying it in Norwegian. In lines 3 and 5, the mother asks the boy what a spider was called in Kurdish, but also in line 3, she repeats the Norwegian word "*spider*" (*edderkopp*). Despite asking her son to say the word in Kurdish, the mother uses his choice of word. The child answers in Norwegian for the third time, with a slightly irritated voice (line 6). In lines 7 to 10, the mother tries to say spider in Kurdish as a correction but is cut off by the child.

As this exchange continues over a few more turns, the child signals his annoyance by raising his voice. Toward the end (line 11), the mother turns the attention to something else in the book. However, the boy does not answer; instead, he becomes quite emotional and almost starts shouting. The boy then said a complete sentence in Norwegian with a raised voice (line 13), and the mother illustrated acceptance of the Norwegian word (line 14). This lengthy back and forth, or *tug-of-war*, showed how the mother made an effort to return to Kurdish, while the child made an equal effort to use Norwegian. In other words, the word "spider" was "tugged" in opposite directions before the mother finally accepted the Norwegian word. This interaction illustrates how insistent the participants occasionally became in negotiations about language choice.

12.5.5. Parent-Initiated Code-Switching to Support the Child's Understanding

The third category illustrates how the parents used both Norwegian and Kurdish to support the child's understanding of the topic. In Example 5, Dyad 1 reads the first book and speaks about bees. The example starts with the boy pointing to the bees and asking what they were (line 1).

Example 5.
Dyad 1 (boy, 52.96 months)
1. CHI: Û eweş?
   And this?
2. MOT: Aha, ew çîye?
   Look, what is that?
3. MOT: Aha, ew hîne (.).
   Oh yeah, it is that thing (.).
4. MOT: Ewe mêşhenge, mêşheng.
   It is a bee, bees.
5. CHI: A.
   Yes.
6. MOT: Mêşheng *lage honning* eken.
   Bees are *making honey*.
7. CHI: A.
   Yes.

As can be seen in lines 2 to 3, the mother seems unable to recall the word for bees at first. After a brief pause, the mother seems to remember and then repeats it twice to secure her son's understanding (line 4). The boy confirms shortly (line

5), and the mother then turns to Norwegian to explain what the bees were doing (line 6), possibly to support a common understanding. Turning to Norwegian as an additional resource when securing a common understanding also happened a few months later, when the same dyad shared the second book. In Example 6, they speak about a picture of trees covered with snow. In line 1, the mother asks her son what snow implies.

> Example 6.
> Dyad 1 (boy, 52.96 months)
> 1. MOT: Ke befir bû, ba yanî çî?
>   When it's snowing, what does it mean?
> 2. MOT: Yanî zistan.
>   It means it's winter.
> 3. CHI: A.
>   Yes.
> 4. MOT: Yanî *vinter* e, *okey*?
>   It means it's *winter*, *okay*?
> 5. CHI: Mhm.
>   Mhm.

The mother explained in Kurdish that when it snows, it means it is winter (line 2). This is followed by a short confirmation from her son (line 3). The mother uses the Norwegian word for winter in line 4, following the boy's minimal confirmation in line 3. A possible interpretation is that the mother used Norwegian as an additional support to make sure the child understood her statement about snow and winter, and in so doing, recognized Norwegian as a language resource for him, despite her own preference for and use of Kurdish (see Figure 12.1).

However, in dyads where the child spoke mostly in Kurdish, the parent also occasionally used Norwegian in addition to Kurdish. In Example 7, the father and child talk about the protagonist and his friends who had gone to the forest. In line 1, the father asks, in Kurdish, where the protagonist and his friends were.

> Example 7.
> Dyad 4 (boy, 61.09 months)
> 1. FAT: Ê, çûn kîve?
>   Yes, where did they go?
> 2. FAT: Ew çûn nav xebata.
>   They went inside the forest.
> 3. CHI: Ê, nav xebata.
>   Yes, inside the forest.

> 4. FAT: Eve *skogen* e, mane?
>   This is *the forest,* right?
> 5. CHI: Ê, *skogen.*
>   Yes, *the forest.*

The father provides an answer that they went to the forest (line 2), with the boy confirming and repeating part of the father's utterance in Kurdish (line 3). In line 4, the father turns to Norwegian to repeat the word and asks for confirmation in Kurdish by saying "*mane*?" (right?). The child responds by repeating the same word (line 5). Since this dyad mostly spoke in Kurdish, and the child actively confirmed that he understood, the father may have said the word in Norwegian to acknowledge that they both also knew how to say it in Norwegian.

12.6. Discussion

The present study examined how code-switching changes over time and how parents use code-switching to scaffold the child's participation in shared reading. Our longitudinal study analyzed recordings of reading sessions from seven dyads over three time-waves. The findings provided us with unique insights into code-switching patterns between and within dyads and revealed several key insights.

First, building on studies that have found that code-switching patterns differ between (e.g. Bail et al., 2015; Byers-Heinlein, 2013) and within (Kabuto, 2010) dyads, we observed both between-dyad and within-dyad differences. A unique contribution of our study is that the dyads exhibited distinctive starting points with respect to the frequency of code-switching and that patterns of code-switching developed in different directions among the dyads (see Figures 12.1 and 12.2). We also observed notable changes in code-switching during a rather short period of only approximately six months. For instance, one might expect parents to use more Norwegian over time due to the child's greater exposure to and use of the language. However, in one of the dyads in our study, the mother used less Norwegian over time, while the son used more Norwegian. Such longitudinal changes in code-switching might reflect a process of negotiating the "rules" of language use. The mother might have used less Norwegian to ensure that her son maintained a command of the Kurdish language, due to her son's increased use of Norwegian. Our results showed that both parents and children played an important role in shaping the language practices in the dialogue by expressing and negotiating their preferred language. According to Gonzales-Barrero et al. (2021, p. 3), families who value bilingualism are more likely to use both languages in their home reading practices. Our findings are consistent with this notion. In the interviews, the parents reported that they wanted their children to grow up bilingual. They also reported that they usually used Kurdish and Norwegian when reading with their children.

Second, the parents and children differed in how often they initiated a switch from Kurdish (the main language) to Norwegian and how often they returned to the main language. Consistent with previous studies showing that children use more of the second language than their parents (e.g. Pan, 1995; Sheng et al., 2013), we found that most initiations of Norwegian language use were performed by the children. This finding is unsurprising, given that all children attended preschool full time, where they were exposed to Norwegian. However, not all children demonstrated greater use of Norwegian over time; some of the children's use of Norwegian remained similar over time. This finding reflects how the dyads differ from each other in important ways. However, most returns to Kurdish were performed by the parents, thus reflecting the parents' desire for their children to maintain a command of the Kurdish language, a fact reported by the parents during the interviews. Studies have shown that parents prefer to use the first language when communicating with their children (e.g. Muysken et al., 1996; Pan, 1995). Adding to these findings, our results illustrate that parents do this in different ways during shared reading. For instance, in Examples 2 and 4, both children initiated a turn to Norwegian, followed by their parents attempting to return to Kurdish. While the father in Example 2 used a more indirect approach to do so, the mother in Example 4 used a more direct approach. Moreover, in countries such as Norway, parents from language minorities are usually the only ones who teach their first language to their children.

Third, and perhaps most notably, our results show that parents use code-switching as a tool to scaffold dialogues. Parents used a combination of both languages in different ways to confirm, extend, and facilitate the child's understanding. Previous studies (e.g. Muysken et al., 1996; Kremin et al., 2022) have illustrated that parents' motivation for code-switching is to develop their children's understanding. We found that one of the most apparent motivations for parents to perform code-switching was to facilitate understanding, but they also used it to confirm and extend the child's contribution. In most dyads, parents actively scaffolded the conversation by attuning to their children's choice of words, which usually included Norwegian words. Parents might have used these approaches to recognize Norwegian as a language resource for their children, despite their personal preference for Kurdish. Parents applied these expressions of recognition, as reflected in their use of both languages, to expand on their children's input. This finding relates to Rommetveit's (1992) discussion of the process of meaning-making and shared attention. Our results show how parents attune to their children by adopting the same words as their children (in the same language) and that they rarely attempted to control the child's language preference and language use.

However, parents who demonstrated less use of Norwegian appeared to be more concerned with what language the child should use in the dialogue. In such instances, it was apparent that the participants adhered to the "contract" of speaking Kurdish during reading. Although children's first-language development may benefit from parents who use the language more (Lanza, 1997), we speculate that such adherence to one language may come at a cost, as children's language preferences may go unrecognized. Our findings also showed instances in which changing the language posed a dilemma for the dyads. In some interactions, the participants appeared particularly persistent in their negotiation of language choice. The children contributed to the dialogue with their own preferences regarding what words to use, and some parents adhered strongly to returning to Kurdish after their child had turned to Norwegian. This situation is best illustrated in Example 4, where there seems to be a clear tension between the mother and son. Their lengthy back and forth—or negotiation—illustrates how the mother tried to return to Kurdish, while the child made an equal effort to use Norwegian. Thus, the children expressed their language preferences and occasionally appeared in negotiations about language choice. This dilemma may be uniquely faced by bilingual dyads, as their two languages can be "tugged" in opposite directions during a dialogue.

The present study has several limitations worth highlighting. First, our study consisted of a small number of dyads and reading sessions. Data from more reading sessions over a longer period would provide additional longitudinal insights into changes in code-switching. Second, the findings with respect to code-switching patterns may not be generalizable to other contexts beyond the specific context of shared reading. It is possible that the same seven dyads would exhibit different patterns during dinnertime or in other settings. Third, we excluded dyads who spoke Norwegian only. We made this exclusion criterion based on our interest in code-switching, but our conclusions may have differed if our sample included Kurdish-Norwegian dyads who used Norwegian as their primary language. Fourth, our findings may not be generalizable to other language minority groups that have different migration backgrounds compared to the Kurds in our sample: all parents in our study were born outside Norway, whereas their children were born in Norway. Finally, we did not distinguish between the different types of code-switching in our analysis, such as single words and complete utterances of code-switching; however, we see value in doing so for future research.

12.7. Conclusion

A large body of research has shown that bilingual children's use of the second language increases over time as they gain greater exposure to the language in settings outside the home, such as in preschool. Thus, parents who wish to raise their children as bilinguals play an important role in ensuring that their children maintain command of their first language. The present study offers insight into code-switching practices between parents and children in the context of shared reading. Across different parent–child dyads, we found that parents used a combination of Kurdish and Norwegian to scaffold their child's language learning. From a dialogic perspective, language is supported in social interaction and "develops in the context of achieving pragmatic goals and for the purpose of contact, interaction, understanding, and knowledge acquisition" (Grøver et al., 2019, p. 2). The parents in our study used both languages to express the recognition of their children as language users who have specific and developing language preferences in a multilingual context in which they are growing up as bilinguals. This chapter has illustrated the ways in which parents and children use their two languages as resources to make sense of each other and reciprocally adjust their perspectives and interests to each other in dialogues about a picture book. Thus, we believe that this empirical study of code-switching within parent–child book-sharing sheds light on an important feature of dialogic theory: how "mutual understanding on the part of conversational partners is contingent upon reciprocally adjusted perspective setting and perspective taking" (Rommetveit 1992, p. 23). Our findings show how parents transcend their own language preferences to adjust to their children's language use to acknowledge and recognize them as dialogically capable participants. In this way, parents "attune to the attunement" of their child.

References

Bail, A., Morini, G., & Newman, R. S. (2015). Look at the gato! Code-switching in speech to toddlers. *Journal of Child Language, 42*(5), 1073–1101. https://doi.org/10.1017/S0305000914000695

Bruner, J. (1985). Narrative and paradigmatic modes of thought. *Teachers College Record, 86*(6), 97–115.

Byers-Heinlein, K. (2013). Parental language mixing: Its measurement and the relation of mixed input to young bilingual children's vocabulary size. *Bilingualism: Language and Cognition, 16*(1), 32–48. https://doi.org/10.1017/S1366728912000120

Dowdall, N., Melendez-Torres, G. J., Murray, L., Gardner, F., Hartford, L., & Cooper, P. J. (2020). Shared picture book reading interventions for child language development: A systematic review and meta-analysis. *Child Development, 91*(2), e383–e399. https://doi.org/10.1111/cdev.13203

Gafaranga, J. (2010). Medium request: Talking language shift into being. *Language in Society, 39*(2), 241–270.

Gonzalez-Barrero, A. M., Salama-Siroishka, N., Dubé, D., Brouillard, M., & Byers-Heinlein, K. (2021). Effects of language dominance on home reading practices of bilingual families. *International Journal of Bilingualism, 25*(1), 77–99.

Grøver, V., Rydland, V., Gustafsson, J.-E., & Snow, C. E. (2020). Shared book reading in preschool supports bilingual children's second-language learning: A cluster-randomized trial. *Child Development, 91*(6), 2192–2210. https://doi.org/10.1111/cdev.13348

Grøver, V., Uccelli, P., Rowe, M., & Lieven, E. (2019). Learning through language. In V. Grøver, P. Uccelli, M. Rowe, & E. Lieven (Eds.), *Learning through language: Towards an educationally informed theory of language learning* (pp. 1–15). Cambridge University Press.

Kabuto, B. (2010). Code-switching during parent—child reading interactions: Taking multiple theoretical perspectives. *Journal of Early Childhood Literacy, 10*(2), 131–157. https://doi.org/10.1177/1468798409345109

Kheirkhah, M., & Cekaite, A. (2015). Language maintenance in a multilingual family: Informal heritage language lessons in parent–child interactions. *Multilingua, 34*(3), 319–346.

Kremin, L. V., Alves, J., Orena, A. J., Polka, L., & Byers-Heinlein, K. (2022). Code-switching in parents' everyday speech to bilingual infants. *Journal of Child Language, 49*(4), 714–740. http://doi.org/10.1017/S0305000921000118

Lanza, E. (1997). Language contact in bilingual two-year-olds and code-switching: Language encounters of a different kind? *International Journal of Bilingualism, 1*(2), 135–162.

MacWhinney, B. (2000). *The Childes Project: Tools for Analyzing Talk, Volume II: the Database* (3rd ed.). Psychology Press. https://doi.org/10.4324/9781315805641

Muysken, P., Kook, H., & Vedder, P. (1996). Papiamento/Dutch code-switching in bilingual parent–child reading. *Applied Psycholinguistics, 17*(4), 485–505. https://doi.org/10.1017/S0142716400008213

Myers-Scotton, C. 1993. *Social motivations for codeswitching: Evidence from Africa.* Oxford University Press.

Pan, B. A. (1995). Code negotiation in bilingual families: "My body starts speaking English." *Journal of Multilingual & Multicultural Development, 16*(4), 315–327. https://doi.org/10.1080/01434632.1995.9994610

Paradis, J., & Nicoladis, E. (2007). The influence of dominance and sociolinguistic context on bilingual preschoolers' language choice. *International Journal of Bilingual Education and Bilingualism, 10*(3), 277–297. https://doi.org/10.2167/beb444.0

Pavlenko, A. (2004). "'Stop doing that, la komu skazala!': Language choice and emotions in parent–child communication." *Journal of Multilingual and Multicultural Development, 25* (2&3), 179–203.

Raikes, H., Alexander Pan, B., Luze, G., Tamis-LeMonda, C. S., Brooks-Gunn, J., Constantine, J., Banks Tarullo, L., Abigail Raikes, H., & Rodriguez, E. T. (2006). Mother–child bookreading in low-income families: Correlates and outcomes during the first three years of life. *Child Development, 77*(4), 924–953. https://doi.org/10.1111/j.1467-8624.2006.00911.x

Roberts, T. A. (2008). Home storybook reading in primary or second language with preschool children: Evidence of equal effectiveness for second-language vocabulary acquisition. *Reading Research Quarterly, 43*(2), 103–130. https://doi.org/10.1598/RRQ.43.2.1

Rommetveit, R. (1992). Outlines of a dialogically based social-cognitive approach to human cognition and communication. In A. H. Wold (Ed.), *The dialogical alternative. Towards a theory of language and mind* (pp. 19–44). Scandinavian University Press.

Sheng, L., Bedore, L. M., Peña, E. D., & Fiestas, C. (2013). Semantic development in Spanish–English bilingual children: Effects of age and language experience. *Child Development, 84*(3), 1034–1045. https://doi.org/10.1111/cdev.12015

Snow, C. E. (2019). So much progress, so much left to do. In V. Grøver, P. Uccelli, M. Rowe, & E. Lieven (Eds.), *Learning through language: Towards an educationally informed theory of language learning* (pp. 257–261). Cambridge University Press.

Vygotsky, L. S. (1978). *Mind in society: The development of higher psychological processes.* M. Cole et al. (Eds.). Harvard University Press.

Yahiaoui, R., Aldous, M. J., & Fattah, A. (2021). Functional and sociocultural attitudes of code-switching and its relation to the meaning-making process: The case of dubbing Kim Possible into Arabic. *International Journal of Bilingualism, 25*(5), 1349–1368.

13
The Importance of Intersubjectivity in Teacher–Child Joint Story Construction

Bente Eriksen Hagtvet, Silje Hølland, Ellen Brinchmann,
Liv Inger Engevik, Jannicke Karlsen, and Jana Kruse

13.1. Introduction

In this article, we report on a study of teacher–child interaction during joint story construction. Its purpose was to elucidate the importance of teacher–child intersubjectivity to story construction and teacher mediation. Intersubjectivity between teacher and learner is presumably a pivot of learning dialogues; yet its importance has attracted limited research interest within the field of education. We carried out an in-depth small-scale study of six teacher–child dyads while co-constructing stories. The dyads were selected for participation because their intersubjectivity was reported to be either very high or very low in an ongoing study by the authors (Hølland et al., in process).

Grounded in sociocultural theory, we assumed that quality teacher mediation aims at supporting skills and knowledge that a learner cannot handle independently but that may be appropriated in collaboration with the teacher (or more competent peers) (Rogoff, 1990; Vygotsky, 1978; Wertsch, 2007). In our study, this collaborative alliance was both the main driver of constructing stories and a focus of study.[1]

Inspired by the phenomenological tradition, and in particular by Ragnar Rommetveit's ideas, we further foregrounded a dialogical perspective on the learning situation. This led us to see intersubjectivity (shared attention/shared understanding) as a basis on which qualified teaching and successful learning is built (Rommetveit, 1968, 1972, 1992).[2]

---

[1] This interactive conceptualization of learning (Vygotsky, 1978) has more recently been expanded in related ideas and perspectives on teaching and learning, such as "dialogism" (Bakhtin, 1981; Linell, 2009), "the multivoiced classroom" (Bakhtin, 1981; Dysthe, 1996), "guided participation" (Rogoff, 1990), scaffolding (Wood et al., 1976), among others.

[2] Being a polysem, "intersubjectivity" has numerous related meanings; its precise meaning therefore depends heavily on its context of use (e.g., "shared understanding", "shared meaning", "shared attention" (Linell, 2009); "shared here and now" (Rommetveit, 1972).

13.2. Teaching and Learning as Communicative Acts, Based on Intersubjectivity

Rommetveit most typically discussed "intersubjectivity" with reference to the ideal "I-You" dialogue with symmetric role relations. In symmetric dialogues, intersubjectivity is achieved by the interlocutors' speaking and listening on each other's premises—by taking each other's perspective (decentering):

> Communicative acts are social and directional: A sent message is encoded in some sign medium [e.g. the language], and the received message is generated by a decoding operation performed upon that medium. Efficiency of communication may in principle be assessed in terms of correspondence between sent and received messages. Encoding and decoding are complementary processes [encoding involves anticipatory decoding and complementarily, decoding takes place on the premises of the sender]. The medium is a tool by which message transmission is made possible. (Rommetveit, 1968, pp. 64–65).

Within these ideal conditions of communication, for example, among close friends, both parties have the will and skill to encode and decode on the other's premises and to (re)establish intersubjectivity via negotiations to clarify misunderstandings. This is most typically *not* the case in *a*symmetric dialogues, such as teacher–child dialogues (Linell, 2009).

13.3. Intersubjectivity and Learning Dialogues

The learning dialogue, or "educational dialogue", is fundamentally a *tool for learning*; its purpose is to increase the learner's insights and skills via dialogically based teacher mediation. Its role relation is *a*symmetric: the teacher is in control and operates from a position of authority, both by dint of role, of mastery of factual knowledge, and of language and dialogical skills. The learner, on the contrary, most typically has complementary disadvantages and often more general problems in taking the perspective of others (decenter) (Piaget, 1954). From a communication perspective, teacher–child dialogues are presumably just as dependent on teacher–child intersubjectivity as are dialogues with symmetric role relations; however, the teacher must typically invest more "communicative labor" (Linell, 2009) to compensate for limitations in cognitive-linguistic skills, insights, and experience of the young learner. Following the reasoning of Rommetveit, the communicative labor involved in compensating for a child's dialogical "limitations" is nuanced in quality and potentially demanding on time.

Establishing intersubjectivity depends on each interlocutor's skills in encoding and decoding on the premises of the partner, via

". . . reciprocally adjusted perspective setting and perspective taking [. . .] achieved by an "attunement to the attunement of the other" by which states of affairs are brought into joint focus of attention, made sense of, and talked about from a position temporarily adopted by both participants in the communication. (Rommetveit, 1992, p. 23).

By inference, a dialogue's core point is "the dialogically established shared social reality" as intersubjectively decided on. If this is not jointly agreed upon, the interlocutors must "endorse contracts" (negotiate) about what knowledge they may take for granted (as tacit information) when something is spoken (Rommetveit, 1972)—most typically by specifications, illustrations, reminders, explanations, etc. From this, it follows that the teacher in learning dialogues has a responsibility to establish at the very least *moments of intersubjectivity* with due attention to the child's perspectives, premises, and presuppositions. And the younger the child, and the more the child's skills of language, cognition, and knowledge deviate from those of the teacher's, the more the teacher must compensate for the child's limitations by taking the perspective of the child and acting complementarily.

Rommetveit did not specifically elaborate on the importance of intersubjectivity to asymmetric learning dialogues. However, his analysis of the asymmetric dialogue between Helmer and Nora in Ibsen's *The Doll's House* (1990) is of some relevance. In the first act, Nora returns home from a pre-Christmas shopping spree fondly showing Helmer all the gifts she has bought, including one to him. Ibsen's voice speaks rather heavily via Helmer's choice of words in addressing Nora: "little squirrel," "skylark," "featherhead," "spendthrift," etc. Rommetveit pursues the message in Ibsen's choice of words arguing that Helmer's condescending use of words is anchored in Helmer's "subjectivity." And as the play develops, this very subjectivity contributes to Nora's distancing herself from Helmer's world and, in the final act, also from his companionship. By this portrayal, Rommetveit draws attention to the potential costs of asymmetric dialogues without intersubjectivity—not only in terms of dialogical distancing but also in feelings of alienation.

While published back in 1879, this aspect of Ibsen's play still appears "modern." It is also relevant to today's schools, for example when a child's learning is slow, or (s)he for other reasons is unhappy. To avoid school failure and students' feelings of alienation, it may then be urgently important that teachers speak with intersubjectivity on the child's premises. We shall argue that Rommetveit's emphasis on the need to aim for speaker–listener-intersubjectivity is also highly relevant to learning dialogues at rather concrete levels.

Rommetveit's argument on this point fits well with Vygotskys (1978) emphasis on the teachers' obligation to guide the learner to new insights by mediating the learning process from the learner's "actual" to "potential" level of competence, via the learner's zone of proximal development (Vygotsky, 1978, 2007). Important concretizations of the process of mediation have been presented, in particular via the concept of "scaffolding" (Wood et al., 1976). Not rarely is it then seen as a process of rather "technically" assisting the child to new insights via subgoals and subcomponents (Stone, 1993). A stronger focus on the "communicative mechanisms" in the scaffolding process has been called for (Wertsch, 1985), for example, on the personal relation between teacher and learner (Stone, 1993), or the subtle verbal directives ("semiotic uptake") that contribute to child involvement and learning (Wertsch & Stone, 1985). Still, systematic studies of one-to-one teacher–child communication in educational settings has, to the best of our knowledge, received limited research attention (but see Brinchmann et al., 2023; Engevik, et al., 2015; Gustavsson, 1988; Røe-Indregård et al., 2022). Rather, when teacher–child interaction *has* been examined, it has most typically focused on teachers' instructional practices vis a vis a group, as for example in observation studies of classroom interactions (Klette, 2003; Pianta et al., 2008).

This state of the affairs presumably partly reflects didactic practices in the classroom: when students within a classroom context work individually (e.g. when writing texts), observation studies indicate that teacher–child interactions tend to be rare (Hagtvet, 2003; Svanes & Klette, 2018). More typically, teachers do desk-based paperwork, or "move around" in the classroom answering questions. In a general sense the importance of teachers' *ways* of initiating and reacting to students' initiatives and responses has nevertheless been emphasized in classroom research. One example regards the ways teachers ask questions, On this background, the which often goes by an "initiative-response-evaluation" pattern: the teacher raises a question, the student(s) respond(s), and the teacher evaluates the respons(es) (the IRE format). While apparently productive when dealing with fact-based knowledge, it has appeared less than constructive relative to other areas of learning. In these "other contexts" the *ways* teachers meet student responses appear to affect learning climate, learning effects, and students' self-efficacy (e.g. Cazden, 1988; Gardner, 2019). Teachers who, rather than evaluating student responses "critically," confirm the correct parts of the student input while at the same time offering an alternative "solution" in a supportive atmosphere (confirmation with reassurance) (the IRC+ format), appear to affect both students' learning and wellbeing positively (Gardner, 2019). This pattern of interaction arguably depends rather heavily on teacher–child intersubjectivity. Overarching aim of the current study is to shed light on these very issues. This is done by elucidating the relations between teacher–child intersubjectivity, teacher mediation, and their ways of interacting during children's learning to construct stories.

13.4. Intersubjectivity in a Developmental Perspective

As a phenomenon, "intersubjectivity" occurs in various appearances depending on philosophical tradition, scientific discipline, domain of study, etc. (Linell, 2009). Of particular relevance to the current study are "developmental perspectives" documenting layers, or levels, of intersubjectivity within various domains—in this study, specifically with reference to development of language and cognition.

Early levels of intersubjectivity between child and caregiver have been extensively studied by Trevarthen and collaborators (1979, 2011). They observed a primary level of I-You-intersubjectivity in the form of shared attention between the gazes of mother and child only a few hours after the child's birth (primary intersubjectivity). A secondary level of intersubjectivity was observed when the child and caregiver some months later documented shared attention toward objects in the room (Trevarthen & Hubley, 1978). This expanded the dyads' opportunities to dialogize with intersubjectivity about objects and persons and an I-It-You-relationship was activated. Trevarthen (2006) further proposed a tertiary level of intersubjectivity (usually mastered around age 4 years). Now the "It" encompassed a more abstract semantic level mediated by symbolic references to actual and fictional worlds via dialogues about words' meanings and storys' events. In the current study we further explored intersubjectivity developmentally, but now with somewhat older children and with a more pronounced emphasis on *variations* in the participants' joint story constructions.

13.5. The Current Study

We carried out a small-scale in-depth study of the joint story constructions of teacher–child dyads at varying levels of intersubjectivity. Young school children (aged 5 through 8 years), some with language and/or cognitive delays, participated in the study together with their teachers. The included teacher-child dyads were selected for participation because they functioned at either particularly high-, or particularly low- levels of intersubjectivity in the abovementioned study by the authors (Hølland et al., in process).

Used for both enjoyment, learning, and assessment, teacher–child co-construction of pictured stories is a highly appreciated activity in preschool and early schooling (Dickinson & Smith, 2001; Grøver et al., 2020; Mol et al., 2009). It is also a much-used research activity. At best it represents a unique combination of joy and learning in a natural, yet defined, setting. From the perspective of intersubjectivity and language learning, it optimizes the chances of talking *about* the "It" of a dialogue at a range of semantic levels. From the perspective of didactics/education, it offers rich opportunities to study *how* teachers mediate the co-construction, in addition to insights into a child's independent and mediated mastery (Vygotsky, 1978). On this background we considered teacher–child story construction a particularly well-suited activity and context for this study. We raised two research questions, first, "how do teacher–child dyads at high- and low levels of intersubjectivity talk about pictures to co-construct stories?"; and secondly, "how does teacher mediation during teacher–child joint story construction vary in dyads at high and low levels of intersubjectivity?". The study's overarching purpose was to elucidate the importance of teacher-child intersubjectivity to children's story construction and teacher mediation.

13.6. Method

13.6.1. Participants

A total of six teacher–child dyads participated in the study. They were sampled from three subsamples participating in the study by Hølland et al., (see Table 13.1). The subsamples involved three groups of children varying in cognitive-linguistic skills: *typical language (TL), impaired language (IL), and Down syndrome (DS)*. From each of these three subgroups, we included the dyads with the highest and the lowest proportion of turns maintaining intersubjectivity, that is two from each subgroup.[3]

The age ranges in the three original samples were as follows: typical language (TL): 5.9–6.0 years; impaired language (IL): 5.3–6.4 years; and Down syndrome (DS): 8.0–8.1 years. At the time of data collection, The TL- and IL-groups were preschoolers/kindergarteners soon to start school; the children in the DS-group were school children (with higher chronological ages, but language ages approximating the ages of the other participating children). The children attended schools in Eastern Norway, most of them in urban areas. All children went to their local mainstream schools. (For more information about the Norwegian educational system, see for example, Hagtvet, 2017).

Information on the current sample as extracted from Hølland et al. are presented in Table 13.1. This includes information on the children's gender, the dyads' length of story construction (total amount of turns produced per dyad (frequency), proportion of turns that were maintained (linked to other turns)

---

[3] Level of intersubjectivity in Hølland et al. was assessed by a simplified version of interaction analysis where the unit of analysis was the turn (Linell et al., 1988). The study's analytical focus regarded the degree to which the teacher–child dyad carried out their co-construction via turns that maintained (level 3), negotiated (level 2), or disrupted (level 1) intersubjectivity. In the current study, we included the two dyads from each subgroup with the highest and lowest proportion of turns maintaining intersubjectivity (relative to negotiations and disruptions).

Table 13.1. Sample characteristics (extracted from Hølland et al., in process).

Dyad Gender (girl/boy)	Total turns (frequency)	Turns maintaining intersubjectivity (% of dyads' total turns)	Level of Intersubjectivity (within each group)*
Typical language (TL): **			
TL04 (g)	167	95 %	High
TL06 (b)	79	55 %	Low
Impaired language (IL): **			
IL11 (g)	206	90 %	High
IL15 (b)	154	65 %	Low
Down syndrome (DS)$_2$: ***			
DS16 (b)	335	95 %	High
DS22 (g)	98	50 %	Low

* Examples of the turns typical at the three levels of intersubjectivity are presented in Hølland et al. (in process): turns maintaining, negotiating and disrupting intersubjectivity. The numbers referring to proportions are rounded.

** The children in groups TL and IL were recruited to the project, Child Language and Learning (CLL). (Department of Special Needs Education, University of Oslo, 2012–2019 / The Norwegian Research Council).

*** The children with Down syndrome were recruited to form a purposive subsample from a national cohort (Næss, 2012), described in two previous studies: Engevik et al., 2015 and Engevik et al., 2016.

(percentage), and the dyad's level of intersubjectivity within his/her language group (High-I dyads and Low-I dyads).

Table 13.1 shows that the children's gender is equally distributed across groups and dyads. Further, the dyads' length of stories (frequency of turns) varied considerably (from 79 turns (TL06) to 335 turns (DS16), as did also, the dyads' proportion of turns maintaining intersubjectivity, ranging from 50% (DS22) to 95% (TL04).

The groups' communication skills also varied considerably: some children had well-developed cognitive-linguistic skills, but considerable expressive language delays (in particular with syntax and articulation), others had more serious language delays, in some cases relying on gestures and manual sign language when communicating, and others again were "typical." In total, the dyads from the three subgroups represented large variations in task-relevant skills of language, cognition, and communication—and also in motivation and endurance during task performance.

The teachers were recruited by virtue of their role as the main teacher of a participating child. The preschool teachers of the children with typical and impaired language development held a degree in early education and care. The teachers of the DS children were either educated as special needs teachers or as teachers trained for general education with many years of experience within special education. All teachers reported an average of five years in their current job position (range = 1–13), and of three years with the target student (range = 2–7). For reasons of anonymity, all teachers are referred to as females; also, qualifications are described by group characterizations. For the same reason, the precise ages of individual children are not given. All preschools and schools were in densely populated areas of Norway, in or near the capital.

By thus aiming for variation with regard to teacher–child intersubjectivity, subgroups' language skills, and teachers' backgrounds, we expected that essential qualities of teacher–child joint story construction and teacher mediation would be more manifest than in more typical teacher–child dyads.

13.6.2. Procedure

The observation setting. According to task instructions, the teacher's role was to construct a story in collaboration with the child on the basis of the story pictured in the book *Frog, Where Are You?* by Mercer Mayer (1969). The book has no text and consists of 24 line-drawings in sepia tones. The story features a boy, his dog, and a pet frog who live together in the boy's room. The frog escapes during the night, and the boy and the dog leave the house to search for the frog in the forest nearby. During their search, they encounter a few animals and events that interfere with their search. Finally, they find the frog at a pond together with his frog-family. The story ends happily: the boy and his dog return home with a small frog and waves goodbye to the other frogs. The task instruction presented by the researcher to the teacher and child was as follows: "Here is a book with pictures that tell a story. Now you can tell this story together".

The data. The joint story constructions were videotaped as unobtrusively as possible at the children's (pre)schools (Engevik et al., 2015; Hølland et al., 2017; Kruse & Hagtvet, in process). The duration of the sessions was, on average, 11 minutes (range: 4 min, 50 sec – 22 min, 00 sec). The dialogues were transcribed verbatim using a simplified version of the transcription conventions of Conversation Analysis (Linell, 2009). Nonverbal communication, such as pointing and nodding, was included in the transcripts and coded on the basis of their functions in the ongoing interactions. The video recordings were transcribed by three of the authors, and uncertainties of interpretation were discussed with a coauthor to resolve potential differences.

13.6.3. Analytical Approach

Levels of intersubjectivity. As mentioned above, the dyads' level of intersubjectivity (low or high) was in the Hølland study assessed by a simplified coding system based on dialogical turns. Representing a dialogical link to the previous turn in an interaction, a turn acts as interactive "glue" between speaker and listener thereby contributing considerably to the intersubjectivity between interlocutors. Teacher-child dialogues with a majority of turns maintaining intersubjectivity presumably affect not only the quality of story construction, but also the quality of teacher mediation and presumably also the students' learning.

The Hølland study revealed great variations in the degree to which the dyads maintained or did not maintain intersubjectivity. In the current study, we expanded on this finding by carrying out a qualitative content analysis of the story constructions of the two dyads within each subgroup with the most and the fewest turns maintaining intersubjectivity (High-I and Low-I, cf Table 13.1).

Qualitative content analysis. In carrying out the qualitative content analysis, key concerns regarded the ways dyads scoring High and Low respectively on intersubjectivity talked about the pictures to co-construct a story (research question 1) and how the teachers mediated the story constructions via invitations, comments, and responses to the children's input (research question 2). Accordingly, the examples presented should shed light on the dyads' typical ways of talking about pictures and the teacher's ways of mediating. By illustrative examples, "thick descriptions" of dialogical qualities were constructed (Derry et al., 2010).

To contextualize the qualitative results below, we will highlight some findings from the study by Hølland et al. (in process) (see Table 13.1): In the total sample of 22 dyads, the proportion of turns maintaining intersubjectivity ranged from 50% (DS22) (the lowest score in the total group), to 95% (TL04), which is the highest. Among other things, this shows that all the participating dyads succeeded in constructing stories with at least 50% of their turns being intersubjectively related (but some with more disruptions than was the case in the dyads defined as "high on intersubjectivity"). This also implies that "high" and "low" are relative terms.

Below we show how the High-I and Low-I dyads talked about pictures to co-construct stories as mediated by the teachers. With teacher mediation being an integral part of the story construction, the two research questions are often addressed concurrently. Also, examples with commentaries are given priority of space. This gives a realistic documentation of the findings in addition to a practice-oriented understanding of the relations studied. A final discussion follows at the end.

13.7. Results

The results are reported dyad-wise, as case descriptions, first the three High-I dyads, thereafter the three Low-I dyads.

13.7.1. Teacher–Child Interactions at High-Level Intersubjectivity

Results from the three High-I dyads are presented in the following order: TL04 (typical language), IL11 (impaired language), and DS22 (Down syndrome).

Dyad TL04—Typical language development: Co-inquiries into story elements. This dyad includes a preschool girl, aged 5 years, and her preschool teacher. A total of approx. 95% of their turns were categorized as high on intersubjectivity (Table 13.1), the highest proportion of its kind in the TD language group (and also in the total data set).

The session started by a relatively long "question–answer" sequence in ways that shared similarities with an interrogation, but in a warm and humorous atmosphere, for example, "What's in the picture?" "Why is it inside the glass bowl?" "Do you think the dog has captured him?" "Do you think it is during daytime (noting a moon outside the window)" "Do you think he (the frog) has run away?"

Already from the beginning, this teacher (T) directed the child's (C's) attention beyond each picture's meaning to the story's meaning, mainly via "there-and-then questions." By this, T showed C a strategy to go by when talking about pictures to construct a story. To each question C briefly responded, with T confirming, clarifying, and sometimes evaluating C's response, for example, by requesting precision ("[you mean] the boy?"). They also co-reflect on the pictures' "messages," relative to a potential story.

Excerpt 1 shows how T and C carried out a coherent sequence of interaction within a context of shared "here and now." The turns are intersubjectively related via joint interpretations of the pictures; in the beginning mediated by T, but at turn 140, C takes on a larger responsibility for the narration. By expanding on events previously introduced via T's mediation, C initiates the co-constructing of the story's climax and resolution.

Excerpt 1: Dyad TL04.

139	T:	Oh no! Oh! What happens Malin? (Å nei! Å! Hva skjer Malin?)
140	C:	The boy falls into the water and then he meets that frog again. (Gutten faller uti vannet og da møter han frosken igjen.)
141	T:	((looks at C)) Do you think so? (Tror du det?)
142	C:	Yes (Ja)
143	T:	Do you really think so? Maybe there was no frog there, but they fell in the water. (Kanskje var det ikke noen frosk der, men de falt ut i vannet.)
144	C:	And then (he hears) the frog. (Og så (hører han) frosken.)
145	T:	Do you think so? (Tror du det?)
146	C:	Yes (Ja)
147	T:	Hush, be quiet ((finger in front of the mouth)) (hysj, vær stille)
148	C:	((peeks))
149	T:	((peeks)) (oh, no, who sits there?) (Nei, men, hvem sitter der?)
150	C:	The frog. (Frosken.)
151	T:	You were right. But what has happened? (Du hadde helt rett. Men hva har skjedd?)
152	C:	(tadpoles) (froskunger)
153	T:	(tadpoles) (froskunger)
154	C:	Small tadpoles (Det er små rumpetroll)

A dramatic climax in the story comes in turn 139, when the boy falls into a pond and C takes the narrative lead by inferring from what happens to what she sees as a probable resolution of the story: "... and then he meets that frog again." (turn 140). By this inferential hypothesizing, C directs T's attention to a more abstract level where the meaning of the story is constructed. With subtlety, T invitingly challenges C's fantasy, "Do you think so?" (turn 141) and subsequently encourages C to interact at the level where the story's meaning is constructed (turn 147). And what is more, the child's prediction (turn 140) turns out to be correct: the frog *is* in fact at the pond, inspiring T to encourage C to deduce what presumably had happened (turn 151).

At the very end, C's concern for the future of the frog is expressed as a dilemma of whether the frog should stay with his frog family at the pond or return to the boy's room: "why did they stea—take the frog from his family?" C thoughtfully questions (turn 158). From the perspective of the frog, enjoying life with his frog family is probably a better option than being imprisoned in a glass bowl in the boy's room. This ethical dilemma is ambiguously presented in the pictures but is quite clearly expressed by C and is a story element of crucial importance to yet another level of intersubjectivity: the story's meaning—its "moral."

In sum, by the largest proportion of High-I turns in the total sample, this dialogue shows how teacher and child, in mutually sensitive collaboration, built a story at different levels of semantic depths: from picture labeling, via the meanings of things and events within the story frame, to interactions at the level of story meaning, and finally its moral. Also, it shows how the teacher's mediating support varied in type as the story developed: in the beginning, T's "interrogative" questioning aimed at aspects of the pictures of essential relevance to the pictured story ("what's in the picture," "why do events take place," "what does the picture signify" (the moon, indicating the time of the day). In short, T's dialogical approach shared many similarities with an advanced form of the IRC+ format (Initiative-Response-Confirmation with Reassurance) (Cazden, 1988; Gardner, 2019), with the confirmation-part inviting inquiries into the story's meaning, but never with corrective remarks ("Do you think so? Why?"). Gradually, as C gains deeper insight into the narrative's plot, the mediation appeared more like a teacher–child co-inquiry into the story's message and moral, which Trevarthen referred to as tertiary, or in this case a fourth, level of intersubjectivity. By this, C co-experienced how to interpret pictures within a narrative frame as guided by T. T's mediating approach functioned as a strategy for C to appropriate and subsequently to use independently (Vygotsky, 1978), which C also did at the end of the session.

Dyad IL11—Impaired Language: Co-construction by encouraging a narrative perspective. The girl in this dyad, aged 5 years, had been referred to a unit for speech and language pathology due to language delays—particularly in articulation and syntax (cognitive functioning was not negatively affected). T started the session by inviting C to "read the book jointly," which C approved of, and T added, "then we have to help each other" while pointing at the pictures on the front page, whereupon C labeled the protagonists:

Excerpt 2: Dyad IL11.
13 C: A frog, a boy ... what ... a (dog) ... boy (En frosk, en gutt, hva en (hund) gutt)
14 T: Very good (turns the page) (Riktig)
15 C: The frog jumps out (looking at C) (Frosken hopper ut)
16 T: Yes, "frog, where are you?" (Ja, Frosk, hvor er du?)
        (T looks in the book and quickly turns the page)
        Look here (pointing) What happens here? (Se her (...) Hva skjer her?)
17 C: The frog. (Frosken)

18	T:	The frog and the dog and the boy ((looks in the book)) (Frosken og hunden og gutten)
19	C:	Mhm.
20	T:	And where is the frog? ((looks in the book)) (Og hvor er frosken?)
21	C:	In there. ((pointing at the glass bowl where the frog is)) (Oppi der)

In this opening scene, T invites C to familiarize herself with the task by labeling the pictures (13, 15) while T confirms (14) and encourages (16) the process. At the end of turn 16, T directs C's attention to the narrative elements that will constitute a story ("what happens here" (16). When C does not respond adequately, T responds by an expansion (18) that would expectantly catalyze a longer sentence by C, which it does not do.

By this, T right from the beginning establishes a variant of the IRC+ format (Initiative-Response-Confirmation with Reassurance). While not always leading to the response requested, at least partly due to C's language problems and uneasiness about trying, this pattern of communication appears to drive the co-construction forward at a level that C can join with engagement.

Excerpt 3 (below) concerns an early conflict in the plot, where the frog climbs out of the glass bowl while the boy and the dog sleep. "What does the frog do?" (30), T invitingly asks, which inspires C to attribute motives to the frog's disappearance: the frog wants to go to the pond . . . (33)) or even run away! (35)). T briefly confirms, before expanding on C's "there-and-then" reflections by asking C what the boy and the dog are thinking when they wake up (and the frog is gone) (36). The pace is slow all along, leaving time for C to think, which C does.

Excerpt 3: Dyad IL11.

30	T:	But what does the frog do? ((T and C look in the book)) (Men hva er det frosken gjør?)
31	C:	Jumps out. (Hopper ut)
32	T:	The frog jumps out, yes. (Frosken hopper ut, ja)
33	C:	Because he would like to go to his pond ((looks at T)) (Fordi han har lyst å gå til dammen sin)
34	T:	((looks at C)) perhaps that is so (4 sec.) (Kanskje det)
35	C:	((yells)) or *runs away* ((looks at T, T looks down)) (Eller stikker av!)
36	T:	((turns the page)) Yes, when the boy and the dog wake up, what do they think then? ((looks at C)) (Ja, når gutten og hunder våkner, hva tenkte de da?)

> 37 C: ((looks in the book)) Where is the frog? ((looks at T—smiles))
>   (Hvor er frosken?)
> 38 T: Where is the frog—that is what I think as well ((nods, looks
>   down in the book))
>   (Hvor er frosken—det tror jeg også de tenker.)

These reflective negotiations about the meaning of the pictures with reference to an overarching story plot (30–35), lift the dialogue to a more abstract, intangible, and hypothetical world of fantasy (36–38). The meanings of the concrete events pictured appear to expand via the dialogue. T contributes to this thematic expansion by inviting C to verbalize what the boy and the dog are thinking when they wake up to discover that the frog has disappeared (37). Implicitly she at the same time encourages C's own thinking ahead, through pauses and a generally slow dialogical pace.

Excerpt 3 further shows how T systematically supports C's engagement and self-confidence by confirming C's input, sometimes with an expansion (38), or by just offering emotional support (verbally and nonverbally (34, 37)). By thus maintaining intersubjectivity within a supportive climate, T and C jointly tell the story as pushed forward by T's invitations to move beyond "the here and now" (34, 36). This takes the dialogue from the "I–It (book picture)–You-level" to a more advanced "There-and-Then" level. Here C and T communicate intersubjectively at a level of "rational fantasy" where links are drawn from the pictures' meanings to the narrative's meaning and where a crucial aim of the dialogizing is to establish intersubjectivity about the resolution and meaning of the story.

The impact of C's language limitations was noticeable all along, although apparently varying with C's involvement in the story under construction. When involved, C spoke in longer sentences. T's focus was mostly on the task of joint story construction and not explicitly on C's language impairments, although she (T) quite often recasted or expanded on deviant uses of words and sentences spoken by C. More rarely, the teacher–child intersubjectivity was challenged by C's syntactical errors, for example, "She breaked the dog the house ((looks in book)) all the honeys" (89) (Norwegian; "Hun ødelagte hunden huset . . . all honningene") (the pictured context was a beehive that had fallen to the ground with a swarm of bees "hunting" the fleeing dog—a rather complex event to verbalize). However, T understood the essence of C's utterances and did not comment on deviant language forms.

In brief, after a short period where C and T communicated about the pictures at a concrete level, they co-constructed their story by a more advanced strategy: first they labeled story elements (who, when, why), followed by T's drawing the attention to narrative elements: first, meaning(s) of picture(s) with reference to story plot; then to the story's meaning. Also, T's mediation via an IRC+ format characterized by expansions at a slow pace, appeared to serve C's contributions well: focusing on communication rather than C's delayed language skills appeared to have both sociopsychological and linguistic advantages.

Dyad DS16—Down Syndrome: Co-constructing by aiming for intersubjectivity. Having a Down Syndrome diagnosis, the boy in DS16, eight years old, mainly talked in one-word utterances, often in combination with signs. Excerpt 4 illustrates how he and his teacher managed to establish and maintain intersubjectivity despite very limited contributions from C, but with T giving priority to shared attention and understanding.

Right from the beginning, DS16 established a systematic, yet flexible, dialogical version of the IRC+ format. The Confirmation part was mainly "implicit," most typically by T confirming or expanding on a correct aspect of the response offered by C. However, the verbal mediation was continuously "explicit"—with as many revisions as needed to establish shared understanding.

Excerpt 4 refers to the first scene in the book where the boy and the dog study the frog in the glass bowl. T starts by questioning C about the characters in the pictures (where (27), who (29), and how (31)). C replies appropriately (although with an erroneous use of a preposition (*oppå* (on) for *oppi* (in)) (28), which T ignores, but indirectly corrects by confirming C's answer via an expanded sentence using the correct preposition ("the frog is inside (*oppi*) the bowl" (29). At a more decontextualized and narrative level, T continues the story construction by asking how the frog got into the glass bowl (31). This invitation to draw relations between a pictured event to an imagined story event obviously confuses C, who first suggests "dog" (32) and then "frog" (36). Drawing inferences from "here-and-now" to "there-and-then" is apparently hard on C. However, imagining what might have happened, or will happen, based on what one sees and experiences, is the very skill needed to explore the relations between a story's characters, setting, plot, conflict, and resolution. T therefore continues to pursue this challenge when jointly constructing a complete story (see Excerpt 4).

Excerpt 4: Dyad DS16.

27	T:	Yes. But . . . , where is the frog? (Ja, men du, hvor er frosken a?)
28	C:	On the bowl ((points)) (Oppå glassbollen)
29	T:	And who is curious about the frog? (Og hvem er nysgjerrig på frosken?)
30	C:	The dog. (Hunden).
31	T:	The dog is curious. But . . . how do you think the frog has got into the bowl? (Hunden er nysgjerrig. Men du, hvordan tror du at frosken har kommet oppi glassbollen?)

32	C:	The dog. (Hunden)
33	T:	Do you think the dog has . . . ? (Tror du hunden har?)
34	C:	Has? (Har?)
35	T:	What do you think? (Hva tror du?)
36	C:	Frog. (Frosk)
37	T:	But . . . who do you think has found the frog and put him inside the bowl? (Men du, hvem tror du har henta frosken og putta'n oppi glasset?)
38	C:	Forest. (Skogen)
39	T:	I would think they have found him in the forest? But who do you think found him in the forest? (De har sikkert funnet den i skogen. Men hvem tror du har funnet den i skogen?)
40	C:	Eh . . .
41	T:	Is it the dog or the boy ((points)). (Er det hunden eller er det gutten?)
4	C:	The boy. (Gutten)
43	T	The boy has found the frog in the forest, I think. (.) . . . Then he has taken him home to his room . . . (Gutten har funnet frosken uti skogen. Så har han tatt den med seg hjem til rommet sitt).

On recognizing that C needs more specific support to move from what is pictured to what may presumably have happened (36), T reformulates her question: "But . . . who do you think has found the frog and put him into the bowl?" (37) "Forest," C replies. Rather than accepting that "forest" (38) is "sort of an ok answer," T takes the dialogue further, aiming for precision. First, she confirms parts of C's reply and secondly, she repeats her question (39): "I suppose they have found him (the frog) in the forest. But who do you think has found him in the forest?" With C not answering, T continues by simplifying her key question into two alternatives (41): "Is it the dog, or the boy? "((points)). "The boy" (42), C answers, causing T to conclude with a confirmatory and explanatory expansion: "I guess the boy has found the frog in the forest . . . and then taken him home to his room." (43) "Yes," C confirms, before T more coherently explains how the story elements fit together (43). In short, at every step in this long process of coming to terms with what made the frog get into the bowl, the teacher made certain that intersubjectivity between T and C was established—before she finally offered a solution.

Overall, Excerpt 4 shows how C's contributions were limited both in vocabulary (28), syntax (38), and, more specifically, in drawing inferences (40). Still T and C most typically attended to the same referent: T confirmed relevant input from C, while at the same time pushing the story further by follow-up questions adapted to C's needs for support. By this mediating approach, T shaped narrative coherence, while at the same time confirming, recasting, and expanding on the content of C's responses. Thereby, T presumably also contributed to C's learning to draw inferences. This collaborative co-construction via sensitive teacher mediation proved productive: they jointly constructed a story of 339 turns, with 90% of the turns intersubjectively related (Table 13.1), and with C engagingly involved to the very end. However, an understanding in C of a link between the meanings of individual pictures and the narrative being told was not clearly evident, despite T's closely designed scaffolding (Wood et al., 1976) and many invitations to draw inferences. This could well be related to both language and cognitive difficulties in the child but also to the fact that children with Down syndrome are at risk of being underestimated during early years and are therefore quite often unexposed to abstract language and reasoning (Engevik et al., 2015). Experience in drawing inferences in collaboration with a teacher, as illustrated in this excerpt, presumably offers important input to reduce this risk.

In summary, the results related to the three dyads with the highest proportion of turns maintaining intersubjectivity (within their subgroups), showed some marked similarities despite substantial differences in the children's cognitive-linguistic skills and in the teachers' professional backgrounds. Within a friendly atmosphere, the teachers made use of a similar dialogical approach to the task (Initiative-Response-Confirmation + Reassurance). This implied that an insufficient or incorrect response was never combined with "critical" feedback; rather, T typically confirmed what was correct in C's response and expanded on, or recasted, the deficient part. Finally, if needs be, the child was "taken through the task" intersubjectively. By not dwelling on a failure or weakness but on C's strengths and interests, C's self-efficacy was consecutively supported, as indicated by the children performing with motivation to the very end.

The unifying quality of these dyads was, by design, their high level of teacher–child intersubjectivity. The examples showed *how* this was manifested in the dyads' story constructions and the teachers' mediation. A major finding regarded the ways these teachers aimed for intersubjectivity: where C's attention was, T's attention joined in; and if C faced a learning challenge, T typically guided C through the hurdle step-by-step with attentive adaptations to the child's needs, in most cases with considerable patience. Differences between dyads most often reflected variations in needs caused by the children's motivation and cognitive-linguistic skills. However, when intersubjectively approached by T, these impacts did not prevent the dyads from co-constructing complete stories (with some noticeable variations in story complexity and narrative language quality).

We will now turn to the co-constructions of Low-I dyads, with the fewest turns maintaining intersubjectivity within their subgroup).

13.7.2. Teacher–Child Interactions with Wavering Intersubjectivity

Examples of the co-construction of the Low-I dyads are presented below. Importantly, intersubjectively related turns dominated the dialogical pattern also of these dyads (see table 13.1). However, compared to the other dyads in their respective language groups, the proportion of High-I turns was in these dyads the lowest (within their subgroups) causing their intersubjectivity to waver. The results are presented in the following order: DS22 (Down syndrome), IL15 (impaired language), and TL06 (typical language).

Dyad DS22—Down Syndrome: When Drawing Inferences Is Demanding. Dyad DS22 involves a girl, aged 8 years, and her teacher of special needs education. The intersubjectivity between T and C was quite regularly disrupted, most typically because C turned the page before they had addressed a picture's content and meaning more thoroughly. Their co-constructions were most typically driven forward by T, who at the same time had to stop C from turning the pages. C contributed with short answers, yet with curiosity and interest.

Referring to the opening scenes, examples of a typical sequence of turns are shown in Excerpt 5. T and C jointly study the bedroom scenes, the first, with the boy and his dog sleeping while the frog climbs out of "his" glass bowl; the second, with the boy and the dog waking up to discover that the glass bowl is empty (the frog has run away?!). T starts by asking questions—with pauses that invite C's answer, but they are answered by T herself, for example, T: "What happens here? (pointing and a pause); there is the little boy . . . there he is happy" (3). C most often answers in one-word utterances or by repeating a question's content (4–10), which T typically confirms with an expansion ("Yes, he has a frog in the glass bowl.") (7). By this interactive pattern, the main story elements are jointly identified via T's mediation.

C responds to most of T's initiatives by naming the characters, repeating already introduced names, or just silently watching the pictures (12, 13). At times T "evaluates" C's responses by confirming (7) or expanding on (11) their content but never by openly paying attention to C's limited language skills. By this practice, T establishes a simple scaffold (Wood et al., 1976), which guides C through the story construction at a concrete level that C masters, most typically via picture descriptions. However, when T encourages C to infer from here-and-now to there-and-then (9), C simply repeats T's invitation, possibly because her inferential thinking and/or language skills for developmental and/or experiential reasons are insufficiently developed. This continued to be a key challenge.

Excerpt 5: Dyad DS22.

3	T:	What happens here? ((points)) (. . .) There is the little boy, there he is happy. (. . .) Who is this, who is this one? ((points)) (Hva skjer her (. . .) Der er den lille gutten, der er han glad. (. . .) (Hvem er det som er, hvem er det da?)
4	C:	Dog. (Hund)
5	T:	And then? ((points)). (Og så?)
6	C:	Frog. (Frosk)
7	T:	Yes, he has a frog in the glass bowl. (Ja, han har en frosk oppi glassbollen).
8	C:	Yes ((picks his hand)) (Ja)
9	T:	Mhm, it is in the evening; can you see? ((points)) (Det er om kvelden, ser du det?)
10	C:	Yes, it is in the evening (Ja, det er om kvelden)
11	T:	Evening, yes (. . .) Maybe he will soon fall asleep. (.) ((turns page)) But what does the frog do? (Kvelden ja (. . .) Kanskje han sovner snart (.) Men hva er det frosken gjør?)
12	C:	((Looks at the picture))
13	T:	Does he attempt to run away? Oh no, oh no. (Prøver han å stikke av? Å nei, å nei)
14	C:	((Looks at the other page))
15	T:	Look, the boy wakes up (.) and the frog has run away. (Se, der våkner gutten og så er frosken blitt borte?)
16	C:	Oh!
17	T:	Where IS the frog? ((points)) (Hvor ER frosken hen?)
18	C:	There he is ((pointing at the former page)) (Den er der)
19	T:	Yes, there he is, but do you see that he leaves the glass bowl? (Den er der ja, men ser du den går ut av glasset?)
20	C:	Yes ((turns page))

At turn 13, T explicitly invites C to infer from here-and-now to there-and-then by asking whether the frog tries to run away when climbing out of the glass bowl (13), C silently looks at the picture (14). T continues by interpreting the events: "Look, the boy wakes up and the frog has run away" (15), to which C utters "oh!" (16). T subsequently repeats, "Where IS the frog?" (17). "There it is" (18) says C, pointing to the picture on the *former* page where the frog tried to get out of the glass bowl.

At this point T changes strategy and continues along an *explanatory approach* stating approvingly, "Yes, there he is. But do you see that it leaves the glass bowl?" (19). "Yes," C confirms and turns the page (20). Drawing inferences from a pictured event to an imagined event, that is from what *is* to what might be, was indeed difficult. This continued to be a challenge during the subsequent co-construction, causing T to change his mediation strategy to more often *explaining* the pictures' content to C. However, this did not make C himself draw inferences from pictured event to imagined event. A more explicit mediation that showed C relations between pictured event and narrative event might have served C well. However, Dyad DS22 did establish shared understanding with reference to an event or person at a concrete level, which Trevarthen referred to as secondary intersubjectivity (I-It-You). And they co-constructed with motivation to the very end.

Dyad IL15—Impaired Language: When Expressing Words and sentences is Demanding. The boy in Dyad IL15 (aged 5 years), had been referred to a speech and language pathologist due to delayed language development particularly affecting his grammar and pronunciation. This made his speech somewhat hard to understand, for example /fsos/ for /frosk/ (Eng: frog), and /ditter/ for /stikker/ (Eng: sting). His verbal and nonverbal behavior indicated that this was socially and emotionally burdensome: C rarely initiated a conversation but showed good comprehension, most typically by answering in one-word utterances, simple sentences, or nonverbally (by pointing, nodding, shaking his head, or making a peeping sound (meaning "no" or "dislike")). T appeared understanding and supportive; she never corrected or commented on T's language deviancies. Rather, she focused on their joint story construction, which C appeared to enjoy.

T's general mediating approach was again a simple version of the IRC+ format, where T asked about the pictures' content or meaning, C answered (mostly semantically adequately, but often after a rather long period of silence), and T confirmed C's responses, often by expansions as illustrated in Excerpt 6 from the opening scene.

> *Excerpt 6: Dyad IL15.*
> 1 T: What do we see in this picture? (Hva ser vi på dette bildet da?)
> 2 C: (makes a sound) ((looks down))
> 3 T: That is a boy, don't you think so? (Det er en gutt, tror du ikke det?)
> 4 C: (nods)
> 5 T: And what do you see? (Og hva ser du?)
> 6 C: A dog and a fsos [frog]. (En hund og en fsos [frosk])
> 7 T: Mhm ((nods)) and where is the frog, can you see that?
>   (... og hvor er frosken hen, ser du det?)
> 8 C: In a dlass [glass bowl] (I et dlass [glass bolle])
> 9 T: In a glass bowl. ((nods)) Why is that do you think?
>   (I en glassbolle ja ((nikker))) (Hvorfor det tror du?)
> 10 C: So that he does not jun away [run away].
>   (For at den ikke skal jømme [rømme]).

Excerpt 6 shows how T makes use of a variety of questions to involve C in the story construction (1, 7, 9). Yet C's contributions are limited. Presumably linguistically and emotionally hampered by his phonological and syntactic limitations, C participates at a language level far below his cognitive level and chronological age. T appears aware of the importance of balancing C's well-functioning cognitive skills with his limited expressive language possibilities. With variable success she invites C to infer from meaning at picture level to narrative level, for example, by asking for qualifications and elaborations (why is that do you think?). This focusing on the pictures' meaning within the narrative's meaning, C seems to enjoy, but verbalizing these "inferential links" is difficult. Alternatively, T asks "simple" "what is this" questions, where C's task is to label elements in the picture. One might think these questions were easier for C to address, and therefore beneficial to his self-confidence. However, with C's many pronunciation errors, this expectation was not always fulfilled (semantically "simple" words were not necessarily easier to pronounce). Rather, C's body language indicated that he was both bored and sad when focusing on details associated with individual pictures.

In brief, the qualitative content analysis exposed some underlying constituents of the wavering intersubjectivity of Dyad IL15. These were apparently related to C's language weaknesses and caused disruptions of intersubjectivity. Although at times visibly uncomfortable and bored, C was attentively involved in the frog's fate. At crucial events in the plot, he even appeared to "forget" his hesitancy about speaking, for example, when a whole swarm of bees came out of a beehive and C yelled "oh, oh, oh!" Why do you say "oh, oh, oh," T intersubjectively asked, and C replied by a 7-word utterance with neither syntactical nor phonological mistakes: "Since all the bees are coming out". However, overall, C's limited expressive language interfered negatively with the story construction and also with C's interaction with T; T's mediation then also became wavering.

Dyad 06—Typical Development: When Motivation is Variable. Dyad TL06 comprised a typically developing boy (age 5 years) and his preschool teacher whom he knew well. On starting the session, T and C apparently went by a plan where C was to tell T a story based on the pictures in the book. However, after a few turns, C bluntly stated, "I do not want to read more," presumably because he felt uneasy or disappointed about the task. T suggested that they instead (and in accordance with the instructions) *jointly* construct a story, which they subsequently did, with C's motivation wavering throughout the session, and with many breaches of intersubjectivity.

C was a thoughtful boy with many considerations about the book's pictures which caused numerous reflections and negotiations about the pictures' meanings. The negotiations progressed at different levels of intersubjectivity and referred to "meaning" at different semantic depths within the story being constructed. A total of four levels of intersubjectivity were revealed.

The most foundational level regarded the negotiation between T and C about *whether* to co-construct a story, that is whether C would involve himself in an "I-You" interaction (primary intersubjectivity), with a "shared here-and-now" between I and You (Trevarthen, 1979). While not an issue of concern in the other dyads, this was important in this one. Next, there were negotiations at a second level of intersubjectivity, that is about "what's in the picture," as revealed in picture labeling (I-It-You), for example, "Do you see what he is doing?". At the third level, T appealed to C's imagination and skills of inferencing by inviting him to infer from the meaning of the pictures' characters and events to their "meanings" within the story being constructed, for example, by asking C where the frog went after climbing out of the glass bowl. By this approach, T and C co-constructed their story by a procedure that gradually encapsulated and integrated the book's increasing number of pictured meanings into a narrative with relevant story elements and with intersubjectivity regarding characters and events at the level of the story's meaning.

Interaction at this fourth level is illustrated in Excerpt 7, referring to the final scene in the book. The boy and the dog wave goodbye to the frogs after visiting the pond. First, T describes the events pictured within their story frame ("the other big frog" is referred to as "girlfriend" and the small frogs as "their children" (68)). C continues at the same narrative level asking, "Why do they take a frog along?" (71) (referring to a little frog in the boy's hands). By this C initiates a rather advanced dialogue at a fourth level of intersubjectivity (shared understanding about the story's meaning). C's main concern now regards what will happen to the little frog the boy is about to take home when he is removed from his frog family.

Excerpt 7: Dyad TD06.

68	T:	He has met a girlfriend and got many baby frogs. That is nice is it not? ((looks at T and smiles)) That is why he left the house. (Han har funnet en kjæreste og fått mange froskunger. Det er hyggelig, ikke sant? Det er derfor han gikk ut.)
69	C:	((looks at T and smiles)) Yes. That is why he left the house. (Ja. Det er derfor han gikk ut.)
70	T:	He had to see his girlfriend of course. There they are. (turning the page) (Han måtte ut til kjæresten sin så klart. Der sitter de)
71	C:	Huh . . . why do they take one along ((points)) [back to their room] (Hæ, hvorfor tar de med en?)
72	T:	Perhaps he got one. (Kanskje han fikk med seg en ())
73	C:	Yes, but what if he, if, if it is a baby frog, he cannot get out [of the glass bowl] (points and looks at T) (Ja, men hva hvis den, hvis, hvis det er en baby så klarer den ikke å komme seg ut [av glassbollen])1
74	T:	Yes, but perhaps the little [frog] wanted to go home with him [the boy] . . . anyway . . . he now says bye-bye to the frog. (Ja, det kan godt tenkes at den lille hadde lyst til å bli med han hjem igjen da . . . . Nå sier han i hvert fall «ha det» til frosken)

We see here how C gets second thoughts about the future fate of the little frog (71) if brought to the boy's room (73): "Oh, why does he take a frog along?" . . . if it is a baby frog . . . "it cannot get out [of the glass bowl]" (73)). By this, a discussion at an ethical level is started which is closed by T's suggestion that the frog perhaps *wanted* to go home with them (74).

With this closure T and C had jointly succeeded in co-constructing a story via four levels of intersubjectivity, despite many disruptions of intersubjectivity and C's wavering motivation. The story nevertheless ended with an intriguing ethical dilemma raised by C unresolved; perhaps because T did not consider it worth pursuing, found it too time-consuming, or was concerned about "losing control" of the situation. Whatever the cause, it was T who called off C's ethical reflections and thereby also the dialogue (which was the shortest in the total sample (79 turns, Table 13.1)).

In summary, like the High-I dyads, the Low-I dyads co-constructed complete stories by an IRC+ format in friendly and supportive atmospheres. The teachers ignored rather than paid attention to the children's language limitations, often by recasting or expanding on the children's utterances.

The content analysis, among other things, revealed the qualities of the verbal interaction associated with the disruptions of intersubjectivity. These breaches of intersubjectivity most typically reflected mismatches between T's and C's understanding of a picture's meaning, the story's meaning, or the task's meaning. Whatever the cause(s), these disruptions offered a leeway, or margin, for significant impacts from C's individual weaknesses (of language, cognition, motivation, etc.) unless intersubjectivity was reestablished by T, which was often *not* the case in these Low-I dyads.

13.8. Summary and Discussion

We have shown how teacher–child dyads co-constructed pictured stories via two research questions: the first, on how dyads at high and low levels of intersubjectivity co-constructed stories; the second, on how the teachers mediated the story constructions. The findings were documented by telling examples that were concurrently commented upon. Some main findings are discussed below. Being interrelated, the two research questions are often discussed simultaneously.

13.8.1. Co-construction of Stories and Levels of Intersubjectivity

Similarities between High-I and Low-I dyads in co-constructing stories. Despite a designed focus on different language groups at different *l*evels of intersubjectivity, the findings revealed several noteworthy similarities across groups and dyads: all dyads co-constructed relatively complete stories with an introduction, a plot, and an ending; the teachers mediated by variants of an IRC+ strategy, and the children carried out the task with overall positive motivation and a sense of achievement.

It came as some surprise that teacher–child dyads, purposely designed to vary in terms of intersubjectivity and children's language skills, shared these fundamental similarities. However, with well educated teachers well-acquainted with "their child," these similarities presumably appear reasonable. Also, observed basic similarities across groups and dyads do *not* of course imply that major differences were not at play as well.

Differences between High-I and Low-I dyads in co-constructing stories. Being designed to vary, differences between dyads high and low on intersubjectivity were pervasive—not only in dyadic skills, such as verbal communication, but also in capabilities, and attitudes, such as teachers' and children's motivation and interests.

Regarding variations in qualities of the stories being constructed dyadic differences were typically associated with more specific aspects: compared to those of the Low-I-dyads the stories of the High-I dyads were generally characterized by a more complex plot, more advanced semantic content, and more complete integration of picture labeling and narrative construction. With the large variations within the three High-I dyads, in particular in terms of children's language skills, this accentuates the importance of teacher mediation to the quality of the story constructed.

13.8.2. Mediating with Intersubjectivity

Overall, the results indicated that children of both Low-I and High-I dyads appeared to profit from their teachers' mediation (e.g., all dyads constructed more or less complete stories in a climate characterized by positive motivation). However, the advantages of being in a High-I dyad nevertheless appeared considerable. As shown in Table 13.1, a high level of intersubjectivity was associated with longer stories (more turns) and therefore more time on the task of constructing story. It was also associated with fewer dialogical disruptions and negotiations to establish intersubjectivity (in each of the three High-I language groups, more than 90% of the turns maintained intersubjectivity, as opposed to 50- to 65% in the comparable Low-I dyads). This implies that the Low-I dyads spent less time on task and more time in disrupted dialogues or in more or less successful negotiations to re-establish intersubjecivity. Experiencing "time on task" within the frames of learning dialogues with high teacher-child intersubjectivity in short offered many opportunities for positive learning experiences. It was presumably also emotionally and language wise beneficial to the students, in particular because the dialogue partner was "one's own teacher".

The results from the content analysis further indicated that children with cognitive- linguistic delays to various degrees were *dependent* on teacher mediation to fulfill the task; a *"high" level of intersubjectivity* apparently compensated for language limitations and for insecurity and low self-confidence (which is not uncommon among children with language delays). In contrast, the "less time on task" experienced by children in *Low-I* dyads, in combination with a number of dialogical disruptions and negotiations to re-establish intersubjectivity not rarely appeared emotionally troublesome on both teacher and child with potential negative effects on motivation and self-efficacy.

Notably, the advantage of taking part in story construction with high teacher–child intersubjectivity appeared to reach beyond the children with language delays who were *dependent* on extensive teacher support. Even the typically developing child who participated in a High-I dyad (TL04) appeared to profit considerably from the mediation: 95% of the turns were maintaining intersubjectivity (versus 55% in the comparable Low-I dyad (TL06, see table 13.1). The content analysis further showed that teacher mediation in TL04 was more detailed, more focused on narrative elements and quality of language and better adapted to C's needs. For the purpose of formulating hypotheses it is interesting to note that, while Dyad TL04 (High-I) co-constructed a rather long story (167 turns) with no disruptions of intersubjectivity in combination with detailed qualitative mediation, Dyad TL06 (Low-I), had a proportion of 16% turns being disrupted and a story length of only 79 turns. Also, the content analyses revealed that the story construction was less detailed in Dyad TL06, with less focus on narrative elements and quality of language. Additionally, the qualities of the Low-I teacher's (TL06) recasting and expansions appeared less adapted to the child's needs.

A final and important finding regards the quality of the mediation of the High-I teachers. Their attentive focus on the need to secure shared attention and shared understanding at every stage of the story construction was notable. Numerous examples showed how High-I teachers patiently, thoroughly, and intersubjectively drew C's attention to important details, in some cases at nearly every turn (e.g., DS16).

This tuning into joint foci was, by definition, considerably less prominent among Low-I dyads. In this sense the children in the Low-I dyads were "left more alone" in their co-construction and learning situation than were the children in the High-I dyads. With shorter stories and more disruptions, they also spent less time on task, and more time dialogizing in more-or-less successful negotiations to re-establish intersubjectivity. Although taking part in disruptions and negotiations to re-establish intersubjectivity may yield valuable learning experiences (for good or bad, depending on emotional climate and quality of outcome), they may also have some costs in terms of reduced learning effects and loss of task motivation and self-efficacy.

13.8.3. Understanding Variations and Relations: Methodological Reflections

There is presumably a complex combination of reasons why the observed similarities and differences in story length, narrative quality, and attuned mediation, varied with predefined categorizations of dyads at High- and Low-levels of intersubjectivity. Being a descriptive small-scale study, assumptions of causality should be carried out with great care. However, main findings that fit a pattern of consistency should be noted, and if supporting theory and relevant empirical research, they are to be highlighted as interesting hypotheses to pursue in future research.

One compelling issue regards the extent to which the language delays of four of the six participating children affected the results. One might presume that these children's language-linguistic weaknesses *caused* their semantically less advanced story constructions. This potential explanation cannot of course be excluded, and oral language skills obviously affect story construction skills, as also indicated by much empirical research. However, in the current study, this factor was to some extent "canceled out" by the design's inclusion of children from three different language groups in both High-I and Low-I dyads: the children in both dyads IL11 and DS16 suffered from cognitive and/or linguistic limitations yet, in collaboration with their teachers, they experienced few disruptions and produced relatively long stories at fairly well-developed semantic levels (Table 13.1). On this basis, and although cognitive–linguistic limitations naturally impacted the results, a child's language skills did not by itself stand out as *the single main* contributor to the long and semantically relevant story constructions of the High-I dyads.

The teacher factor is the other obvious explanatory factor, also often seen as a main cause of student's learning and performance. Again, the teacher of course matters. Being an asymmetric educational dialogue (Linell, 2009) the teacher is in *more control* of dialogical premises and contents than is the case in more symmetric dialogues. Yet, in this sample all the teachers were both experienced and child-oriented; the Low-I-teachers in fact made use of similar general task approaches as did the High-I teachers.

From this follows that the single variable that systematically differentiated between Low-I and High-I dyads was their dyadic skill in maintaining intersubjectivity. This invites a dual perspective in interpreting the results. Rather than seeing the causes of poor story constructions in "limitations" in the child's language skills *or* the teachers' quality of mediation in a general sense, a dialogical approach sees the quality of interaction as a major factor: C's behavior is both a cause and a result of T's initiatives and responses. In these six dyads there were numerous examples of mismatches between C's needs for support and the support offered by T, leading to dyadic disruptions and negotiations to re-establish intersubjectivity. However, there were more of them in Low-I dyads than in High-I dyads causing the Low-I dyads to depend more on clarifying negotiations between C and T to fulfill the task. The extent to which these negotiations were successful was quite decisive in their success in constructing their stories.

Within all three language groups, the High-I dyads systematically produced the longer and more detailed stories. This leads to the hypothesis that level of intersubjectivity is a main determiner of both quality of construction, of story length, of story quality and potentially also of the child's learning (which was not assessed in this study). The findings further suggest that children with language delays, or variable motivation, not unexpectantly appeared *more dependent* on teacher–child intersubjectivity to construct complete stories at fairly advanced cognitive-linguistic levels. This suggests that dialogues with intersubjectivity were crucially important to the children's performance and learning.

13.8.4. Three Dimensions of High-I Teacher Mediation

In conclusion, and in elucidating qualities associated with High-I teacher mediation as inferred from the findings, we will highlight three dimensions: teacher competence, teacher attitude, and time.

The dimension of *teacher competence* has many qualities and layers. In the current study it broadly refers to the teachers' professional knowledge and skills as applied when mediating children's learning during their co-construction of a story. In this broad sense, all the teachers in the current study showed "a level of professionalism" by securing that "their dyad" jointly constructed relatively "complete stories." However, the teachers in the High-I dyads "took their child longer," with fewer disruptions and longer and more complete stories, often with rather advanced semantic content and narrative structure.

The *attitude* dimension regards the teacher's "settled way of thinking about her role," in this case as a mediator of story construction. At a basic level, the High-I teachers went by a practice of "adapting to the child" by ensuring shared understanding. This attitude was projected as a superstructure on the High-I teachers' professional competence and guided T's approach to the task of co-constructing. Relative to the Low-I teachers, the High-I teachers appeared more highly aware of the importance of securing intersubjectivity (by shared attention and shared understanding) at every stage in the story construction, particularly when facing misunderstandings, when a child appeared hesitant, or when (s)he lacked relevant knowledge or skills. This willingness to stay where the child's attention, understanding, and learning needs were, dominated the High-I teachers' practice like an obligation to continuously establish "moment-by-moment intersubjectivity." This also included a willingness to co-construct by mediating beyond "a needed minimum." If needs be, the High-I teacher appeared inclined to "work harder" than the Low-I teacher to compensate for less-qualified contributions of the learning child.

The third dimension regards a more practical priority: the High-I teacher allocated the time needed to mediate on the premises of the child. She consistently took the time required for the child to "join in" actively during their co-constructing.

The issue of time is a multifaceted phenomenon in educational practice. Among other things, it may be a costly scarcity good for which reason it often takes both professional insight, patience, and generosity to prioritize the time necessary to mediate with teacher–child intersubjectivity. However, in the current study, the teachers' willingness to mediate by maintaining intersubjectivity appeared to be a prerequisite for constructing complete stories, in particular with a complexity that was within reach at the upper boundary of the child's level of competence. The labor involved in the two High-I dyads, including children with language delays, supports this statement: DS16: 338 turns, 0% disruptions, 5% negotiations to establish intersubjectivity, and IL11: 206 turns, 1% disruptions and 5% negotiations (Hølland et al. in process).

13.9. Implications

Taken together, these results indicate that teacher–child intersubjectivity stands out as a fundamentally important professional "phenomenon" with educational implications that should be more systematically evaluated in future research. At a general level, the findings presented accord with sociocultural ideas underscoring the importance of the teacher who sensitively guides a child through a learning process in their zone of proximal development (Vygotsky, 1978). However, the findings expand these Vygotskyan ideas by highlighting the importance of the dialogue itself, particularly the importance of securing *teacher–child intersubjectivity* at every step of the learning process.

To view teaching as a "two-sided act" with ownership anchored in both the teacher and the student is in some sense contrary to educational conventions. By tradition, teaching is often seen as one-directional, with the teacher telling and/or showing the child what to learn and what to do. Although teachers are often available to "help the child if needs be," individual teacher–child interactions are, for practical or other reasons, not regularly prioritized in schools of today. More typically, dialogical activities are carried out in student groups, which may also be of great value as, for example, illustrated in Chapters 11 and 12 in this volume. However, student–student interaction cannot *replace* dyadic teacher–child interaction with intersubjectivity in educational settings, in particular not when learning for different reasons is demanding, as it was in those of our dyads which included a child with delayed language development.

These findings have implications for parents and teachers in preschool, school, special needs education, and teacher training. They are also relevant to policy makers in the field of education, particularly when the child, for different reasons, struggles.

In the context of this volume on dialogic perspectives in times of change, the findings also provide an optimistic note by suggesting that dialogues with intersubjectivity may be attained even in the face of seeming impediments. This provides a glimpse into the foundations and development of human dialogue and may even be a glimpse into what successful dialogue could be at all levels in today's troubled world.

References

Bakhtin, M. M. (1981). *The dialogic imagination:Four essays by M. M. Bakhtin*. (M. Holquist, Ed., C. Emerson & M. Holquist, Trans.). University of Texas Press.

Brinchmann, E. I., Røe-Indregård, H., Karlsen, J., Schauber, S., & Hagtvet, B. E. (2023). The linguistic complexity of adult and child contextualized and decontextualized talk. Child Development, 94(5), 1368–1380. doi: 10.1111/cdev.13932

Cazden, C. (1988). *Classroom discourse. The language of teaching and learning*. Portsmouth, NH: Heinemann.

Derry, S. J., Pea, R. D., Barron, B., Engle, R. A., Erickson, F., Goldman, R., Hall, R., Koschmann, T., Lemke, J. L., Sherin, M. G., & Sherin, B. L. (2010). Conducting video research in the learning sciences: Guidance on selection, analysis, technology, and ethics. *The Journal of the Learning Sciences*, 19(1), 3–53.

Dickinson, D. K., & Smith, M. W. (2001). Supporting language and literacy development in the preschool classroom. In D. K. Dickinson & P. O. Tabors (Eds.), *Beginning literacy with language: Young children learning at home and school* (pp. 139–147). Paul Brookes Pub. Co.

Dysthe, O. (1996). The multivoiced classroom: Interactions of writing and classroom discourse. *Written Communication*, 13(3), 385–425.

Engevik, L. I., Næss, K.-A. B., & Hagtvet, B. E. (2016). Cognitive stimulation of children with Down Syndrome: A study of inferential talk during book-sharing. *Research in Developmental Disabilities*, 55, 287–300. https://doi.org/10.1016/j.ridd.2016.05.004

Engevik, L. I., Hølland, S., & Hagtvet, B. (2015). Re-conceptualizing "directiveness" in educational dialogues: A contrastive study of interactions in preschool and special education. *Early Childhood Research Quarterly*, 30, 140–151. https://doi.org/doi:10.1016/j.ecresq.2014.10.004

Gardner, R. (2019). Classroom interaction research: The state of the art. *Research on Language and Social Interaction*, 52(3), 212–226. https://www.tandfonline.com/doi/full/10.1080/08351813.2019.1631037

Grøver, V., Rydland, V., Gustafsson, J.-E., & Snow, C. E. (2020). Shared book reading in preschool supports bilingual children's second-language learning: A cluster-randomized trial. *Child Development*, 91(6), 2192–2210. https://doi.org/10.1111/cdev.13348

Gustavsson, L. (1988). *Language taught and language used: Dialogue processes in dyacic lessons of Swedish as a second language compared with non-didactic conversations* (Ph.D. Thesis). University of Linköping, Sweden.

Hagtvet, B. E. (2003). Skriftspråkstimulering i første klasse: faglig innhold og didaktiske angrepsmåter. Literacy stimulation in grade one: content and didactics In K. Klette (Ed. *Klasserommets praksisformer etter Reform 1997. The teacher's classroom work after Reform 1997*. Department of Education, *University of Oslo* (pp. 173-219). UniPub. Department of Educational Research, University of Oslo.

Hagtvet, B. E. (2017). The Nordic countries. In N. Kucirkova, C. E. Snow, V. Grøver, & C. McBride (Eds.), *The Routledge international handbook of early literacy education. A contemporary guide to literacy teaching and interventions in a global context* (pp. 95-112). Routledge.

Hølland, S., Engevik, L. I., & Hagtvet, B. E. (2017). The dialogical dynamics of mediation in educational dialogues: A study of child-teacher interactions during shared book reading. In S. Hølland (Ed.), *Samspill i læringsdialoger. En studie av interaksjon, dominansmønstre og mediering. [Interaction in educational dialogues. A study of interaction, patterns of dominance, and mediation]*. PhD Thesis. University of Oslo.

Hølland, S., Hagtvet, B. E., Engevik, L. I., Kruse, J., Brinchman, E., & Karlsen, J. (in process). Degrees of intersubjectivity in teacher–child dialogues. Unpublished journal article.

Klette, K. (2003). Lærerens klasseromsarbeid; Interaksjons-og arbeidsformer i norske klasserom etter Reform 97. [The teacher's classroom work after Reform 1997]. *Department of Education, University of Oslo. (39-76) UniPub*.

Kruse, J., & Hagtvet, B. E. (in process). Teacher–child dialogues in language delayed children. Unpublished journal article.

Linell, P. (2009). *Rethinking language, mind, and world dialogically: Interactional and contextual theories of human sense-making*. Information Age Publishing.

Linell, P., Gustavsson, L., & Juvonen, P. (1988). Interactional dominance in dyadic communication: A presentation of initiative-response analysis. *Linguistics, 26*(3), 415–442. http://dx.doi.org/10.1515/ling.1988.26.3.415

Mayer, M. (1969). *Frog, where are you?* Dial Books for Young Readers.

Mol, S. E., Bus, A. G., & de Jong, M. T. (2009). Interactive book reading in early education: A tool to stimulate print knowledge as well as oral language. *Review of Educational Research, 79*(2), 979–1007. https://doi.org/https://doi.org/10.3102/0034 65430933256

Næss, K. (2012). *Language and reading development in children with Down Syndrome*. Ph.D. thesis. Faculty of Educational Sciences, University of Oslo.

Piaget, J. (1954). *The construction of reality in the child*. Basic Books.

Pianta, R. C., La Paro, K. M., & Hamre, B. K. (2008). *Classroom assessment scoring system™: Manual K-3*. Paul H. Brookes Publishing.

Rogoff, B. (1990). *Apprenticeship in thinking: cognitive development in social context*. Oxford University Press.

Rommetveit, R. (1968). *Words, meaning, and messages: Theory and experiments in psycholinguistics*. Academic Press.

Rommetveit, R. (1972). *Språk, tanke og kommunikasjon: ei innføring i språkpsykologi og psykolingvistikk*. Universitetsforlaget (Scandinavian University Press).

Rommetveit, R. (1992). Outlines of a dialogically based social-cognitive approach to human cognition and communication. In A. H. Wold (Ed.), *The dialogical alternative: Towards a theory of language and mind* (pp. 19–44). Scandinavian University Press.

Røe-Indregård, H., Brinchmann, E., Rydland, V., Rowe, M., Hagtvet, B. E., & Imbrana, I. M. (2022), Teacher–child Interactions during toy play and book sharing. *Early*

Education and Development. Published online Nov. 2022; https://doi.org/10.1080/10409289.2022.2142028

Stone, C. A. (1993). What is missing in the methaphor of "scaffolding"? In E. A. Forman, N. Minick, & C. A. Stone (Eds.), *Contexts for learning* (pp. 169–183). Oxford University Press.

Svanes, I. K., & Klette, K. (2018). Teachers' instructional practices during pupils' individual seatwork in Norwegian Language arts. *Education Inquiry, 9*(3), 247–266. https://doi.org/https://doi.org/10.1080/20004508.2017.1380485

Trevarthen, C. (1979). Communication and cooperation in early infancy. In M. Bullowa (Ed.), *Before speech. The beginning of interpersonal communication* (pp. 321–347). Camebridge University Press.

Trevarthen, C. (2006). The concepts and foundations of intersubjectivity. In S. Bråten (Ed.), *Intersubjective communication and emotion in early ontogeny* (pp. 15–46). Cambridge University Press.

Trevarthen, C. (2011). What young children give to their learning, making education work to sustain a community and its culture. *European Early Childhood Education Research Journal, 19*(2), 173–193. https://doi.org/https://doi.org/10.1080/1350293X.2011.574405

Trevarthen, C. & Hubley, P. (1978). Secondary intersubjectivity: Confidence, confiding and acts of meaning in the first year. In: A. Lock (Ed.), *Action, gesture, and symbol* (pp. 183–229). Academic Press.

Vygotsky, L. S. (1978). *Mind in society: the development of higher psychological processes*. Harvard University Press.

Wertsch, J. V. (1985). *Vygotsky and the social formation of mind*. Cambridge, MA: Harvard University Press.

Wertsch, J. V. (2007). Mediation. In H. Daniels, M. Cole, & J. V. Wertsch (Eds.), *The Cambridge companion to Vygotsky* (pp. 178–192). Cambridge University Press.

Wertsch, J. V., & Stone, C. A. (1985). The concept of internalization in Vygotsky's account of the genesis of higher mental functions. In J. V. Wertsch (Ed.), *Culture, communication, and cognition: Vygotskyan perspectives* (pp. 162–179). New York: Cambridge University Press.

Wood, D., Bruner, J. S., & Ross, G. (1976). The role of tutoring in problem solving. *Journal of Child Psychology and Psychiatry, 17*(2), 89–100. https://doi.org/10.1111/j.1469-7610.1976.tb00381.x

SECTION 5
COMMENTARIES

In this last section we present three commentaries on the volume's content and perspectives; two by scholars in the field, the third by the Editors. We invited two experts in the field, Jay Lemke, City University of New York, and Alfredo Jornet Gil, University of Oslo/University of Girona, to write personal reflective notes on the book's main topics. Specifically, we asked them to reflect on the thematic relevance of the book chapters to the times of great changes and increasing polarization in which we live. Both colleagues accepted the invitation. With different scholarly backgrounds, and representing different generations, they naturally solved the task from different positions.

Lemke has written a commentary analysis of basic phenomena associated with "the role of dialogue in times of increasing social polarization and rapid cultural change." His analysis is, among other things, a reminder that communication does not only regard the interpersonal level; it also regards the larger sociocultural frameworks of conflicting group interests, divergent cultural narratives, and distinct collective histories. With reference to the notion of "double dialogicality," Lemke also argues that there is a difference between "the ideal dialogue" and the "messy" real-life dialogues: "The genesis of true intersubjectivity requires not only that we understand the viewpoint of the Other, but that we come down from the Ideal . . . and engage with real persons, messy situations, ambiguous narratives, and fuzzy norms."

In turn, Gil has written a commentary analysis of the times of crisis which contextualize our lives as of today, with a specific focus on climate change and on the hope offered by qualified education and authentic enlightening dialogues. He discusses the book chapters as inspirational sources of critically important issues of our time, such as climate change, pollution, and biodiversity. In particular, he addresses aspects of sustainability as an educational challenge of our time.

Together, Lemke and Gil add complementarity to the depth and scope of ongoing debates. They also offer some hope, despite wars, migrations, plagues, and a planet on the verge of taking a stranglehold on man and humanity.

At the very end, the volume's messages are channeled by the Editors' final note and above via Rommetveit's own words. We close by leaving the floor to Ragnar, who for more than two generations inspired those who wanted to listen: gentle in form, but strong in words.

14
Dialogue, Polarization, and Change: Reflections
A Commentary
Jay Lemke

The chapters in this volume address critically important issues regarding the role of dialogue in times of increasing social polarization and rapid cultural change. They remind us—and further develop—both conceptually and with many rich examples, that dialogue is not simply interaction at the interpersonal level and the conversational timescale, but is always also taking place within larger sociocultural frameworks of conflicting group interests, divergent cultural narratives, and distinct collective histories. I take this to be the core message of the notion of "double dialogicality" as framed by Per Linell in this volume and elsewhere.

This double dialogicality is essential as we consider a critical practical issue: when and why do local and global dialogues contribute to the peaceful reconciliation of conflicts or instead to increasingly dangerous social polarization?

The chapter authors draw upon, and enter into dialogue with, seminal theorists who have engaged with these matters and greatly influenced succeeding research and conceptualization, prominently Rommetveit, Bakhtin, Vygotsky, Habermas, and Wittgenstein. I would myself also underline the useful contributions of Gregory Bateson (see Reference Note below), both his interpersonal scale work on the dialogic ("double bind") genesis of some types of schizophrenia and, even more so, his community scale notion of "schizmogenesis" in the broader sense of processes that increase social polarization and can lead to divergent cultural norms, civil strife, and community partition—or even destruction.

It is critically important to recognize that dialogue, both interpersonal and intersocial, can lead to increased polarization as well as to constructive transformation and reconciliation. This is so, in large part, because dialogue across differences always takes place within an already existing matrix of social viewpoints, narratives, and discourse formations (cf. Bakhtin's core notion of *heteroglossia*). Not only the oppositions of a highly polarized community but even the normal contrasts in viewpoint arising from the social division of labor—or

Jay Lemke, *Dialogue, Polarization, and Change: Reflections* In: *Education and Dialogue in Polarized Societies*. Edited by: Ola Erstad, Bente Eriksen Hagtvet, and James V. Wertsch, Oxford University Press. © Oxford University Press 2024.
DOI: 10.1093/oso/9780197605424.003.0014

differences of age, gender, status, and power—insure that no "neutral" word can be spoken.

Each utterance carries connotative meanings for members of a multivoiced community (and all communities are such). Even if unconsciously, we are always asking ourselves how is this speaker positioned in the larger web of social voices? How is this occasion being constituted as part of the routines and expectations of this or that social subgroup? Whose norms are being invoked or alluded to? What is the history of the relationships between the groups whose norms and narratives are (even implicitly) engaging with each other (or rejecting engagement)?

Taking this logic of heteroglossia one step further (following on from Bateson's notion of "meta-learning" to more recent concepts such as meta-discourse and meta-pragmatics), we need to recognize that whether or not two cultural narratives (or sets of norms, typical utterances, etc.) represent "incompatible worldviews," "irreconcilable differences"—or even just categorically opposed claims—depends on some particular cultural framework for deciding such matters (and is not an absolute consequence of the content of the narratives per se).

Social processes that increase polarization are as much built into the affordances of dialogue as are those that may reduce it. Communities with different histories and cultures do not simply mesh without resistance and transformation. New communities and cultures arise from preexisting ones by processes of divergence and separation ("schizmogenesis") as well as by processes of transformation and fusion. Communities and cultures preserve their identities as much by rejecting the Other as by reinforcing their Own.

Or so it seems when we think only in terms of ideal types and perfect social categories (which are also a mainstay of deliberately polarizing rhetorics). In the real lifeworld to which phenomenologists like Rommetveit seek to return us (and without denying the conceptual value of semiotic categories as such), there is always *slippage*. There are always overlaps, hybrids, multiple identities, polyvalence, strategic deployment of multiple social voices even by single actors, and degrees of loyalty and group identification. In the life-stream, realities are complicated and messy, and therefore more fuzzy, flexible, and robust than in our idealized models.

Dialogue by itself does not guarantee movement toward reconciliation. The genesis of true intersubjectivity requires not only that we understand the viewpoint of the Other but that we come down from the Ideal (or rise to the concrete) and engage with real persons, messy situations, ambiguous narratives, and fuzzy norms. But we all know, or at least we unconsciously feel, that doing so is risky. When we slip out of the meshwork of generalities and categories, we slip our moorings, we may make serious mistakes, we may be held (even unfairly) to account by those who rely more strictly on the canons. The less secure we are in our social status, the less social capital we have available to risk, the harder it is to open ourselves to potentially transformative dialogue (cf. the rich examples in the chapters by deHaan and others).

Polarizing dialogue is conservative (or reactionary) because it relies on, reinforces, and, above all, exaggerates preexisting categories and norms. Its appeal is that we think we know its consequences, where it is leading us. Potentially transformative dialogue, on the other hand, will most likely lead us into uncharted waters; where it will lead is inherently unpredictable. Polarizing dialogue requires conviction. Transformative dialogue requires courage.

And it requires resources and support. To entice people away from familiar certainties, we need to offer more than ideological support. Material support is necessary. Social polarization grows when the material support needed for risk-taking is lacking, and we live in times when material resources are ever more rapidly concentrating in fewer hands. It should be no surprise that certainties are growing ever more strident, social polarizations ever more extreme.

Neo-authoritarians openly disparage democratic norms, appealing to categorical nationalisms and racisms. Their polarizing rhetorics succeed more often when the concrete results of wealth-corrupted democracies in people's real lives are impoverishment, downward mobility, underemployment, and ill-health. Young people in diverse communities are summoned to monologic norms of group identity and fixed and canonical gender roles and sexualities not only by polarizing discourses but by the threat of ostracism and loss of material support in communities where such support is essential to survival.

It is, however, not just the character of the discourse and the material circumstances of a community which may tilt toward polarization. As noted in the discussions in this volume around themes of digitalization, the technologies of communication are also changing in ways that, despite initial hopes for constructive interaction across boundaries, afford the comforts and intensifying effects of echo-chamber monologic bubbles of already like-minded interlocutors. Choirs that preach to themselves.

In such environments monologic and polarizing discourses thrive and drive out the complexity of real lives and moral uncertainties. So-called cancel culture and the reactionary movement to cancel it are both grounded in the intolerant norms and self-organizing, transient certainties of mass social media.

Contending monologisms do not afford transformative dialogue. No less so when one of them is our own, liberal democratic values or progressive social justice norms. Dialogues are not just monological when they occur in echo chambers for like narratives and categories. They are also monological when two category and value systems that view each other as opposed volley one monologic viewpoint against the other, leading to greater, not lesser, polarization.

If there is an escape from this ultimately destructive downside of dialogue, I think it must lie in a return to the lifeworld, to real lives and real people, to the concrete consequences of group histories and material conditions in the beings of persons and the feelings we can have for another. Not as a reductionist neo-individualism but in our focus on specificity. The specificity of the here-and-now dialogue—not just in terms of persons but of circumstances and conditions—interpersonal networks and histories, the unique but never unprecedented.

A key feature of the lifeworld is that each next moment, no matter how dependent on all the moments that preceded it, can still surprise. Across many timescales, the new continues to arise. We continue to become what we could not have imagined, and we do so because we are in constant dialogic interaction with the real specificity of moments that escape all possible delimitation by categories.

Genuinely new ways of being, and the hope they offer, arise from the essential unpredictability of true dialogue. If we have the courage and resources to take the risk.

Reference Note. For the contributions of Gregory Bateson noted above, see his *Naven* (1936) on schizmogenesis and *Steps to an Ecology of Mind* (1972) on double-bind theory and the logic of meta-learning as well as for its emphasis on dialogue.

15
Not Just Change: Dialogue in Times of Crisis
A Commentary

Alfredo Jornet

15.1. A Perennial Theme of Acute Contemporary Relevance

The present volume takes up the longstanding, foundational problem—at least in sociocultural research—of the role of language, and more specifically *dialogue*, in the development of human subjectivity and human culture.[1] In this regard, the insights and elaborations presented in this volume are truly perennial. For the issues it raises have been, are, and will continue to be foundational to sociocultural research as a relevant academic field or discipline. At the most general level, these questions concern the relation between humans as individual organisms and their cultural environment, which is collective in nature. Here, dialogue becomes the link between the two. For there is no human relation without some form of dialogue, no dialogue without some form of language, and no language without some form of culture.

Ragnar Rommetveit—who is "a crucial inspiration for this book," as per the editors' introduction—drew on Ernst Cassirer's notion of *animal symbolicum* to capture this irreducible unity between human organism (nature) and human culture and argued for a *psychology of the second person* (Rommetveit, 2003) in which it is understood that, in humanity, there really is no "I" without "you." Between I and you, or perhaps more precisely, in uniting I and you, there is dialogue. In a similar vein, Lev Vygotsky—another source cited in several chapters in this volume—paraphrasing Ludwig Feuerbach, stated that "the word is a thing in our consciousness ... that is absolutely impossible for one person, but that becomes a reality for two" (Vygotsky, 1986, p. 256). In Vygotsky's cultural-historical psychology—which, it could be argued, is akin to a "psychology of the second person"—the most primary form of dialogue starts already in the relation between mother and

---

[1] Strictly speaking, from a sociocultural perspective, culture and subjectivity are indeed inherently related and so not really two different things. They can be understood as the expression of two different aspects of the broader notion of humanity (Roth & Jornet, 2017).

Alfredo Jornet, *Not Just Change: Dialogue in Times of Crisis* In: *Education and Dialogue in Polarized Societies*. Edited by: Ola Erstad, Bente Eriksen Hagtvet, and James V. Wertsch, Oxford University Press. © Oxford University Press 2024.
DOI: 10.1093/oso/9780197605424.003.0015

child, a relation that itself is immersed in a cultural universe that is always already in place, a cultural universe that becomes the means and medium for this relation to unfold. From these perspectives, an inquiry into dialogue is always also an inquiry into the meeting point between experiences, memories, personalities, or any other individual "psychological" phenomena, and collective ways of experiencing, remembering, of becoming a subject in any given culture and society.

This otherwise perennial concern of sociocultural inquiry acquires undeniable contemporary relevance in the present volume, where dialogue and dialogical perspectives are drawn on to address what the volume's title refers to as "times of change." More specifically, the editors identify three aspects or dimensions that characterize these times of change and that the diverse chapters in the book address: increased polarization of political discourse and of dialogues between segments of society (what the editors refer to as the political dimension); the possibilities and complexities of new technologies and digital communication (including, of course, social media, and which the editors refer to as the technological dimension); and the role of dialogue as a tool for learning and interaction (which the editors refer to as the learning dimension). In many ways, every chapter in this book builds upon and contributes to advancing our understandings of how dialogue, generally, and dialogical perspectives, more specifically, can become helpful means to addressing the emerging challenges and opportunities that contemporary global societal phenomena pose for all of us.

15.2. Crisis, Not Just Change

Societies are indeed changing, and the three overall themes that organize this book, along with the chapters that actualize them, do describe central dimensions involved in this change. Increased polarization, digitalization, the emerging forms of learning and learning ecologies that new technologies afford, and the sort of challenges and opportunities that these bring for and through dialogue are undoubtfully crucial aspects of what defines the sort of global issues that characterize our times.

And yet, if one considers what these global issues are more concretely—think of the great recession of 2008–2009, the Covid-19 global pandemic that still lingers as a serious health and sociopolitical issue in many parts of the world, or the horrifying and deplorable wars of our time, including Russia's violent and unrightful invasion of Ukraine[2] with its renewed threat of nuclear

---

[2] During the production of this book, another equally horrifying invasion is taking place in Gaza, where war crimes and genocide are taking place, making evident the inability of a global order in crisis to safeguard and guarantee the most basic human rights.

catastrophe—one may argue that the notion "change" may not capture the essence of "these times" as aptly as the notion "crisis" does. And perhaps the global issue in which this is most salient—the one that the United Nations (UN) has labeled as the "defining challenge of our age" (Rosenthal, 2007)—is the *climate crisis*, which poses the great dark backdrop against which all these other crises unfold.

On the point of contrasting crisis and change, it is illustrative that, in the media and in the scientific literature, the notion of and narratives around "climate crisis" have become commonplace as a means to refer to what otherwise could have been termed "climate change" (Carey, 2012). It is in fact possible to speak of three ongoing, interrelated planetary crises: climate change, pollution, and biodiversity loss (United Nations Environment Programme, 2021). References to a climate and a planetary "emergency" are no longer strange in scientific journals either (e.g. Inman, 2010; Serrao-Neumann et al., 2021), and the sense that we are approaching a point of no return keeps growing among media and academia discourses when it comes to defining "our times."

Of course, these discursive and narrative realities may be seen as "just" that: ways in which we—scientists, journalists, international organizations—make sense, through discourse, of the sort of issues that are at stake when considering today's global conjuncture. It may also be argued that this is no news: that the looming of planetary crises has been on the public, governmental, and intergovernmental imaginary several times before. Just as Wertsch (this volume) shows how collective, national narratives both reflect and shape a nation's memory and understanding of its own past, present, and, by extension, its future, it is also possible to trace back a history of how and when planetary crises have been conceptualized through public narratives and culture. Anthropologist Joseph Masco's (2010) examines, for example, how the threats of nuclear crisis and of ecological crisis have been brought into focus several times in recent history, most saliently during the Cold War. According to Masco, during the Cold War and the nuclear arms race, nuclear fear became not only a narrative but also, and at the same time, an "instrument of state power" that "established a nationalized vision of planetary danger of very specific terms" (p. 9). It also produced "an unprecedented commitment to research in the earth sciences, enabling a new vision of the globe as integrated political, technological, and environmental space" (p. 9).

Just as it was then, narratives about planetary crisis today have very real implications that relate to our capacity to envision and imagine past, present and future possibilities. These narratives also refract an equally objective reality that should indeed be of great concern. The fact is that, as the available scientific evidence shows, unless profound societal transformations in the ways we exploit and relate to our environment take place, critical tipping points in the climate and in the ecosystems that support human civilization may be crossed within our lifetimes (Armstrong McKey et al., 2022; Boulton et al., 2021). And whereas planetary crises (including global health issues, social justice crises, and economical crises) have all happened before, there is good reason to think that what we are living today is not just another crisis. Certainly, it is not just "change." Rather, the current conjuncture presents itself as a rupture or disruption in which problems that have been with us for a long time—war, inequity, social and ecological injustice—are exacerbated in such a manner that they seem to be pushing local and global systems of human subsistence beyond the sort of irreversible "tipping points" that are otherwise referred to in the climate science literature.

A growing number of scholars are arguing that what we see unfolding today is, in fact, a crisis of a different order, an *epochal turning point* (Fraser, 2022; Moore, 2010). This is not only because the continuity of our species and of the vast majority of species on Earth are at stake in unprecedented ways. It is also because, as several scholars studying the history and politics of the environmental crisis argue (e.g. Charbonnier, 2021; Moore, 2015), the crisis is not just about "the environment" but about the ways in which our social, political, and economical forms of organization have developed during the last centuries and, more concretely, during the last five centuries of *capitalism* development. In this view, capitalist societies are not simply a way of organizing and producing social objects and social beings but also, and at the same time, a way of organizing and producing a natural environment that, in turn, further shapes society and its possibilities. Accordingly, what we see unfolding today is a compound of environmental, social, political, and economical crises that are inherently tied to capitalism as a way of organizing both societies and nature. As Charbonnier (2021) puts it, "the atmospheric accumulation of CO_2 not only compromises the Earth's ability to function as a habitat, but requires a new conception of our political relation to resources" (p. 4).

15.3. The Implications of Considering Crisis

Understanding today's planetary crisis as the expression of a socio-economical system of human relationships and struggles that configures "how human and extra-human natures get bundled" in the web of life (Moore, 2015, p. 47) is indeed very much in line with the dialogical premises that were presented at the outset of this chapter and which assert the irreducible unity, in humanity, of biology ("nature") and culture (Rommetveit, 2003; Vygotsky, 1986). The notion of language and dialogue as foundational to what connects us with each other and with our (cultural, natural) environment also seems to align well with the reflections on how narratives on crisis, and on what is possible and not possible to do within this crisis, both refract material, objective relations and shape our perceptions about them.

How then, does a consideration of the current times as times of crisis allow us to say anything about the significance of the current volume that would not have already been said? First, on a critical note, it should help us reconsider our analysis of current global societies and how and on which narratives we draw when characterizing the problems and ambitions of education in view of contemporary global issues. A case in point are narratives on the challenges of the 21st century—widely held across educational policy-making and research—as mostly of an entrepreneurial nature and responding to a rapidly developing and changing "knowledge society" (Ananiadou & Caro, 2009). From that view,

> success lies in being able to communicate, share, and use information to solve complex problems, in being able to adapt and innovate in response to new demands and changing circumstances, in being able to marshal and expand the power of technology to create new knowledge, and in expanding human capacity and productivity. (Binkley et al., 2012)

Communication, solving complex problems, and being able to adapt to changing circumstances are of course important educational values in contemporary societies. However, considering the growingly unjust depletion and exploitation of natural and human resources—what Patel and Moore (2017) refer to as capitalist's "cheaps"—which in turn contribute to the continuous acceleration of the planetary crisis of climate, pollution, and biodiversity loss—one wonders what "expanding technology, human capacity, and productivity" tells us about education's role.

Consider the Covid-19 pandemic as a societal challenge characteristic of the 21st century. There is evidence suggesting that the likelihood for the occurrence of such global pandemics has increased during the last century (Morse et al., 2012). Of course, a global pandemic may be considered a complex problem in the 21st-century skills framework. But when the World Health Organization's (WHO) director addressed global audiences at a media debriefing on Covid-19 in June 2020, he chose to emphasize the following as values and skills on demand:

> We're all in this together. And we're all in this for the long haul. We will need even greater stores of resilience, patience, humility, and generosity in the months ahead.
> We have already lost so much, but we cannot lose hope. (Ghebreyesus, 2020)

Resilience, patience, humility, generosity, hope. Inventiveness, solidarity, and kindness were other qualities the WHO's director emphasized through his speech. These are keywords that fit uneasily into narratives of human capacity and productivity, and words that are more generally all too absent in discourses about education.

The point is not to suggest that WHO has a more adequate analysis of what is required for living, learning, and thriving in the 21st century, but rather that we, dialogical educators, need to draw on adequate analyses that address the hard truth of planetary crisis; of its historical, social, political, and economical causes and conditions. The point is not to suggest that the current volume builds upon or draws on the 21st-century skills framework specifically either. In fact, values of equity and of democratic dialogue are thoroughly represented throughout the book. But the framing analysis on today's context and its educational challenges seems to fall short of considering the full scale and quality of the problems we face.

Identifying a proper method and approach to understanding the sort of problems and educational challenges we face today also implies the possibility of opening new educational horizons, ways of imagining what sort of futures we can achieve in and through our educational research practices. As cultural–historical theorist Anna Stetsenko has recently argued, what we need is an "emphasis on a close interlinking of our ability at diagnosing the ongoing crisis by going to its roots . . . on one hand, *and* at envisioning a better future and making a commitment to its realization, on the other" (Stetsenko, 2022, para. 4). In my reading, this implies that articulating dialogical perspectives as relevant to our ongoing crises—or to any issue of relevance and societal concern, really—demands not only thoroughly examining what the nature of the sociohistorical context being addressed is but also making clear what the *commitment* of a dialogical perspective is with regards to those contexts. Reminding us that "any research/theorizing, at its core, can never be apolitical, removed from struggle, or devoid of human dimensions such as intention, stance, desire, and commitment," Stetsenko (2022, Beyond Vygotsky: Activist-transformative methodology, para. 11) contends that "both our practice *and* our scholarship . . . demand of us a definition of *where we stand and where we want to go next.*"

Throughout the chapters of this volume, a stance on humanistic and democratic values of social justice and equity is tangible, from the commitment of relevance to the wider societal context articulated in the introduction, to chapters of relevance to inclusion (e.g. on reading in bilingual families by Nomat et al.) or democratic civic coexistence (e.g. on active citizenship and participation by Ligorio et al.). There is also a definitive commitment to activist scholarship—in the sense of scholarship that takes a stance and presents a project of resistance and change, as visible in chapters such as that by de Haan's, which explores "the limits and potential of dialogue to *counter polarization* in educative settings" (emphasis added). If the ambition is to better understand and meaningfully address, through dialogical scholarship, the sort of eco-social struggles and injustices that characterize the current sociohistorical conjuncture, a critical and precise analysis of the sociohistorical precedents and conditions that characterize our times should be of utmost importance.

15.4. The Significance of Dialogical Perspectives in a Time of Planetary Crisis

Having argued that a more critical analysis of the current "changing times" should allow us to more precisely position the dialogical perspectives as relevant to ongoing social and ecological challenges and struggles, to conclude this commentary, I would like to make the (obvious) case that all chapters included in this volume do present contributions of relevance to contemporary issues, including those chapters which do not directly address salient contexts of crisis, such as the Covid-19 pandemic (thematized, among others, but perhaps also most saliently in Bisgaard et al.'s chapter on Layered Attunment). I do so by revisiting some of the notions in the book as they are mobilized to address an empirical illustrative example from sustainability education.

The question of sustainability[3] is not directly addressed in any of the chapters, but, in the reminder of this commentary, I would like to exhibit the volume's significance by drawing on some of the chapters' arguments and contributions to address some of the aspects of sustainability as an educational challenge of our times. To begin with, it should be said that the relevance of dialogue in issues of sustainability is beyond question: in the fight for a more just, sustainable future, sustained and committed collective action is required. Accordingly, understanding and ensuring the conditions to engage in dialogue within and across social groups, sectors, and nations is of utmost relevance. Beyond the question of collective action, and no less importantly, dialogue and dialogical perspectives are of paramount relevance for understanding and promoting the emergence of new ways of collectively imagining alternative ways of organizing our societies and of imagining possible socially just and sustainable futures. Dialogue is indeed a core condition for the implementation of "utopian methodologies," that is, design-based methodologies for "envisioning, implementing, sustaining, and critically evaluating . . . educational activity systems that prefigure the utopian goal of an equitable and humane education system" (Rajala et al., 2022).

In our own work, we have focused on investigating the ways in which different discursive and narrative aspects around sustainability intermesh with teachers'

---

[3] Here, and in line with the historico-material perspectives on planetary crisis discussed in the previous section, I am using the term sustainability to refer to an interdisciplinary concern that relates to the "environment" as much as it does to the social, political, and economic relations of production and consumption that characterize humans' relationship with the environment.

and students' positioning, through education, as historical actors in the struggle toward a more sustainable and socially just future (e.g. Svarstad et al., in press; Tasquier et al., 2022). Similar to the type of research-practice partnership we find in Ligorio et al.'s chapter and their "Dialogues in the Square" project, we engage with students, educators inside and outside of the school, as well as with public and private organizations and actors in the school's local communities to codesign and engage in action toward local and global sustainability challenges. As part of this engagement, we get the opportunity to discuss and generate opportunities for the discussion of sustainability issues as they involve the participants' lives.

The following excerpts are extracted from an interview with two upper secondary students, part of a larger set of interviews that took place following a school project in which the students, in collaboration with several actors including environmental organizations, had explored and evaluated possible climate change solutions with regard to their own visions and hopes for the future (Røkenes & Jornet, 2023). The excerpts are helpful to illustrate some of the issues that characterize sustainability as an educational issue and as an educational research issue. They are also helpful to illustrate how several of the ideas and discussions included in this volume may contribute to the subject. Rather than attempting to present a proper (dialogical) analysis of these excerpts, I use them to present an overview of some of the chapters in this volume and how the ideas presented in these chapters become relevant to the themes of sustainability and planetary crisis.

15.5. A Brief Illustration

Student 1: I do not think so much about sustainability, actually. Like, I try—but I do not have any strong thoughts about—I do want, of course, I don't want lots of plastics in the sea. I don't want that the world is destroyed and all of that, but I do not do so much about it either. . . . I feel this is the same for most, because they do not feel that they do have much influence. [long pause]. You can have it, but it is more difficult to get it. Like Greta Thunberg. Because, she is one person, and she manages to get a lot—she manages to make a great impact. But it is very rarely that one achieves that. So, there is very little hope in that one person manages that. It's like voting, like few—there are many who do not vote because they think their vote makes no difference. But it does make a difference if there are more votes, it's like an irrational thought many have.

In the excerpt, the student admits that, despite being concerned about the issue and not wanting that "the world is destroyed," he does not do or think much about it, and further provides a reasoning or justification that he extends to "most" people more generally. The reasoning is that, since most people think their actions most likely won't change much, they do not really engage. The student further draws an analogy with voting: one can think that just one vote does not make a difference. But, the student admits, this is "irrational" since a vote makes a difference if it adds to more such votes.

Without being able to go in detail within the scope of this commentary, the excerpt illustrates some issues that we find to be characteristic of the subject of sustainability when taken up and addressed in educational settings. As existential threats to both human and nonhuman species that are increasingly becoming presented as such in the media, the planetary crises of climate change, pollution, and biodiversity loss are generally recognized by students and educators as a collective issue of importance—at least to some extent and with varying degrees of awareness and concern. What is characteristic across the cases we have documented is that the quality of the students' concern, interest, and engagement is often modulated by their sense of agency with respect to the issue, both in how they perceive it to concern *them* personally, but most importantly how they perceive whether and how their actions (or thoughts) can make any difference at all (Røkenes & Jornet, 2023).

In the student's account, one can hear the sort of *multivoicedness* that Wertsch, making reference to Bakhtin, describes in his chapter on the role of narratives in dialogue and intersubjectivity. Multivoicedness is not just about there being multiple arguments or positions that co-exist in the student's utterance—which there are—but, more fundamentally, about the fact that, when we speak, we do so using a language and narratives—that is, symbolic tools—that are not just ours. They bring "a history and structure of their own into what a speaker says" (Wertsch, this volume), allowing her or him to say more than what one could alone "intend" to say. What the students' say in conversations, such as the one reported here, thus, does reflect narratives, and *narrative templates* (see Wertsch, this volume) that are characteristic of a national or global community, in this case, with respect to what individuals can (and cannot) do to address large societal issues on their own. These narratives, which today reach us through multiple digital media, including digital social media, deeply shape the possible dialogues that can be had on the issue, and therefore both afford and constrain the possibilities for envisioning possible paths to knowledge and action. As the excerpt below shows, students not only express but also become aware of this multivoicedness and wonder about where they "get it from."

Student 2: I just feel that the reasoning of most people, it's a bit strange, because I do not know where we get it from, but like, [clothing] trademarks are popular among youth . . . there is high value in like showing that you have money, something that is a bit stupid, because it does not make sense.

We also find in the student's accounts a certain *dialogical tension* of the kind Bisgaard et al. elaborate on in their chapter on internal dialogues and intersubjectivity, according to which, having internalized a diversity of voices, "individuals are able to inhabit several I-positions which can create tension in the meaning-making process following contradictions and oppositions between the relevant voices" (Bisgaard et al., this volume). Such contradictions are visible in the coexisting narratives—coexisting in the students' accounts but also and at the same time in the pool of sense-making resources available in today's dialogues on sustainability—that (i) individuals' actions cannot make a difference and that (ii) individuals' actions can make a difference (because they add to collective action). There is also contradiction, or at least ambiguity, in the students' recognition of ways of reasoning that they disagree with (as in the second excerpt, where giving value to luxurious clothing marks is labeled as "stupid" and as difficult to understand) while at the same time counting themselves among those who endorse those thoughts, the "young." These are contradictions that pervade society as much as they permeate individuals' sense-making, both cognitively and affectively, as Bisgaard et al.'s chapter argues (see also Roth & Jornet, 2014). Part of the analytical task, therefore, must include examining the historical and cultural origins and logic of these tensions and contradictions, as real forces that become entangled in our and our students' ways of speaking, thinking, and acting and which, in the case of the ongoing crisis, need to be seen in relation to the struggle against an unsustainable geopolitical order, the fight to degrowth and to subvert the fossil fuel-based capitalist regime.

Given the existential nature of the crisis that educators and educational researchers confront when addressing sustainability in and through education, it is necessary to consider what the role and positioning of dialogical education is with respect to the social struggle of radically transforming societies—which is what is required to open for the possibility of generating more sustainable futures (Morrison et al., 2022). Here, dialogical spaces—as the ones argued for in de Haan's and Ligorio et al.'s chapters—are to be conceived as developmental, transformative spaces with the potential to support participants in the struggle toward better, more just futures.

During interviews such as the one reported here, students (or teachers, or any other interviewee for that matter) often change their ways of talking and thinking about issues, since interviews too can be dialogical spaces where development takes place.[4] In the course of the interview, interviewers (two educational researchers)

---

[4] This is a universal trait of interviews, but also of conversations more generally, and one that is presumed in Vygotsky's (1986) understanding of thought and language, according to which thoughts are not expressed but developed in speech. Accordingly, spontaneous speech never is a direct reflection of what one thinks, but in speaking a developmental process unfolds in which both thinking and speaking develop, mutually constituting each other (Jornet & Roth, 2017).

participated in the exploration of these contradictions, for example, by following up with questions and remarks on the example, brought about by the students, on Greta Thunberg as a young individual who, nonetheless, has had tremendous impact in the environmental movement. Such an inquiry led participants—researchers, students—to further explore and question their own assumptions about themselves as individuals, and as humans capable of change (or not), more generally. For example, the assumption that counting on people to willingly contribute to societal transformation was hopeless (since, according to Student 1, "it is in our nature to want to show off" and therefore difficult to assume we will want to reverse consumption and pursue degrowth and alternative forms of organization), and that state-driven interventions focusing on innovations in technology and energy should be pursued instead. By questioning these narratives, their origin, and what they do or do not do for us to be able to achieve collective action, alternative horizons of being engaged with the societal issue opened.

The latter issue points back at our and responsibility as educators (and educational researchers) for, as Linell (this volume) reminds us when referencing Rommetviet, "participants in communication must take on some responsibility for their utterances and other actions" and that "if somebody asserts something publicly, he or she must remain epistematically responsible." As participants in the dialogues that we make possible through our scholarly activities in projects focusing on sustainability, or, as the remainder of this book does, on any other societally and locally relevant issue of praxis, we are also epistemically responsible to, as Stetsenko puts it, not pretend political neutrality and to take a stance. Beyond well-established notions of socioscientific issues as involving controversy along social and ethical aspects of science, the environmental crisis presents profound educational dilemmas as it concerns the students' very right to a livable environment, their right to having a future. The environmental crisis is not just symptomatic of a changing world, but of a global system in profound turmoil, a system of human environment-making and environment-transforming socio-economical and political relations (Charbonnier, 2021; Moore, 2015).

The students' thinking and feeling as articulated throughout their conversations on the topic are not just theirs, but also expressions of this very crisis. As Wertsch (this volume) states by reference to the notion of *double dialogicality*, "dialogue between interlocutors also involves dialogue with the sociocultural conditions in which they are embedded." It is up to us, educators and educational researchers who work in and for the field of educational praxis, to create an educational, sociocultural, and dialogical context in which conditions for becoming aware of the real, historical, and cultural conditions for making a difference and being able to contribute to more socially and ecologically just and sustainable societies exist. I believe contributions like this book are invaluable resources for that cause.

References

Ananiadou, K., & Claro, M. (2009). *21st Century skills and competences for new millennium learners in OECD countries*. OECD Education Working Papers, No. 41. OECD Publishing. http://dx.doi.org/10.1787/218525261154

Armstrong McKay, D. I., Staal, A., Abrams, J. F., Winkelmann, R., Sakschewski, B., Loriani, S., Fetzer, I., Cornell, S. E., Rockström, J., & Lenton, T. M. (2022). Exceeding 1.5°C global warming could trigger multiple climate tipping points. *Science, 377*(6611). DOI: 10.1126/science.abn7950

Binkley, M., Erstad, O, Herman, J., Raizen, S., Ripley, M., Miller-Ricci, M., & Rumble, M. (2012). Defining twenty-first century skills. In P. Griffin, & E. Care (Eds.), *Assessment and teaching of 21st century skills* (pp. 17–66). Springer.

Boulton, C. A., Lenton, T. M., & Boers, N. (2022). Pronounced loss of Amazon rainforest resilience since the early 2000s. *Nature Climate Change, 12*, 271–278.

Carey, M. (2012). Climate and history: A critical review of historical climatology and climate change historiography. *WIRES Climate Change, 3*, 233–249.

Charbonnier, P. (2021). *Affluence and freedom. An environmental history of political ideas*. Polity Press.

Fraser, N. (2022). *Cannibal capitalism. How our system is devouring democracy, care, and the planet—And what we can do about it*. Verso.

Ghebreyesus, T. A. (2020). WHO director-general's opening remarks at the media briefing on COVID-19, 29 June 2020. https://www.who.int/director-general/speeches/detail/who-director-general-s-opening-remarks-at-the-media-briefing-on-covid-19---29-june-2020

Inman, M. (2010). Planning for plan B. *Nature Climate Change, 1*, 7–9.

Jornet, A., & Roth, W.-M. (2017). Design {thinking | communicating}. A sociogenetic approach to reflective practice in collaborative design.

Masco, J. (2010). Bad weather: On planetary crisis. *Social Studies of Science, 40*(1), 7–40.

Moore, J. W. (2010). The end of the road? Agricultural revolutions in the capitalist world-ecology, 1450–2010. *Journal of Agrarian Change, 10*, 389–413.

Moore, J. W. (2015). *Capitalism in the web of life. Ecology and the accumulation of capital*. Verso.

Morrison, T. H., Adger, W. N., Agrawal, A., Brown, K., Hornsey, M. J., Hughes, T. P., . . . Van Berkel, D. (2022). Radical interventions for climate-impacted systems. *Nature Climate Change, 12*, 1100–1106. https://doi.org/10.1038/s41558-022-01542-y

Morse, S. S., Mazet, J. A., Woolhouse, M., Parrish, C. R., Carroll, D., Karesh, W. B., . . . Daszak, P. (2012). Prediction and prevention of the next pandemic zoonosis. *The Lancet, 380*(9857), 1956–1965.

Patel, R., & Moore, J. W. (2017). *A history of the world in seven cheap things: A guide to capitalism, nature, and the future of the planet*. University of California Press.

Rajala, A., Cole, M., & Esteban-Guitart, M. (2022). Utopian methodology: Researching educational interventions to promote equity over multiple timescales. *Journal of the Learning Sciences*. DOI: 10.1080/10508406.2022.2144736

Rommetveit, R. (2003). On the role of 'a psychology of the second person' in studies of meaning, language, and mind. *Mind, Culture, and Activity, 10*, 205–218.

Roth, W.-M., & Jornet, A. (2014). Towards a theory of experience. *Science Education, 98*, 106–126.

Roth, W.-M., & Jornet, A. (2017). *Understanding educational psychology. A late Vygotskian, Spinozist approach*. Springer.

Rosenthal, E. (2007). U.N. chief seeks more climate change leadership. *The New York Times*. https://www.nytimes.com/2007/11/18/science/earth/18climatenew.html

Røkenes, H., & Jornet, A. (2023). *Affective contradictions in meaningful open schooling sustainability education: A critical, cultural-historical approach*. [Manuscript submitted for publication]. Department of Teacher Education and School Research, University of Oslo.

Serrao-Neumann, S., Moreira, F. de A., Fontana, M. D., Rodrigues Torres, R., Montengro Lapola, D., Hidalgo Nunes, L., Marengo, J. A., & Marques Di Giulio, G. (2021). Advancing transdisciplinary adaptation research practice. *Nature Climate Change*, 11, 1006–1008.

Stetsenko, A. (2022). Radicalizing theory and Vygotsky: Addressing crisis through activist-transformative methodology. *Human Arenas*. DOI: https://doi.org/10.1007/s42087-022-00299-2

Svarstad, H., Jornet, A., Peters, G., Griffiths, T. G., & Bejaminsen, T. (in press). Critical Climate Education is crucial for fast and just transformations. *Nature Climate Change*.

Tasquier, G., Knain, E., & Jornet, A. (2022). Scientific literacies for change making: Equipping the young to tackle current societal challenges. *Frontiers in Education*, https://doi.org/10.3389/feduc.2022.689329

United Nations Environment Programme. (2021). *Making Peace with Nature: A scientific blueprint to tackle the climate, biodiversity and pollution emergencies*. Nairobi. https://www.unep.org/resources/making-peace-nature

Vygotsky, L. S. (1986). *Thought and language*. MIT Press.

16
Legacies and Prospects of Dialogue
Editor's Final Note

Ola Erstad, Bente Eriksen Hagtvet, and James V. Wertsch

16.1. A Final Note

Since we began planning this volume in 2018 the world has experienced several devastating crises and conflicts, often leading to increased polarization, both within and between nations. Expressions of protectionism, nationalism, and what used to be considered extreme political parties are now dominating politics in growing numbers of countries. Even in traditionally strong social democracies, like the Nordic countries, right-wing parties have grown in influence, not only in gaining votes, but also in the ways other parties have popularized their political messages. Still, the most concrete expression of increased polarization is the war in Ukraine and the Middle East, which has created a global crisis and a gap between the East and the West that recalls the Cold War period. And, as if this was not enough, the global Covid-19 pandemic made us all experience isolation and dependence on digital forms of communication. These changing and accumulating barriers to dialogue have most likely influenced the book's content—maybe not so much its *semantic* meaning as its *emotive*. The book's *emotive* meaning has presumably become more dominant during these years—the authors' awareness of *the importance* of dialogue is stated throughout this book. An important message is the emphasis on the facilitators of true dialogue and the dangers of taking it for granted. While the collection of the volume's chapter topics was largely preplanned, the times we have lived through during the delivery of this book have presumably strengthened our awareness of the ideals of authentic dialogue being an urgently important, yet fragile, quality of living. On this background, this book is also a defense of authentic dialogues and the need to nurse them in school.

As mentioned in the introduction to this book, there is nothing new in societies and communities being polarized. However, the escalating tensions, both in the physical and the virtual worlds, bring increased complexities to how these issues are experienced today and to our perceptions of possible futures. There are numerous attempts to understand contemporary processes of polarization today, but in general there seems to be a struggle on the international level of using dialogue as an approach to counter polarization. As such, we believe there is a need to raise broader debates and increase understanding of how authentic dialogues may be used to reduce tensions in societies around the world today. By this volume we aim at contributing to increased awareness of the potentialities of authentic dialogues (see *Dialogic approaches and tensions in learning and development. At the frontiers of the mind* (Muller & Dos Santos, 2021), and the journal "Dialogic Pedagogy: An International Online Journal," as well as other publications by authors in this volume.)

This volume brings together key authors from different fields, all reflecting the legacies of Ragnar Rommetveit's writings. Of particular importance for the positioning of the volume is the role of education as an arena for developing students' skills of communication and also for developing increased awareness of the dialogue's potentially misleading power in the forms of, for example, sarcasm intended to harm, betrayals, lies, etc. In educational arenas, dialogical skills may be both aims and means, and this volume addresses both of these—often interrelated—functions and knowledge areas. Inspired by the broad variety of works by Ragnar Rommetveit, some chapters document how education may promote knowledge and mutual understanding across borders and individuals via dialogues as *tools* of interaction and learning. Other chapters show how education via activities and discussions *foster* dialogical skills and competence. By diverse approaches, the chapters further cover a broad variety of research issues ranging from macro- to micro-perspectives: some studies showing how macro-contexts, such as cultural narratives and culturally situated forms of understanding, affect citizens' understanding of situations and words; others report "micro studies," such as the effects of diverse forms of mediation on children's learning in specific contexts.

16.2. With Inspiration from Ragnar Rommetveit

This book has been written in respect and gratitude to Ragnar Rommetveit. By placing himself in the interface between philosophy, linguistics, sociology, and psychology, he was in many respects ahead of his time. And he still appears modern, maybe in particular in his later writing between 1980 and 2010 (Hagtvet et al., 2020). Most of the chapters in this book draw on this scholarship, especially his explorations into the concept of intersubjectivity and perspectivity, as has been discussed in several of the chapters.

Rommetveit also had an artistic side—he wood-carved shapes, drew illustrative pictures, and wrote poetry in his local dialect of Norwegian. His poetic skills were sometimes noticeable in interviews and on informal occasions.

In an interview with Ragnar, carried out by Ingrid E. Josephs (*IJ*) (Josephs, 1998) and published in *Culture & Psychology*, this combination of academic skills, sense of humor, and self-irony is often revealed. Ragnar (RR) reflected on how he positions himself in opposition to other thinkers and academics, especially within psychology. In elaborating on his truly interdisciplinary approach, the impacts of other cultural resources such as humor and poetry are clearly revealed:

IJ: *In your oeuvre you often refer to your philosophical and sociological roots, to Wittgenstein, Schütz and Luckmann, for instance. What are your psychological roots?*

RR: I don't know. My first teacher of psychology at the University of Oslo was the philosopher Arne Naess. He had been in Vienna, knew very well the Vienna Circle, and had also spent some time at Berkeley, studying Tolman while Tolman was studying rats. . . . Arne Naess had written a small piece: "Notes on a Foundation of Psychology as a Science." That was one of the first things I read. . . . He taught me always to reflect upon and question my own epistemological premises for empirical psychological research.

IJ: *So, at that time language was not your main interest?*

RR: No, not my first interest, but I gradually moved into it after having conducted research on social norms and roles, person perception and experiments on reflectively monitored vs intuitive' cognition. . . . The point of departure for my wondering about language and mind was not at all the eternal sentence, but rather *the cryptic yet*—to quote Vygotsky (1962)—*perfectly understood utterance*. And if I were to choose a canonical utterance within a dialogical approach, it has to be *the answer*. . . . I think that in most dialogues there is an *openness of meaning*—Wittgenstein called it indeterminacy of sense. . . . we are held personally and individually responsible for what we "mean". . . . Dialogic theory is in some sense counterintuitive: The fact that we are multivoiced and only "shareholders" in what is meant by what we assert goes contrary to the morally warranted claim that we must be accountable as individual monological speakers. And this is very much in line with the whole of psychology—and in particular with the American psychology of the individual organism. Every kind of mental activity in the gray zone of intersection of the individual and the collectivity—that's out. The mutual infiltration of the individual and the collectivity is a terra incognita in post-cognitive revolutionary mentalism. The dialogical paradigm provokes us to recognize and reflect upon moral aspects of communication without disguising them.

Ingrid E. Josephs also asked Ragnar about his conception of the dialogue and intersubjectivity—it appeared rather circular she indicated:

IJ: *The concept of "attunement to the attunement of the other" seems to refer to a circular process from which nothing new can emerge. How can anything new emerge in such a dialogue? If everybody were attuned to the attunement of the other, nothing could change, and there would be no reason for communication at all.*

RR: I definitely do not equate intersubjectivity with consensus. The taken-for-grantedness is one thing, but in the most fruitful dialogues novel ideas emerge as a result of fruitful misunderstanding. A person says something, and I read something into it beyond what he or she meant. . . . So the dynamic aspects are very essential. When I first used the expression "intersubjectivity" in my writing, I think some of the examples I gave could be interpreted in the direction of consensus. But I would definitely not constrain my investigations of intersubjectivity to cases of consensus. For example, take teaching situations, dialogues between student and teacher. He or she, who let's say is a novice in some respects, starts phrasing something and you listen carefully with the intention to capture and feedback what the student's utterance could be developed further, rather than hasten to mediate your own ready-made answer to her or him.

By these words, Ragnar guided us to design a book on the importance of dialogue with a specific focus on education.

References

Hagtvet, B. E., Linell, P., Wertsch, J. V., & Wold, A. H. (2020). Ragnar Rommetveit: A full life. *Culture & Psychology, 26*(3), 528–539. https://doi.org/10.1177/1354067X19898679

Josephs, I. E. (1998). Do you know Ragnar Rommetveit? On dialogue and silence, poetry and pedantry, and cleverness and wisdom in psychology (An interview with Ragnar Rommetveit). *Culture & Psychology, 4*(2), 189–212.

Muller, M., & Dos Santos, M. (Eds.). (2021). *Dialogic approaches and tensions in learning and development. At the frontiers of the mind.* Springer Nature. https://doi.org/10.1007/978-3-030-84226-0

Index

For the benefit of digital users, indexed terms that span two pages (e.g., 52–53) may, on occasion, appear on only one of those pages.

Please note: Tables and figures are indicated by *t* and *f* following the page number

abductive generalization, 62*f*, 62–63
America
   Civil War and competing narrative templates, 23–24
   and competing narrative templates, 22–26
   and national narratives as coauthors, 20–22
Anthropocene age, and educational technology, 122
attendance to others, microblogging and, 145–47
   classroom interactions, 149–50, 150*f*
   dialogic classroom, 148–49
   technology-mediated dialogue, 147–49
   technology-mediated learning and intersubjectivity, 160–63
   vignettes of classroom attunement, 150–59, 152*f*, 156*f*, 159*f*
attunement
   abductive generalization, 62*f*, 62–63
   communities, tension and negotiation between, 67–68
   and dialogical negotiation, 60–61
   dialogic classroom, 148–49
   layered attunement and intersubjectivity, 50–60, 55*f*, 71–72
   microblogging and, 145–47
   microblogging in classroom interactions, 149–50, 150*f*
   polysemic multivoiced self, 55*f*, 61–67, 69*f*, 70*f*
   and technology-mediated dialogue, 147–49
   technology-mediated learning and intersubjectivity in, 160–63
   vignettes of classroom attunement, 150–59, 152*f*, 156*f*, 159*f*

Bakhtin, Mikhail
   dialogue and intersubjectivity, 17–19
   dialogue and "voice," 169–70
   narrative as symbolic tool, 19–20
bilingual families, shared reading in, 219–20, 235–36
   child-initiated code-switching and parental confirmation, 227–29
   child-initiated code-switching and parental extension, 229–31
   dialogic perspective, 220–21
   parent-initiated code-switching, 231–33
   patterns over time, 224–27, 225*f*, 226*f*
   scaffolded dialogues, 227
   study design, 222
   study discussion, 233–35
   study methods, 222–24
Binkley, M., 281
Brown, John, 23–24
Bruner, J., 219–20

change
   characteristic aspects or dimensions, 278
   epochal turning points, 280
citizenship education and participation, 96–98
   "Dialogues in the Square," constraints and opportunities, 113–17
   "Dialogues in the Square," cross-generational dialogue, 110–13
   "Dialogues in the Square," dialogue development, 106–8, 107*t*
   "Dialogues in the Square," on sustainability, 283–84
   "Dialogues in the Square," origins of project, 102*f*, 102–4, 104*f*
   "Dialogues in the Square," participants and partners, 104–6, 105*t*
   "Dialogues in the Square," types of dialogue, 108–10, 109*t*, 110*f*
   theoretical framework, 98–101
   Trialogical Learning Approach (TLA), 101
"City on a Hill," as American national narrative, 20–21, 22–26
classroom attunement, vignettes of, 150–59, 152*f*, 156*f*, 159*f*
classroom discussion, promoting reflection in, 204–6, 211–13

classroom interactions, microblogging and, 149–50, 150f
classroom methods, and collaborative learning, 207–8
classroom supports, for active learning, 202–6
coauthorship of meaning, dialogism and, 168
code-switching, and shared reading in bilingual families, 219–20, 235–36
  child-initiated code-switching and parental confirmation, 227–29
  child-initiated code-switching and parental extension, 229–31
  dialogic perspective, 220–21
  parent-initiated code-switching, 231–33
  patterns over time, 224–27, 225f, 226f
  scaffolded dialogues, 227
  study design, 222
  study discussion, 233–35
  study methods, 222–24
collaborative reasoning, 203
communication, contexts of, 32–42
  cultural context, 39–40
  and enculturation, 187–88
  Putin on war in Ukraine, 40–42
  remote contexts, 42–44
  sexual abuse of children, 37–39
  threatening phone calls, 35–37
  and video games, 181–85
communicative acts, teaching and learning as, 240
communities, tension and negotiation between, 67–68
connection, educational technology for, 134–35
connectivism, or learning as networking, 132–34
contact zones, and dialogue to counter polarization, 92–93
contexts, of communication, 32–42
  cultural context, 39–40
  Putin on war in Ukraine, 40–42
  remote contexts, 42–44
  sexual abuse of children, 37–39
  threatening phone calls, 35–37
conversation analysis, 42, 44–45
conversation theory, and educational technology, 130–32
COVID-19 pandemic, social challenge of, 281–82
crisis, dialogue in times of
  COVID-19 pandemic, 281–82
  dialogical tension, 286
  epochal turning points, 280
  implications of, 280–83

pervasiveness of dialogue, 277–78
in planetary crisis, 283–84
social crisis *versus* social change, 278–80
student interviews, 284–87
sustainability, educational challenge of, 283–84

debate
  and classroom supports for active learning, 202–4
  hybrid debate and discussion, 210–11
developmental perspective, intersubjectivity in a, 243
dialogical interventions, implications for designing, 89–92, 90f
dialogicality, and importance of dialogue, 2–3, 273
dialogical negotiation, 60–61
dialogical perspective, 2–3
Dialogical Self Theory, 59
dialogical spaces, designing inclusive, 82–84
dialogical tension, 286
dialogic classroom
  "possibility thinking" and, 160
  role of teacher in, 148–49
dialogic education theory, 98–101
dialogic gap, 126
dialogic relations, 127
dialogic space, 127
dialogic theory, of educational technology, 129–30, 137–39
  and Anthropocene age, 122
  connection, technology for, 134–37
  connectivism, or learning as networking, 132–34
  conversation theory, 130–32
  defining education, 125–26
  defining technology, 123–24
  definitions and scope, 121–26
  dialogic gap, 126
  dialogic space, 127
  dialogism, aspects of, 126–29
  double-voicedness, 128
  nature of dialogic relations, 127
  nature of learning, 127–29
  participation, educational technology for, 135–36
  theory *versus* practice, 124–25
  time, educational technology for expansion of, 136–37
dialogism
  aspects of, 126–29
  and contexts of communication, 32–35
  definition, 29–31

INDEX

dialogic gap, 126
dialogic space, 127
double-voicedness, 128
indicators for, 100–1
and life and career of Ragnar Rommetveit, 31–32
and macro-level phenomena, 45–46
nature of dialogic relations, 127
nature of learning, 127–29
dialogue
 and action in a public space, 106–8, 107t
 cross-generational, 110–13
 between different worldviews, 85–86
 importance of, 1–2
 influence of Ragnar Rommetveit, 16–19
 and intersubjectivity, 86–89
 learning dialogues, 240–42
 and narrative, 15–16, 26–27
 as remedy for polarization, 79–81
 specificity of, 276
 technology-mediated, 147–49
 transformative dialogue *versus* polarization, 275
 types of, 108–10, 109t
 viability in polarized settings, 77–79
 See also video games, intersubjectivity and dialogue in
dialogue, in times of crisis
 COVID-19 pandemic, 281–82
 dialogical tension, 286
 epochal turning points, 280
 implications of, 280–83
 pervasiveness of dialogue, 277–78
 in planetary crisis, 283–84
 social crisis *versus* social change, 278–80
 student interviews, 284–87
 sustainability, educational challenge of, 283–84
"Dialogues in the Square"
 constraints and opportunities, 113–17
 cross-generational dialogue, 110–13
 dialogue development, 106–8
 origins of the project, 102–4
 participants and partners, 104–6, 105t
 on sustainability, 283–84
 types of dialogue, 108–10, 109t, 110f
digitalization, and current monologic approaches, 5–6
discussion
 and classroom supports for active learning, 202–4
 hybrid debate and discussion, 210–11
Doll;s House, The (Ibsen), 241
double dialogicality, 169–70, 273

double-voicedness, 128
Down syndrome, and teacher-child story construction, 253–55, 256–58
dual-language learners, and parent-child shared reading, 219–20, 235–36
 child-initiated code-switching and parental confirmation, 227–29
 child-initiated code-switching and parental extension, 229–31
 dialogic perspective on, 220–21
 parent-initiated code-switching, 231–33
 patterns over time, 224–27, 225f, 226f
 scaffolded dialogues, 227
 study design, 222
 study discussion, 233–35
 study methods, 222–24

economic crises, dimensions of living through, 1
education
 citizenship education and participation, 96–98
 contact zones and dialogue, 92–93
 definition of, 125–26
 dialogical interventions, implications for designing, 89–92, 90f
 dialogical perspective in, 2–3
 dialogical spaces, designing inclusive, 82–84
 dialogic education theory, 98–101
 dialogue and learning, 8
 and dialogue as a remedy for polarization, 79–81
 and dialogue between worldviews, 85–86
 "Dialogues in the Square," constraints and opportunities, 113–17
 "Dialogues in the Square," cross-generational dialogue, 110–13
 "Dialogues in the Square," dialogue development, 106–8, 107t
 "Dialogues in the Square," on sustainability, 283–84
 "Dialogues in the Square," origins of project, 102f, 102–4, 104f
 "Dialogues in the Square," participants and partners, 104–6, 105t
 "Dialogues in the Square," types of dialogue, 108–10, 109t, 110f
 and fostering dialogical skills and competence, 291
 intersubjectivity and differing worldviews, 86–89
 limits of countering polarization, 77–79
 traditions, addressing incommensurable, 91
 Trialogical Learning Approach (TLA), 101

educational technology, dialogic theory of, 129–30, 137–39
  and Anthropocene age, 122
  connection, technology for, 134–37
  connectivism, or learning as networking, 132–34
  conversation theory, 130–32
  defining education, 125–26
  defining technology, 123–24
  definitions and scope, 121–26
  dialogic gap, 126
  dialogic space, 127
  dialogism, aspects of, 126–29
  double-voicedness, 128
  nature of dialogic relations, 127
  nature of learning, 127–29
  participation, educational technology for, 135–36
  theory *versus* practice, 124–25
  time, educational technology for expansion of, 136–37
enculturation, and online video games, 187–88
  example, 188
epochal turning points, 280

Frog, Where Are You? (Mayer), 246

Grant, Madison, 24

Habermas, Jürgen, 82–83, 84

Ibsen, Henrik, 241
intersubjectivity
  abductive generalization, 62*f*, 62–63
  communities, tension and negotiation between, 67–68
  and dialogical negotiation, 60–61
  and differing worldviews, 86–89
  grammar of, 90–91
  and importance of dialogue, 2–3
  influence of Ragnar Rommetveit, 16–19
  and layered attunement, 50–60, 55*f*, 71–72
  levels of in co-construction of stories, 262–63
  mediating with, 263–64
  and narrative, 15–16, 26–27
  and online gaming, 180–81
  polysemic multivoiced self, 55*f*, 61–67, 69*f*, 70*f*
  and technology-mediated dialogue, 147–49
  in technology-mediated learning, 160–63
  and vignettes of classroom attunement, 150–59, 152*f*, 156*f*, 159*f*
  See also learning opportunities, intersubjectivity; video games, intersubjectivity and dialogue in
intersubjectivity, and joint story construction, 239
  analytical approach, 247–48
  developmental perspective, 243
  dimensions of high-level teacher mediation, 266–67
  and Down syndrome, 253–55, 256–58
  interactions at high-level intersubjectivity, 248–56
  and language impairment, 250–53, 258–60
  learning dialogues, 240–42
  levels of intersubjectivity, 262–63
  mediating with intersubjectivity, 263–64
  observational setting, 246
  study description, 243–44
  study discussion, 262–67
  study implications, 267–68
  study method, 244–48
  study participants, 244–46, 245*t*
  study procedure, 246–47
  teaching and learning as communicative acts, 240
  and typical language development, 248–50, 260–62
  understanding variations, 264–66
  with wavering intersubjectivity, 256–62

Jefferson, Thomas, and competing narrative templates, 22–23

language development, and teacher-child story construction, 248–50, 260–62
language impairment, and teacher-child story construction, 250–53, 258–60
League of Legends, and dialogue in online gaming, 181–85, 182*f*
  analysis, 188–93
  enculturation, 187–88
  example 1, 184
  example 2, 185
  toxicity, and elements of communicative media, 185–86
learning
  as communicative act, 240
  as expansion of dialogue, 128–29
  learning dialogues, 240–42
  as networking, 132–34

as response to a call, 127–28
technology-mediated, 160–63
learning opportunities, intersubjectivity and, 199–202
classroom supports, 202–6
suggested practices, 214–15
See also tasks, collaborative learning with authentic

MacIntyre, Alasdair, 19, 21–22
Masco, Joseph, 279
mathematics, and examples to promote reflection, 204–6
Mayer, Mercer, 246
microblogging, and space to attend to others, 145–47
and classroom interactions, 149–50, 150*f*
dialogic classroom, 148–49
technology-mediated dialogue, 147–49
technology-mediated learning and intersubjectivity, 160–63
vignettes of classroom attunement, 150–59, 152*f*, 156*f*, 159*f*
monologic approaches, current dominance of, 3–6
monologisms, and transformative dialogue, 275
Mouffe, C., 83–84
multivoicedness, in student interviews, 285–87

narrative
influence of Ragnar Rommetveit, 16–19
narrative templates, 20
narrative templates, competing, 22–26
national narratives as coauthors, 20–22
plot and, 19–20
role in dialogue and intersubjectivity, 15–16, 26–27
as symbolic tool, 19–20
templates in student interviews, 285–87
national narratives, as coauthors, 20–22
negotiation, tensions and, 67–68

online communities, dialogic activities in, 167–68, 175–76
chatting activities, 173–74, 175
chatting sequence, 174
coauthorship of meaning, 168
double dialogicality, 169–70
groups, creating and maintaining, 172–73
profiles, creating, 171–72

Space2cre8 as illustrative case, 170–74
See also video games, intersubjectivity and dialogue in

Papastergiadis, N., 85
participation, educational technology for, 135–36
Pask, Gordon, 130–32
Passing of the Great Race, The (Grant), 24
personalization, and current monologic approaches, 4–5
perspectivity, and importance of dialogue, 2–3
plot, narrative structure and, 19–20
polarization
versus constructive transformation, 273–76
contact zones and dialogue, 92–93
and current monologic approaches, 3–4
dialogical interventions, implications for designing, 89–92, 90*f*
dialogical spaces, designing inclusive, 82–84
versus dialogue and learning, 8
dialogue as remedy for, 79–81
evidence of increased, 290–91
polarized settings, viability of dialogue in, 77–79
political crises, dimensions of living through, 1
polysemic multivoiced self, 55*f*, 61–67, 69*f*, 70*f*
"possibility thinking," and dialogic classroom, 160
professional development
and collaborative learning, 208–10, 213–14
and intersubjectivity, 200–1

reading, dual-language learners and, 219–20, 235–36
child-initiated code-switching and parental confirmation, 227–29
child-initiated code-switching and parental extension, 229–31
dialogic perspective on, 220–21
parent-initiated code-switching, 231–33
patterns over time, 224–27, 225*f*, 226*f*
scaffolded dialogues, 227
study design, 222
study discussion, 233–35
study methods, 222–24
reconciliation, *versus* polarization, 273–76
reflection, promoting in classroom discussion, 204–6, 211–13
Rommetveit, Ragnar
coauthorship of meaning, 168

Rommetveit, Ragnar (*cont.*)
  communicative acts, 240
  contexts of communication, 6–8, 32–35
  on contextures and shared understandings, 29–31
  on conversation analysis, 44–45
  dialogical negotiation, 60–61
  dialogic education theory, 100
  dialogue and interaction in learning, 219–20
  dialogue and intersubjectivity, 86–89
  dialogue in times of crisis, 277–78
  importance of dialogue, 2–3
  influence of, 16–19
  intersubjectivity and learning dialogues, 241
  interview with, 291–93
  and layered attunement, 50–60, 55*f*, 71–72
  legacy of, 15–16, 26–27
  life and career, 31–32
  polysemic multivoiced self, 55*f*, 61–67, 69*f*, 70*f*
  on remote contexts, 42–44
Russia, narrative templates in, 20

SCALE model, 209–10, 212–13
schizmogenesis, 273, 274
slavery, and competing narrative templates, 22–26
social crisis
  dimensions of living through, 1
  versus social change, 278–80
social media, toxicity and, 181
socioscientific reasoning, and technology-mediated dialogue, 147–49
Space2cre8, 170–74
specificity, and transformative dialogue, 276
Stetsenko, Anna, 282
story construction, teacher-child, 239
  analytical approach, 247–48
  developmental perspective, intersubjectivity in, 243
  dimensions of high-level teacher mediation, 266–67
  and Down syndrome, 253–55, 256–58
  at high-level intersubjectivity, 248–56
  and language impairment, 250–53, 258–60
  learning dialogues, 240–42
  levels of intersubjectivity, 262–63
  mediating with intersubjectivity, 263–64
  observational setting, 246
  study description, 243–44
  study discussion, 262–67
  study implications, 267–68
  study method, 244–48

  study participants, 244–46, 245*t*
  study procedure, 246–47
  teaching and learning as communicative acts, 240
  and typical language development, 248–50, 260–62
  understanding variations, 264–66
  with wavering intersubjectivity, 256–62
sustainability
  educational challenge of, 283–84
  student interviews on, 284–87
Sustainable Coaching and Adaptive Learning for Education (SCALE) model, 209–10, 212–13

Talkwall, 149–50, 150*f*, 159*f*
tasks, collaborative learning with authentic, 206–7, 213–14
  classroom methods, 207–8
  hybrid debate and discussion, 210–11
  and professional development, 208–10
  and promoting reflection, 211–13
  suggested practices, 214–15
teaching, as communicative act, 240
technology, definition of, 123–24
technology-mediated learning, attunement and intersubjectivity in, 160–63
tensions, in negotiation, 67–68
time, educational technology for expansion of, 136–37
toxicity, in online gaming, 180–81, 185–86, 188–90, 192–94
traditions, addressing incommensurable, 91
transculturation, 85–86
Trevarthen, C., 243
Trialogical Learning Approach (TLA), 101

UNION Project, Utrecht city schools, 78, 79–81
United States
  Civil War and competing narrative templates, 23–24
  and competing narrative templates, 22–26
  and national narratives as coauthors, 20–22

video games, intersubjectivity and dialogue in, 178–80, 194–95
  data and analysis, 188–92
  disagreement, online and offline, 192–94
  enculturation, 187–88
  example 1, 184
  example 2, 185
  League of Legends and contextual background, 181–85, 182*f*

online gaming and notions of
    intersubjectivity, 180–81
toxicity, and elements of communicative
    media, 185–86
toxicity, example of, 188–90
Vygotsky, Lev
    dialogue and intersubjectivity, 17–19
    dialogue in times of crisis, 277–78
    zone of proximal development, 219–20, 242

White supremacy, and competing narrative
    templates, 24–26
Winthrop, John, 20–21
Word Generation program, and classroom
    discussion, 203
worldviews
    dialogue between different, 85–86
    intersubjectivity and, 86–89
    traditions, addressing incommensurable, 91